Reflecting the Audience

STUDIES IN THEATRE HISTORY & CULTURE

Edited by Thomas Postlewait

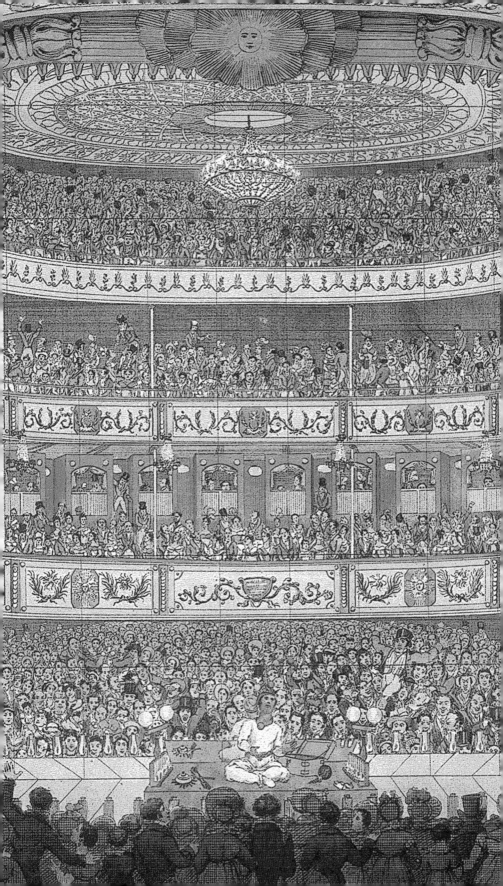

Reflecting the Audience

London Theatregoing, 1840–1880

JIM DAVIS & VICTOR EMELJANOW

University of Iowa Press ᴪ Iowa City

University of Iowa Press, Iowa City 52242
Copyright © 2001 by the University of Iowa Press
All rights reserved
Printed in the United States of America
Design by Richard Hendel
http://www.uiowa.edu/~uipress

The publication of this book was generously supported
by the University of Iowa Foundation.

Printed on acid-free paper

Library of Congress
Cataloging-in-Publication Data
Davis, Jim, 1949–
Reflecting the audience: London theatregoing, 1840–1880 / by
Jim Davis and Victor Emeljanow.
p.   cm.–(Studies in theatre history and culture)
Includes bibliographical references and index.
ISBN 0-87745-781-6 (cloth)
1. Theater–England–London–History–19th century. 2. Theater
audiences–England–London–History–19th century.
I. Emeljanow, Victor. II. Title. III. Series.
PN2596.L6D38 2001
792'.09421'09034–dc21   2001034729

01 02 03 04 05 c 5 4 3 2 1

CONTENTS

TO OUR FAMILIES

ACKNOWLEDGMENTS

Any study of nineteenth-century theatre owes an inestimable debt of gratitude to Michael Booth. He pointed the way and has remained a friend and mentor during the long gestation period of this book.

We also are immensely grateful to friends and colleagues who have encouraged and supported us: Leonard Connolly, Veronica Kelly, and David Mayer supported this project in its early stages. Tracy Davis and Bruce McConachie provided invaluable advice when an earlier version of our chapter on the Surrey and Victoria Theatres was presented at an ASTR conference and later published in *Theatre Survey*. Joseph Donohue helped with some enlightening comments on the final manuscript. We are particularly indebted to Tom Postlewait for his faith in the book and his enthusiastic and detailed suggestions as editor.

We thank the Australia Research Council for awarding us a large research grant from 1995–1997 toward the realization of this project. We are grateful to the Society for Theatre Research (London) for a grant toward the cost of illustrations for this volume. We are also indebted to colleagues and postgraduate students in our respective departments in the Universities of New South Wales and Newcastle for the interest taken and feedback given at various seminars.

We would not have been able to reach this point without the efforts and dedication of those who helped directly with our research: Jennifer Aylmer, MBE, who facilitated the work in its early stages; and our research assistants, Sonya Langelaar, Margaret Leask, Georgia Macbeth, Julie Pavlou-Kirri, Karina Smith, and Rayma Watkinson.

We are also indebted to the curators, librarians and staff who unfailingly helped us mine the rich resources at their disposal. In particular we would like to thank the staff of the Harvard Theatre Collection, the Theatre Museum (London), the British Library, the Public Record Office (London), the Greater London Record Office, the Guildhall Library, the New York Public Library, the Hoblitzelle Theatre Arts Library (Texas), the John Howard Library (Southwark), the Minet Library (Lambeth), the Rose Lipman Library (Hackney), the Bancroft Library (Mile End), the Holborn Local History Library, and the Finsbury Library.

The aim of this book is to fill a very obvious gap — the lack of any full-length study of nineteenth-century British theatre audiences. Insofar as a comprehensive study would be impossible in one short book, we have limited our work to one city, London, and to the period from 1840, immediately prior to the deregulation of the London theatres, to 1880. Yet London theatre audiences themselves defy easy categorization, for they varied according to the neighborhood in which individual theatres were situated, while each audience member was individuated by class, race, age, and gender, as well as specific motivations for attendance. For these reasons, our study is not primarily concerned with or limited by a discussion of audiences that patronized the theatres of the West End.[1]

At the beginning of the nineteenth century, theatrical activity in London had centered on the patent houses, Drury Lane and Covent Garden, which operated throughout the year, and the Haymarket, which opened in the summer.[2] An expanding population, however, necessitated more entertainment than the patent monopoly allowed. The consequence was a large number of "minor" theatres which sprang up in the early years of the century. These years saw a dispersal of this audience, especially as theatres opened in specific neighborhoods to serve the local inhabitants. Although the Select Committee on Dramatic Literature of 1832 investigated the implications of the patent house monopoly and the official restriction of legitimate drama to these theatres, it was not until the passing of the Theatre Regulation Act in 1843 that the monopoly was broken. The act made the legal position of the minor theatres clearer and less arbitrary — previously they had depended on the local magistracy for the annual renewal of their licenses — and brought them under the central control and censorship of the Lord Chamberlain's office. It also removed some of the legislative confusions that had been inherited from the eighteenth century and dissolved the separation between "major" and "minor" theatres; and between "legitimate" and "illegitimate" drama. In many respects, however, the act was a two-edged sword. Although it deregulated theatres, it placed unprecedented powers in the hands of the Lord Chamberlain, whose decisions were not subject to appeal. The act was also significant in establishing free enterprise and commercial competition as the basis on which London theatres operated.

Not only were the minor theatres licensed at this time, but so also were a number of saloons. These were theatres that functioned within or as part of a public house. Any discussion of London theatre audiences in the mid-nineteenth century must therefore take cognizance of saloon theatres and also the music halls, many of which were the progeny of those saloons not licensed as theatres. Out of the former grew a number of popular London neighborhood theatres in the 1840s, whereas the latter were being blamed by the 1860s for depriving the theatres of their audiences. While any assumption that there was a massive drift by working class audiences to the music halls, thus paving the way for quieter and more respectable audiences to reclaim the theatres, is a complete misreading of history, the music halls did create competition. Yet it is erroneous to divide the two venues on a class basis: both theatres and music halls catered to mixed clienteles, sometimes within one building, sometimes according to neighborhood.

By the 1860s, the minor theatres and former saloons had ceased to be a problem, although a new financial threat was posed by the music halls. Theatre managements now tried to apply pressure on magistrates to prevent the issue of music hall licenses and employed informers to give evidence against unlicensed halls, the same kinds of strategies that the former patent theatres had used against the encroachments of the minor theatres before 1843.[3] Yet the financial implications were downplayed at the various parliamentary hearings that sought to control the spread of popular entertainments, which the saloons and music halls epitomized. Rather, the arguments were couched in the familiar terms of moral corruption, particularly as it affected young people, and the debasement of dramatic art. Curiously, no legislative measures resulted from these hearings despite efforts by theatres after the promulgation of the 1843 act to extend the definition of stage plays. The unsatisfactory state of the law culminated in a new Select Committee appointed in 1866 to investigate the state of theatrical licensing. Once more protectionism versus free trade became the main issue. By this stage however it was no longer possible to label music halls as essentially a working class entertainment, particularly in the West End.

In response to the theatres' complaints that the music halls were depriving them of their audiences, W. B. Donne, the Examiner of Plays, wrote:

> I doubt the managers' allegations that the Halls have materially diminished their profits. The increasing population of London — and where does London not now extend to — have prevented them from any permanent, though there may have been occasional, loss. I am in the way of hearing a good deal about theatre business, and with one or two exceptions, the managers report very fair — or — very good business.[4]

Yet, despite the attention paid to the complaints of the theatre managers, the Select Committee of 1866 did not establish the need for new legislation to protect the theatre managers. Consequently, the free market predominated with theatres and music halls continuing to compete for audiences — or, in many instances perhaps, continuing to share them. Thomas Wright, the journeyman engineer, actually indicates that working people preferred a visit to a theatre gallery over a visit to the music hall on grounds of expense. Whereas they could take their own provisions to the theatre gallery, they were obliged at the halls to purchase "the more than moderately dear" provisions, at the same time enduring the intimidating expectations of waiters that glasses would be frequently refilled and tips readily given. Despite the low prices of admission, says Wright, music halls were "about the dearest places of amusement that a working man can frequent."[5] Although Dagmar Kift makes it clear that music halls catered for differing levels of income,[6] Wright's complaints should at least alert us to avoid the simplistic assumption that the working class audience was swallowed wholesale by the music halls in the middle years of the century.

The state control of London theatres and what they offered, which commenced in 1843, ended one set of restrictions by imposing another. Moreover, there were many other interested parties who wished to control these places of entertainment: religious reformers and conservative clerics, who wished them closed down or converted to other uses; commercial entrepreneurs, who were to play a major part in the development of the newly regulated theatres; artistic and cultural arbiters, with agendas for the English theatre that at times were idealistic or even impracticable; and social reformers, who saw the theatre as a scourge or alternatively as a form of rational recreation. Indeed, it is impossible to comprehend fully some of these issues without reference

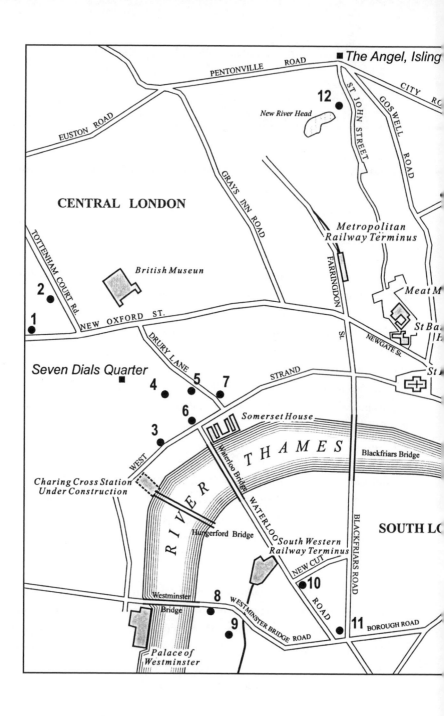

The Angel, Islingi

PENTONVILLE ROAD

CITY RO

EUSTON ROAD

GRAYS INN ROAD

ST JOHN STREET

GOSWELL ROAD

New River Head

12

CENTRAL LONDON

Metropolitan
Railway Terminus

TOTTENHAM COURT Rd.

British Museun

FARRINGDON St.

Meat M

2

1

NEW OXFORD ST.

NEWGATE St.

St Ba
H.

DRURY LANE

St

Seven Dials Quarter

STRAND

4   **5**   **7**

6

Somerset House

3

WEST

Waterloo Bridge

R I V E R   T H A M E S

Blackfriars Bridge

Charing Cross Station
Under Construction

WATERLOO

SOUTH LO

BLACKFRIARS ROAD

Hungerford Bridge

South Western
Railway Terminus

NEW CUT

10

ROAD

Westminster
Bridge

8

WESTMINSTER BRIDGE ROAD

11 BOROUGH ROAD

9

Palace of
Westminster

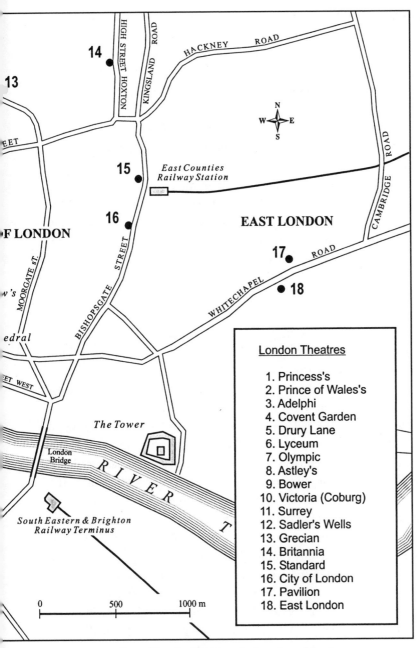

Map of London showing the location of the theatres.
Courtesy of Olivier Rey-Lescure.

to the social and cultural contexts in which they occurred and to the audience members whom they affected. Commentators moreover described theatre audiences in terms that implied deep social stratification, so that we need to examine carefully references to "respectable" and "fashionable" audiences, frequently described in newspaper accounts in the mid-nineteeth century, as well as to the "lowest orders" or even the working, middle, and upper classes. The relationship of income and working hours to theatregoing is also significant in any socioeconomic consideration of audiences and their habits, together with the ways in which emerging middle-class values of privacy and social discrimination in the nineteenth century coincided with the commercial imperatives of theatre managers.[7] Equally, when we talk about "neighborhood" theatres we need to understand concepts of neighborhood and community as they existed between 1840 and 1880, especially within a period of increasing urbanization and population growth.

In the ensuing chapters we explore these concerns through a series of case studies. We focus on representative theatres from four areas of London. To the south we concentrate on the Surrey Theatre and the Royal Victoria; to the east, the Whitechapel Pavilion and the Britannia Theatre, Hoxton; to the north, Sadler's Wells and the Queen's, which was transformed into the Prince of Wales's in 1865. Within the West End we focus on Drury Lane, as representative both of that area and of aspirations towards a National Theatre. Other theatres are also referred to, often for comparison and contrast, but the emphasis is placed firmly on these seven theatres. Our immediate aim is to examine the possible composition of these theatres' audiences, as well as their behavior and patterns of attendance, through a variety of means. In particular we look at topography, social demography, police reports, economic and social factors, communications, and managerial policies in relation to the chosen theatres. This project entails an examination of maps, census returns, transport data, playbills, government papers, dramatic texts, local and national newspapers, as well as memoirs, journals, diaries, and letters. Using this data we demonstrate the diversity of the London theatre-going public from 1840 to 1880 and challenge some of the received orthodoxies currently in existence.[8]

Part One

THE SURREY-SIDERS

London Audiences South of the Thames

1. The Surrey and the Victoria Theatres

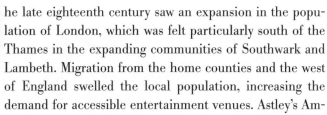he late eighteenth century saw an expansion in the population of London, which was felt particularly south of the Thames in the expanding communities of Southwark and Lambeth. Migration from the home counties and the west of England swelled the local population, increasing the demand for accessible entertainment venues. Astley's Amphitheatre and what was to become the Surrey Theatre already existed as centers for equestrian entertainment, while the Coburg (later Victoria) Theatre came into existence in 1818 in response to the opening of Waterloo Bridge. In time the Surrey and Victoria theatres played a major role in providing entertainment for these new communities. Although the Surrey was located in Southwark and the Victoria in Lambeth, they were actually situated quite close to each other (about a ten minute walk) and must at times have shared the same audiences. This chapter reevaluates what is meant by a "transpontine" or "Surrey-side" audience.

THE SURREY

Originating as the Royal Circus in 1782 near the Obelisk in Blackfriars Road, the Surrey Theatre was situated at the point south of the Thames where the roads to Westminster and Blackfriars Bridges intersected. Blackfriars Road was an important thoroughfare, linking the city of London and Southwark and sustaining their joint commercial interests: a straight, broad, well-lit road, it was also deemed a magnificent entry into London. The Surrey Theatre was originally built to emulate Astley's, and initially the playbills announced that a horse patrol was provided from bridge to bridge because of the footpads prevalent in the area.[1] Rebuilt and remodeled in 1801, it burnt down in 1805 and was again rebuilt, reopening the following year. Renamed the Royal Surrey from 1811, the theatre gradually became the focus for a small commer-

Surrey Theatre exterior, Blackfriars Road,
drawn by Thomas H. Shepherd, 1828.

cial district, and its strategic setting was further enhanced by the opening of Waterloo Bridge and the Waterloo Road in 1817. In 1823 *The
Times* described the theatre as "very neatly and creditably appointed,"
adding that "if the idle boys were kept away from about the doors, and
the money-takers would shave themselves, it is such a place as people
might go into."[2] The theatre's reputation was considerably enhanced
by Robert William Elliston's two periods of management, although he
proved unable to persuade the authorities to "legitimize" the theatre.
Under his second period of management (1827–30) the theatre attempted to broaden the range of its audience beyond the immediate
neighborhood. By 1827 tickets for the theatre could be purchased in the
West End at Sam's Royal Library, St. James's Street, and at Mr. Charles
Wright's, a Haymarket wine merchant, while a July playbill for that year
announces that "for the convenience of the Public Mason's Greenwich
and Deptford Coach calls at Johnson's Coffee House every night after
the Performance to convey Passengers from the theatre."[3] In December 1836 it was announced that "An Omnibus will call at this Theatre
at Quarter past 11 every Night for Fleet-st., Holborn Hill, the Post Office
and Islington."[4] Although the Surrey was in essence a neighborhood
theatre, even drawing complaints about the filthy mess left behind by
sweeps in the audience on one occasion,[5] Elliston evidently sought a

{ *Audiences South of the Thames* }

cosmopolitan audience and frequently boasted the theatre's superiority to the neighboring Coburg. An 1829 playbill categorically states that "nothing can be so abhorrent to the feelings of the Conductor of this theatre, than any collusion, or association in an assumed rivalry, with the Coburg Theatre."[6]

David Osbaldiston, who became manager in 1831, gave evidence to the 1832 Select Committee on Dramatic Literature that all social classes were represented at the theatre and that more people from the immediate vicinity attended the Surrey than from the west end of town, although he hastened to add that the audiences were always of a respectable description.[7] T. P. Cooke, giving evidence to the same committee, confirmed that the South London theatres were "in a large measure supported by the surrounding neighborhood."[8] After 1831 this neighborhood had been depleted of some of its more affluent residents, who had moved on account of the cholera epidemic.[9] Earlier Charles Dibdin had referred to the somewhat mixed constituency of the Surrey audience, recounting how he inserted two scenes into *The Apprentice's Opera* (1826) at the request of the local Superintendent of Police: one showing a burglary, so householders would know how to protect their homes; the other illustrating the ease with which police officers arrested thieves in the public houses where felons gathered, in order that impressionable young thieves in the audience might be given a warning.[10] Edward Fitzball, who wrote a number of plays for the Surrey, recalls how his play *Jonathan Bradford* restored the theatre's dwindling fortunes in 1833, specifically on account of one scene in which simultaneous action occurred in four different rooms. It was witnessed, according to Fitzball, by at least "four hundred thousand of the public," not merely the middling and working classes, but also "some thousands of the highest order of intellect and society."[11] Although this figure may be an inflated one, the social mix discerned by Fitzball is supported by subsequent accounts. Visiting other Surrey productions in 1837, Charles Rice states that "the house was crowded by a very respectable audience" and that "the company was orderly, well dressed and cool."[12] By 1842, located at the center of a now densely populated neighborhood, the Surrey was reputedly the leading minor theatre in London.

There are a number of more recent views of Surrey audiences that have also gained currency, particularly through that theatre's association with such dramas as *Black Ey'd Susan* and *The Factory Lad.*

Michael Booth writes that "a theatre like the Surrey, the headquarters of nautical melodrama, drew a considerable proportion of its patrons from sailors, Thames watermen, shipwrights, dock workers, and all those who lived on the river or sailed on it to the open sea."[13] J. S. Bratton refers to the "dockyard and sailor audiences at the Surrey," and to their special relationship with the Surrey nautical melodramas.[14] Marvin Carlson echoes Booth when he states that "Such melodrama houses as the Royal Coburg . . . and the favoured home of nautical melodrama, the Surrey . . . were both located on the South Bank, in a district with close ties to the sea and shipping. Thus they attracted many off-duty sailors to their productions."[15] Equally problematic are Robert Estill's class-based assumptions about *The Factory Lad* (1832), which lasted for only six nights at the Surrey. Estill states that "At the Surrey possibly the regular audience in the pit would be skilled artisans and small masters, the people likely to have taught themselves to read and the ones who would support the illegal press and radical organisations."[16]

He also suggests that the arrest of a certain Thomas Hansbury for selling the *Poor Man's Guardian* at Astley's in September 1832 may imply that theatres attracting less affluent audiences, such as the Surrey and the Coburg, were more probable venues for the sale of such literature. This seems unlikely considering the dependence of these theatres' livelihoods on the good will of local magistrates and the concern of the Select Committee of 1832 with the possible use of the minor theatres as centers for political dissent. Hartmut Ilseman refers to *The Factory Lad*'s first performance at the Surrey Theatre, Blackfriers Road [*sic*], adding that "Blackfriers was a workers' quarter at the time."[17] Yet, as the Surrey continued to draw a broad range of spectators, we may question these assertions.

THE VICTORIA

At the outset, the Coburg was built as a speculative venture deliberately calculated, in the wake of the opening of Waterloo Bridge in 1817,[18] to challenge the Surrey and its perceived up-market clientele. Marvin Carlson has drawn attention to the elaborate exterior and interior of the Coburg,[19] as well as to the rococo fancies that suggested a sophisticated cultural awareness totally at odds with the surrounding topography. Edward Fitzball in 1822 commented upon the rural setting of the

{ *Audiences South of the Thames* }

Surrey Theatre interior. Detail from "Pit Boxes and Gallery" by George Cruikshank, from 400 Humorous Illustrations, *London, originally published 1836.*

theatre,[20] while Crabb Robinson in 1819 and Macready in 1833 both commented on the prettiness of the theatre's interior.[21] Nevertheless the choice of location and the nature of the building itself reflected, not the reality of what actually existed in the area, but rather what the speculators anticipated the area might become. Since 1785, warehouses, wharves, breweries, timber yards and woollen cloth factories had existed in Lambeth particularly in the vicinity of the Thames. The first determined attempt, however, to develop the area for commercial and residential purposes took place after 1810, when it was decided to proceed with the building of a new bridge.[22] Unlike the Surrey, which had been built at the confluence of arterial roads, the Victoria was built inauspiciously on a corner of reclaimed land below the level of the river with the Lambeth Marsh to the west and market gardens to the east. From the northern side of the river, looking southwards, the onlooker would have been confronted by a vista of timber yards, the Lambeth Water Works, Coade's Artificial Stone works, and boat building facilities. From the south side, however, the view was somewhat different: from this perspective the Waterloo Bridge set against Somerset House, with St. Paul's Cathedral as a backdrop, might well have justified Canova's assessment of it as "the noblest bridge in the world."[23] The ornate buildings constructed shortly after the bridge and the theatre were opened, all testified to a business optimism on the part of timber merchants like John Lett or gold refiners like John Roupell (who would develop the area of the New Cut in the 1820s), that the area would develop profitably and perhaps even fashionably.[24]

Yet unlike the Surrey Theatre, which fashionable audiences continued to attend until well into the 1860s, the Coburg (renamed the Royal Victoria in 1833) was from the outset identified with a local audience whose composition was described in terms ranging from the dismissive to the patronizing. Certainly much of the surviving evidence indicates that the Victoria attracted an audience whose composition reflected the neighborhood in which the theatre was located. In 1832 Davidge, the theatre's manager, stressed his reliance on a local audience who would not cross Waterloo Bridge to visit theatres on the northern side.[25] By 1861 the *Era* (16 June) could report that the Victoria was "depending largely upon the patronage of a class unable to get far from the immediate scene of their daily labors." The discrepancy with the dreams of the speculators was soon apparent. Shortly after the theatre was built, Hazlitt was appalled to find himself "in a bridewell, or a brothel,

Victoria Theatre: "View from the New Cut" 1879, from G. W. Thornbury and E. Walford, eds., Old and New London, *1879.*

amidst Jew-boys, pickpockets, prostitutes and mountebanks."[26] This low view was reiterated by F. G. Tomlins in 1840, who situated the theatre "in one of the lowest neighborhoods, its audience are of the lowest kind,"[27] and perpetuated at the end of the century when Barton Baker described the audience as "the lowest and vilest in London, the very scum of Lambeth."[28] Social apologists, however, like Dickens and Sala were careful to differentiate between the oppressive environment of the New Cut and Waterloo Road and the transmogrifying capability of the theatre itself. In 1838, Dickens described the "dirt and discomfort" of the area surrounding the Victoria, characterized by oyster, flat fish, and fruit vendors, while identifying the local "ragged boys" as enthusiastic half-price patrons of the theatre.[29] Later, in 1850, he identified the packed gallery and pit as filled with "good-humoured mechanics," their wives and children, and urged social activists to lose no time in capitalizing on their rapt attention and thus "effecting any mental improvement in that great audience."[30] Henry Mayhew commented on the throng of costermongers in the gallery of the Victoria after a day of grinding work and on the youth of the audience (young men between twelve and twenty-three and young girls with babies) in the early 1850s.

Dickens's moral concern was echoed in 1859 by George Sala. He found the New Cut to be "one of the most unpleasant samples of London you could offer to a foreigner," its tenements filled with an "unwashed, unkempt, wretched humanity." At the same time, he distinguished between the eager rush of gallery audiences to the gin palaces and public houses opposite the theatre itself — and the "highly healthful and beneficial" moral tone of the plays actually performed, and asked:

> Which is best? That they should gamble in low coffee houses, break each other's heads with pewter pots in public houses, fight and wrangle at street corners, or lie in wait in doorways and blind alleys to rob and murder, or that they should pay their threepence for admission into the gallery of the "Vic."[31]

Sala and Dickens saw the theatre as redemptive and the Victoria as an ideal opportunity to demonstrate this capacity. At the end of the period their dream appeared to have become a reality through the temperance meetings and Sunday night services held at the theatre and through the managerial policy of Emma Cons. She renamed it the Royal Victoria Coffee Music Hall, miraculously transforming a noisy disruptive audience brought up on the New Cut's "cheese, butter, bacon piles, cheap yellow and willow crockery," into patrons who now quietly conversed with each other in the gallery, enjoying "the purity of the higher stage," sipping cocoa, coffee, or tea for 1d or "beef and ham and soup at two pence a plate," who presented themselves "in every detail except for costliness (crimson wool-stuff having to do duty for Utrecht velvet and tabinette) — as if they had been on the fashionable side of the river and in a fashionable house."[32] This is a far cry from the old Victoria gallery described by John Hollingshead:

> most of the men in shirt-sleeves, and most of the women bareheaded, with coloured handkerchiefs round their shoulders. . . . This 'chickaleary' audience was always thirsty — and not ashamed. It tied handkerchiefs together . . . until they formed a rope, which was used to haul up large stone bottles of beer from the pit, and occasionally hats which had been dropped below.

These same responded with blasphemous yells as E. F. Saville playing Bill Sikes dragged Nancy round the stage by the hair and looked "defiantly at the gallery" before murdering her.[33]

Nevertheless, Hazlitt, Sala, and Dickens set in motion a dismissive or condescending commentary about working-class audiences in general and the Victoria Theatre in particular that has been accepted and repeated by subsequent scholars. George Rowell, for example, is prepared to dismiss the Victoria audience as "illiterate . . . simple and undiscriminating,"[34] while Richard Findlater refers to the fact that "the 'Vic' changed for the worse in the six decades since it was built," describing the theatre in 1880 as "a massive, boozy melodrama house rearing high above the Lambeth slums, a minute's walk from Waterloo Station and some of the worst brothels and thieves' kitchens in late Victorian London."[35] This commentary needs to be examined further.

TRANSPORT AND COMMUNICATION

The Victoria

It was quite clear from the outset that the Coburg/Victoria would be affected by the success with which the proprietors of the Waterloo Bridge Company could induce people to cross the Thames. The company contributed to making up the shortfall when Jones, Glossop, and Dunn, the Coburg's original developers, were unable to raise sufficient funds to build the theatre by public subscription. The company also contributed to lighting the approaches from the bridge down to the theatre itself. The bridge, however, cost £937,000, which had been loaned by wealthy speculators. They naturally wanted a return on their investment and therefore a toll was imposed of 1d per person and 2d for vehicular traffic.[36] The pedestrian toll was reduced to 1s 2d in 1841.[37] The article on Waterloo Bridge in Charles Knight's *London*, while admiring its construction and *aesthetic* appeal, commented on its sense of desertion, which was directly attributed to the toll, since toll-free Westminster and Blackfriars Bridges were crowded.[38] In 1854 the Select Committee on Metropolitan Bridges heard evidence that on any given day between 10 A.M. and 6 P.M., Waterloo Bridge was far less utilized by pedestrian, equestrian, or vehicular traffic than Westminster or Blackfriars Bridges.[39] The figures suggest that the imposition of a toll may indeed have militated against its use. The toll profits enabled the Waterloo Bridge Company to pay an annual dividend of 4s for every pound invested in 1854.[40] The toll would remain an issue throughout the period. In 1872 the *South London Press* (4 May) directly suggested that property values in Lambeth would be enhanced if the toll were removed. Although the fashionable West End clientele, which the early managers like Glossop, Davidge, Abbott, and Egerton hoped to encourage to the Coburg, would not have been deterred by the toll, it would have tended to emphasize the theatre's relative isolation. The preponderance of a local audience may in turn have militated against the theatre's attractions for a middle-class audience, thus giving credence to the accounts of Hazlitt and others cited previously. Moreover its location, together with the imposition of the toll, possibly inhibited casual working-class visitors from the north bank. A statement in a playbill from 1833, "Tickets to any part of the theatre purchased at Mr Griffiths, Bookseller, Wellington St, Strand, with pass to Waterloo bridge toll-free" implies that considerable inducements were necessary to attract visitors from the Middlesex side of the Thames.[41]

John Coleman recalled how, as a lad, he had walked to theatres in the 1830s and 1840s: "There was no penny omnibus in those days, so in most instances each visit to the play was attended by a walk of six or eight miles."[42] The significance of public transport soon made itself felt. A notice on a playbill of 1819 alerted patrons "For the accommodation of numerous visitors from Greenwich, Deptford, etc a coach calls at the theatre a quarter before eleven at which time the performances terminate."[43] This information, however, may not reflect the actual presence of visitors from Greenwich or Deptford, but rather an inducement to persuade such distant visitors that the theatre was not a remote one. In 1840 *The Stranger's Guide* listed the omnibus and steam boat timetables of use to theatrical visitors. It listed two bus routes from Islington and King's Cross every quarter of an hour which went to the Elephant and Castle down Blackfriars Bridge Road to the Surrey Theatre, making the return journey via Kennington, and the Vauxhall Bridge Road at a cost of 6d. There is no reference to the Victoria. The steamboats plying between London Bridge and Chelsea every quarter of an hour did indeed stop at Waterloo Bridge but on the northern or Strand side. They then proceeded to Westminster Bridge now stopping on the Surrey side for a cost of 4d.[44] What this suggests is that direct access to the Surrey Theatre could easily be obtained from the City or the western boundary of the West End by way of toll-free bridges or by regular public transport. The Victoria, on the other hand, had direct access hampered by an obligatory toll and certainly in 1840 by the absence of regular transurban public transport. But some transportation was available because by 1843 a playbill notice assured patrons that an omnibus passed the theatre every 10 minutes from 9 A.M. to 11 P.M., traveling from Regent's Park via the Strand to the Elephant and Castle.[45] Moreover the description by Charles Dickens in 1838 of Waterloo Road at 1 A.M. suggests that special theatre omnibuses were in operation and that watermen ferrying passengers provided a significant means of transport:

> One o'clock! Parties returning from the different theatres foot it through the muddy streets; cabs, hackney coaches, carriages, and theatre omnibuses roll swiftly by; watermen with dim, dirty lanterns in their hands and large brass plates upon their breasts, who have been shouting and rushing about for the last two hours, retire to their watering houses . . . the half-price pit and box frequenters of the theatres throng to the different houses of refreshment.[46]

Dickens's description refers both to those returning to the Waterloo Road from elsewhere and to local inhabitants leaving theatres like the Victoria.

The advent of the railway appeared once more to offer opportunities for attracting an audience from outside the Lambeth area. When Waterloo Station opened in 1848, it seemed as if its proximity to the theatre would be an inestimable advantage. Its significance is articulated in a burletta, *Adventures at a new Railway Station!!!* which contained views of the station's exterior and waiting room.[47] It was hoped that the terminus would offset the relatively light use of the bridge by people from the northern bank. In 1847 a playbill averred: "Amongst the manifold advantages of railways . . . none can be greater than the opportunity they present . . . of enabling parties to come and witness the superior performances of the Victoria Theatre." It declared the notice to be a response to the numerous inquiries from patrons about return trains.[48] But by 1866 it became apparent that trains held a far greater potential for taking people out of the locality than for bringing them in. Cheap excursion tickets, for example, encouraged Lambeth inhabitants to travel to the seaside — a holiday trip of eight hours for 3s 6d.[49] In 1869 a playbill noted that trains "bring passengers from the suburbs within a few yards of the theatre" and that "The Railway Fare and Admission to witness this costly production [is] less than the entrance alone into other theatres." By this stage, such comments might have appeared as a pathetic plea rather than as a confident affirmation.[50] By 1878 the playbill notices possessed the qualities of weariness and resignation:

> The Theatre is opposite the Waterloo Station, Waterloo Road. Trains run to and from Woolwich, Greenwich, Deptford . . . also Clapham Junction, Battersea, Chelsea, and all other stations. The Entertainments are always of the most varied and best descriptions commencing at 7 o'clock and terminating . . . after 11 o'clock thus allowing visitors time to reach home by early trains."[51]

Far from bringing visitors to the Victoria, trains merely brought them closer to the Lyceum, Drury Lane, and the eastern end of the Strand. Moreover, the location of the railway terminus and its exits to the north of the theatre, rather than enhancing attendance at the Victoria, accentuated its marginalization. Regardless of accessible public transport, it would appear therefore that Davidge's evidence in 1832, in which he stated that his theatre depended on local patronage; the description of the Victoria audience that appeared in the police report of 1843 as "principally mechanics in the neighborhood"; and the opinion in the *Era* in 1861, quoted above, may all well reflect the reality that, unlike the Surrey, the Victoria's audiences were largely local and working class.[52]

The Surrey

Since the Surrey relied not only on local audiences but also on attracting audiences from further afield, the communications system must have been adequate to draw audiences from other areas of south and north London.[53] In the 1840s and 1850s private boxes could still be hired for the theatre from venues such as Regent Street, Bond Street, and St. James's Street in the West End. Audiences from the West End and other areas of London had various forms of transport at their disposal by road and river. While the more affluent spectators would have used hackney coaches or cabs, others may well have used steamers or ferries as a means of transportation, although the Surrey was still a 10 to 15 minute walk from the Thames.[54] Omnibuses may also have been used as a means of transportation. However, not all routes were operative in the evenings: indeed, omnibuses were a largely middle-class form of transport for respectable passengers and certainly beyond the means of the working classes.[55] A playbill for Astley's circa 1848, which was a short walk along the Westminster Bridge Road from the Surrey Theatre, indicates the sort of transport available locally. It advertises "steamboats and omnibuses from all parts of town to Westminster Bridge," mentions that "the South-Western Railway new Terminus is now open, and is within five minutes walk of the amphitheatre," and draws attention to "Mason's Omnibuses" to Greenwich and the "Atlas Association" to Paddington, "at the termination of the performance every evening." An Astley's bill for 13 March 1856 mentions that the performance ends in time for late trains from Waterloo and London Bridge plus buses to Greenwich and Paddington.[56] Although the Surrey continued not to advertise transport details in the 1850s and 1860s, by 1872 it was promoting itself to the suburban inhabitants of South London, announcing: "Tramways from Brixton, Clapham, Kennington, Greenwich, Deptford, New Cross, &c, convey Passengers to the Door of the Theatre and return after the Performance."[57]

Cheaper omnibus fares also provided another form of access: a critic for the *Illustrated Sporting and Dramatic News* (22 June 1878) says he got to the Surrey "by twopenny bus." Towards the end of the 1870s persons booking private boxes at the Surrey were informed that they "will have a well-appointed brougham placed at their disposal (provided they happen to live within the cab radius) to bring them to the theatre and take them home again."[58] Yet despite such incentives, at least one critic writing in 1880 suggests that the residents of Middlesex county found it inconvenient to get to the Surrey Theatre.[59]

Many of the audience who came from further afield quite possibly walked to the Surrey.[60] A particularly useful witness is P. P. Hanley, who makes it clear that the Surrey's audiences in the early 1840s were not confined to its immediate neighborhood. Living in Camden Town near Regent's Park, he writes that "in my school-boy days, and indeed for years afterwards, the Surrey was my favourite house, as, like the majority of lads, I liked something stirring and exciting."[61] His father offered him as a twelfth-birthday treat a visit to *Rory O'More* at the Adelphi, but he insisted on going to the Surrey instead to see *Wapping Old Stairs* and *The Whistler*, as his schoolmates had spoken highly of Saville and the Honners. Two years later he walked several miles from his home in Camden Town to see *Martha Willis* and the pantomime at the Surrey, having obtained permission to go with a school fellow. He recalls how they bought buns and oranges on the way and how they found such an immense crowd at the pit entrance that, after fighting their way

in, there was not even standing room, so they had to console themselves with tickets given for another night.[62] That audiences visited the
theatre from across the Thames and that actors might also reside further afield is further substantiated in newspaper reports, which mention audience members from Hyde Park and Westminster, and benefit
bills, from which we learn that the Honners, engaged in 1842, lived at
19 Homer Street, Pentonville, while B. S. Fairbrother, stage manager
and treasurer, lived in High Holborn.[63] An indication of the distances
it was anticipated potential audiences might travel is implicit from the
benefit bill of Mrs. J. Furzman, formerly of the King's Arms, Smart's
Buildings, Holborn, on 11 March 1845. Tickets were available not only
from venues in Southwark, but also in St. John's Wood, Holborn, Tich-
borne Street, Windmill Street, Leicester Square, Portland Town, and
Hammersmith Bridge. Whether spectators walked or used some form
of transport, the transpontine location of the Surrey Theatre was arguably no impediment to those who wished to visit from north of the
Thames or to actors and theatre personnel who lived the other side of
the river.

THE EVIDENCE OF THE CENSUS

The Surrey

In order to test claims about neighborhood audiences at the Surrey and
Victoria we look at census abstracts for 1841–1861 and at local census
returns from a cross-section of streets within the immediate vicinity of
the Surrey and Victoria Theatres for this period.[64] In 1841 the population in Southwark had grown over the previous ten years by 5.5 percent
from 92,970 to 98,089 and in Lambeth by 20.5 percent from 87,856 to
105,887.[65] In 1841 about 50 percent of inhabitants in the streets surveyed in the vicinity of the Surrey Theatre were of local origin, while
there is also evidence of migration from counties close to London, the
west country, and Ireland. Families predominantly live in the area and
the census abstracts for Southwark record children under five and men
and women between twenty and thirty as the two largest groups. There
is also a small but substantial population between thirteen and twenty
and of single people between twenty and thirty-five.[66] Many of the inhabitants close to the theatre are tradesmen, shopkeepers, skilled artisans, and small merchants. Frequently cited trades include carpentry,

painting, engineering, bricklaying, chair making, laboring, dressmaking, tailoring, and shoemaking. Butchers, bakers, printers, cabmen, as well as sempstresses, needlewomen, and laundresses frequently appear. There are a few plasterers and a small number of costermongers, but few related to nautical or marine trades and professions, apart from the odd waterman and chandler. The published census abstracts for 1841 record 360 seamen and 211 watermen as living in Southwark, relatively insignificant figures (0.6% of the working population) compared with 5,001 servants (13.2%), 3,985 laborers (10.5%), 1,665 employed in the boot and shoe trade (4.4%), 969 tailors (2.5%), 932 clerks (2.4%), or the 926 employed in carpentry (2.4%) in the same area. At this point in time Lambeth and Southwark residents tend to follow similar occupations, with some fluctuations. Southwark has far more policemen, chairmakers, and hatters, for instance. Only 26 seamen and 61 watermen are resident in Lambeth. Of seamen resident in the London area in 1841, 7.1 percent live in Southwark, 0.5 percent in Lambeth, but the majority (69%) live in the Tower District.[67]

By 1851 the Surrey appears to be surrounded by a more socially mixed community, though there is little change in the places of origin recorded. About half of the inhabitants had been born locally or in the London area. The Irish form the largest single group after this (2,667 in St. George's parish alone). A large proportion originate from neighboring counties such as Kent or from Norfolk, Suffolk, and Oxfordshire, all relatively close to London. A significant number of residents had come from the west of England, while a smaller proportion hailed from the Midlands and the north of England. Families still predominate, as do offspring of all ages. The number of single people in the area is proportionately smaller, but where they are evident, they tend to be divided by gender: different streets appear to have either a preponderance of single men or single women.[68] In the streets sampled tradesmen, shopkeepers, skilled artisans, and merchants are still among the most conspicuous inhabitants, but laborers, dressmakers, needlewomen, charwomen, and servants are also significant. The shoe and clothes trades remain prominent, with shoemakers, shoe binders, and boot makers to be found everywhere, not to mention drapers, milliners (the most frequently cited female occupation after housewife and domestic servant in St. George's parish as a whole), and hatters. Printers, book binders, book folders, chair makers, engineers, bricklayers, carmen, coach makers, and carpenters are much in evidence.[69] However, despite the indications of the census abstracts, the local returns show that more clerical workers appear to have moved into the neighborhood (indeed, commercial clerk and laborer are the two most frequently cited male occupations in St. George's)[70] and some roads seem to be occupied only by white-collar workers and skilled artisans.[71] A number of police constables and police sergeants reside in the vicinity, as well as the odd musician; again, nautical and seafaring employment is limited, in the streets sampled, to two midshipmen, two mariners, and a master sailor. Other areas in London are still far more densely populated by sailors.[72]

Ten years later, in 1861, the inhabitants living in the vicinity of Surrey, both in major roads and side roads, still tend to be tradesmen, shopkeepers, skilled artisans, merchants, clerks, and laborers. There are still a lot of families, many with children under twelve. Frequently cited jobs include carpenters, clerks, engineers, charwomen, chairmakers, plumbers, printers, dressmakers, needlewomen, book binders, cordwainers, hawkers, shoemakers, french polishers, bricklayers, butchers, carmen, servants, and shopkeepers such as bakers, butchers, grocers, porters, tailors, laundresses, laborers, needlewomen, mantle makers, hat-makers, and general dealers. Again there are few nautical inhabitants in the local streets sampled: a marine-store dealer, a waterman, a merchant seaman, and a dock laborer. There is the odd solicitor's clerk or tax officer, but the potential for gentrification and white-collar settlement, evident in 1851, seems to be on the decline. Indeed, the parish of Saint George reflects Lambeth with respectively 3.5 percent and 5 percent professional residents, 35.4 percent and 42.2 percent residents in domestic service, 8.9 percent and 7.8 percent in commercial employment, and 44.6 percent and 35.1 percent in industrial employment. If the Surrey looked beyond its immediate vicinity for its audiences in Southwark, the parish of Saint Olave's with 22.9 percent in commercial employment and 30.8 percent in industrial employment may have provided a potentially more variegated audience for the theatre. Consequently, it is possible that the Surrey's status as a neighborhood theatre depended on a much wider local radius than did the Victoria. Certainly its repertoire and managerial policies, discussed below, would support this assumption.

The popularity of nautical drama at the Surrey in this period may thus have had more to do with the attractions of T. P. Cooke and the

{ *Audiences South of the Thames* }

genre itself rather than a maritime presence in the Surrey neighborhood. Theatres like the Pavilion in Whitechapel, where Harry Rignold enacted nautical roles, were much better placed to attract the seafaring community. In 1843 a survey carried out for the Lord Chamberlain's Office had described the Surrey audience as "sometimes nobility and gentry, tradespeople, mechanics in the gallery, 4 women to 1 man in pit, the husbands, brothers being in the gallery to save expense."[73] This would seem to corroborate Osbaldiston's statement to the Select Committee in the previous decade. The Pavilion, Whitechapel was attended by "Persons in the neighborhood and many from the Docks, many Sailors,"[74] which tallies with the evidence of the census returns and abstracts. Equally, while the presence of workers and artisans within the local community is evident, Southwark's population is sufficiently diverse to prevent easy categorization of the neighborhood.[75]

Further evidence as to the residency of Surrey audiences, as well as occupation, surfaces in the occasional newspaper report. In 1858 a man between thirty and forty, "obviously a mechanic," dressed in cord trousers, black jacket, and a black hat, precipitated himself towards the front of the gallery at such a speed that he fell over the edge and killed himself. Two witnesses to this event were John Hatch, who lived locally in Tower Street, Lambeth, and Henry Watkins, who lived across the Thames at St. Ormond's Hill, Westminster. A dispute near the pit refreshment bar over an alleged pickpocketing incident in 1867 involved William Davis of 8 Albion Street, Hyde Park; Charles Madden, a commission agent of 10 Walworth Road; a friend of his, James Newberry, described as "a gentleman of property"; and Richard Vincent, a warrant officer of Westminster County Court.[76] Such instances suggest that both local residents and audiences from across the Thames visited the theatre and that they represented a range of occupations. Many of those associated with the Surrey Theatre also lived locally; indeed at one time the area around St. George's Circus was occupied by so many performers from the Surrey and Coburg Theatres that it was allegedly known as the Actor's Barracks.[77] Quennell, a scene painter involved in a backstage fracas at the theatre, lived in Park's Place, Walworth, while Mary Hall, a dresser who witnessed the incident, lived at 34 Grosvenor Place, Borough Rd. In 1842 two performers from the theatre, Mr. Dixie, the Harlequin, and Mr. Staples, stopped to help a woman in distress as they walked home along the Walworth Rd. and were assaulted for their pains.[78]

An examination of the census returns in the period 1841 to 1861 suggests that a demographic pattern that had already established itself at the end of the eighteenth century would continue until the end of our period. Despite the expectations of speculators and the confident Doric columns with which they adorned their early houses, Lambeth retained its identification as a region of wharves, timber yards, and heavy machinery. Indeed, these industries acted as the magnets for the numbers who immigrated to the area from Ireland and elsewhere. In 1841 the census returns that included Lambeth show those who were born in the county jostling with new immigrants: young people with children, single men and women who found work as bakers, blacksmiths, boot makers, bricklayers, carpenters, joiners, and coach makers.[79] In Webber Street, for example, which ran past the rear of the Victoria, apart from 37 unemployed single women and children, there were 20 housewives, 5 servants, 3 carpenters, 2 bricklayers, a smith and his apprentice, and 5 dressmakers among the total of 109 surveyed.

By 1851 the population of Lambeth alone, which rose from 52,728 males and 63,160 females in 1841 to 63,673 and 75,652 respectively (an increase of about 20.7%), had outstripped the increases in Southwark. It now boasted more inhabitants than any area in London, except the Saint Pancras and Marylebone districts north of the Thames.[80] Of the 59,003 under twenty included in the 1851 Lambeth census, 37,329 were born locally (63.2%), 9,803 in the Middlesex areas of London (16.6%), and 809 in Ireland (1.3%). Of the 80,322 over twenty, 19,101 were born locally (23.7%), 17,756 were born in the Middlesex areas of London (22.1%), and a significant number came from Ireland (3,563 or 4.4%) and the West Country (5,529 or 6.8%).[81] Proportionally the numbers of those working as mechanics, servants, or as dressmakers had increased.[82] In 1851, Webber Street listed 5 cordwainers, 4 carpenters, 2 beer sellers, 2 general shopkeepers, 3 comb makers, as well as 7 hatters, boot and shoe makers, and needlewomen. Just as importantly, however, 133 had no listed trade or occupation. Ten years later, in 1861, 40.7 percent of those twenty and over in metropolitan Surrey were employed domestically in one capacity or another, and 36.4 percent were in industrial trades.[83] Lambeth mirrored these statistics almost exactly: of the 92,042 over twenty, 42.2 percent or 38,813 (including housewives) were involved in domestic duties, 32,326 (35.1%) in industrial trades, while an additional 7.8 percent, including dealers of all

{ *Audiences South of the Thames* }

kinds and porters, engaged in commercial trades. Though engine and machine makers remained an important element, shoemakers, brass foundry workers, and boilermakers were fewer in number.[84]

The census abstracts and returns show a rapidly expanding neighborhood attracting immigrants from other parts of London, as well as the West Country, Suffolk, Norfolk, and Ireland (the Irish presence had already been felt by the 1820s). By 1861 there were also a significant number of German, Dutch, and French immigrants, especially around the arterial roads like Waterloo Road. Although most of the working population were absorbed into dressmaking, engineering, book making, and the shoe trade, the relative containment of the Lambeth area encouraged its early identification as a marketplace as well. Large numbers of shopkeepers, especially butchers, bakers, grocers, cheesemongers, and fishmongers, together with their associated assistants and errand boys, dotted roads like Waterloo Road and the New Cut.[85] Interestingly there is little to suggest the dominance of costermongers in the area — there is one listed in Webber Street in 1851, one in Waterloo Road in 1861, and nine in Granby Street. Given Mayhew's calculation of 300 in the area around the New Cut, their absence from the census return may suggest that they were part of a large seasonally driven population of street vendors or that many of those who listed no trade in their return might have hired barrows on particular occasions without being formally described as costermongers.[86] Immediately after the opening of the Coburg, the area began additionally to attract people associated with the theatre. Its relatively cheap housing also meant that performers, musicians, and dancers could live there within striking distance of the Strand and booking agents.[87] In 1841 the published census return counted 56 male and 18 female performers in the Lambeth Church district. By 1851 these had risen to 87 male and 29 female, 13 of whom were attached to theatres in some form as lace makers, costumiers, shoemakers, an inspector of theatre bills, and porters.[88] The benefit playbills moreover show that both the managers as well as many performers lived locally.[89]

Both the census returns and police newspaper reports corroborate the significance of the young population in the area. This presence complements the observations of Sala and others that the overwhelming impression, certainly in the galleries of the Victoria, was of a throng of young people between the ages of twelve and twenty. The Victoria gallery and its approaches were the scene of a number of accidents, particularly during the Christmas pantomime season when overcrowding became particularly noticeable. In 1848 two boys were killed and others injured in a crush on the stairway. Identification of the victims showed that the two boys, aged fourteen and eleven, lived in Chelsea and Regent Street West, while one of the injured lived near Vauxhall Bridge Road.[90] In 1858 fifteen people were killed when two pantomime audiences collided: the matinee audience trying to exit at 4:30 P.M. were met by an eager audience crowding for the 6:30 performance. The dead were all boys between fourteen and twenty-one, who lived round the immediate vicinity of Waterloo Road, Bermondsey, and Southwark. Others had lived at slightly more distant addresses such as Holborn. *The Times* (28 December 1858) noted that no females were among the injured. In 1867 a similar accident resulted from patrons discovering too late that prices to the gallery had been raised from 3d to 6d for the Boxing Night performance of the pantomime and deciding to turn and leave. The consequence was the death of a boy aged eleven who had traveled from Blackfriars with his brother aged sixteen.[91] In 1842 two boys sixteen and fourteen and a girl described as "a little prostitute" aged eighteen, from Whitechapel, were arrested for a burglary in Spitalfields. They had walked by way of London Bridge "to the Victoria theatre to enjoy themselves on the proceeds of the plunder."[92] In 1843 a Mrs. Allen was the victim of pickpockets at the pit entrance. Although one was fashionably dressed, the police recognized them as part of a gang operating around the St. Giles's area, roughly one-and-a-half miles north of the theatre.[93] Local gangs also operated near the theatre: in 1868 a fifteen-year-old boy "connected with a gang of youth ruffians and thieves infesting the New-cut" attacked and robbed Henry Grey, a groom on the gallery stairs.[94] Not all victims however were necessarily young: in 1842 Ellen Gunton, aged fifty, after visiting the theatre with friends, was knocked over by a horse and rider and killed.

Such reports help to document the presence in the gallery of both a local audience and one which had traveled from other parts of London. The reports of accidents also indicate the presence of professionals living in the area, particularly doctors — the 1858 reports show the presence of at least five who assisted with the dead and injured.[95] Census returns corroborate this: in 1851, for instance, Upper Stamford Street, in addition to carpenters, draper's assistants, errand boys, lodging house keepers, and plumber's apprentices, housed clergymen, civil engineers and surveyors, solicitors, retired annuitants, and "gentle-women." There is little evidence however to suggest that pockets of middle-class professionals lived in a sea of working-class housing. Indeed, professional and artisan occupations appear to have existed side by side in the same streets.

The evidence of census returns, reports by the police to the Lord Chamberlain, and newspaper accounts of disasters and assaults imply a period of rapid growth in the area from 1830 into the 1860s, particularly of people associated with machine trades and the various service industries providing food, clothing, and housing. Many settled in the area with young families and this combination provided a degree of demographic stability until the early 1860s. The presence, however, of a large marketplace in the New Cut and Waterloo Road attracted numbers of transient workers and street vendors. The *South London Press* (28 January 1865) commented that the composition of the neighborhood by the 1860s had changed, especially around the densely populated New Cut. Since the cost of living increased by 18 percent between 1858 and 1872 (including a rent increase of 10%) and wages failed to keep up with inflation, there may well be good cause for the impression of deterioration which Sala and others noted in the Lambeth area. By 1866 the journal *All the Year Round*, which had generally viewed Lambeth with good-natured curiosity, depicted it as a derelict area inhabited by "swarms of creeping, crawling, mangy-looking people who constantly throng the thoroughfare . . . suggestive rather of vermin than of human beings." [96]

REPERTOIRE AND MANAGEMENT

The Surrey

After Elliston's death in 1830, the Surrey maintained a relatively popular repertoire, with a strong emphasis on nautical and domestic melodrama. Even though nautical melodrama represented only one aspect of its offerings, a playbill announcing T. P. Cooke in *Poor Jack* and *My Poll and Partner Joe* in 1841 claimed:

This undeniably fortunate establishment, so long pronounced to be THE FIRST NAUTICAL THEATRE IN EUROPE is maintaining its proud pre-eminence, and almost eclipsing all former popularity: — Innumerable crowds flock from every quarter of London and the vicinity to greet their old favourite."[97]

In 1845 the *Weekly Dispatch* (4 May) commented, "If we want to see 'a true British sailor,' it is at the Surrey.... Yes, if we wish to hear true British courage extolled, and some feats of daring performed by the British tar, let us haste to the Surrey." Both Osbaldiston, who briefly managed the Surrey in the 1830s, and William Davidge, who succeeded him, presented dramas similar to those presented at the Victoria. A memorandum to the Lord Chamberlain shortly before the Theatre Regulation Act of 1843 describes performances at the Surrey and Victoria Theatres:

> The Surrey — nautical melodramas, Pantomimes and occasionally the regular Drama — the latter not more than a month throughout the year.
> The Victoria — Melodramas, Domestic Melodramas of 3 Acts, Burlettas, Comic Interludes, Pantomimes. The regular drama at intervals of six weeks continued for two and three weeks.[98]

Both theatres are recorded as charging the same prices for boxes, pit, and gallery (respectively 2s, 1s, and 6d), opening during the same hours (6 to 11:30 P.M.) and playing to a capacity of over two thousand plus in the case of the Victoria and of over three thousand at the Surrey. They often competed with rival versions of the same play, as in December 1841 with *The Two Locksmiths*. Under Davidge the nautical and domestic dramas of J. T. Haines (*My Poll and My Partner Joe, The Ocean of Life, The Phantom Ship, Alice Grey, Jack Sheppard*, and *Claud Duval*), as well as other melodramas such as *Jane of the Hatchet* (with its 100 female warriors), were all drawing audiences. The *Weekly Dispatch* (9 May 1841) characterizes the Surrey audiences as "not over fond of sterling acting. Murders, suicides, highway robberies, crying women and women in hysterics, hair-breadth escapes, with uninterrupted discharges of fire-arms, blue lights and trap-door tricks, are alone calculated to please them."

The passing of the Theatre Regulation Act in 1843, which made very little difference to the Victoria's repertoire, gave scope for a broader range of performances at the Surrey, to some extent achieving the breadth that Elliston had argued for earlier in the century. Mrs.

Davidge, who assumed control after her husband's death in 1842, Alfred Bunn, who briefly shared the management with Mrs. Davidge in 1847, and Richard Shepherd, who managed the theatre from 1848 to 1869, developed a policy that mingled melodrama, farce, Shakespeare, the legitimate drama, and the opera and also attracted many visiting stars, who would not have been willing to appear at the Victoria. The intention was evidently to offer a diversity of attractions, presumably to draw and/or cater to a diversity of playgoers. Since two classical actors shared the management during much of Shepherd's tenure – William Creswick from 1850 to 1862 and 1866 to 1869, and James Anderson from 1863 to 1865 – there were further incentives to perform the legitimate drama, perhaps partly in emulation of Samuel Phelps's success at Sadler's Wells, although the Surrey audiences were never considered as dedicated as those of Sadler's Wells. However, press reports of the Surrey from 1843 onwards are generally favorable; indeed, any lapse into too popular a repertoire tends to be reprimanded, as if expectations are higher of this theatre than of the neighboring Victoria. Throughout the 1840s and 1850s its policies reflect a conscious desire to present high quality drama and acting and to mount high quality melodramas and pantomimes, usually enhanced by spectacular staging. Nevertheless, these more popular forms of entertainment invariably came second in the bill whenever legitimate drama or opera were also on the bill, suggesting the possibility of two distinct types of audience at different times in the evening.[99]

Both the evidence of the census and of the press suggest mixed rather than specifically working-class audiences. Nevertheless, this does not mean that the audience or some of its members could not be unruly or express political views on occasion. Thus Charles Rice describes a performance of *Venice Preserv'd* in 1837, during which the audience applauded "the radical sentiments of Pierre." [100] In *Cinderella or Harlequin and the Little Glass Slipper*, staged in 1846, "the political allusions . . . running counter to the Chartists and their Kennington Common gathering, were not received with cordial approval, and discords instead of concords smote the ear." [101] The Surrey could be unruly for other reasons as well. In 1842, during a performance of *La Sonnambula*, two members of the audience who were in the gallery disrupted the performance by using improper language during a scene in which Miss Romer was discovered lying on a couch. Being drunk and becoming turbulent when an attempt was made to eject them, they were subsequently fined 5s each. When George Stansbury, the musical director, had his benefit in 1843 the *Weekly Dispatch* (24 September) reported that:

> The doors were thronged and a great rush into the theatre ensued; women shrieked, men boxed and children cried vociferously. The women found the clothes torn off their backs and their fronts, and their shrieks might have been attributed partly to this cause. The overture was performed but indignation from the whole house smothered even the crash of the trombones. A general cry arose of "Give us back our money" . . . At last the authorities of the theatre, with the music director, returned the entrance money to more than 400 persons, but this was not until the justly indignant audience assaulted the money-takers in the house.

In 1869 a youth was badly bruised when he was knocked over as he left the gallery, after witnessing a performance of *True to the Core*, by some rough fellows "rushing unmannerly down the gallery stairs, for a lark as they called it." [102]

Much of the time the gallery audience was relatively restrained, if W. B. Donne's observations in 1859 are to be trusted. Donne, the Examiner of Plays, visited the Surrey to observe behavior at the gallery bar:

> At the end of the first price, about 9 o'clock, about 20 people of both sexes went to the bar, without any noise or confusion and called for porter or spirits &c, which they drank standing (there are no seats) and almost immediately returned to their seats. After the second price the same movement was repeated in similar good order. I did not hear a word uttered that I could not write down; and I purposely put myself in the midst of the roughest batch, who seemed most likely to take license. There seemed much more anxiety to regain places than to remain near the counter on these occasions. Neither did I see in anyone an approach to drunkenness.
>
> Having satisfied myself that on the particular occasion, at least, there was neither tumult or excess, I had a little conversation with the Check-taker of the Gallery; and he assured me that a disorderly person was a most unusual occurrence, and there was always a watchman on ken in the Gallery, to shew him out, if troublesome or drunken. [103]

Donne further discovered from the manager, Shepherd, that the refreshment bars were an advantage insofar as spectators no longer left the house for refreshments, consequently no longer interrupting the performance on their return.[104]

The varied nature of the Surrey's repertoire, which could attract audiences for opera, Shakespeare, and the legitimate drama, not to mention melodramas and farces on a variety of non-nautical topics, militates against the assumption of specifically nautical and working-class audiences. The audience was not only local but also from further afield. When the theatre reopened in April 1843 the *Weekly Dispatch* (23 April) claimed the Surrey was now "a very fine theatre, and will attract not only those who live in that quarter, but those at the other extremity of London." On 29 April 1846 the *Weekly Dispatch* stated that the Surrey "is well worth a visit, and we think the bill of fare they continually present will induce hundreds to cross the river now the spring season is advancing." This may also explain the success of the opera seasons each summer, which appealed both to the local community and to a broader cross-section of the public. The doors opened half an hour later for these seasons than at other times of the year, indicating an audience traveling from further afield. Certainly, against all odds, the opera seasons, which had commenced prior to 1840, drew crowded audiences.[105] In June 1842 there was scarcely standing room in any part of the theatre when Bellini's *La Sonnambula* was performed. The *Sunday Times* (11 June 1843) claims that the opera company was delighting "the denizens of Lambeth, Kennington and Vauxhall," implying an extensively local patronage. (Evidence of a local presence also emerged in 1841, when "the inhabitants of St. George's Fields' made up the nightly audience while Ducrow was performing *Mazeppa* at the Surrey.) [106]

In 1844 the *Weekly Dispatch* (1 September) stated that the Surrey deserved to be classed with its rivals in the West End and was drawing large audiences through its presentation of legitimate drama. A year later, in July 1844 the same journal noted a strong improvement in the Surrey:

As the importance of our large theatres has gradually diminished from causes too well known and too often discussed to be now dilated upon, the character or standing of our minors has proportionately been exalted and respected. It has been found to be far better in the long run to make expensive engagements with talented performers, and give us specimens of good dramatic composition, than to continually present us with "raw head and bloody bone" melodramatic abortions, abounding in clap-trap and having a very questionable moral effect upon the minds of audiences. What an immense improvement is there in the direction of the Surrey Theatre. We now have excellent operas, admirably performed, in lieu of the series of horrors and absurdities of the Radcliffe School, which was given a few years back.

Subsequently in July and August 1846, the Surrey engaged Mathews and Vestris, although accounts of their reception are contradictory.[107] In the same year Macready was engaged and drew large crowds, leading the *Weekly Dispatch* (18 October 1846) to suggest that the legitimate drama was flourishing with Macready at the Surrey and Phelps at Sadler's Wells. *The Times* (9 November 1846) inferred that the crowded theatre was evidence of "that taste for the legitimate English drama which is now becoming so prominent a feature among the less aristocratic classes." In 1847 the *Satirist* (30 May) noted that "the pit was crowded with a class of person of much higher respectability than ordinarily are attracted by the extremely moderate charge for admission." Three months later (29 August) it implied that not even "West-end admirers of genuine theatricals" could be sure of a private box during T. P. Cooke's reengagement. On 11 June 1848 the *Weekly Dispatch* reported of Lord John Russell's five-act tragedy *Don Carlos* at the Surrey that "the pit and gallery were tolerably full," but that "the boxes were indifferent; we suppose Ascot Cup Day had drawn the fashionables." Yet, when Phelps appeared in *The Lady of Lyons* two months later, the theatre was crowded "almost to suffocation." Despite its hyperbole, the announcement in a playbill for January 1849 that the Surrey was "the nightly resort of all the Rank and Fashion in London" demonstrates the aspirations now held for the theatre by its management.

The press continued to wonder at the capacity of Surrey audiences to listen quietly to Shakespeare or the opera. The *Sunday Times* (10 August 1851) refers to the silence with which the opera *The Mountain Sylph* was listened to as a testimony of "the improvement of taste among all classes." After *The Huguenots* played to overflowing houses the same paper (24 August 1851) commented:

It was strange indeed to see the class of people who usually compose the audience of the pit and gallery flocking eagerly to hear a grand opera; their response proved there was no lack of appreciation for good music "amongst the mechanics and laboring classes of London."

Between 9 June and 20 December three new operas, including *Don Giovanni*, were mounted, and twenty operas were revived.[108] On 9 October 1851, the *Sunday Times* referred to the high quality of productions under Creswick and Shepherd at the Surrey; on 23 November 1851, it surmised that only a few years before it would not have been thought possible that such quality would be appreciated south of the river. On 28 December it stated that the patronage bestowed on the Surrey was not only extensive in its character, "but . . . stamped with the seal of respectability and intelligence." However, the press, although praising some audience members, could still be dismissive of the local audience. The *Illustrated News* (31 July 1852) reported that *The Devils* (a new opera by Balfe) drew one of "the largest and most respectable audiences ever collected within the walls of the Surrey Theatre. The pit and galleries were filled with the usual southern aborigines – coatless, and in many cases waistcoatless, but the boxes and private boxes were tenanted by almost every professional and amateur of note in the metropolis, including the principal members of Her Majesty's Theatre."

Despite the condescending tone implicit in this review and occasional sneers in other publications about the "great unwashed," the Surrey was arguably attracting a local community from a wider social range than such an account suggests. Even in 1845 there was reference to the Surrey's appeal to a range of classes from the local community:

A successful piece may be regarded as a standard of the dramatic taste with which the middling classes and those a shade lower are imbued. . . . The most favourite productions are those laid among the domestic circles in which the majority of the audience move.[109]

The *Era* (9 June 1861) complained about the unsuitability of William Searle's summer season at the Surrey, commenting that the pieces were more appropriate to the City of London Theatre than the Surrey and that it was equivalent to "transferring the manners of Whitechapel to

Belgravia." Such comments certainly help to explain the Surrey repertoire during the 1840s and 1850s, as does Creswick's own statement that:

> We commenced our managership of the Surrey by taking as an example Mr Phelps's conduct of Sadler's Wells Theatre, and endeavoured to do at the Surrey side what he had effected at the north end of the metropolis, by creating a taste for a better kind of amusement than that to which the people had been accustomed. We determined to exert ourselves to raise the character of the house by providing an intellectual fare for its patrons — to choose good pieces, and with the means at our command, to present them to the public in the best possible style.[110]

Thus in 1852, for instance, Creswick appeared in *The Duchess of Malfi* with Isabella Glynn and in *Virginius*. During the 1850s *Richard III, King Lear, King John, Othello, Julius Caesar, Henry IV Part I*, and *Much Ado About Nothing* were among the many Shakespeare plays staged. Samuel Phelps often played special seasons at the Surrey Theatre from the late 1840s until the early 1860s. Although Creswick lacked a company equal to Phelps's and had to moderate his policies by also presenting more popular fare, he maintained that the objective of presenting more elevated entertainment was "kept steadily in view." [111] *The Times* (30 April 1860) certainly recognized this:

> The present managers of the Surrey are not violent reformers, who would effect such a thorough change as that of Sadler's Wells by Mr Phelps, but they have an evident disposition to elevate their public, and in these decentralising days we should not be at all surprised if their house — one of the best built in London — became a recognized place for the production of important novelties.

If Creswick could not quite emulate Phelps, it may be partly due to the different demographic constituencies of north and south London audiences.[112] Nevertheless, it is clear that the Surrey cannot be dismissed as a mere purveyor of melodrama to the lowest common denominator of spectator during this period.

The demographic shift away from the pockets of respectable residents discernible in the 1860 census may help to account for the change in the Surrey's fortunes in the late 1860s, although the appeal of opera had declined from the mid-1850s. (Shepherd and Creswick had put on an opera in Italian instead of in English and doubled their prices in 1856. The opera failed to draw and the season was abandoned; this disaster also signalling the end of the Surrey's in-house opera company.[113] Yet its policy of presenting opera in English had been very successful up until this time.) In 1863 the Surrey was addressing its advertisements for *Jessie Ashton; or, London By Day and Night: Being the Career and Adventures of a Barmaid* to "the Barmaids of London and all parties in or out of the trade." The theatre also continued to present new dramas with a broader social appeal, such as Watts Phillips's *Theodora, Nobody's Child,* and *Land Rats and Water Rats* (replete with a sensational scene in which a young girl was bound to a railway track in front of an oncoming express train), and to win praise for the order kept in the auditorium.[114] However, although a new farce, *A Night at the Bal Masque,* drew a fashionable audience in 1866, the *South London Press* (17 March 1866) lamented that the dress circle and boxes presented "a sight too rarely seen in a theatre this side of the Thames." In the same year the opera season proved something of a failure, suggesting that the Surrey Theatre could no longer count on such entertainment to attract audiences. Insofar as the theatre's fortunes began to change during the 1860s, the period between the destruction of the theatre by fire in February 1865 and its subsequent reopening in December 1865 may mark the beginning of the transition. Despite Creswick's return in 1866 and such successes as *East Lynne* (with Avonia Jones) in 1866 and *True to the Core,* the T. P. Cooke prize drama, a number of factors may have contributed to this situation, including the development of the suburban railway network, which made the growing number of theatres in the West End more accessible, and competition from music halls such as the South London Palace of Varieties and the Surrey Music Hall.

Creswick and Shepherd relinquished the management in 1869, to be followed by a succession of short-lived managements, and a policy of playing more popular dramas.[115] In 1872 there were rumors that the theatre would be sold and converted for commercial purposes,[116] despite the fact that several notable actors and actresses, including Madame Celeste and Henry Neville, appeared at the theatre. The performances early in 1873 of Watts Phillip's *Lost in London* and of Murray Wood's *Innocent,* a "social evil" play about slum-dwellers and the need for "clean, healthy houses," which drew strong reactions "from all parts of the house," may indicate a response to a more locally based and less affluent audience.[117] From December 1873 to 1881 William

Holland, the self-styled "People's Caterer," took over the management of the theatre. *All the Year Round* (19 May 1877) characterized the Surrey audience under Holland's management:

> It was an enthusiastic, nay, a noisy audience which crowded Mr Holland's theatre from floor to roof; but it was well-behaved, most cordial, and most sincere, if most vehement in the applause which it showered on its favourites. There was nothing specially instructive about it unless, indeed, it be its countenance of delight. There were visible social gradations in the audience. The two rows of stalls — the rest of the area was occupied by the pit — were filled by the elite of the vicinity of Kennington and a few pilgrims from the West End; the boxes were occupied, for the most part, by the magnates of local trade and by young gentlemen, who had formed a party for the evening.

The emphasis placed by Holland on popular melodrama drew audiences reminiscent of those that had earlier characterized the Victoria Theatre:

> The pit seemed a seething mass of plebeian humanity. The gallery loomed portentous in a motley crowd of noisy witnesses; while, even the dress-circle was infected with the wild abandon of transpontine labor let loose, and joined in the irrepressible tumult.[118]

The effervescent, if formulaic tones of these accounts belie the fact that Holland's management was to end with a debt of £10,000. Despite a return to a more popular repertoire than that played under Creswick and Shepherd (although Creswick returned to play brief seasons in 1875 and 1880), the Surrey was not to succeed again financially until the Conquest management commenced in 1881.

From the time of Shepherd's and Creswick's management, the Surrey Theatre had established and maintained a reputation for its annual pantomimes, providing something of a magnet for the inhabitants of South London. George Conquest had previously established himself at the Grecian Theatre as one of the leading pantomime performers of the period. Now he also engaged comedians such as Dan Leno and Tom Costello for his Surrey pantomimes, thus doubly ensuring their success. A reputation for sensational melodrama (Arthur Shirley and Paul Merritt numbered among his authors), often in local and contemporary settings, also ensured the prosperity of the Surrey under the

Conquest family into the twentieth century. In many ways the Surrey Theatre provided for the suburbs of South London the sort of mixture that Augustus Harris had found so effective at Drury Lane.

The Victoria

As we have seen, managers attempted to come to terms with the location of the Victoria theatre by stressing the availability of transport and by attempting to attract patrons used to theatregoing on the northern side of the Thames. In common with other minor theatres during the period up to the end of the 1830s, the Coburg managers were exercised by rapid increases in population, which juxtaposed newcomers with those who had already settled in the various neighborhoods, and which made choices of repertoire highly problematic. As well, managers were forced to balance ticket prices with profitability as they tried to come to terms with what the theatrical marketplace could tolerate.

The period from 1819 to the end of Davidge's management in 1833 was marked by the belief that the basis of the theatre's clientele would be patrons attracted from elsewhere, who would be prepared to accept a price structure of 3s and 4s in the boxes, 2s in the pit and 1s in the gallery. Both the theatrical nomenclature (The Royal Coburg), which identified the theatre with specific members of the royal family, together with the personal visits by dignitaries such as the Duke and Duchess of Kent in 1819 and Queen Caroline in 1821, seemed to justify the establishment of West End ticket offices for "the Accomodation [sic] of the Nobility and Gentry." [119] At the same time managements made no secret of the fact that they were placing themselves in direct competition with the Surrey and even Astley's and challenging the repertoire of the major theatres themselves. In order to do so, visiting celebrities would need to be seen in the theatre, and productions of plays comparable in quality to those concurrently being performed either at the Surrey or the West End would need to be offered. Thus Junius Brutus Booth played a version of *Richard III* in 1819 with the result that Glossop the manager was promptly prosecuted. [120] In 1831, when Edmund Kean opened on June 27 in *Richard III*, Davidge not only installed 4s stalls in the pit, but asserted that he was following the practice of the opera:

those of the Theatrical Public who have hitherto only witnessed the efforts of this great tragedian in the vast spaces of the Patent

Theatrical Reflection, or, a Peep at the Looking-glass Curtain at the
Royal Coburg Theatre, 1822.
Courtesy Harvard Theatre Collection.

Theatres, will find their Admiration and Delight at his splendid Powers, tenfold increased by . . . seeing them exerted in a Theatre of
moderate Dimensions, allowing every Master look and fine Tone of
the Artist, to be distinctly seen and heard.[121]

Explicitly, this points to the expectation that theatregoers would follow
their stars to other theatres and that the Coburg's intimacy would en-

hance performances. To an extent the policy appeared to be working, although E. L. Blanchard's estimation that in 1821 the receipts of the Coburg "indicated a period of good business" is questionable.[122] In 1821 the novelty of the looking-glass curtain, which reflected the entire audience, was intended to flatter those who spent time looking at themselves in mirrors and who could afford them. In actual fact the curtain's weight made it unmanageable and in any case poor ventilation coated it with a misty, opaque film, thereby defeating its whole purpose.[123] By 1828, however, the rivalry with the Surrey, the realization that the actual Coburg audience was not predominantly fashionable, and the need to retain the goodwill of local shopkeepers by distributing free orders to those prepared to display playbills, forced the management to reassess its ticket prices. Davidge reduced prices in 1832 to boxes 3s and the pit 1s 6d, while retaining the gallery at 1s; a further reduction took place in 1833, with boxes at 2s, pit at 1s, and gallery at 6d. This last price structure would last until the 1840s. It was an admission that box prices were unsustainable and it threw particular emphasis upon the gallery.

The period until Davidge's bankruptcy in 1833 has few documentary sources of information: playbills are rare and information is derived secondhand. Increasingly after this period it is possible to chart managerial policy and repertoire. The period to 1841 saw attempts on the part of managers to adhere to elements of a policy evidently out of touch with the theatre's surroundings. A change of name to the Royal Victoria in 1833 maintained the myth of royalty's personal involvement in the fortunes of the theatre. A production of Bellini's *La Sonnambula*, which stressed the similarities with the production offered at Drury Lane (15 April 1840), clearly sought to challenge the Surrey's operas. On the other hand J. T. Haines's *Wizard of the Wave*, which played for four weeks in 1840, was more appropriate and, as the playbill for 25 September asserts, had been "witnessed by 24,000 persons." This exciting melodrama, with N. T. Hicks playing identical twins and set in an exotic Sierra Leone, with pirate ships, government spies, and gold bullion, was paired with *Cherokee Chief; or, the Dogs of the Wreck*, which brought Indians, Cony's celebrated dog, Hector, and a combat with sword and dagger to the stage. These dramas were much more appealing, as was the last pantomime under John Ratcliffe's management, *Jack of Newbury, or; Baa, Baa, Black Sheep and the Old Woman of Berkeley*, written by Moncrieff, with contemporary references to a railway terminus, the exterior of Drury Lane Theatre (mocking at its patent pretensions), and the interior of a local paper mill. The portrayal of the "exterior of a Fanciful and Architectural residence in the Vicinity of the Metropolis" (playbill 4 January 1841) could just as well have been a comment on the fancies that speculators had attempted to build round the theatre itself.

The turning point for the theatre came with David Osbaldiston and Eliza Vincent's partnership. It began in 1841 and, after Osbaldiston's death, the theatre continued under Eliza Vincent's sole management until her death in 1856. Both were actors who lived in the area and were thus attuned to the nature of its socioeconomic structure. The changes in respectability noted by the papers did not in fact signal a change in demography, but rather the fact that managerial policy was consistent with the tastes and wishes of its patrons. Osbaldiston recognized that the Victoria's audiences responded to performers who identified themselves with their patrons. The playbill for Dibdin Pitt's *Simon Lee, or; the Murder of the Five Fields Copse* (17 May 1841) announced:

> This most beautiful and truly Pathetic Domestic Drama has already aroused the feeling of thousands of delighted Spectators! – Look around, and behold the moist tear of compassion flowing from the o'ercharged heart, as it sympathizes with the wretched sufferings of the wreck'd and broken-hearted! – Who can restrain these, the best feelings of our nature, at the representation of such Domestic Woe, rendered still more poignantly acute by the reflection, that the occurrence in Real Life is but too frequent and too fatal.

Although this play had been written originally for the City of London theatre in 1839, Dibdin Pitt followed with a play written expressly for the Victoria, *Susan Hopley, or, the Vicissitudes of a Servant Girl*, which opened on 14 June 1841 and, by 7 August was being announced for its sixtieth night. The play, which took as its point of departure the occupation of many of the young single girls who lived in the neighborhood, was a moral lesson in domestic loyalty. It traced the events which befall a young servant girl, played by Eliza Vincent, who "leaves the country, disgraced but innocent," journeys to London, and is exonerated at the end of the play. Her lover was played by E. F. Saville. It was a play calculated to appeal to the gallery, demonstrating that the managers recognized the need to cater to this section of patrons. The playbill for 2 August 1841 announced that:

> To Parties frequenting the Gallery of this Theatre. The Management begs to announce that Many and Efficient Alterations have been made in this part of the House . . . Numerous Additional Seats have been most conveniently constructed, from all of which the Spectator can command a view of the stage as full and uninterrupted as from the very center. New openings have been made on both sides . . . Another New Passage has also been made from this part of the Theatre to the Pit, in order to give every facility to the Hundreds who pass down nightly after the Gallery has been completely filled.

In September 1842 a revival of *Susan Hopley* was announced with a notice that "female domestics wanting to see *Susan Hopley*" could be assured that the performance ended at 8:30 in order to gain permission to see the play from their mistresses.

At the same time Osbaldiston added revivals of established plays to the domestic dramas, including *Virginius* and *The Iron Chest* in 1841, *Katherine and Petruchio* and *The Merchant of Venice* in 1842, and *Othello* and *Hamlet* in 1844. Generally these appear to have been due to his own desire to perform or in response to requests for benefits. Yet the great successes of this management were the numerous plays, often with Welsh, Irish, or West Country settings, juxtaposing the contrasts between idyllic village settings and city squalor and corruption, and featuring Eliza Vincent as the heroine. Though this thematic concern was not unique to the Victoria, it had particular relevance to the neighborhood's composition and to the experience of its immigrants.

In 1846 managements throughout London were beginning to feel economic hardship. Osbaldiston attributed this in particular to the competition from the beer shops and dancing rooms, as well as the attractions of steamboat and railway excursions.[124] The causes could equally be laid at the door of the economic climate generally and it was necessary to actively promote the theatre to its now regular patrons. A playbill (4 April 1847) states:

> In the present state of the times, the industrious mechanic (in too many instances) is unable to afford to take his wife and children on

the usual pleasure trips as formerly; the increased demands upon his pocket rendering the expense almost more than he can retrieve even by a week's hard toil; but HERE, for a small amount saved from his week's earnings, he can, surrounded by his family, witness AN ENTERTAINMENT, novel, varied and instructive; while with feelings of delight, he looks upon the happy group, sees their smiling faces, and can go to work cheerfully on the morrow, with the conscience that he has not purchased a too dearly bought gratification.[125]

It is a sentiment with which Dickens would have agreed. At the same time Osbaldiston was actively seeking the patronage of temperance societies and others who would take the theatre for a special occasion. By the end of 1846 he had dropped the price of the gallery to 4d;[126] by 8 May 1847 prices were further dropped to boxes 1s, half-price 6d, pit 6d, and gallery 3d, and he could state the theatre's prices were "within the means of all classes of society."[127] On 4 October 1847 a playbill for Dibdin Pitt's *The Merchant's Clerk; a Love Story* announced that "This establishment being now the only theatre on this side [of] the water where . . . the true domestic drama can be represented."

After Osbaldiston died in 1851, "domestic drama" in the theatre's repertoire seemed to decline, although plays which referred to local trades and preoccupations remained. The performance of historical dramas like Stirling's *White Hoods, or, the Revolt of Flanders* as well as the revivals of past successes suggest either a loss of purpose or a return to an insecurity about the nature of the theatre's audience. In 1859 the introduction of pit stalls at 1s 6d indicate an attempt at gentrification. In March 1863 in an effort to retain their audiences, the management of Frampton and Fenton announced that refreshments in the theatre's saloons — wine, beer, fruit, sandwiches and pork pies — were no more expensive than at the public houses outside, to counter the kind of rush at half price to which Sala alluded in 1859.[128] A further attempt to regulate behavior also found an expression in 1868, when the lessee J. Arnold Cave announced that "Any person whistling or making any other disturbance will be expelled by the police. No encores will be allowed during the pantomime."[129] The final attempt to restore the theatre to the vision which had animated the earliest lessees occurred in the 1870s, when Cave introduced programs at 1d (with a full page advertisement for Rimmell's Toilet Waters and Restoratives on the inside cover) and when a list of refreshments in 1878 included not only beer at 2d a glass and spirits at 4d and 6d per glass, but champagne at 1s a large bottle, undoubtedly to celebrate the fact that Waterloo Bridge could now be crossed toll-free.

SUMMARY

By 1871 Southwark's population had grown to 208,725 and Lambeth's to 208,342. Yet, although the local population had therefore almost doubled during the previous thirty years, both the Victoria and the Surrey were in difficulties. The increase in theatre building throughout London and the competition from the music halls may partially explain this, just as cheaper fares and improved transport facilities may have encouraged local inhabitants to look to the West End for an evening's entertainment. Many neighborhood theatres experienced difficulties during the 1870s and had to make fundamental policy changes to keep afloat.[130] The Surrey and Victoria were no exceptions. Additionally, a decrease in the disposable income available to local audiences may also have been a factor in their decreasing attendance. In the preceding years, however, both theatres had played a significant part in the life of their immediate neighborhoods. Nevertheless, the Victoria's proximity to the New Cut and the general squalor of its immediate environment set it apart from the Surrey, which enjoyed a more salubrious and accessible location. The Osbaldiston/Vincent management at the Victoria and the Shepherd/Creswick management at the Surrey had consequently established quite diverse policies: the Victoria's emphasis on domestic drama arguably catered to a local, popular audience; whereas the Surrey's combination of legitimate drama and opera with the more popular forms of melodrama, burletta, and farce, appealed to both a mixed local audience and to visitors from further afield.

The gradual establishment of differing programs, aimed at potentially different (but still local) audiences, by neighboring theatres, is a phenomenon that we shall also find in the East End. The evidence of the census suggests that locally both family audiences and unaccompanied children and adolescents would have attended both theatres and that the social range of such audiences would have been broader than that represented merely by the laborers, artisans, and mechanics who lived locally. It also demonstrates that the local community was not particularly representative of maritime or nautical occupations, despite the popularity of nautical melodrama at the Surrey and the Vic-

Victoria Theatre, children at the Royal Victoria Coffee Music Hall, 1882.

toria. Given the capacity of Londoners to walk long distances in the nineteenth century and the increasing availability of new, inexpensive forms of public transport, it is dangerous to assume that audiences even at neighborhood theatres were specifically local. Equally, it may be erroneous to overcategorize audiences by class: the interior divisions within both theatres separated out spectators according to income and social preference. What can be ascertained, however, is that the composition of the "transpontine" or "Surrey-side" audiences was far more complex than is indicated by Dickens, Sala, and many later accounts of the two theatres.

Part Two

ORIENTALISM & SOCIAL CONDESCENSION
Constructing London's East End Audiences

INTRODUCTION

In 1858 two large, ornate theatres in the East End of London opened after rebuilding: the Pavilion in Whitechapel and the Britannia in Hoxton. Both were considered as elaborate as any West End theatre, for no expense had been spared and the most up-to-date building technologies had been used. Both held large-capacity audiences and both attracted comment that raise significant issues about east London audiences. In the case of the Britannia, Dickens's well-known account creates a portrait of a generic East End audience, although this portrait is carefully constructed to support his argument in favor of popular amusements. The "motley assemblage" of all age groups, some less clean in their attire and habits than others, but all attentive and orderly, in a large new theatre built especially for them, illustrates Dickens's belief in the efficacy of popular entertainment and the need for its proper provision. The initial response of the *East London Observer* to the new Pavilion, however, indicates the dangers inherent in assuming that East End audiences could be described generically in the first place. Although these two theatres will be the focus for a discussion of East End audiences, it is necessary initially to look more closely at generic accounts of East End audiences and to contextualize the East End of London and its theatres.

Typical portraits of the generic East End audience occurred in two accounts of the Britannia Theatre published in the 1870s, during a period which also saw changes in local demographics.[1] The first was *L'International* (11 and 12 May 1870), which desired to provide an account of a popular London theatre for its French readership. The author arrived at 9:00 P.M., just before the commencement of the second piece, and visited the refreshment room common to the stalls and boxes, the inhabitants of which reminded him of the average barroom in an ordinary public house. Two "fish wives" were drinking gin; two young men in their Sunday best were talking to two female laborers; others were sitting alone. As soon as it was announced that the next play was about to start, they all quitted the bar immediately. On entering the auditorium the author was struck by its ornateness, equivalent to any West End theatre; its "strong smell of poverty," and "the sea of moving heads" receding into darkness in the gallery. Even in their shirt sleeves, the gallery occupants still sweated and their clothes stuck to their skin. In the stalls and pit were many young female laborers from the neighborhood with their sweethearts; also many children but few older people. No one removed their hats. The noise was tremendous, particularly from the gallery, where people were passed back and forward over the heads of those already seated. Throughout the first act of the play the noise continued, as did cries of "Order! Order!" so that little could be heard. Throughout the play the audience kept up a running commentary: whenever it became too loud there were again cries of "Order!" although these might merely provoke fresh outbursts. At the end of the play the crowd went wild, their cries, however, being overwhelmed by shrill and piercing whistles, which seemed to be the normal mode of applause at the Britannia. The actors seemed used to performing against all the noise; when the leading actress was called back on stage, she was showered with orange peel. Again, this is an impressionistic account, but it does suggest something of the vitality, combined with self-regulation, of the audience, even if it cannot resist the perennial urge to exoticize them.

On 19 May 1877, *All the Year Round* published an account of audiences at the Surrey and Britannia Theatre under the title "Some Theatrical Audiences." The gulf between east and west is emphasized in this account; indeed, the cab driver hired to take the writer to the East End clearly does not know his way to the Britannia and the journey itself is exotic:

How very few of those who live West know anything of that world which we have traversed in our drive due East — have any idea of the better and more attractive aspects of the most unfashionable quarter of London! True we have threaded some stifling thoroughfares, where flaming gas-jets have lit up hulks on which malodorous fish are exposed for sale, and whose surface is covered with decaying vegetables and unsightly morsels; have seen many signs of misery and vice; much squalor; much of dirt, and rags, and drunkenness. But we have emerged from all this now. We find ourselves being whirled through broad streets, in which are bright, cleanly shops, full of cleanly, sober people, flanked by houses, unpicturesque, it may be, but substantial and healthy. The whole place is airy and light; there is much bustling about on the part of neatly-clad women, and children and men; for it is Saturday night and the week's shopping is in process.

Having traversed the threatening terrain that divides east from west, the author is taken to his box, noticing in passing "a component odour, whose chief ingredients seem to be the perfume of disinfecting fluids and the fragrance of very coarse tobacco smoke." Most impressive, however, is the audience itself:

The great proportion are working men and women clad in their working clothes; a few are mechanics and artisans, in broad cloth and dark tweed. As for the women, they are all neatly but more showily attired. There is a fair sprinkling of children in arms; some thirty per cent of the entire audience are possibly boys between the ages of twelve and sixteen. It is not a polished assemblage; the faces are for the most part grimy, and the hair unkempt, but the patient attention and tranquillity of the huge concourse are quite admirable.

The lavish provision of "Brobdignagian sandwiches" and "foaming pots of porter" is also noted. Yet, despite all of this, nothing prevents the audience from "diligently noting all that is said and done on the stage." The account concludes with the usual moral truisms. It is formulaic in its exoticization of the journey east and tells us little about the Britannia that is not already available in earlier accounts.[2]

If we wish to explore the complexity and variety of East End audiences, which such accounts tend to conceal or even erase, then we must investigate the nature of the East End itself. From the late eighteenth century the East End had developed as the major center of trade, industry, and shipping in London. Separated from the fashionable West End by the City, it increasingly took on an identity that was fostered by its isolation. Bounded by the Thames to its south and stretching as far as Shoreditch and Hackney to its north it sprawled northwards and eastwards throughout the nineteenth century. It seemed a world apart to those who lived elsewhere, although not necessarily to its own inhabitants. In time the East End developed its own mythology; whether through the notoriety of the Ratcliffe Highway (allegedly dominated by knife fights, prostitution, and squalid drinking saloons), the extreme poverty of Bethnal Green, the waves of immigrants (particularly Irish and Jewish), or the efforts of journalists and commentators who sought to create and perpetuate its myths. It was another country, foreign and even terrifying territory to those who lived in the more comfortable districts and suburbs of London. It was also an area which, because of its close proximity to the City, was being depopulated to make way for the building of warehouses and other commercial developments. Its richer inhabitants moved out to the new suburbs of Dalston and Hackney; its poorer inhabitants moved more slowly outwards or, like the Jewish migrants at the end of the century, concentrated in ghettoes.

The population of East London expanded considerably in the nineteenth century, except in those areas cleared for redevelopment, warehousing, or industry, from about 125,000 in 1780 to almost one million in 1888. To the north the population of Shoreditch grew from 43,930 in 1811 to 124,009 in 1891, while that of Hackney expanded from a mere 16,771 in 1811 to 198,606 in 1891. Shipping and merchandizing determined employment in the early part of the century. The opening of a series of new docks also had an appreciable impact on the development of employment prospects, demographics, and communications. The West India Docks opened in 1802; the London Docks in 1805; the East India Docks in 1806; and St. Katherine Docks (closer to the city) in 1828. Commercial Road, providing easier access to the East End, was laid out in the early 1800s. As a result of such activity the area around Wapping, in Wapping High St. and Ratcliffe Highway materialized into a sort of shanty town of brothels, pubs, and cheap lodging houses, inhabited by sailors, prostitutes, and dock laborers. Marine-related trades and occupations made the area exotic insofar as they were specific (at least in London) to the East End and connected with access to strange and distant places overseas. To the north, in Spitalfields and Bethnal Green, lived many weavers.[3] Because of their closeness to the Regent's Canal and to the Docks, which meant that timber could be easily transported, Shoreditch and Curtain Road became the center of furniture and related trades from 1820. Other East End industries included ironworks, and rope and cable manufacture. Ships' joiners, carpenters, mast makers, sail makers and ships' chandlers plied their trades until disrupted by the advent of iron and steam ships later in the century. Clothing was another prominent industry, gradually overtaken by the "sweating system," dependent on cheap labor in the home, as was the footwear industry, situated more closely to Shoreditch and Stepney. Other forms of employment included candle and wax making, the manufacture of paint and of soap, beer brewing, sugar refining, and confectionery.[4]

The majority of inhabitants in the East End had either been born locally or had migrated from rural areas in search of work. Also among the inhabitants of the East End were the Spanish and Portuguese Sephardi Jews, who had settled there from 1656, while the Jewish population was enhanced during the century by Jewish settlers from Holland, Germany, Russia, and Poland. This certainly contributed to the exoticism and to the "otherness" of the East End. Between 1770 and 1914 about 120,000 Jews settled in London, becoming associated with street trading in east London and also with the clothing trade. L. P. Gartner claims that Jewish immigrants originated largely from Holland and Germany prior to 1865, but that the transition to greater migration from eastern Europe occurred from 1865 to 75. Around 1860 the Dutch Jews were particularly engaged in the tobacco and cigar-making trades in the East End. At the time, when Dutch Jews outnumbered Polish Jews by three to one, tailoring was very much a poor second to cigar-making as a Jewish occupation in Whitechapel and the neighboring parish of St. George's-in-the-East.[5] In the eighteenth century Irish migrants had also arrived, at first concentrating in the parish of St. Giles's and then gradually spreading along the banks of the Thames to the east. After the potato famine in Ireland more Irish migrants settled in east London than the entire population of Dublin; they preferred to congregate around Wapping and in the district around Devas Rd. in Bow.[6]

"All kinds of suppositions, associations, and fictions appear to crowd the unfamiliar space outside one's own," writes Edward Said.[7] Although Said's discussion of orientalism raises many issues that do not apply to an investigation of London's East End theatres, it would to some extent be correct to say that our perceptions of East End theatres are the constructs of West End critics, journalists, and social commentators, who tended to treat them as something remote and "other." Poor communications from west to east provided the starting point for investigative accounts by journalists fascinated by east London's promise of the exotic, the strange, and the sordid. An "orientalism" as pervasive and as fictive as that created by nineteenth-century European travelers to the Middle and Far East (not to mention those with a political agenda) permeates the accounts of those who braved the narrow streets of the City to arrive eventually in the strange outposts of Hoxton and Whitechapel. Even the theatrical journalists treat the locals like exotic species: accounts of the Britannia Theatre's productions in the *Era*, for example, often refer to the "natives" as "Hoxtonians," a tribe which not only celebrates a strange yearly "Festival" within the theatre, but can even be observed specifically for its unique and peculiar eating habits. Inevitably, as with accounts of the Victoria Theatre south of the river, gallery audiences are the most frequently described by journalists, just as they are the part of the audience most frequently investigated in police reports. Thus the "great unwashed" (hardly surprising in an area of London in which sanitation and water supplies were so inadequate) and the "lowest orders" are often represented in such accounts. Edward Said has written that the European representation of Muslim, Ottoman, or Arab:

> was always a way of controlling the redoubtable Orient, and to a certain extent the same is true of the methods of contemporary learned Orientalists, whose subject is not so much the East itself as the East made known, and therefore less fearsome, to the Western reading public.[8]

Similarly the East End audience is often represented as ultimately knowable and controllable, so that the fear of the "other" is appeased as the audience and its habits are defined and effectively "orientalized." Yet it is still difficult to define precisely the typical East End audience, almost certainly because there was no such thing. The bleak, depressed view of the East End at the end of the nineteenth century, as perpetuated by Charles Booth and Walter Besant,[9] had also colored accounts of East

End life earlier in the century. Socially, economically, and demographically, the East End was constantly changing. If, at the end of the century, it was gloomy and depressed, in the earlier years it had been a vibrant, confident hub of trade and industry. It was out of such a community that East End theatre originally grew.

The East End established itself as a generic theatrical area during the nineteenth century.[10] Following the expansion in trade and industry partially fostered by the intensive dock-building program of the early 1800s, a number of theatres that were to assume great significance in the area came into existence. These included the Pavilion Theatre, also known as the "Drury Lane of the East," and the Effingham Saloon (later the East London Theatre) in Whitechapel; the Garrick Theatre, just southeast of Houndsditch and the city in Leman Street; the Standard Theatre, opposite Bishopsgate Railway Station; the City of London Theatre, just along the road in Norton Folgate; the Britannia Saloon (later Theatre) in Hoxton, just north of the Standard and the City of London Theatres; and the Grecian Saloon (also to become a theatre) along the City Road and the furthest west of the significant "East End theatres."

East End audiences were arguably neighborhood audiences, many of whom had a choice of two or three theatres within walking distance. These audiences were probably quite diverse, not necessarily comprising a majority from the most cited occupations in the neighborhood and almost certainly including a wider social mix than many accounts imply. Yet, like West End audiences, the East End audiences tended to be defined generically. When asked by the 1866 Select Committee about the character of East End audiences as compared with those in the West End, the commissioner of police, Sir Robert Mayne, commented:

> They are a totally different class of people; in some part of the East end, the Whitechapel district and Wapping, there are rather the very lowest class of men and boys, the working classes of the neighborhood, but I'm bound to say that they were perfectly well behaved; they all seemed so much amused; the performances were not of a very high order but there was nothing demoralising.[11]

The remoteness of the East End theatres [12] is further highlighted by the *Builder* (25 September 1858):

Many of those, from whatever part of London, who frequent the chief theatres, or extend their tastes, once in a few years to Astley's or the Surrey, would be surprised to find the theatres that there are in the eastern part of London, which attract immense audiences, and which, with very low prices of admission, have proved the best-paying speculations.

The congruence of sailors, dock laborers, tradesmen, weavers, tailors, and other modes of employment in the East End suggests some aspects of audience composition in this area, but not in a sufficiently systematic way to establish East End playgoers as sui generis.

The earliest official attempt to categorize East End audiences was made in a series of police reports requested in 1843 on the deregulation of the London theatres. These claim that the City of London Theatre drew "persons in the neighborhood, many weavers," while the neighboring Standard drew tradesmen, mechanics, their children, and silk weavers from Spitalfields. Further south, the Garrick also drew a neighborhood audience, including tradespeople and mechanics, while the Pavilion drew persons in the neighborhood, "many from the docks, many sailors." [13] A petition on behalf of the Effingham commented that "many hundreds of the working Tradespeople, Housekeepers and their families and seafaring men from Whitechapel, Spitalfields and Stepney in the immediate vicinity have weekly resorted to this theatre for public amusement." [14] The audience at the Effingham was characterized as "tradesmen and their children from the neighborhood of St George's Parish, Whitechapel, Stepney; sailors when the river is full of shipping Families 2 or 3 times a week." Unaccompanied children were generally not admitted.[15] A report on the Grecian described its audiences as respectable tradesmen, clerks from the city, mechanics, and neighbours.[16] Yet there remained pockets of affluent inhabitants who also needed local theatres to cater to them, if they were to avoid the journey to the West End for entertainment. Equally, it was more convenient for the middle-class residents of Hackney, Dalston, and Stoke Newington (if they wanted theatrical entertainment at all) to travel directly south for entertainment than to the West End, which was still inconvenient to access by road or rail for much of the century.[17]

Both the orientalization and social mythologization of the East End are particularly noticeable in occasional pieces on East End audiences and in police and parish endeavors to suppress theatrical activity. The Jewish element in East End audiences and in the vicinity of the theatres particularly contributed to the orientalizing tendency, as in this description of a visit to the Pavilion Theatre:

> A night walk through Whitechapel is not exactly similar to an evening stroll through Regent Street. At every step we met Jew brokers, shops filled with an indescribable assortment of second-hand trumpery, locomotive fish stalls, baked 'tater establishments and penny pie warehouses. After threading our way through the crowds of Israelitish-looking people . . . we at length reached the Pavilion Theatre.[18]

Interestingly, a major West End thoroughfare is the norm against which the street is judged. The City of London Theatre also attracted a Jewish audience, again exoticized in this account:

> It was literally a house of Israel, as if all Bishopsgate, St. Mary Axe, Shoreditch and Finsbury Circus had disgorged their fusty tenantry in one huge mass of Anglo-Jewish capitalists. There were Moseses and Jacobses and Solomons and Isaacs, enough to have stormed and retaken old Jerusalem.[19]

In the early 1850s Mayhew described how this theatre, the Standard Theatre, and East End playhouses in general, were "greatly resorted to by the Jews, and more especially by the younger members of the body, who sometimes constitute a rather obstreperous gallery."[20] For over 100 years the Jewish playgoers of the East End are invoked in numerous such accounts.

Police reports tend to provide an equally colorful view of East End audiences. Although there is obviously some truth in what is reported, the number of youthful thieves and prostitutes readily identified in such reports, especially in the 1840s, also suggests a degree of prejudice. This may have been connected with a generally held belief that theatrical entertainments had a corrupting influence on young people. Thus at the City of London Theatre a police report for 1845 claimed:

> The audience in this part of the house was composed of the youth of both sexes, whose ages varied from 11 to 18, and chiefly of the very lowest class of society; the majority of the males being with-

out coats or jackets – I, and the officers who were with me, saw several males the associates of thieves – There were also between 40 and 50 young prostitutes, some apparently not more than 14 or 15 years old.[21]

In 1844 a police report had complained that the Britannia was resorted to "by the lowest class – prostitutes and thieves – old and young – who are admitted nightly for . . . 3d each."[22] A subsequent report stated that the theatre was resorted to by "the lowest grade of both sexes viz. Watercress girls, Hearth stone and match boys and girls from about 10 to 16 years of age" and that there could be no doubt that it was "calculated to corrupt the morals of the growing youth in that low and thickly populated neighborhood to a great extent."[23] A further police report claimed that the Britannia was resorted to "by the lowest class of Prostitutes and Juvenile Thieves who are supposed to form one half of the audience."[24]

The assumption that the boys and girls who formed the audiences at East End theatres were either thieves or prostitutes or soon would be through the corrupting influence of the drama resurfaces again and again. A police report on the Garrick Theatre in 1868 claimed "the persons attending consist principally of boys of the poorer class, many of them very young (from 10–12 years of age)."[25] In 1872 the parish authorities turned their attention to the Garrick, complaining that "children of tender age" were admitted in large numbers to "performances of an exciting nature and utterly unfit to be witnessed by (them)." They requested that the theatre's license be suppressed, since the theatre was "a perfect scandal to the neighborhood and causes immorality and vice."[26] Juvenile audiences also attended the penny gaffs, small unlicensed venues for cheap theatrical entertainment. The *Church Times*, c.1851, claimed the majority of these audiences were the children of the poor, particularly boys who couldn't read or write, and wondered what could be done to keep one's children and servants away from such places. In one of them in the east of London, it stated, "the policeman assured us that the audience scarcely contained an honest youth and there is little doubt that the means to attend these places of amusement are frequently procured by theft."[27]

The strange, uncouth habits of East End audiences are well documented. Lack of urinals and water closets meant that audiences often relieved themselves on the gallery stairs or in alleys and streets adja-

{ *East End Audiences* }

cent to the theatre, as at the East London Theatre, creating "scenes which can only be described as beastly," according to the Rector of Whitechapel, Reverend James Cohen.[28] The noise, especially on Boxing Day and at benefits; the smells, despite gradual improvements in ventilation and sanitation; the never ending supply of refreshments are all well documented. Yet, there is little evidence to substantiate either the journalistic fantasies or antitheatrical prejudices which strove to depict the East End theatres as lurid centers of depravity or disorder. Thefts were occasionally committed in the theatres and prostitutes occasionally attended, although usually as audience members. A girl of fifteen was indecently assaulted at the City of London Theatre in 1870, but such an occurrence was a rarity if the outraged response of the local press is anything to go by.[29] There were also few recorded instances of disorderly conduct or drink-induced violence. The theatre was more an alternative to the public house, rather than a simulacrum, especially once the saloon theatres had disappeared. Youthful audiences between twelve and twenty were regularly noted, especially in the galleries, but complaints concerning them were often a result of their crowding the pavements when awaiting admission. In fact, whereas some of the police reports may have told the authorities what they wanted to hear, others served as a corrective to the rather extreme nature of the complaints directed at East End theatres. Thus a day after the City of London Theatre was condemned for the presence of thieves and prostitutes in its audience, a further police report commented:

> there were between 4 & 500 persons in the house, all orderly and paying great attention to the performances . . . such as were in the Boxes and the pit were as respectable as one may expect to find at a Theatre, surrounded by the working classes of the Metropolis. Those that were in the Boxes consisted of Tradesmen and their wives and families, all cleanly dressed and very respectful.[30]

A subsequent visit to the gallery during a performance of *Jack Sheppard*, a drama about a notorious highwayman, later banned from representation on stage by the Lord Chamberlain,[31] also revealed an audience which was attentive and whose conduct was orderly:

> I saw a great number of young Boys and Girls ages varying from 7 to 20 years, also a great many elderly persons amongst them. I could not distinguish one from the other, as to their character in life. They

might have been the Depraved of the Depraved. But I saw nothing to give me any reason to say the least thing against them.[32]

The Britannia also began to draw more favorable reports from the very source which had originally condemned it. Samuel Lane, the Britannia's manager, had felt the earlier reports highly colored and flatly denied the presence of prostitutes in the theatre, claiming his house was resorted to by "respectable working people and Tradespeople and their families."[33] Within a year complaints had ceased: a police report of 24 March 1845 stated that the theatre was conducted in an orderly and proper manner,[34] an improvement confirmed by a police report of 1847:

> A great many respectable Tradesmen and Mechanics, with their wives and children, generally frequented the Boxes there, the Galleries being frequented by the lower classes of both sexes from the age of 12 years and upwards. Children under the age of 12 years are generally accompanied by their parents or friends.[35]

Such reports imply an audience determined by local demographics, but hardly the journalistically constructed audiences of popular mythology.

Exotic representations of "native" East End audiences persisted throughout the century. In 1868 the *Dramatic and Music Hall Review* (1 February 1868) suggested that the inhabitants of the West End of London were ignorant of the Britannia's existence or, if they had heard of it, of its whereabouts. However, the journal believed that a visitor to the theatre would be well repaid by a journey "to the remote locality" in which it was situated:

> Most other East-end houses are in main thoroughfares, but the Britannia is located in a region, known only to its natives, or by those who have been induced by some special object to explore it. If any of our readers have never visited this theatre, and are desirous of witnessing a somewhat novel sight, let them sally forth on a Saturday evening, during the run of the pantomime, and follow the course of the Old Street Road, until they arrive within a few hundred yards of Old Street Church; then turn to the left, and they will soon arrive at their destination.

The unease apparent in defining East End audiences occurred even in accounts of the Standard Theatre, which was to gain a reputation for bringing West End plays and performers to the east. The demographics of the local neighborhood and the theatre's accessibility by public transport were equivalent to the City of London Theatre, only a few hundred yards away. The Standard's repertoire and reputation were very different, however. According to Albert Douglass, "the residents of Hackney and Kingsland (very opulent districts then) flocked to the neighborhood to do their shopping and generally finished up at the Standard — And what an audience! — keen — critical — pulsating with life and easy to seize every point."[36] Most accounts, however, defined the theatre through comparison with the West End. A clipping c.1850 comments that:

What the Adelphi Theatre, from its situation, is to the Strand and the West End, this house is to Shoreditch and the East End; standing as it does in a leading thoroughfare, directly opposite the terminus of the Eastern Counties Railway, and in the midst of a dense neighborhood, it is nightly filled to overflowing.[37]

In 1856 *The Times* commended Douglass for his attempts to improve the theatre through "the engagement of a series of Western (West End) 'stars' who . . . shed the light of their talent *on a public entirely isolated from the rest of London*" [our italics].[38] It also commented on the "intelligence" with which this supposedly undiscriminating audience listened to the vocalist, Sims Reeves, not interrupting a song in the middle with untimely applause, but waiting until the end to show their appreciation. In 1869 the *Entr'acte* (10 July 1869) commended the theatre for its engagement of Phelps and Sothern:

The management of this house has completely demonstrated the fact that the population of the eastern districts of the metropolis is quite able to appreciate plays of the highest class when represented by artists of real ability. When a dramatic poem like "Manfred" . . . attracts immense audiences to a house situated in Shoreditch, it is sufficient proof that people at the East-end can enjoy works that do not depend for their interest on the apotheosis of a thief, nor upon the introduction of a real pump or of a real potato-gun. Anyone glancing round the dress-circle of the National Standard might well ask himself if he had not by some misconception entered a new West-end theatre built with a view to eclipsing Drury Lane. The ladies and gentlemen in this part of the house and in the stalls are dressed *de rigueur*, and many of the costumes of the fairer sex display a refinement of taste suggestive of their being the work of a George-street *modiste*.[39]

Within these accounts lurks a set of prior assumptions, which the Standard Theatre clearly belies, about East End audience behavior and composition, and a surprise that "they" respond and behave just like "us." In order to examine the problems created by such assumptions more closely, we shall now consider two representative theatres in detail, the Pavilion and the Britannia.

2. The Pavilion Theatre, Whitechapel

he history of the Pavilion Theatre compels us to challenge the conventions through which East End audiences were usually depicted. Situated opposite the London Hospital and on the site of a former clothing factory[1] in the busy Whitechapel Road, one of the major thoroughfares in and out of London, the Pavilion opened in 1828. The first of the major East End theatres to open in the nineteenth century, stimulated no doubt by the expansion in local population that the docks and increased trading had fostered, it was constructed by a local cat's meat man, Wyatt,[2] and Farrell, an actor. The new theatre's luxurious accommodation was advertised, particularly its "elegant and commodious boxes [which] have been constructed and adapted for respectable Family Parties and which the Proprietors flatter themselves are fitted up in a manner to give satisfaction and ensure Patronage."[3] The Pavilion evidently mirrored the patent theatres in its magnificence and aspirations. A. E. Wilson cites a court case in 1829, in which a prostitute appeared before the magistrates on a charge of disorderly conduct, after being refused admission. Farrell claimed that the management was resolved no female "of light character" should be permitted to enter the boxes. Yet this indication of aspirations towards respectability is offset by a newspaper report the same year, which referred contemptuously to "river pilots, its distinguished patrons."[4] Further, although it is dangerous to overargue the relationship between repertoire and neighborhood, it is clear that its early emphasis on nautical melodrama may well have been aimed at a local population in part familiar with marine pursuits. T. J. Serle's evidence to the Select Committee in 1832 also implies the Pavilion was drawing local audiences.[5] Douglas Jerrold's powerful indictments of naval and domestic abuses, *The Mutiny at the Nore* (1830) and *Martha Willis the Servant Girl* (1831), both first performed at the Pavilion, may have marked the theatre not only as a home of melodrama, but of plays that were critical of aspects of British society in those turbulent years leading up to the first Reform Bill of 1832. The theatre was surrounded by "a typical low-income working class neighborhood, comprised of small businesses, coffee shops, pubs, greengrocers and assorted enterprises."[6] Yet the commercial energy of the district, with its reliance on docks and trade, had been noted by C. A. B. Goede as early as 1807.[7] The Reverend H. Hadden, writing of St. George's-in-the-East Parish in 1880, suggests that in 1820 the East End was far less poverty-stricken than later in the century:

> Sixty years ago St. George's was in the zenith of its prosperity. It was not then, as now it fairly may be called, an almost entirely poor parish. The London Docks had it all their own way . . . and a large proportion of the imports which came to the Thames were discharged within their boundaries. Many wealthy merchants and traders resided in the parish, and on Sunday morning one might have seen a line of carriages drawn up outside the church gates, waiting to take their owners home from service. Houses, each of which now give a dwelling to three or four separate families, were then the town residences of the parochial merchant princes, Wellclose Square being pre-eminently the most fashionable quarter, as containing the house of the Danish Ambassador. Ratcliffe Highway was a busy mercantile thoroughfare.[8]

Millicent Rose also provides a sense of the industrial vitality of the East End in the early and middle years of the century with its cabinet making and tailoring, docks and ship building, and breweries and sugar refineries, the latter being one of the chief sources of occupation in Whitechapel.[9] It is for this vital community that the Pavilion was presumably catering, at least until the slump of the late 1860s.

Throughout the 1830s the Pavilion continued to present melodrama yet also aspired to a respectable audience. Wilson quotes a panegyric by a manager of the theatre in 1840, announcing the Pavilion as "an eastern national theatre where the cause of moral improvement will be strenuously advocated and supported in the selection of dramas calculated to instruct and improve the youthful understanding," adding that "parents and guardians may visit the theatre with their females without the fear of having the young mind contaminated by ribald and trashy productions which have too long been the order of the day."[10] Yet the theatre's failure to achieve its social aspirations is implied in an account of Buchanan's Shakespearean engagement in 1853:

In the heart of that region where the tribes of Israel have found an abiding place and where the steaming fragrance of fried flounders, blending with strong meaty exhalations of the butchers' shambles down the Whitechapel Road, keep the atmosphere dangerously odorous from morning to eve, is the Pavilion Theatre. . . . The aristocratic playgoers ignore the existence of the Pavilion and it would require a greater genius now to lure the denizens of the West End into this locality. The audience, however, possess the acceptable characteristics of being easily pleased and what they lack in refinement they make up for in earnestness of applause.[11]

Yet, as in so many neighborhood theatres, Shakespeare remained a constant in the repertoire.[12]

That the East End community, and consequently the Pavilion's potential audience, was a mixed one, in which the more debauched and more respectable inhabitants lived in close proximity, is implied by the *East London Observer* (10 October 1857) in an account of the Ratcliffe Highway, which was also a plea for better policing. A community "connected with pitch, tar, marine stores and the Thames Tunnel" might be thought to exist there, yet, "strange though the fact may appear in this long street of crimp slopsellers, flaring gin palaces, sailors' Boarding Houses, equivocal coffee shops, and flash Dancing saloons there are steady, hard working, respectable . . . and *wealthy* tradesmen with staid matrons, and pure-minded daughters growing up amidst all the filth and depravity that defective public arrangements permit to pollute the local atmosphere." In *London Labor and the London Poor* Bracebridge Hemyng, one of Mayhew's co-reporters, describes Whitechapel and its places of entertainment:

Whitechapel has always been looked upon as a suspicious, unhealthy locality. To begin, its population is a strange amalgm of Jews, English, French, German and other antagonistic elements that must clash and jar, but not to such an extent as has been surmised and reported. Whitechapel has its theatres, its music halls, the cheap rates of admission to which serve to absorb numbers of the inhabitants, and by innocently amusing them soften their manners and keep them out of mischief and harm's way.[13]

Such a view is reflected in the *East London Observer* (24 October 1857), which argued of the saloons that "places of rational entertainment —

of light entertainment, such as appeals to the hearts of the low and uneducated, should always be encouraged when their tendency is beneficial." Hemyng, however, is concerned with the theatres. Significantly, he refers to the Earl of Effingham, which had recently been "done up" and held three thousand people. "It has no boxes," he says. "They would not be patronised if they were in existence. Whitechapel does not go to the play in kid-gloves and white ties." Having established a general picture of the Effingham's clientele and melodramatic repertoire, Hemyng turns to the Pavilion which:

> Perhaps ranks higher than the Effingham. The Pavilion may stand comparison, with infinite credit, to itself and its architect, with more than one West-End theatre. People at the West-end who never in their dreams travel further than the dividend and transfer department of the Bank of England in Threadneedle Street, have a vague idea that East-end theatres strongly resemble the dilapidated and decayed Soho in Dean Street, filled with a rough, noisy set of drunken thieves and prostitutes. It is time that these ideas should be exploded. Prostitutes and thieves of course do find their way into theatres and other places of amusement, but perhaps if you were to rake up all the bad characters in the neighborhood they would not suffice to fill the pit and gallery of the Pavilion. On approaching the play-house, you observe prostitutes standing outside in little groups and knots of 3 or 4, and you will also see them inside, but for the most part they are accompanied by their men.[14]

Hemyng's comments are a welcome antidote to the orientalist and myth-making tendencies at large in so many other popular accounts of East End theatres and their audiences.

In 1856 the Pavilion Theatre burned to the ground. On its reopening it was to provoke a controversy, which demonstrated that social aspirations for the theatre were not only the concern of the management, but also of the community at large. The new Pavilion, which was double the size of the old theatre, now had the largest pit of any theatre in London, capable of seating two thousand people.[15] The pit also included eight rows of stalls and had good sight lines and an adjacent refreshment room. Saloons and waiting rooms immediately connected with the ground entrance, while minor entrances to the galleries were to be opened, one facing White Street, Mile End New town, and the other facing into Charles Street. The galleries held twelve hundred, the

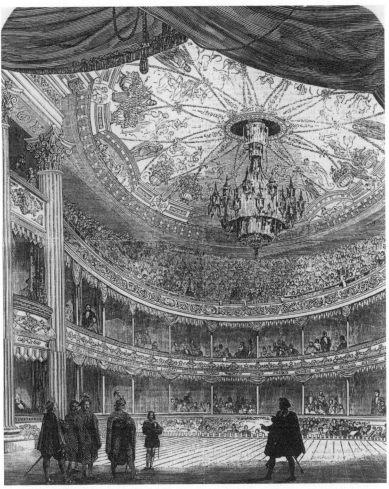

Royal Pavilion interior, Illustrated London News, *November 6, 1858.*

majority paying 6d, but some paying 1s for the front seats. Three tiers of boxes were planned, the lower tier dress and private boxes seating 750. Overall the theatre was designed to accommodate comfortably 3,500 to 3,700 patrons (one thousand more than estimated for the new Covent Garden on crowded nights).[16] John Douglass (who also managed the Standard Theatre) took over the management of the Pavilion, advertising it as "the great nautical melodramatic theatre" and as "the people's own theatre, built for the million."[17] He opened the new theatre with *The Sailor's Return,* claiming that he wished to render it "the Porte St Martin of London, the nautical Temple of the British Public" and also calling it "The Great Nautical Theatre of the Metropolis."[18] The unabashed populism of Douglass's policies roused the ire of the *East London Observer* (6 November 1858), which commented:

> We fully expected an attempt would be made to raise still higher the class of performances at the east end, and to provide at least one theatre to which respectable people might go, with a reasonable expectation of enjoying what has been called the highest form of intellectual amusement — a fine play, finely acted. We expected to see a step in advance of the Royal Standard, where good plays are presented with one or two of the characters efficiently and the remainder wretchedly filled. . . . There were many things which promised that a bold step of this kind would be rewarded with success. The numerous elocution classes and dramatic clubs that have sprung up during the last few years have done much . . . to foster a taste for dramatic representations among people to whom the theatre was once abhorrent. . . . The spread of education among the masses has removed much of that mental darkness which is requisite to make a drama of the "blood and thunder" class endurable; and — let us do Mr Douglass justice — the pieces he has brought out at the Standard . . . have assisted in completing what we may call the dramatic refinement of "the people."
>
> Putting, therefore, entirely out of consideration the large class of residents at the east-end whose intelligence and education require some resemblance to nature in the characters they see upon the stage and are either playgoers or would be if good plays were more accessible, and east-end theatres not associated with every thing vulgar and dreary . . . we do not think a manager would do wrong in speculating on a high class of entertainment.

For the *East London Observer* "the taste and judgement of the locality" were compromised by Douglass's proceedings, especially in the light of critical responses of those coming from the west to see what was served up in the east.[19] Worst of all was the theatre's failure to become "a place for refined and intellectual amusement, into which respectable people might, with propriety, introduce their wives and families" instead of "a receptacle for the lowest of our population."

A week later the *East London Observer* (13 November 1858) revisited its grievances and also published a letter in support of its views:

{ *East End Audiences* }

It was apparent to all who knew the district well, that there was a fair opening for a theatre which, without aiming at too much, proposed to afford amusement and even instruction to the trading and intelligent working population of the district. . . . Surely the tradesmen are as refined, and the working people as intelligent in the Tower Hamlets as they are in Southwark and Lambeth, where flourishes the Surrey Theatre, or Bagnigge Wells, where Mr Phelps so deservedly proceeds.

This significantly links Whitechapel with Islington and south London, two other areas with demonstrably mixed populations, which required a diversity of entertainments. A second visit to the theatre confirmed Douglass's failure to take this into account, for "the house was not one quarter filled, there being very few persons in the boxes and about 300 in the pit. A few sailors and their 'girls' seemed to occupy some seats at the front of the dress circle." Douglass had mistaken the local population; he should have realized that "the East-end population is not entirely composed of sailors and prostitutes, but that there are respectable people seeking intelligent amusement." A letter in the same edition praised the newspaper for its nonpartisan approach, stating that the previous article must surely echo "the ideas of every east-end lover of the drama." The correspondent felt that Douglass had been too swayed by profits, but believed that "had he made the theatre such a one that respectable people might visit it, it would have been a much more profitable speculation than it is likely to prove." The correspondent, who called himself "An East-ender," felt that the Surrey Theatre provided the model which should have been followed.

It was almost a year, however, before an attempt was made by the management to attract a totally different type of audience to the theatre. In October 1859 the engagement of Tully's English Opera Company drew to the Pavilion "an audience such as we never saw within these walls, cramming every part, even the extensive boxes, and leaving some scores standing behind them."[20] A few days later the theatre was "filled by a respectable and discriminating audience. The appearance and conduct of the audience is entirely changed from what it was, when the most violent melodrama was the stock commodity."[21] At last the *East London Observer* felt validated, even commenting on the theatre's accessibility from all the East End parishes and predicting attendance "by those families that have hitherto been in the habit of visiting the west end whenever they desired to go to a theatre."[22] Yet the Pavilion could not survive solely on opera nor fully meet the expectations of the *Observer*. While it provided a wider range (and higher quality) of entertainment than the neighboring Effingham/East London, it could not afford to limit its appeal merely to the more affluent and educated sections of the community.

DEMOGRAPHICS AND TRANSPORT

The following interview with an East End factory worker might imply that a predominantly local audience attended East End theatres such as the Pavilion:

> I am a working man. . . . I go to my factory every morning at six, and I leave it every night at the same hour. I require, on the average, eight hours' sleep, which leaves four hours for recreation and improvement. I have lived in many places at the outskirts according as my work has shifted, but generally I find myself at the Mile End. I always live near the factory where I work and so do all my mates, no matter how small, dirty and dear the houses may be.[23]

If local residents did seek local entertainment, we need to consider employment opportunities offered locally. In 1848 (for instance) dock laborers were the largest group of employees in St. George's-in-the-East, one of the parishes most likely to supply the Pavilion with a neighborhood audience.[24] However, audiences would not only have journeyed to the Pavilion Theatre from the southern areas closest to the docks. Those living to the north and east in Spitalfields and Bethnal Green were also within walking distance of the theatre, as were the inhabitants of Whitechapel itself and of the communities developing to its east.[25] Many of the Whitechapel inhabitants appear to have been involved with food provision, street trading, clothing and shoemaking, carpentry and related trades, laboring, and with local industries such as sugar refining or brewing.

A survey of selected streets close to the Pavilion Theatre, taken from the 1841 and 1851 censuses, indicates the range of employment locally. In Osborn Place and Osborn Court, five to ten minutes west of the theatre, lived laborers, tailors, carpenters, shoemakers, cabinet makers, clothiers, small tradesmen, shopkeepers, a pencil maker, an engineer, and a cooper, among others. A similar range is found in nearby Chicksand Street: laborers and general dealers predominate, while other occupations include a cabman, an umbrella maker, and a plate glass worker. Coopers, boot makers, shoemakers and binders, seamstresses, and even a scum boiler resided in Old Montague Street. Finch Street's occupants included sugar refiners and sugar bakers, silk dyers and winders, tailors, a fur dyer, timber bender, slop worker, and iron founder. Closer to the Pavilion Theatre, Thomas Street's inhabitants were involved in an even wider range of occupations such as laboring, bell founding, hawking, starch making, horse slaughtering, bone boiling, grease melting, mangling, omnibus conducting, distilling, weaving, and stay making. Court Street included a costermonger, several hawkers and shoemakers, some laborers, some charwomen, and an assortment of other trades. In 1851 a large number of handloom weavers and silk weavers were living in the vicinity of the Pavilion, together with those pursuing related trades. Laborers, especially dock laborers, were common, as were shoemakers and binders. Seamstresses, laundresses, slop workers, and needlewomen were prominent, but there were no discernible trends beyond this. A range of occupations were listed, but there is no indication of any pockets of white-collar workers in the streets selected. Families and their children predominated, although there were a small percentage of young single males over twenty (but fewer single females). Most of the inhabitants were born locally; a significant minority originated from counties close to London.[26] There is little evidence of Irish and Jewish settlement in the streets surveyed.[27]

In 1861, just three years after the new Pavilion Theatre had opened, John Liddle, medical officer to Whitechapel Board of Works, reported on the census returns for that year. The population had in fact decreased by 995 from 79,959 in 1851 to 78,964 in 1861. The decrease in numbers had occurred since 1858, when the houses of the poor had been pulled down to make way for the construction of new warehouses. Such demographic changes were caused also by "the building of the Victoria Docks at the extreme east of the metropolis, which has induced a great many habitations, and to locate themselves in the vicinity of the newly constructed works in the expectation of employment."[28] A further two factors were "the operation of the common lodging house act which has limited the number of persons to the cubic dimensions of each room, – and . . . the emigration of families to other parts of the world."[29] A sampling of the occupations of the inhabitants of streets close to the Pavilion Theatre in 1861 census reveals engineers, carmen, porters, a furniture broker, and a goldsmith among the inhabitants of Green Street. Court Street contains a number of laborers and dock laborers, brush makers, general dealers, a hearth rug weaver, an assistant ship agent, and a cap maker and his family from Russia. Thomas Street contains a wide range of trades including laborers and shoe and boot makers, tailors, a silk weaver who doubles as an undertaker, a skin dyer, a coal whipper, a tobacco stuffer, and a cigar maker. A small number of occupants in this street originate from Russia, Poland, and Ireland.[30] Again, the occupants are largely working class, involved in local trades and industries or small shopkeepers. Across the road from the theatre, in Vine Court, hawkers, costermongers, charwomen, laborers, and a cat gut maker [sic] resided.

Just across the road the occupations of residents in Mount Place and Mount Street suggest a slightly more diverse community and give some credence to the complaints aired in the *East London Observer* in 1858. Although many of the houses reveal multiple occupancy, some are singly occupied and a number of the inhabitants can afford their own servants. Inhabitants include a clergyman and his family, several surgeons, a maker of medical instruments, a retired draper, bookkeepers, a cigar manufacturer (from Holland), ship agents, clerks, a master mariner, a commercial traveler and agent, a customs house agent, a ship brokers' manager, a telegraph clerk, actors, a ticket sorter, as well as the dressmakers and carpenters to be found everywhere.[31] This suggests that there were pockets of more affluent or more educated inhabitants in close proximity to the theatre, who might well have visited it and contributed to a wider social range among the audience than many outside commentaries lead us to believe. The clerks, revenue officers, warehouse keepers, engineers employed at the docks; the school teachers; the white-collar workers attached to various East End industries all needed entertainment as well. Moreover, a regular audience could only be supplied when there were enough spectators with a sufficiently regular income (and at a sufficient level) to make theatre-going possible. This is not to argue for a white-collar audience at the Pavilion, although it certainly seemed to aspire towards a relatively respectable audience in the early 1860s, but to suggest that the equation of East End poverty and East End theatregoing is in need of careful examination. The casual laborers, shopworkers, and seamstresses, for example, were often too poorly paid to constitute a likely or regular audience for the East End theatres, although they may have managed the occasional visit. Indeed, a survey of 1,651 heads of families living in St. George's-in-the-East in 1848 revealed that approximately two-thirds of the families surveyed lived on less than 25s per week and that only 17 percent earned more than 30s.[32] Such figures do not preclude regular visits to, say, the galleries of local theatres, but they should also encourage us to proceed with caution in defining potential audiences.[33]

The population of the East End and, indeed, its industrial vitality, began to decline after the slump of 1866. The coming of the railways had already contributed to the exodus of respectable families from the East End, not only through demolition and improved communication patterns from the outer suburbs, but also through the grime they brought with them. Thus, "once select residential areas – Well Close Square, Prescott Street, Spital Square and other places of handsome building were now completely given up to industry or inhabited by working class people."[34] The 1871 census details a somewhat depressed population with "unemployed" or "out of employment" sometimes listed against Whitechapel inhabitants. Yet close to the theatre a road like Court Street was still inhabited by a variety of shopkeepers, tradesmen and laborers, butchers, dressmakers, needlewomen, laborers, dock laborers, cigar makers, together with the odd mariner, hackney carriage driver, and horse slaughterer.[35] Similarly, in Thomas Street tailors, dock laborers, a toymaker, and a bookseller could be found amongst the inhabitants. Baker's Row included staymakers, shoemakers, cigar makers, gas fitters, tripe dressers, firework makers, and even a translator. A little further afield, in lodgings in Osborn Place or in Wentworth Street as well as further west towards Aldgate, lived many dock laborers. In Union Street and Montford Street, on the other side of the Whitechapel Road close to the rectory where the Reverend James Cohen M.A. resided, lived cab drivers, compositors, sugar bakers, and police. Also across the road from the theatre, in Raven Street lived a Baptist minister, an omnibus conductor, a boot maker, a shoemaker, and a cabman. Pockets of mixed and even predominantly white-collar workers could still be found close to the theatre in East Mount Street and Mount Street, where residents included a chief engineer, numerous commercial clerks, an accountant, a mining engineer, the collector to the Guardians of the Whitechapel Union, a Metropolitan police inspector, a registrar of births and deaths, a shorthand writer, and a schoolmaster. Yet mingled with these inhabitants, few of whom were sole occupants of their homes, were plumbers, carpenters, tailors, and cabinet makers, while in Green Street, running parallel to Mount Street, dock laborers, washerwomen, and porters lived side by side with clerks and accountants.[36]

The Pavilion Theatre enjoyed the advantage of being situated on a busy thoroughfare in a densely populated area. Within a mile's radius were Limehouse, Stepney, Bethnal Green, Spitalfields, and the eastern part of the city itself, while the crowded parishes of Whitechapel and St. George's-in-the-East were even closer. The Whitechapel Road could be reached from Bishopsgate via Houndsditch or Commercial Road[37] and from the area north of the London Docks via Cannon Street Road. Westward, the Whitechapel Road connected directly with the City, while eastward it provided a link with the growing populations of Mile End and Bow. It was therefore within walking distance of a large potential audience, while also accessible by omnibus and, later, by tram and railway.[38] As early as March 1829 a playbill informed patrons that the "performances invariably close before 11 o'clock" and that "Stebbings's Limehouse, Poplar and Black Wall stage will leave the theatre nightly at the conclusion of the performances." This suggests that the theatre was looking for patrons to the east and southeast of the theatre, as these areas began to expand.[39] Subsequently, omnibuses were a potential form of transport to and from the Pavilion. *Bradshaw's London Guide Book* for 1857 states that omnibuses ran from 9 in the morning to 12 at night, detailing one principal route running from east to west, from Mile End (the London Hospital), which was just opposite the Pavilion Theatre, along Whitechapel Road, to Aldgate, Leadenhall Street, St. Paul's, Ludgate Hill, Fleet Street, the Strand, Charing Cross, Regent Street, Piccadilly, Knightsbridge, and Chelsea. In the 1850s, both before and under Douglass's management, playbills advertised that "Omnibuses pass the Theatre every five minutes for the City, and all parts of the West End, Bow and Stratford," which suggests the theatre had aspirations to attract patrons from beyond the immediate confines of the East End.[40] When the *Daily Telegraph*'s critic visited the Pavilion pantomime in 1860, however, he complained about the difficulties of returning from the theatre "on a snowy night . . . when the last omnibus is full, and the last be-mused cabman refuses to hear the call of the would-be fare."[41]

Although railway connections had come early to the East End, they did not particularly benefit the Pavilion. The London and Blackwall

Railway connected Fenchurch St. with Cannon Street Road, Shadwell, Stepney, Limehouse, and West India Docks from 1841. By 1853 the North London Railway had built a line running from Islington through Hackney to Bow Station, which had opened in 1850, and on to Fenchurch Street. There was also a station at Mile End, connecting with Bow and with Bishopsgate. It seems unlikely that these railway connections facilitated visits to the Pavilion, although Bank Holiday excursions may have deprived the Pavilion, along with other East End theatres, of its holiday audiences.[42] The underground railway did not reach Whitechapel until after 1880, but in 1870 a new tramway was opened by the North Metropolitan Railway between Whitechapel Church and Bow Church, later extending to Aldgate and Stratford. The horse-drawn trams had much more capacity than the horse-drawn omnibuses, which had been prevalent in east London since mid-century. It was intended that trams should run every five minutes and that the exorbitant omnibus fares — 3d even for short trips — would be undercut. Workmen, in accordance with a new act of Parliament, would be conveyed for a 1d on particular journeys in the morning and evening. Otherwise, the minimum fare was 2d.[43] Traveling along Whitechapel Road was no easy matter, since hay and manure carts from the Essex agricultural districts clogged the thoroughfare several times each week. W. B. Donne's relief at canceling a meeting with Morris Abrahams in Whitechapel because of the snow and his comment that "if it changes the mud will render Whitechapel and Poplar more abominable than even the snow,"[44] suggests that traveling to the district may also not have been that pleasurable in inclement weather.

MANAGEMENT POLICIES AND REPERTOIRE

The Pavilion Theatre ostensibly balanced the demands of a largely working-class audience with the needs of a smaller middle-class clientele. In the 1820s and 1830s and beyond, an enormous number of nautical melodramas were performed,[45] but the legitimate drama was also well represented. In 1835 *Figaro in London* suggested that the Pavilion was competing with the Garrick Theatre for the local Jewish audience.[46] A number of plays were presented using local settings. These included *The Lone Hut of Limehouse Creek or The Sailor and the Miser* (1832), which was set "in the days before Limehouse was so densely populated and covered with its hundreds of magnificent re-

positories of wealth and commerce."[47] Also of interest to local inhabitants may have been the "great panorama of a Homeward Bound East
India Fleet" in *Homeward Bound* the following year. *A London Tradesman's Life* and *London Labor and the London Poor*, the latter of which
included scenes in Farringdon Market and at the back of Whitechapel
Road, also evoked local interests and conditions. The pantomimes inevitably capitalized on the theatre's locale: *Whitechapel Needle* (1844)
incorporated settings in Courtship Lane in Bow, a toy shop and pork
butcher's at Stratford, a quiet street in the neighborhood of Hackney,
and New and Old Streets in the City of London, while the 1859 pantomime included a scene in Lyons' Clothing Establishment, Whitechapel
Road.[48] None of this proves conclusively that the theatre was attracting
a primarily local audience, but it does suggest that managements were
aware of the drawing power of depicting familiar local settings on
stage.

Seat prices varied at the Pavilion Theatre. Between 1828 and 1830
boxes cost 3s, the pit, 2s, and the gallery, 1s. Such prices and a regularly
changing repertoire suggest a small and relatively affluent audience.
By 1833 boxes varied from 1s 6d to 2s, the pit was 1s, and the gallery,
6d. Prices continued to fluctuate, dropping to 1s for boxes (although
private boxes cost 2s), 6d for the pit and 3d for the gallery in 1848.[49]
That the Pavilion still aspired to attract respectable patrons, however,
emerges in a playbill for 10 July 1853, which announces that "The numerous and Highly Respectable Families that now frequent the Boxes
are most respectfully informed that children under Twelve years of age
will be admitted at half-price for sixpence."[50] When the new theatre
opened in 1858 the boxes in the center circle, the public boxes, and the
upper tier cost 1s; private boxes were £1 10s, or 2s per seat; the stalls
were 1s, the pit, 6d, and the gallery 3d. By mid-December the private
boxes had been reduced to a guinea and the stalls to 9d, although the
boxes in the center circle had been raised to 1s 6d. In May 1859 the
management assured family audiences that:

> Private Families visiting the 3s. and 2s. Boxes are assured that no
> improper characters are allowed upon any pretence to occupy those
> seats; they can therefore rely upon not suffering the annoyance so
> much complained of at other places of amusement.[51]

The 1858 prices were still operative in early 1861, although the center
circle boxes were now 2s, while a playbill announced that, for the con-

venience of patrons who wished to avoid the crowds when the theatre opened at 6:30 P.M., the stage door in Baker's Row would be opened an hour earlier every evening. As if in recognition of the type of audience attracted to the opera seasons, children in arms were not admitted.[52] After the financial crisis in the mid-sixties the Pavilion's prices were dramatically reduced. In 1869 admission to the gallery was 2d, to the stalls 4d, to the gallery 6d, to the boxes 8d, and to the dress circle 1s. Private boxes cost 7s 6d and 15s. In 1871 prices were even lower: gallery, 1d; pit, 2d; stalls, 3d; boxes, 6d; and reserved seats, 1s; although the prices rose again in the 1870s.

In the 1820s and 30s the theatre was quite successful in attracting actors of quality such as Edward Elton. In 1838, Yates of the Adelphi managed the theatre for a short time and announced to "the Gentry, Inhabitants of the East-end, that the Royal Pavilion has undergone a thorough renovation, and has been tastefully redecorated."[53] If the theatre appeared to be in decline in the early 1850s, its rebuilding in 1858 gave it a new lease of life, as discussed above. In August 1860 work was completed on converting the Pavilion into "a permanent Italian and English Opera House" and it was renamed the East London Opera House. Fifty private boxes, as well as balcony and amphitheatre stalls, were constructed. Yet between 1858 and 1862 the most popular presentations, other than the annual pantomime, were *Fifteen Years in a British Seaman's Life, The Colleen Bawn*, and *Kathleen Mavourneen*. Most of the operas performed during this period had respectable, if not extensive runs, although *Der Freischutz, Il Trovatore*, and the operatic drama *Guy Mannering* did better than most.[54] In May 1862, when Campbell and Chappell had become lessees of the theatre, the policy of upgrading the quality of entertainment offered still seemed to be working.[55] That such a situation did not last throughout the decade, however, is implied by the *Tower Hamlets Independent* (6 February 1869), which suggested that, as the West End moved into the ascendant, through the opening of new theatres and an improved transport infrastructure, the old neighborhood theatres declined, citing the Pavilion Theatre as a particularly notable victim. In fact the Pavilion failed in April 1869, a state of affairs reflecting the difficulties that theatres like the Surrey, Victoria, and Sadler's Wells were now facing.[56] A new lease of life came when Morris Abrahams, the manager of the East London Theatre, took over the Pavilion in the 1870s and, with his stage manager, Isaac Cohen, restored it to prominence.

The audience for the Pavilion Theatre is not easy to identify. Nevertheless, the evidence of the census, as well as the comments of the *East
London Observer* and of Bracebridge Hemyng, should warn us against
placing too great an emphasis on the authenticity of exotic or derisory
accounts. Unfortunately, as the century progressed and greater emphasis was placed on the East End's "otherness," the tendency emerged
even more strongly. Thus on 29 March 1879 the critic of the *Saturday
Musical Review* provided a rather formulaic account of a visit to the
Pavilion and of its audience. After "a long and somewhat tedious journey" from the West End, the critic arrived at the theatre and was shown
to a box, already occupied by five ladies "of portly dimensions." He
noted that the Pavilion audience lacked the social divisions of the West
End:

> There is no foolish pride amongst Pavilion audiences, or, as far as
> we could see, any of those stupid social distinctions which divide the
> sympathies of other auditoriums. There were no stalls, and the pit
> was quite full; the dress-circle and upper-boxes were occupied by
> apparent pittites; and the private-box people were just as jolly as
> anybody else. In fact it appeared as if, strange to say, everybody had
> come determined to be interested and amused.

Such an account, which depends on the relativity of West End audience
behavior, is typical in its characterization of the East End. Equally, although it occurs after the period discussed here, St. John Adcock's description of an audience leaving the Pavilion Theatre on a Saturday
night at the turn of the century suggests that little changed. Having
described the vitality of the Whitechapel Road, he writes:

> The curtain has not fallen in the Pavilion yet, but there is as much
> life here as in the Strand when the theatres are emptying.
>   It is five minutes to eleven. Two ancient four-wheelers, and a
> single hansom have driven up and are standing forlornly hopeful,
> opposite the theatre. An attendant bolts the door back, and a mo-
> ment later a dark mass surges up the long bare passage from the pit,
> and a second less compact mass simultaneously flows by the broader
> exit from the stalls and boxes.
>   As the earliest to emerge from the gallery doors round the corner

"Leaving the Pavilion Theatre, Whitechapel" from St. John Adcock, "Leaving the London Theatres," in George R. Sims, ed., Living London, *1903.*

are batches of rampant, hooting boys, so the first hundred or so to burst into the open air from the front entrances are all men.[57]

Adcock goes on to describe what this audience does on leaving the theatre:

So, for some ten minutes the crowd streams out from the front and round from the gallery door, and the larger crowd moving up and down the Whitechapel Road easily absorbs it. Passing trams or 'buses are besieged; a young man is regaling his much befeathered sweetheart at the baked-potato can; two men in tall hats and a miscellany of less-imposing persons congregate around the whelk stall, and hand the pepper and vinegar around with gusto. There is an influx of trade to the public houses; the boxes of an adjacent fried-fish shop are full of hungry revellers, and faces of men and women peer in increasing numbers over its counter, demanding "middle pieces" well browned. You meet these customers strolling a little later eating fried fish out of newspaper, or carrying it wrapped up to be eaten more comfortably at home. Nobody has hired any of the cabs, but the drivers linger still, on the chance of finding a fare among the actors and actresses.[58]

This is a companion piece to an account of a West End audience. Although not disputing the accuracy of its observations, the treatment of the East End audience as something of a curiosity, as something distinct from (but defined by) the western end of town, is very much evidenced in its tone.

The Pavilion Theatre's history challenges many of our assumptions about East End theatregoing. It is clear that, in the mid-Victorian period, it catered for a diverse audience rather than the "great unwashed" of popular mythology. Despite the formulaic nature of many accounts of this theatre, culminating in Adcock's well-known description, the Pavilion cannot be characterized in so facile a way. Neither, on closer examination, can the Britannia.

3. The Britannia Theatre, Hoxton

n 1840 Samuel Lane became the proprietor of the Britannia Tavern, located in Hoxton Old Town, in the central area of Shoreditch. The first saloon theatre associated with the tavern, built with a loan from the brewers, Elliots', was opened on Easter Monday, 1841, with a capacity of about one thousand, but its license was withdrawn by the local magistracy in October of the same year and it was not licensed again until after the Theatre Regulation Act of 1843. In the 1843 petition for a license submitted to the Lord Chamberlain, Samuel Lane implied that the theatre had been erected at the request of the local neighborhood, to supply a need for entertainment, and because otherwise they "were compelled to walk or incur (in addition to the price of admission) the extra expense of riding a considerable distance to a theatre, there not being one nearer than the City Theatre in Bishopsgate, which in the Winter season was found by them to be most inconvenient."[1] Lane clearly had the support of the local community when he petitioned for a license. Not only were the local trustees, overseers and churchwardens of the parish behind him, but also the local tradesmen (shoemakers, cheese mongers, drapers, dyers, coal and timber merchants, cabmen, auctioneers, and pocket-book makers among them).[2]

Lane's initial difficulties with the authorities seem surprising, given his subsequent reputation as a manager and the regard in which such figures as W. B. Donne and Charles Dickens held him. In the early 1840s, however, the authorities harbored an innate prejudice against the saloons, particularly if obstruction of any sort occurred outside them and if children or prostitutes were assumed to attend them. Such obstructions did occur (and Lane may well have been right in attributing their inception to rival managements), but, although it is clear that gallery audiences were youthful in the cheaper theatres, the real issue goes back to the antitheatrical prejudice — to the belief that theatrical entertainment corrupted the morals of young people. As for the presence of prostitutes and thieves, police reports often refer to this, but it is unlikely that any minor theatre or saloon would have flourished for any time if this had been the most conspicuous aspect of its clientele. Indeed, Hoxton was largely an industrious, hard-working community, very much in need of entertainment and recreation to fill the leisure hours of its inhabitants.

A. L. Crauford writes that Hoxton mainly depended upon the upholstery trade and that the bulk of its inhabitants were respectable workers.[3] The local population in 1841, enumerated in the census a month before Lane opened his first Britannia Saloon, worked in a range of trades including shoemaking, plastering, cabinet making, tobacco pipe manufacturing, bricklaying, dyeing, carpentry, printing, and tailoring. Such a range can be found all around the theatre in Upper John Street, Myrtle Street, Huntingdon Street, or Bacchus Walk. Yet, if we take as representative streets Old and New Gloucester Roads, within five minutes walk of the theatre, we find that local inhabitants are more mixed than either the police reports or Crauford might lead us to believe. In 1841 the most common occupations in these two streets are clerk and servant, followed by laborer, cabinet maker, carpenter, tailor, needlewoman, dressmaker, and laundress. In the ensuing years the range of occupations remains relatively stable, although the number of clerks, servants, and carpenters decline. There is a sudden expansion in shoemakers and bootmakers in 1851, as well as in needlewomen, milliners, and laborers, although all of these groups have declined again in 1861 and 1871. There is also a notable decline in the number of occupants who list themselves as being of independent means after 1841. Most of the inhabitants were born locally in London or in the neighboring counties, with a small number coming from further afield and a negligible number from Scotland, Ireland, or elsewhere in Europe. Among Britannia employees we find Frederick Marchant, an up-and-coming actor and dramatist, and Thomas Swayne, a check taker at the theatre, living there in 1861. Ten years later another dramatist and leading actor at the Britannia, William Pitt, lived there, as did William Kelsey and his wife, both of whom were employed as "supers" at the theatre.[4]

The distribution of Britannia employees within the neighborhood of Hoxton should also alert us to the dangers of categorizing neighborhoods through generalities. In 1861 Cecil Pitt, prompter and actor, lived in Parr Street, about half a mile northwest of the theatre. Catherine Atkinson lived in Wenlock Street, about a quarter to a half a mile west of the theatre and close to the Grecian, where she was subsequently engaged. Sarah Lane's brother-in-law, William Crauford, and his wife, lived in Hoxton Old Town (where the theatre was situated and where Samuel and Sarah Lane had resided in the 1840s). Two other leading actors also lived close to the theatre: its tragedian, Joseph Reynolds, was in Alma Street, a short walk away, while G. B. Bigwood, its leading low comedian, was in Long Alley in Holywell, close to the City of London Theatre and to Worship Street. Further south, Frederick Wilton, the stage manager, lived over the grocer's shop his wife ran in Houndsditch, a brisk half-an-hour's walk from the theatre. Ten years later Joseph Reynolds had moved a few hundred yards further away to New North Road, Cecil Pitt had moved in closer to Upper John Street, as had Bigwood, who was now less than a quarter of a mile southwest of the theatre in Great Chart Street. The Newham family, many of whom had appeared at the theatre, lived just across Hoxton Street in Huntingdon Street. Henry Hope (leader of the orchestra) also lived a few hundred yards from the theatre in St. John's Road, while another musician, William Wade, was about a quarter of a mile north in Newton Street, as was the bill poster, Jacobs, in the parallel Grange Street. Five minutes across the Kingsland Road, in the attractive Nichol's Square, lived Edward Elton, second low comedian, and Wilton, who had moved there in 1863. A leading actor at the Britannia earned £4 per week, its stage manager £2, the leader of the orchestra £2 5s and a super 9s, which was probably representative of the span of wages across Hoxton itself. Like other local workers they could not have afforded to pay for transportation to and from their place of work, but needed to live within walking distance. The Lanes themselves followed other local entrepreneurs in moving north: they were living in rural Tottenham by 1849 and commuted to the Britannia by carriage.

Between 1841 and 1851 the population of Shoreditch had increased from 83,432 to 109,257 (30.9%) and of Hackney from 37,771 to 53,589 (41.8%). In 1849 Lane rebuilt the theatre, which had become too small for the audiences it was attracting, and provided better quality staging facilities and accommodation.[5] A sense of the potential audience(s) targeted in the 1850s emerges in a playbill for *The Life and Struggles of a Working Man*, a partly temperance drama, which suggests that:

ALL WORKING MEN, THEIR WIVES AND CHILDREN should see this real and affecting picture of a Working Man's career. The beautiful tableau of the Mason's death calls forth repeated bursts of applause![6]

The 1851 census also reveals the appropriateness of such a play for the Britannia: the most common occupations for men in Shoreditch included shoe making, cabinet making and upholstery, carpentry, printing, tailoring, bricklaying, plumbing, and portering. There were also quite a few commercial clerks and travelers, while washerwomen, seamstresses, domestic servants, and milliners predominated in female fields of employment.[7] However, the pattern for our perception of Britannia audiences in the 1850s has been established by Dickens's account of the theatre in *Household Words*. Dickens particularly notes the youthfulness of the audience, the refreshments available, and the audience's attentiveness:

> The place was crowded to excess, in all parts. Among the audience were a large number of boys and youths, and a great many very young girls grown into bold women before they had well ceased to be children. These last were the worst features of the whole crowd, and were more prominent there than in any other sort of public assembly that we know of, except at a public execution. There was no drink supplied, beyond the contents of the porter-can . . . which was seen here everywhere. Huge ham sandwiches, piled on trays like deals in a timberyard, were handed about for sale to the hungry; and there was no stint of oranges, cakes, brandy-balls, or other similar refreshments.

Proper provision had also been made for the gallery audience to see and hear, instead of packing it away in a dark gap in the roof, as at Drury Lane or Covent Garden. In consequence:

> The audience . . . was very attentive. They were so closely packed that they took a little time in settling down after any pause; but otherwise the general disposition was to lose nothing and to check (in no choice language) any disturber of the business of the scene.

Dickens cannot restrain his fastidiousness, noting that "the outer avenues and passages of the People's Theatre bore abundant testimony to the fact of its being frequented by very dirty people," nor can he refrain from burlesquing *Lady Hatton*, the melodrama he witnessed. His prurience regarding the "young girls grown into bold women" suggests a certain squeamishness, but he does not categorize them or the boys and youths in the audience as thieves and prostitutes, which often seemed to be the case in the early police reports. Yet there is also a polemic embedded in his description:

> Ten thousand people, every week, all the year round, are estimated to attend this place of amusement. If it were closed tomorrow — if there were fifty such, and they were all closed tomorrow — the only result would be to cause that to be privately and evasively done which is now publicly done; to render the harm of it much greater and to exhibit the suggestive power of the law in an oppressive and partial light. The people who now resort here, *will be* amused somewhere.[8]

His comments are both a validation of the 1843 Theatre Regulation Act and of the Britannia itself. Yet his object is not only to counter the antitheatrical prejudices still at large in the midcentury, but also to make the case that the theatre is easier to regulate (and therefore control) if it is openly allowed to function.[9]

In 1858 the theatre was rebuilt with a capacity of forty-seven hundred (allowing for standing).[10] The *Builder* (25 September 1858) commented on how much importance was given to the pit and the gallery in the new building, and how the latter was more advantageously provided for, "as regards seeing and hearing than the gallery in other theatres, — being better, of course, than the excellent gallery of Covent Garden Theatre, inasmuch as it is nearer . . . to the stage." However, on viewing the full gallery, the journal (13 November 1858) commented that:

> When crowded on Monday with the "unwashed" . . . it formed a curious sight, not altogether in harmony with the decorations. These last, however, may help to induce habits — the want of which is the chief cause of any prejudice against what are called the lower classes — or at least so help when the means of cleanliness are supplied in towns.

The seating capacity of the pit was one thousand persons and of the stalls two hundred; a further three hundred could be accommodated in the promenade and at the back of the pit. There were about six hundred seatings in the lower tier of boxes, with about fifty standing places in the adjoining refreshment rooms, and room for about 1,250 in the gallery and upper tier of boxes. The journal also details the extensive provision for refreshments, aimed at avoiding trouble with checks and readmissions. The new Britannia Theatre also boasted separate entrances to the dress circle and boxes and also insisted on appropriate dress being worn by spectators in the stalls and boxes. In other words it was attempting to attract a more socially diverse audience than before.

The *Builder* also emphasized the moral responsibility of the theatre to its community:

> Here then is a school for 500,000 to 600,000 persons annually, where instruction, evil or good is conveyed . . . and will most powerfully operate on the moral and social condition of society at large. We are amongst those who believe that the mere decorative features of places of public amusement, if marked with propriety and taste, are not wholly without influence . . . of mollifying the manners of whatever the class.[11]

As if in response to the *Builder's* concerns, the Britannia Theatre's audiences were described in a second account by Dickens, this time in *All the Year Round* (1860), again providing a highly impressionistic point of view against which other available evidence needs to be measured. Dickens wrote:

> We were a motley assemblage of people, and we had a good many boys and young men among us; we also had many girls and young women. To represent, however, that we did not include a very great number, and a very fair proportion of family groups, would be to make a gross misstatement. Such groups were to be seen in all parts of the house; in the boxes and stalls particularly, they were composed of persons of very decent appearance, who had many children with them. Among our dresses were most kinds of shabby and greasy wear, and much fustian and corduroy that was neither sound nor fragrant. Besides prowlers and idlers, we were mechanics, dock-laborers, costermongers, petty tradesmen, small clerks, milliners, stay-makers, shoe-binders, slop workers, poor workers in a hundred highways and byeways. Many of us — on the whole, the majority — were not at all clean and not at all choice in our lives or conversation.[12]

Dickens was struck by the ventilation which rendered the theatre "fresh, cool and wholesome" and prevented unwholesome smells.

Exterior of Britannia Theatre, 1858, from Illustrated News of the World,
25 December 1858.

Dickens was very much on the side of theatres like the Britannia and
Victoria: his 1850 and 1860 articles are in part polemical, demonstrating that theatres are morally educative, orderly, and self-regulating. He
may mythologize the audience, as he did in his earlier descriptions of
the Victoria and Britannia audiences, but he does so with a purpose:
his aim is to counter the antitheatrical prejudice still at large in Victorian society. That his 1860 account has also provided the premises for
Janice Carlisle's Foucauldian analysis of the theatre and its audience
is consequently problematic, because Dickens is pursuing an agenda
rather than presenting an objective description. Carlisle believes that
Dickens "offers the most striking evidence of what Michel Foucault

would have recognized as a panoptical perspective. . . . The person on the stage is not the object of the audience's gaze, but the overseer of the audience as spectacle. What can be seen, as Foucault has pointed out, can be controlled or, more importantly, self-controlled."[13] The disciplinary function of the performance operates through the close attention (and separation) it exacts from the audience. Yet the Foucault paradigm ignores the close relationship that existed between the performers and audience: demographic surveys prove that "the Britannia's company lived with and as its audience."[14] The *Porcupine* (29 December 1866) comments that the performers were known to the audience "as real living and well-known acquaintances; and yet this duality of appearance does not seem to diminish the relish of the audience for the drama." The relationship suggested here is not so much one of control as of complicity. Equally, when Carlisle describes the empty Britannia, as depicted in an illustration in the *Builder* (1858), as "a vast, sterile hall that might be construed as an architectural mechanism of intimidation,"[15] she ignores the fact that, in its provision of an exceptionally well-raked stage and auditorium, the unusual adoption of an elliptical form (or oval) within the auditorium and unrestricted sight lines (no chandelier blocking the view from the gallery here), the theatre is designed to facilitate a shared and integrated experience rather than a cold act of control. The theatre's program also militates against such an analysis. Carlisle writes of the pantomime Dickens saw on his visit to the Britannia:

> According to Dickens "The Spirit of Liberty" plays to an enthusiastic crowd in a theatrical inspection house, and the illusion of freedom fosters the willing subjection of its inhabitants.[16]

Carlisle, drawing specifically on Dickens's perceptions, sees embodied in the Victorian pantomime a discourse of control and improvement, equivalent to the motives of the Sunday services that were also held in theatres like the Britannia. Yet the transgressive nature of the harlequinade, a feature of the Britannia pantomime throughout the Victorian period, and the social concerns of many of the melodramas performed there, might lead us to resist such assumptions.[17] Thus, while Carlisle's invocation of Foucault as a means of explaining the dynamics of Victorian popular audiences attempts to provide a theoretical basis for analysis, the evidence and ideological implications discussed above seem to counter a total acceptance of this particular perspective.

Interior of Britannia Theatre, from The Builder, *13 November 1858.*

Just over a year before the *Illustrated Times* (11 December 1858) had described the Britannia audience as "rough, but very attentive to the performance, and they have the aspect of working-people and small tradesmen."[18] Another account of this period provides evidence from quite a different perspective. Thomas Erle depicts the Britannia's audience in a much broader, more burlesqued fashion:

> The youths in the gallery . . . are gifted with a flow of exuberant animal spirits which find a safety-valve in shrill whistlings. . . . Since the temperature up in their sixpenny heaven is so high . . . they find it "cool and convenient" to sit without their coats. They evince, too, a noble independence of sentiment towards the swells in the body of the house (who are in this case the counter-skippers of Kingston and Dalston) by turning their backs to the chandelier, and sitting along the gallery rail like a row of sparrows on a telegraph wire. In this position they confront their friends in the back settlements, and exchange with them a light fusillade of *bandinage*, [*sic*] principally couched in idiomatic expressions of remarkable vigour and terseness, which is sustained with much animation during the time that the curtain is down between the pieces.[19]

Oddly enough, this seems quite a credible account: the whistling can be substantiated from other sources; gallery audiences without coats because of the heat were common; and the presence of shop assistants from Kingston and Dalston in the pit is both geographically and economically feasible. However Erle's description of the food and drink partaken at the theatre seems rather far-fetched. He says that the young woman seated next to him at the Britannia must now be in a state:

> After rashly embarking, as she did, on "'am sandwidges" and open tarts, with a glass of gin and treacle imprudently called sherry. It is a misfortune that the cold pease pudding, which used to be offered as an aristocratic delicacy to the occupants of the private boxes and dress circle at the old Britannia, is now, under mistaken notions of progress in refinement, withheld from them.[20]

Through such descriptions Erle too contributes to the conventions through which East End audiences are represented.

In fact, the consumption of food and drink was an integral part of a visit to the Britannia. Responding to a solitary complaint about its provision in 1864, W. B. Donne expressed surprise, for he had never noted anything to lead him "to infer discontent or disorder of any kind"[21] when he visited the theatre. Indeed, so impressed was he with the exemplary orderliness of the Britannia Theatre and with Charles Dickens's *All the Year Round* account that he added it as an appendix to his annual report in 1860. That the theatre was orderly owed something to the quality of facilities provided and also to the audiences it attracted in consequence. The fact that the Britannia was a theatre drawing a local clientele who did not go to the West End, while not drawing audiences itself from further west, is implicit in Boucicault's statement to the 1866 Select Committee that *The Colleen Bawn* played simultaneously at the Adelphi and the Britannia, because the Britannia was "so far off that it would not interfere with the piece at the Adelphi."[22] Yet the diaries of F. C. Wilton, the Britannia's stage manager from 1846 to 1875, demonstrate that not only natives of Hoxton attended the theatre.[23] In the early 1860s occupants of the boxes included Mrs. Burdett Coutts (philanthropist), Lord Alfred Paget (commodore of the Thames Yacht Club), and Frederick Peel (chief railway commissioner and son of Sir Robert Peel). Other visitors noted from beyond Hoxton include Mr. Frith of Frith & Smith (Silk Pressers & Calenderers) of Brook Rd., Dalston, and Wilton's friends Mr. and Mrs. Askew from Victoria Park. Further visitors included his son-in-law and daughter, Fred Rountree (a clerk in the railway clearing house) and Harriet, and his friend Fred Dewar, the West End actor.[24]

Wilton also provides evidence that boys were still attracted to the theatre when the pantomime was on or a highwayman drama like *The Ride to York* was revived. Wilton often played the latter for his benefit, noting in 1865 that it had drawn over one thousand persons to the gallery, including "about 30 boys waiting outside the gallery door at 4 o'clock in the afternoon, a sight which has not been seen since Xmas."[25] In 1869 he repeated the experiment, drawing to the theatre precisely the sort of audiences and problems that had so bedeviled Lane in the early 1840s:

> Hundreds of people last night turned away from the doors! Mr Borrow laughed & said he felt really ashamed last evening when he looked out of his window before the Doors were opened to see the mob waiting for admission (ragged shoe-less boys). . . . During the Performance Fred Rountree saw a man in the gallery, after drinking a pint of Beer, throw the empty pot over his head behind him and as it flew through the air, the other people in the gallery did not seem at all surprised but quietly raised their eyes and watched its flight! The Gallery was filled in half an hour after the doors were open & then the doors were closed, & there was such a number of people disappointed & grumbling at not gaining admission that there were 3 policemen appointed to pace the pavement & keep the people quiet. During the dialogue of *The School for Scandal*, the boys in the gallery were singing *a rousing chorus* & scarcely a single speech was heard.[26]

A year later *The Ride to York* was again revived for Wilton's benefit, this time with Marie Henderson in the title role. The aim was to draw a young female audience, which significantly would bring money into the stalls or pit rather than the gallery. However, Wilton was disappointed, for "[s]carce anybody in the stalls! So that the expectation of a great number of girls to see Miss M. Henderson ride the horse was not fulfilled!"[27]

Another perspective on the Britannia's potential local audience can also be gleaned from accounts of other audiences in the vicinity at this time. In the late 1870s the New Variety Theatre in Pitfield Street, Hoxton, was certainly either competing with the Standard and Britannia for audiences or drawing an alternative audience from within their catchment area. In 1878 a letter to the Lord Chamberlain complained that by 8:20 P.M. the New Variety's pit was full of people, the "best part of the greatest roughs in London."[28] In response, the proprietor George Harwood wrote that "as regards roughs, Hoxton being a poor district of London, my audience comprises working men (mechanics) who come for rational amusement for a couple of hours and [sic] probably keeps them from getting too much drink."[29] Yet three months later Thomas Pelham (who wrote to inform the Lord Chamberlain that, because he was "a great deal interested in the boys of London," he was visiting the places of amusement they frequented) drew attention to the Variety, which "was crowded with boys and girls, 90 per cent must have been under 20 years of age, and many under 15," who were watching a performance much of which was immoral and indecent.[30] A police report of 24 December 1878, however, felt that there was not much that was vulgar: "The theatre contained at most about 400 persons, chiefly boys and youths ranging from ten to twenty years of age. There were very few girls — scarcely a dozen — present." It also pointed out that immediately before Christmas places of entertainment in the East End were "but meagrely attended" and that the theatre itself had police and officers on duty.[31] Harwood explained his audience as follows:

> In reference to the audience, you will always find Saturday nights in east end places of entertainment are noisier and rougher than the middle nights of the week, you get more juveniles and less women. Being the working classes this is easily explained. Females have their marketing to do, also domestic work for the Sunday and youths get their week's pay and they will go to places of amusement to pass away their evening — as no doubt their homes are not the most comfortable.

Harwood believed his establishment provided "a public education" and that there should be many more cheap places of entertainment since it kept "many men, women and youths from spending their time in Public Houses. They get two hours rational entertainment which enables them to get home at a reasonable time and does not interfere with their next day's work."[32]

The closest theatre to the west of the Britannia was the Grecian, whose clientele in the 1870s seem to have come from the City Road, where the theatre was located, and from Islington, Pentonville, and

Hoxton. In 1873 the *Hackney and Kingsland Gazette* (27 August) undertook an analysis of the audience's social composition. It claimed that both the highest and the lowest were absent, "yet between the two grades almost every variety of mankind was present." The crowd around the gallery door were "a swarthy lot, begrimed withal with elements of toil; for there were hardy workers among the throng." At the main entrance quite a different group had gathered, for they "were of a different stamp and more than one grade higher in the social scale" and "the greatest order and decorum prevailed." They were well dressed and clearly belonged to the "middle dominion of society" and, unlike the rush that occurred when the gallery doors were opened, they entered the theatre in an orderly manner. The writer inevitably felt obliged to visit and describe the gallery "where many gentlemen were voluptuously regaling themselves by gnawing lumps of ice, while they made copious cushions of their coats. Bonnetless women abounded, and so did the sweetmeats which they drew in abundance from the remote corners of their capacious pockets."

John Hollingshead tells us in 1885 that the Britannia was essentially "a local house. It is self-supporting and self-supported. It draws none of its attraction and none of its audience from the western districts. Its audiences, its actors, and its pieces are more or less of native growth, and more or less fixed and immutable."[33] However visitors from further afield were still noted in the 1870s and the *Hackney and Kingsland Gazette* (10 January 1876) refers to "visitors from distant regions" being among those visiting the pantomime, even a fortnight into its run. The constituency of the Britannia audience may have remained stable until the end of the century, although it is likely that, as the district of Hoxton grew poorer and transport facilities to the West End improved (not to mention the growth of a network of suburban theatres around London), the local audience was less often supplemented by visitors from further afield. Walter Besant, writing in 1888, suggests that Hoxton was sealed off from its surroundings by the Kingsland Road to the east, Old Street and City Road to the south, and canals to the west and north, almost like a secluded city. "Travellers come not within its borders; few, even Londoners, wot of it; foreigners never hear of it . . . it is content with one line of omnibuses to connect it with the outside world; there is no cabstand within its precincts; it has no railway station." Besant characterizes its inhabitants as "quiet and industrious" and indicates a pronounced lack of a criminal class.[34] Barker makes a cogent case for the accuracy of his description, but also draws attention to the impoverished, depraved and criminal Hoxton depicted by Booth at the end of the century.[35] In 1896, the theatre's manager, A. L. Crauford, told the *Sketch* (24 June 1896) that the audience was "a local one for everything but the pantomime, that it is well-behaved, but very exacting, requiring frequent change and very strong fare." The janitors were quite capable of dealing with any "rowdy elements" and only temperance drinks were now available in the auditorium, although other types of drink were available at the bars. The gallery audience was described (almost a cliché by now of any visit to a south or east London theatre) and had changed little since Dickens's two famous descriptions.

MANAGEMENT AND TRANSPORT

The Britannia's management policies were evidently responsible for the long-term success of the theatre. Samuel and Sarah Lane entrusted most of the managerial roles to members of Sarah Lane's family and created what was to be the longest continuous management of any London theatre during the nineteenth century. In the 1840s performances started at 6:30 P.M. In 1846, when F. C. Wilton asked if 6:30 P.M. was not too early to start the performances, as the class who supported the theatre were working people, William Borrow, who managed the front of house, told him the theatre usually filled up the minute the doors were opened.[36] Prices were always kept low: in the early 1840s, when Wilton had advised against lowering prices, Lane still went ahead and reduced the gallery, for instance, from 3d to 2d. Far from losing money the theatre's business rose rapidly.[37] Thus in 1846 boxes were 8d; stalls, 6d; upper stalls, 4d; and the gallery, 2d; while children in arms were not chargeable — and children under ten were admitted at half price to the boxes and stalls. Although no persons were admitted to the lower stalls or the boxes without being suitably attired, throughout this period the Britannia was designated "The People's Theatre." By July 1847 the boxes and pit cost 6d (with half-price at 8:30 P.M.) and the gallery 3d, with no half-price. The playbill which announces these prices asks:

> Why do 20,000 people visit the Britannia every week? Because it is the best and cheapest theatrical establishment in the world.[38]

By 1853 prices had crept up slightly: stage boxes were 1s 6d; boxes, 1s; gallery "equal to boxes in any other theatre," 4d; and the back of pit,

3d; while children under seven were admitted half-price to the boxes and pit.[39] Three years later a private entrance to the boxes was open at no extra charge at 5:30 P.M., a move which suggests that some sort of social distinction existed amongst the audience.[40]

The rebuilding of the theatre in 1858 was an astute managerial move. The comfort of the audience; the sight lines from the gallery and pit; the acoustics; the refreshments provided have all been enumerated. The *Illustrated Times* (11 December 1858) praised the new facilities and added:

> The bill has to be varied pretty frequently, the first piece, after running a fortnight, generally going second for another fortnight, after which it dies out for ever. . . . With this provision a steady audience for the pit, gallery and common boxes is always found.

This suggests that a regular audience visited the theatre on a monthly and/or fortnightly basis. It is impossible to give an accurate figure, but one might surmise that the theatre could rely on a nucleus of between 15,000 and 30,000 regular playgoers, plus other more casual visitors both locally and from further afield. Given that the Grecian and Standard (and even Sadler's Wells at times) were advertised as local theatres for the inhabitants of Shoreditch and Hackney, a regular theatregoer could be assured of at least something totally new at each of these theatres once a month and a partial change of program once a fortnight. During the pantomime season it is possible that more people, both locally and from further afield, visited the theatres; that enthusiastic theatregoers did the "rounds";[41] and that local inhabitants probably revisited pantomimes they had particularly enjoyed.

Much has been made of the problems faced by the Britannia in the 1870s after the death of Samuel Lane and through the influence of bookmaker and boxers' manager, Johnny Gideon. Certainly the Britannia presented a number of French plays, including the highly successful *Dolores* (adapted from Sardou's *Patrie*), and also allowed French influences to creep into its pantomimes. However, French plays such as *Frou-Frou* (1873) were often not successful as they contained too much "talkee-talkee" for a Britannia audience.[42] In 1869, when Marie Henderson played Juliet to Adelaide Ross's Romeo and *Mary Stuart* was also performed, the house was not as large as expected, but "Mr Borrow said a large proportion of the audience highly respectable."[43] Such programs, as well as the 1870s French plays, may have been aimed at the middle-class inhabitants north of the theatre,[44] as much as at the local audiences. However the old repertoire still continued into the 1880s, until a taste for productions of West End hits became prevalent. Prices remained attuned to the neighborhood. In 1866 a stage box had cost 1s 6d; box & stalls, 1s; pit and box slips, 6d; lower gallery, 4d; and upper gallery, 3d. Children under seven were half price, infants, free. Throughout this period management appears to have viewed the Britannia as a neighborhood theatre. A clipping of 1856 states:

> In the great race for novelty Mr Lane never allows the Hoxtonians to be left behind, and determined that there should be no necessity for going further a-field in search of amusement, a bill crammed with alluring promises of entertainment threw the neighborhood into a feverish condition of excitement and anticipation.[45]

It was this sort of attentiveness to audience needs that made the Britannia such a successful theatre among its local community. A camaraderie between performers and audience existed there unlike that at any other theatre: "There surely never was a warmer-hearted or more appreciative audience than that of the Hoxton theatre."[46] It was also evinced in the annual Britannia Festival, which had commenced well before the opening of the new theatre in 1858, on the occasion of Sarah Lane's benefit just before Christmas. Chance Newton recalls how:

> You saw hurtling down from the gallery or up from the stalls or pit, or flying out of the private boxes, pipes, tobacco pouches, umbrellas, walking sticks, a batch of neckties, pairs of boots, hats, comforters, pairs of socks, and even pairs of trousers. . . . All these and other useful articles were for the actors. For the ladies of the company . . . the present-givers pelted gifts of another kind. These included rounds of beef, a fine parcel of sausages, a goose, pairs of ducks, legs of pork, and sundry articles of wearing apparel. . . .
>
> Some of the audience — especially the sweeter sex — mostly humble shop assistants, servant girls and artificial flower makers (very numerous in that district) would hand over the footlights cheap (and often gaudy) clocks, glass cases of wax fruits, and flowers. Sometimes they would throw at the feet of their favourite actresses sprays of artificial flowers — the work of their own deft hands.[47]

The enthusiasm of the audience is also indicated by a description of a Boxing Day audience gathering from an early hour outside the theatre, young and old, despite heavy rain.[48]

The majority of this audience (like the Britannia company) probably traveled to the theatre on foot. The widening of Shoreditch High Street between Bateman's Row and Old Street slightly eased northern egress from the City and relieved a chronic bottleneck of licensed cabs and horse-drawn omnibuses in 1877, but there were no other street improvements in the immediate vicinity of the theatre. Even if there had been, it is unlikely that they would have made much difference to the majority of the audience. Yet between 1853 and 1857 playbills announced that "omnibuses for all parts of London stop within 2 minutes walk of the Britannia every quarter of a hour,"[49] while relatively expensive trains provided an alternative form of transport from the early Victorian years. New railway routes potentially increased the Britannia's reach in a wide arc. A railway was built from Shoreditch (directly opposite the Standard Theatre) to Bow, Stratford, Romford, and Brentford in 1840, with extensions to Camden Town and Stepney in 1851; its efficiency was aided by ancillary tram and omnibus routes along the Shoreditch High Street and Kingsland Road. In 1855 the Standard Theatre advertised that trains departed from Shoreditch Station at 11:30 P.M. for Stratford, Lea Bridge, Tottenham Park, Water Lane, Ponder's End, Waltham, Bradborne, St. Margaret's Ware, and Hartford, all within a twenty-mile radius north and east of the station.[50] In 1867 the Britannia Theatre certainly advertised the existence of Shoreditch Station on its playbills, announcing:

> Extension of the North London Railway. The Patrons of this Theatre, and the Public generally, are respectfully reminded that the NEW STATION recently opened opposite Shoreditch Church is within Three Hundred Yards of the Britannia, which is also the nearest Theatre to any Station of the above Railway, an advantage that gives the inhabitants of Hampstead Road, Chalk Farm, Kentish Town, Camden Town, Holloway, and their vicinities, easy access to and from this, the largest Theatre in the North or East of London. The last train leaves Shoreditch every night at 10 minutes before 11 o'clock for the before mentioned places. Last Train for Dalston, Hackney, Victoria Park, Bow and Poplar at 10 minutes past 11.[51]

Later in the year the train times were revised to 11:15 P.M. and 11:25 P.M., although such advertising ceased at the end of the year.[52] The Metropolitan line from Paddington to Farringdon opened in 1863, but it was very expensive.[53] The electric trams favored by the poorer classes did not radiate north, west, or east from the theatre until after 1871. A comment by a correspondent in the *Hackney and Kingsland Gazette* (2 April 1870) that "from Dalston Junction to the Shoreditch Station is but a ride of five minutes" and that it takes only a further five minutes to walk via Old Street to the New Theatre of Varieties in Pitfield Street is also useful, in that the Britannia was situated only a further couple of minutes away. However, a review of the Standard Theatre's pantomime in the *Hackney and Kingsland Gazette* (16 January 1875) states of Shoreditch Station that "a more bitterly bleak waiting place after coming out of the warm theatre, for children especially, could not be," while a correspondent in the *Referee* (3 February 1924) recalls how tedious it used to be to journey from "the northern heights of London" to see the Britannia pantomime.

Even if the journey to the Britannia pantomime could be tedious, it was evidently worth making. The Britannia Theatre clearly attracted not only an audience in the immediate neighborhood but also, at least for its pantomime, one from further afield. As with the Victoria Theatre the Britannia's audience, as constructed by Dickens and a number of Victorian journalists, is formulaic and contrived. Closer investigation leads us to question such perspectives and to explore the possibility of a more diverse audience, even within the locality of Hoxton itself, than these earlier accounts allow.

A DIVERSITY OF AUDIENCES

Any account of East End audiences over a period of forty years is likely to be inadequate. At the start of our period the East End was a lively, thriving community, more socially diverse than the mythologized East End with its degradation and poverty. It was the hub of commerce and trade in the most industrialized country in the world. Only from the late 1860s did a decline set in, but at least three major theatres – the Standard, Pavilion, and Britannia – survived until the end of the century and beyond. The East End was certainly isolated from other parts of London, although omnibus, tram, and rail services improved as the century progressed. Nevertheless, at least for those who visited from outside, it seemed to be a world apart. Yet, if its theatres drew a predominantly neighborhood audience, the constituency of that audience is still open to question. To talk about a Britannia or a Pavilion audience is too limited. The proximity of East End theatres suggests that audiences identified not with one theatre but with several. In particular, the Pavilion and East London Theatres and the Standard and City of London Theatres must have competed, at times, for the same clientele.[54] Moreover, the Hoxton audience were within easy walking distance of the Grecian, the Standard, and the City of London Theatres. Thus the notion of a generic audience should be replaced with the concept of something more mobile. Moreover, the presentation of opera at the Grecian and, later, at the Pavilion and Standard provides one example of an attempt to draw diverse audiences not only from the immediate neighborhood but also (one assumes) from the new middle-class suburbs to the north and perhaps from even further afield. We are not necessarily talking about one audience at a specific theatre but a diversity, according to what was playing. There was also an increasingly educated section of the working-class communities. Although the poverty of the East End and a taste for popular entertainment are repeatedly emphasized in accounts of the area, it is interesting to note that, during Easter 1878, four large venues presented *The Messiah* to packed audiences:

It was a grand conclusion to the day . . . for some eight thousand persons and these, we may say, East-enders, to testify by their presence as auditors a rationality and intellectuality which little more than a generation ago would be deemed an impossibility and laughed at as an absurdity.[55]

We should also remember that among the theatres that flourished most in the East End were the Pavilion, Britannia, and Grecian, all located "in pockets of contrasting well-to-do and chronically poor residents."[56]

The journalistic construction of East End audiences also had repercussions in the behavior of visitors from the West End, who seemed sometimes to believe that the accounts they read licensed their own transgressions. Early in January 1869 some "gentlemen" were accused of disorderly conduct at the Pavilion, according to the *Tower Hamlets Independent* (16 January 1869):

Frederick Mordaunt, twenty-one, living in Edwin Terrace, Victoria-park road, Jeffrey Foot, twenty-six, of 5 Albion-place, Blackfriars-bridge, William Rix, twenty, of the same address, Hugh Woodsworth, nineteen, of 18, Inverness Terrace, Bayswater, John Williams, twenty, of 5, Stamford-street, Blackfriars rd, Thomas Maxwell, twenty-five, of 95, Ebury-st, Pimlico, all described on the police charge sheet as "gentlemen," were charged with riotous and disorderly conduct in the Pavilion Theatre, Whitechapel.

About eight o'clock on the previous Friday evening they were placed in a private box, "according to order" and "began talking and laughing aloud, smoking, and knocking each other's hats off." When reprimanded because they were annoying the audience, they moved to a "stage-box" and repeated the conduct. Several of them became violent and created a further disturbance when attempts were made to remove them. However, although they assaulted the sergeant who arrested them, they were merely ordered to pay bail. A clipping in Wilton's diary c.1876–77 details a fracas at the Britannia Theatre between an attendant and some law students/solicitors from west central London and Surbiton.[57] This would also suggest that disturbances were not always caused by local audiences but by younger men in middle-class occupations possibly "slumming" it for the night.

Another factor to be considered with caution is the relationship of repertoire to audience. The Pavilion Theatre presented an enormous number of nautical melodramas in its earlier years and there is clear evidence that it was attended by sailors. Yet nautical melodramas enjoyed widespread popularity in the 1820s and 1830s, reflecting a taste shared by a much wider cross-section of the community. It is clear, for instance, that many of the Jewish community were enthusiastic theatregoers, but this does not mean that every play with a Jewish subject was aimed exclusively at this community, any more than plays on Irish topics were aimed at Irish East Enders. Yet the repertoire of theatres like the Britannia was often ideologically in line with the likely attitudes and aspirations of its local community and many East End melodramas contain passages critical of social injustices. Such plays are often empowering, especially in their presentation of strong female characters.

A further issue that has to be addressed is the social diversity of the East End as its more affluent inhabitants moved northwards, potentially creating a middle-class audience that might more easily travel directly south to the East End theatres than undertake a longer journey to the West End. Alternatively, such communities might even require their own theatres, although we should be wary of assuming that this was the case. On 10 October 1853 a petition to open a theatre in Dalston, immediately to the north of the Britannia and Standard Theatres, was sent to the Lord Chamberlain. The neighborhood inhabitants were described as "persons of great respectability principally persons engaged in London in mercantile pursuits or retired from business [who] feel that the distance of places for dramatic entertainment are [sic] too far removed for their enjoyment." Sadler's Wells was two-and-a-half miles away and, although the Britannia, Standard, and City of London Theatres were closer, Dalston inhabitants wished "to have a place for select society to witness dramatic performances" and "would not visit either the Britannia, the Standard or City of London, the class of persons visiting these places of amusement being such as your petitioners ... would not like to mix with." Consequently, their only choices were the West End (too far away) or Sadler's Wells (still a two-and-a-half-mile distance). As further confirmation of the need for a theatre, the petitioners added that "Within the last four years there has been a neighborhood built and occupied in the district of Hackney, Dalston, De Beauvoir Town and Kingsland to the extent of fifteen thousand houses and ... there is no place of dramatic entertainment in the above districts."[58] As a result of further enquiries, the police reported that the Dalston inhabitants were very much against a theatre being built: "The neighborhood is inhabited by respectable families the male portion being generally engaged in the city during the day, and I was informed by many of them that they seldom visited Theatres."[59] Nor is it likely that the inhabitants of Stoke Newington, a suburb developing alongside Hackney, journeyed south to the Britannia or other East End theatres (let alone desired a theatre of their own) for the neighborhood consisted of "a great population of dissenters, including many Quakers, who will go to Readings, Recitations etc., but would not enter a Theatre proper, on any pretext."[60]

However much the population increased, the East End theatres were inevitably in competition for audiences. Clearly, those theatres situated close to each other found the most satisfactory option was to present somewhat different repertories. Yet it becomes clear that it is impossible to consider any of these theatres in isolation. In Whitechapel the Pavilion has to be considered in relation to the Effingham and, to a lesser extent, the Garrick. In Shoreditch the Standard and City of London set up a similar connection, while the Britannia was also close enough to affect and be affected by the proximity of these two theatres. Similarly, the Grecian was in competition with the Britannia to the east and Sadler's Wells to the west. One can only surmise, but it seems likely that patterns of theatregoing may have been, first, spread across two or three neighborhood theatres and, second, decided by repertoire and the social tone that this set at one or more theatres. Of the six major East End theatres, three evidently aspired at times to attract a more sophisticated audience. The Grecian, Pavilion, and especially the Standard provided opera and, in the latter's case, various examples of West End fare. The Britannia, the Effingham, and City of London presented more popular fare and perhaps appealed more to their specifically local communities.[61]

The uncouthness of the East End audience, so often fostered by popular journalism, is also open to question. Accounts of rowdy gallery audiences for the pantomime on Boxing Night are no more representative than contemporary media accounts of football hooliganism are of the average football supporter. In fact, the theatres served to keep people off the streets and out of the public houses and were generally well ordered. The comfort of patrons was attended to at prices that were affordable and audiences were generally attentive. Exceptions to the rule, especially if arrests were made and charges laid, are well documented, but relatively scarce. Audiences were generally self-regulating, more lively, and also more engaged than their West End equivalents, often watching performers (the Standard apart) who lived as members of their local community.

By 1889, according to Charles Booth, music hall had replaced the theatre as the predominant mode of entertainment in the East End. Yet he also refers to those East End theatregoers who indulge their passion for the theatre by also visiting the West End or belonging to dramatic clubs:

There are three theatres in the East End: the Standard in Norton Folgate, the Pavilion in the Mile End Road, and the Britannia in Hoxton; all homes of legitimate drama. Everywhere in England theatregoers are a special class. Those who care, go often; the rest, seldom or not at all. The regular East End theatregoer even finds his way westwards, and in the sixpenny seats of the little House in Pitfield I have heard a discussion of Irving's representation of *Faust* at the Lyceum. The passion for the stage crops up also in the dramatic clubs, of which there are several. But by the mass of the people, the music-hall entertainment is preferred to the drama. There are fully half a dozen music halls, great and small, in the district, and of all of them it must be said that the performances are unobjectionable — the keynote is a coarse, rough fun, and nothing is so much applauded as good step-dancing. Of questionable innuendo there is little, far less than at West End music-halls, and less, I noticed, than at the small benefit concerts held in public houses.[62]

The absorption of so many East Enders into the music hall is yet another effect of the social engineering commenced by W. B. Donne, who, as we shall see in the ensuing section, may have partially succeeded in restoring the drama to its former glory as a branch of literary endeavor and an emblem of social respectability, but who also fostered its decline in so many communities beyond the West End. Equally, those journalists and commentators who recorded (or rather created) quasi-fictive East End audiences during the Victorian era participated in an act of social hegemony that could be described, as Said himself describes Orientalism, as "a reminder of the seductive degradation of knowledge."[63]

Part Three

MYTH AND NINETEENTH-CENTURY
THEATRE AUDIENCES

INTRODUCTION

Narratives of Victorian theatre history, both in the nineteenth century and in early twentieth-century accounts, such as those of Nicoll and Rowell, have created an orthodox, yet mythologized picture of a progression towards the restoration of literary drama, improved standards of production, and greater social respectability, both on and off the stage. Nicoll's view is that the nineteenth-century theatre opened badly, partly on account of the audience, which "in the larger theatres in the first decades of the nineteenth century were often licentious and debased, while those in the minor playhouses were vulgar, unruly and physically obnoxious."[1] Noise and riotous behavior predominated, leading Nicoll to infer that "the auditorium of an early nineteenth century playhouse was a place lacking both in taste and in good manners, a place where vulgarity abounded, where true appreciation of the drama was subordinated to rude and foolish practical jokes, to the roaring of a drunken bully, to the besotted solicitations of a prostitute."[2] Nicoll sees in the gradual introduction of the stalls during this period the development of a more decorous tone, but attributes the popularity of melodrama in the early nineteenth century to the "comparative simplicity of the average spectator" and among the causes he attributes to the contemporary "decline" of the drama is the power of the gallery audiences. In his view:

The stage in the early part of the century was largely a "popular" affair, and for the most part bourgeois opinion regarded its delights with cringing disapproval. Typical audiences were composed mainly of lower-class citizens with a sprinkling of representatives from the gayer or more libertine section of the aristocracy. The staid middle class and the respectable, dignified nobility tended to look upon the stage as a thing not to be supported in an active manner.[3]

The cure, says Nicoll, was partially effected through the efforts of actor-managers such as William Macready and Samuel Phelps and by the increasing interest taken in the stage by Queen Victoria[4] and in turn by the development of "a more decorous and better-mannered" audience. In Nicoll's view the rowdy elements had been drawn away by the music halls and the respectability of the theatre was also improved by a growing alliance between church and stage. Refinements to the auditorium, of the sort undertaken by Marie Wilton at the Prince of Wales's Theatre, once more drew a fashionable and more sophisticated audience. Overall, Nicoll's narrative is very much one of triumphalist progress as the century draws to its conclusion, a view corroborated by Rowell. "By the outset of the nineteenth century," says Rowell, "butcher and barber had driven . . . fashionable clients from the pit to the boxes, or in many cases out of the playhouse altogether"[5] and it was not until the reforms of the Bancrofts in the 1860s, followed by the Lyceum productions of Henry Irving and Savoy operas of Gilbert and Sullivan, that respectable audiences returned. Like Nicoll, Rowell tends to see the theatre as the preserve of a particular class and neither of them explore the variety or diversity of theatre audiences in Victorian London or consider alternative interpretations of the evidence.

Hayden White, however, has suggested that myth and history are not antithetical; indeed, myth may be a relatively displaced way of ordering historical material.[6] He also refers to the notion that, if any set of facts is "variously and equally legitimately" describable, then a range of narratives can exist. Yet, in questioning the orthodox narrative of the theatre's social and literary reclamation during the nineteenth century, we argue that Victorian narratives of theatre history should be treated with caution. As White demonstrates, the language with which we discuss any historic event carries its own nuances and assumptions to the extent that we are not only creating myths and fables, however inadvertently, but we are also moving into the territory of ideology.[7] Terry Eagleton has written:

> The relationship between myth and ideology is not easy to determine. Are myths the ideologies of pre-industrial societies, or ideologies the myths of industrial ones? If there are clear parallels between the two, there are also significant points of difference. Both myth and ideology are worlds of symbolic meaning with social functions and effects; . . . [Myths] are also pre-historical or dehistoricizing, fixing events in some eternal present or viewing them as infinitely repetitive; ideologies, by contrast, may and often do dehistoricize, but the various nineteenth-century ideologies of triumphal historical progress hardly fit the bill. (One may argue, however, that such ideologies of history are historical in their context but immobilized in their form; certainly Claude Levi-Strauss sees history as simply a modern myth).[8]

In fact, if the notion of triumphal historical progress in the nineteenth century is ideologically driven, the application of this narrative to so many aspects of nineteenth-century life has engendered myths that in some instances are still allowed to pass as fact. Of course there is always the possibility that the demolition of one myth merely leads to the construction of another to take its place, although the breadth of discourse and even uncertainty allowed by new historicism arguably frees the historian from so narrow an agenda.

When we come to investigate the theatre audiences of the nineteenth century, we have eyewitness reports by sympathetic and discriminating social observers like Charles Dickens, George Sala, James Greenwood, Henry Mayhew, and William Bodham Donne on whose judgments we assume we can depend. Yet the closer we get to the evidence, the more we are aware that the theatre in the nineteenth century was itself subject to myth-making and the invention of traditions, to paraphrase Eric Hobsbawn, propagated by those same detached and discriminating observers on whose evidence we have come to rely. As the evidence becomes more questionable we begin to notice recurring descriptive patterns and rhetorical formulas that erode the boundaries between fact and fiction. Dickens and his coevals shared an uncompromising belief in the achievement of two complementary nineteenth-century goals: the reclamation of a golden age and the amelioration of society and the individual. Both these goals have considerable implications both for theatrical practices and for the role that theatre audiences performed. The first goes some way towards clarifying both the bardolatry that encouraged Dickens and Macready to support the purchase of Shakespeare's birthplace in 1847,[9] and their support of Knowles, Talfourd, and Browning in the hopes of bringing about a nineteenth-century theatrical golden age equivalent to that of Shakespeare and the Elizabethans. In so doing, they felt such dramatists would reinforce tradition and precedent, dissolve the differences between "legitimate" and "illegitimate" forms of drama, and by personal example reclaim the moral and spiritual high ground, which they believed was the traditional theatrical vantage point. Once this was achieved, a better and more appreciative audience would inevitably evolve. The second goal from a populist perspective could be identified as the trajectory from rags to riches. This tied the yearning for a golden age to the belief in the inevitability of progress and evolution. Indeed, such a trajectory informed the narrative structures of many Victorian melodramas, pantomimes, and novels. One might also argue that accounts, generated by late nineteenth-century commentators and accepted by many twentieth-century scholars, which depict the rise of the actor, the emergence of the playwright, and the evolutionary process of the drama from the domestic comedies of T. W. Robertson to the issues-based drama of Ibsen, form part of the narrative of social amelioration.

It is with an awareness of the cultural agendas held by Dickens and his circle and enshrined by subsequent critics and scholars, as well as that of W. B. Donne, that we would like to reexamine the mythopoeia that surrounded the apparently miraculous transformations of two Victorian theatres: Sadler's Wells and the Prince of Wales's. The two myths show some remarkable similarities. In the case of Sadler's Wells, the distinguished Shakespearian actor Samuel Phelps took over in 1844 an inaccessible neighborhood theatre, remarkable only for its longevity and its identification with so-called "aquatic dramas." During his management, which terminated in 1862, he presented almost the entire Shakespearian canon, and miraculously transformed the misbehaving members of the working classes into an attentive and discriminating literary audience. In the case of the Prince of Wales's, Marie Wilton, a performer distinguished for her popularity in burlesque, took over in 1865 the management of the Queen's Theatre, a disreputable fleapit, popularly known as "the Dusthole," renamed it, and together with her husband, Squire Bancroft, reclaimed a popular melodrama theatre as a center for middle- and upper-class entertainment.

In considering Sadler's Wells, the myth of miraculous transformation is complemented by one that postulates that the period 1844 to 1862 marked a golden age, during which the literary high ground had been recaptured for the theatre through the management of Samuel Phelps. After the departure of Phelps, late Victorian nostalgia would reinforce the status of this myth, in particular using it as a yardstick to measure subsequent London productions of Shakespeare. In order, therefore, to test the legitimacy of these mythological constructs we examine the socioeconomic context in which Sadler's Wells operated in the years immediately before, during, and immediately after Phelps's management. This reveals something of the actual nature of the neighborhood and the changes that occurred during the period, and provides some real evidence to support a radical transformation in the audience and its behavior in 1844 and in the period after 1862. We also examine the evidence supplied by observers of productions at Sadler's Wells and of the Islington environment. Moreover, we consider aspects of the managerial policies of Phelps, his predecessors, and successors, and the extent to which these policies coincided with or helped to fashion new audience tastes.

We have seen the ways in which Charles Dickens intervened in order to demonstrate the role of the theatre in the regeneration of theatregoers in the East End and in South London. The success of the Phelps management at an out-of-the-way suburban theatre seemed to prove the validity of lower-class responsiveness to enlightened cultural policy. Not surprisingly Dickens was a significant contributor to the myth of miraculous transformation at Sadler's Wells. We should also remember that Phelps undertook the management of Sadler's Wells at a crucial moment in his professional career. Since his London debut at the Haymarket in 1837, he had been in Macready's Covent Garden and Drury Lane companies, where he felt that his potential was unrecognized. Fortuitously, Macready's management of Drury Lane came to an end in 1843, thereby releasing Phelps from an ongoing commitment, while the passing of the Theatre Regulation Act in the same year dissolved the differences between "legitimate" and "illegitimate" forms of drama. Both these circumstances enabled Phelps to undertake, at the invitation of Greenwood, the lessee of Sadler's Wells, a term of management that would allow him a free rein in his choice of repertoire and the roles which he played. The Islington area was regarded as sufficiently remote to allow him the luxury of failure. There is at the same time no evidence to support the contention that he undertook the management in a spirit of missionary zeal.

Writing in 1851 in *Household Words* under the title "Shakespeare and Newgate,"[10] Dickens together with his collaborator R. H. Horne chose the apparent transformation of a suburban theatre situated north of the Smithfield Market and the City of London to exemplify the need of the English people for "sound rational amusement." Such a need could be met only by the intervention of a strong personality and this from Dickens's perspective had occurred in 1844, when Samuel Phelps became the theatre's manager. Prior to the advent of Phelps, according to Dickens's reconstruction, Sadler's Wells had been "a bear garden, resounding with foul language, oaths . . . [and] . . . obscenity." Phelps "conceived of the desperate idea of changing the character of the dramatic entertainments presented at this den, from the lowest to the highest, and of utterly changing with it the character of the audience." The article goes on to describe the actions of Phelps in terms that parallel those of Christ banishing the money changers from the Temple. He first rid the theatre of "the fryers of fish, vendors of oysters and the costermonger-scum accumulated round the doors." He then followed this up by the banishment of vendors of beer in the theatre, and finally and less Christlike, the children in arms.

During his opening summer season, Phelps allegedly stopped performances to eject users of bad language and on occasions "went into the gallery, with a cloak over his theatrical dress" to point out offenders to the police. Realizing the error of their ways and "sensible of the pains bestowed on everything presented to them" the audiences by 1851 "[had] really come to the Theatre for their intellectual pursuit." The result, concluded Dickens, was a gallery "as orderly as a lecture room" and a pit "filled with respectable family visitors" sitting decorously as though in their own homes. The place which was a Nuisance is become quite a household word." The choice of the concluding phrase is a deliberate one, which completes the identification between Phelps's actions and Dickens's own ideological standpoint.

Such was the authority of the journalistic accounts which appeared in *Household Words* both of the exotically distant colonies and the exotic reaches of London, that the consumer of his myths read them, to borrow Barthes's analysis, as a factual system, instead of recognizing

them as a semiological one signifying the efficacy of cultural intervention, and in the case of Phelps himself, embodying its very presence. The actions of the "costermonger-scum" moreover contain the
elements which describe lower-class behavior in public places in es-
sentialist terms: the alcohol-induced obscenities and shrieks, the consumption of copious food, and the proliferation of unidentifiable offspring. Dickens's account thus becomes accepted as a narrative of
social reclamation. Subsequent storytellers about Sadler's Wells height-
ened the aesthetic contrasts within the narrative and endowed his actions retrospectively with enlightened social reform. For example, J. R.
Towse, writing in 1916, after a lifetime as theatre critic for the *New York
Evening Post*,[11] recalled his childhood in London and the one occasion
that he visited Sadler's Wells as a very young boy to see Phelps's production of *A Midsummer Night's Dream*. He remembered nothing of it
and confesses that his memories of Phelps date from the late 1860s,
when Phelps was a starring actor at Drury Lane. Nevertheless, despite
remarking that he had avoided any recourse to books of reference, he
felt able to write:

> The old Prince of Wales's Theater, before the occupation of it by
> the Bancrofts, was not so disreputable a hole as "The Wells." . . .
> Islington, indeed, was densely populous, but exceedingly poor and
> shabby. It abounded in small shops, taverns, cheap lodging-houses
> and slums, and small tradesmen, mechanics, the commoner kind of
> clerks, peddlers, innumerable wage-earners of different kinds, with
> a plentiful sprinkling of degraded 'sports', constituted the great bulk
> of the inhabitants. "The Wells" had been devoted to what would
> now be described as vaudeville, to tenth-rate boxing matches, comic
> concerts, acrobatic shows, and so on. It was one of the dingiest,
> dirtiest, and in every way most objectionable resorts imaginable.[12]

He continued:

> To the illiterate denizens of Islington, or most of them, his [Phelps's]
> representations must have been strange and phenomenal, but they
> hailed them with enthusiasm and soon learned to applaud them
> with discrimination. . . . There has never been a more striking in-
> stance of the educational power of the theater or of the natural ca-
> pacity of the masses to comprehend . . . what is noblest and best in
> the drama.[13]

Similarly Michael Williams writing about Sadler's Wells from the perspective of 1883 described it before Phelps as offering:

> Melodrama of the coarsest type . . . to a class of frequenters, in themselves so utterly vicious, that no respectable tradesman would dream of taking his wife or daughters to the place. The lessees [Phelps and Greenwood] had not only to purify the nature of the performances, they also had to <u>unmake</u>, as well as to create, their audience.[14]

Though muted and qualified, the myth of Sadler's Wells as a site for miraculous transformation finds its way into Shirley Allen's account of Phelps when she characterizes the theatre before him as reflecting "the tastes and attitudes of the relatively uneducated lower middle class typical of suburban London in 1840."[15] Thus the original narrative, itself based on flimsy and perhaps imagined evidence, becomes transformed into a myth attempting to explain the phenomenon of social change itself. The action ascribed to Phelps by Dickens not only transformed an opening night but also succeeded in changing the very nature of Islington society. Yet the whole question of Phelps's intervention was discounted as inaccurate by his nephew W. May Phelps on the evidence of Phelps himself,[16] and neither the *Athenaeum* nor the *Theatrical Journal*, both of which reviewed the occasion, saw fit to mention Phelps's personal intervention. Indeed, when Dickens addressed the Royal General Theatrical Fund dinner, held at Drury Lane on 6 April 1857, and attempted to characterize the Sadler's Wells audience as low and very bad, his words received a hostile reception from the floor. He was forced to modify his comments and describe the audience as a mostly "vagabond" one.[17] Moreover, the comments about Islington audiences and their environment were strangely at odds with the respectability of Sadler's Wells audiences noted by the *Theatrical Journal* when it visited Sadler's Wells in 1841 or the description in the same year by James Cook in *The Actor's Notebook* that the theatre was set within a "neighborhood . . . vastly picturesque, what may be called the barrier walls between the bustle and noise, and country quietude, being only a little way off."[18]

The case of Sadler's Wells demonstrates one of the central problems in theatre historiography: that of breaking through the myths that have grown up over time. Sadler's Wells purveying education via the medium of Shakespeare to the workers or the Prince of Wales's reclamation of a popular melodrama theatre into a center for middle- and upper-class entertainment answer utopian and Darwinian notions of progress and enlightenment, but also support a carefully contrived "Victorian" view of history. The concern with moral improvement and social order is also fundamental to the way W. B. Donne conceived of the relationships between theatres, drama, and their audiences. So closely did his own agenda and that of Dickens coincide (at least in some respects), concerning the uplifting purpose of the drama, that, as we have seen, he included Dickens's account of the Britannia Theatre (after it had been rebuilt and reopened in 1858) in one of his annual reports on London Theatres.[19] The Lord Chamberlain's Papers are a particularly rich resource for research into nineteenth-century London audiences, but we must bear in mind that Donne was a man with a mission. What might, at first glance, appear to be a relatively objective source is in fact a heavily loaded set of comments and reports, many of which are driven by Donne's own obsessions and concerns.

Although we no longer interpret the past as a journey towards a utopian present, it is quite clear that W. B. Donne saw his own function as propelling the drama towards a utopian future and that he attempted to use his powers as Examiner of Plays to bring this about. Unlike Dickens, who wanted popular theatre to uplift the morals of the lower classes, Donne really wanted the drama to be uplifted by the exclusion of the lower orders. The better classes of spectator would oust their social inferiors and herald in a new golden age of elevated drama. (We must remember that Donne, a contemporary of Tennyson and Hallam, had belonged to the Apostles at Cambridge and possessed a strong sense of English dramatic traditions). "The nation which boasts of Shakespeare and his great contemporaries," wrote Donne, "should continue to boast of its stage. But in order to become a subject of legitimate pride, the stage itself must retrace many a long and heedless step in the path of error, and by assuming to itself a vocation to guide rather than follow the caprices of the public, regain the grounds at least of self-respect, before it can re-acquire its true position among the arts which minister to the instruction as well as to the amusement of an age."[20] Donne also desired that managements would seek to win back "the educated and intellectual classes of the community" and that the nineteenth century would develop "an intellectual, moral, and vigorous national drama."[21] Donne believed that the drama should elevate its audiences, but that a more elevated drama depended in turn on drawing to the theatres a more elevated class of patron. In 1858 he commented in his annual report that theatres were beginning to attract back a better class of person as the quality of their buildings improved (under strong pressure from the Lord Chamberlain's Office), but that although the morality of the drama had also improved, a few theatres were still attracting audiences through the representation of crimes of violence and fraud.[22] Amongst the latter was the Queen's Theatre in Tottenham Street, just north of Oxford Street and west of Tottenham Court Road. Insofar as Donne's wishes were fulfilled, one of the greatest success stories during his years of office was the transformation of the Queen's Theatre, the only theatre to provide the citizens of central London with popular melodramatic fare, into the Prince of Wales's Theatre.

The myth of the Prince of Wales's Theatre is a commonplace of nineteenth-century British theatre history: H. Barton Baker provides the typical rags-to-riches narrative, which was to become common in subsequent accounts. Of the melodramas performed under the previous management he writes (without substantiation) that "the style in which these plays were rendered may be imagined; no burlesque was ever half so extravagant."[23] His description of the Queen's prior to Marie Wilton's arrival prepares us for a transformation worthy of the most spectacular of Victorian pantomimes:

> The Queen's shared with the Bower Saloon in Stangate the reputation of being the lowest theatre in London; and then the neighborhood! always impregnated with "an ancient and fish-like smell" from the fried fish, which was the staple commerce of the street. Such was the house that Miss Marie Wilton, in 1865, being at that time in search of a theatre, fixed upon as a home for elegant comedy.[24]

The *Era* (16 April 1898) retrospectively referred to how the Bancrofts [*sic*] "had taken almost in fear and trembling, a dirty little playhouse near the Tottenham-Court-Road." Marie Wilton paints a far from glowing picture of the theatre of which she became manager in 1865:

> I was implored by everyone I consulted to reflect before entering upon such an enterprise. 'The neighborhood was awful.' 'The distance too great from the fashionable world,' and 'Nothing would ever make it a high-class theatre'.[25]

One night prior to the commencement of her management, she visited the theatre:

It was a well-constructed, clean little house, but oh, the audience! My heart sank! Some of the occupants of the stalls (the price of admission was, I think, a shilling) were engaged between the acts in devouring oranges (their faces being buried in them), and drinking ginger-beer. Babies were being rocked to sleep, or smacked to be quiet, which proceedings, in many cases, had an opposite effect! A woman looked up to our box, and seeing us staring aghast, with I suppose an expression of horror upon my face. first of all 'took a sight' at us, and then shouted, 'Now then, you three stuck-up ones, come out o' that, or I'll send this 'ere orange at your 'eds'.[26]

Yet the evidence suggests that, as with Sadler's Wells, the transformation itself may have been less overwhelming than the subsequent myths which have encapsulated it.

4. Sadler's Wells Theatre

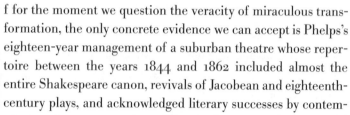f for the moment we question the veracity of miraculous trans-
formation, the only concrete evidence we can accept is Phelps's
eighteen-year management of a suburban theatre whose repertoire between the years 1844 and 1862 included almost the
entire Shakespeare canon, revivals of Jacobean and eighteenth-
century plays, and acknowledged literary successes by contemporary nineteenth-century authors. That such a repertoire remained
constant throughout the period may itself testify to the existence of a
constant audience demand. Certainly, comparisons with other theatres
corroborate that it was the only London theatre with such a policy. The
fact that the price structure also remained constant may indicate the
social and economic stability of those who attended and may have
implications about production values that identified the theatre's offerings throughout the period. The only other hard evidence we can
accept is that after Phelps relinquished Sadler's Wells in 1862, the theatre declined rapidly. Successive managements, which tried to emulate
Phelps's policy of legitimate drama or to capitalize on his managerial
stability, largely failed.

Sadler's Wells was the oldest theatre in London. It had operated as a
place of entertainment since the late seventeenth century, its attractions tied in part to its identification as a summer holiday resort. Indeed
by the middle of the eighteenth century it was at the center of a thriving tourist industry comprising pleasure gardens and spas clustered
around the New River. These catered to the extraordinary zest for
country rambles, afternoon teas, and escapism, which affected all Londoners especially during summer.[1] Such gardens were set among fields
approached along country lanes, and in Islington among dairy farms —
indeed, this area retained its identity as a supplier of milk for London
into the nineteenth century. Sadler's Wells, however, seems to have
been the only spa that possessed a permanent theatre, certainly after
Rosoman's rebuilding of it in 1765. The decline in the fortunes of the

Islington spas began at the end of the eighteenth century, as the carriage trade declined and as building spread from Clerkenwell in the south to Highbury and Canonbury in the north, especially after 1810. The prospect of traveling to a northern rurality increasingly built out and remote would rapidly prove less attractive to potential tourists and pleasure seekers than the opportunities afforded by public transport to reach the seaside to the south and southeast of London.[2]

Yet it would be misleading to identify the Islington area merely as a summer resort that had outlived its patrons. It was immediately north of the City and a main arterial road from York and Essex (St. John's Road) bisected Finsbury and Clerkenwell, and terminated at the Smithfield Market. The Angel Inn at the junction of this road and New Road (later Pentonville Road) was an important staging post for coaches. It was also an area noted for its evangelical churches, schools, hospitals, and reformatories.[3] Town houses for City merchants were established in the Finsbury district in the eighteenth century, and from 1773 the area to be known as Pentonville became identified with "gentlemen and affluent tradesmen,"[4] while Penton Street was described as the "Belgravia" of Islington. From 1820 the number of formal streets and squares increased dramatically and this reflected the increase in population: for example 23,396 persons lived in Clerkenwell in 1801, rising to 49,634 in 1831.[5] At the same time, even though the spas declined as watering holes, the proximity to water encouraged the setting up of breweries and distilleries: Whitbread in the southern Bunhill district of Clerkenwell from 1750, followed by Gordon's in Goswell Street, and Booth's in Britton Street in the early nineteenth century.

Thus, by the beginning of the nineteenth century, Sadler's Wells stood physically at the interstice between a retreating countryside and an encroaching urban development. The fashionable patronage of the eighteenth century could be found in the elegant town houses, especially in the areas north of the theatre in Canonbury, which preserved the sense of a retreat from the bustle of the City. At the same time new streets and squares were being built to accommodate a middle class looking for housing: Exmouth Street, Myddelton Street, Spencer Street, and Ashby Street between 1800 and 1821; Myddelton Square, Wilmington Square, and Upper Rosoman Street between 1821 and 1831. Myddelton Street, moreover, linked the main north-south St. John's and Goswell Roads, thus bringing into the area traders, innkeepers, and farmers with their cattle, whose presence was preserved in the names of Exmouth Market and Chapel Market. Such increases in building and the concomitant possibility of a changing demography of the Islington area after 1821 demanded a reappraisal of managerial policy at Sadler's Wells, which indeed took place under Thomas Dibdin's management in 1825.[6]

Throughout the eighteenth century the policy of the various spas had accommodated the patronage of summer visitors by presenting music concerts, dancing, and entertainments, which complemented the holiday atmosphere of fairground vitality and visceral attractions, as well as presenting opportunities for social intercourse over tea, coffee, or alcoholic beverages. The comparative isolation of the Sadler's Wells area also encouraged the presence of those who regarded the visitors as easy pickings — the footpads and pickpockets. The theatre's management tried to allay the fears of patrons by providing watchmen to monitor journeys back to the City. Yet despite the collapse of the fashionable carriage trade and the decline of other spas and pleasure grounds from the end of the eighteenth century, the artistic policy of Sadler's Wells appears to have changed little in the period between 1780 and the early 1820s. A notice of 12 April 1785 announces a program featuring dancing dogs, a "learned pig," the appearance of the Irish Giant, Patrick O'Brien, together with singing, dancing, and an Easter pantomime, *Oriental Magic, or, Harlequin Nabob* (with the footnote "Patroles of horse and foot stationed from Sadler's Wells along the different roads from the hours of seven to eleven"); and on 21 July 1822, a subsequent notice announces *The Rival Indians, or, the Faithful Dog*, the "extravaganza" *Tom and Jerry*, featuring pony races in and around the pit in Act III, as well as a real bear in the forest scene of *Valentine and Orson*. Moreover, it was still possible to attract a fashionable audience during the summer, as can be seen from a report in July 1822 that the theatre had been visited by the Earl and Countess of Darlington, the Dutch ambassador, Lord Clanwilliam, and Sir Charles Laurie and Lady Laurie among others.[7] Equally significant is the evidence for the continuing presence of a mobile nonfashionable audience. At the end of a long summer season (15 October 1807) a panic about a fire at Sadler's Wells killed eighteen people. Reports reveal the presence of both local people and those who had traveled to the theatre: the dead included those who were residents of Temple Bar, Westminster, Leicester Square, Hoxton, Whitechapel, Shoreditch, Bloomsbury, and London Wall, as well as Goswell Street,

Pentonville, and Battle bridge (King's Cross). The age range was between nine and thirty: eight of the victims were female. No full list of occupations appears, although the reports note that nine-year-old Rebecca Saunders was in service and had come with her mistress from London Wall to look after a baby; John Greenwood was an apprentice living in Hoxton who was identified by his master; James Binks was a sixteen-year-old who helped his father, a porter in the Hoxton area; John Wood was a twelve-year-old errand boy living in Aldersgate; and a sailor reported that he had accompanied an "unfortunate female" who was killed and had been living in Whitechapel.[8]

In 1825 Dibdin decided to extend the Sadler's Wells season to a full year, to introduce half-price and to reintroduce the sale of liquor, which had been discontinued after the disaster of 1807. He announced that the saloons would be open from 11 A.M. to 11 P.M. This signaled a radical change: an acceptance of the fact that the theatre could no longer exist as a summer theatre dependent on a holiday trade and that the creation of residential squares like Myddelton Square immediately around the theatre after 1821 heralded increases in the population living permanently in the area. The sale of liquor, though it preserved an element integral to the eighteenth-century pleasure gardens, was now an added drawcard. Additionally, half-price signaled not only an acceptance of the fact that some of the theatre's patrons might now be drawn from those whose working hours were long and who could no longer pay the full price, but also that the surrounding squares might house a significant number of middle-class people whose dining habits precluded them or their servants from attending the theatre at 6 P.M. The newspaper responses to Dibdin's managerial innovation suggest both a wish to retain elements of the past and an admission that the neighborhood was changing:

> Sadler's Wells re-commences its operations at Christmas; a speculation which we think likely to answer, as a playhouse will be a great acquisition to the pastoral inhabitants of Mecklenburgh, Tavistock, Brunswick, and Russell-squares, and the sequestered glades of Guilford-street, Pentonville, Woburn-place, Islington, and St. John's-street.

The same notice points to the need for adequate street signs and the fact that the native watchmen in the area "speak a *patois* peculiar to the district."⁹ At the same time *Life in London* places Sadler's Wells, after Dibdin's expenditure on refurbishment, in the midst of a new development:

> The fields and dreary roads, which of yore isolated the spot, have now, as by pantomime magic, given place to a new and populous town, entirely surrounding the Wells, and presenting avenues in every direction abounding in lamps, watchmen, and hackney vehicles of all descriptions.¹⁰

As with all minor theatres, the period from 1825 to the end of the 1830s was an insecure one as the population of London spread rapidly and managerial concern about audience composition saw rapid shifts and changes in repertoire in order to determine the tastes of the new patrons. Sadler's Wells's theatrical reputation had rested on the popularity of Grimaldi in the Easter pantomime since the 1780s and the novelty of aquatic dramas since 1804. After Grimaldi's departure, effectively from 1823, the theatre found itself facing the problems of other minor theatres, although it seemed to retain an immunity from the complaints and prosecutions instigated by the patent theatres when they felt that their rights were being infringed by performances of quasi-legitimate plays. The theatre's perceived distance from the theatrical center of London lent it a degree of enchantment. Nevertheless, its repertoire mirrored the melodramas and farces of theatres like the Surrey and Victoria, while retaining elements of its earlier incarnation as a pleasure garden and a house noted for speciality acts by musicians, acrobats, balloonists, and animals.

The period until 1838 saw the theatre pass through the hands of a number of managers: Campbell, 1828 to 1832, who tried to put on Shakespeare, but with poor results because of his inadequate company; George Almar, 1833 to 1836; Osbaldiston with Eliza Vincent in 1836 and 1838; and finally Robert Honner, who had been stage manager of the Surrey and became the lessee in 1838. Throughout this unsettling period of change, prices fluctuated considerably. During the eighteenth century the summer theatre had charged boxes, 4s; pit, 2s; and gallery, 1s. In 1832 prices were dropped, although in 1835 pit and box seats were 1s 6d and 2s 6d respectively. In the period 1835 to 1836, Almar tried a policy of half-price in the pit together with a free gallery. By 1839, however, the admission price of boxes, 2s; pit, 1s; and gallery, 6d was set, and this would remain constant for the next twenty-five years.

{ *Nineteenth-Century Audiences* }

Honner mounted a repertoire that included adaptations of Dickens's novels like *Oliver Twist*, Thomas Greenwood's adaptation of *Jack Sheppard*, T. E. Wilks's locally based dramas *The Ruby Ring, or, the Murder at Sadler's Wells*, and *The Fair Maid of Tottenham Court*. He also invited well-known actors like William Elton from Drury Lane to play in *Othello*, Massinger's *A New Way to Pay Old Debts*, and *The Merchant of Venice*, alongside Daniel Terry's adaptation of Scott's *Rob Roy* and the appearance of Mr. Carter, the American Lion King, with a pride of lions. In 1840 he brought Elton to Sadler's Wells with Henry Marston to play in *Hamlet*. In 1842 Thomas Greenwood, whose connection with the theatre spanned three generations and who had become responsible for the annual Christmas pantomime under Honner, became the theatre's manager with Marston as stage manager. In 1843 it was they who invited Phelps and Mrs. Warner to appear at a benefit for Elton's widow and who commenced negotiations with them to assume the management of Sadler's Wells from 27 May 1844.

When Phelps moved his family from Chelsea to Canonbury in 1844, he moved into an area whose populations reflected both change and respectability. The Finsbury Division, which included Islington, Canonbury, and Clerkenwell had a population of 185,174, of whom 55,720 lived in Islington itself and by far the greatest proportion of whom had been born in Middlesex.[11] The increases in building meant that large numbers of bricklayers, plasterers, carpenters, joiners, painters, plumbers, and glaziers lived in the area, while at the same time there remained considerable evidence of Islington's farming connection: the area had, for example, the largest numbers of drovers, agricultural laborers, cowkeepers, and nurserymen in London. The presence of the arterial road between York, Essex, and the City inevitably encouraged blacksmiths, carriers, carters and wagoners, coachmen, coach guards, and postboys to live near its vicinity. Just as important was the presence of a large professional and skilled artisan class. The area was already noted for its jewelers, and gold- and silversmiths, as well as its watch, clock, and instrument makers. These were complemented by skilled metal workers: embossers, engravers, and brass finishers. It was also a center housing booksellers, binders, newspaper publishers, and reporters. The area had the second largest London population of attorneys, solicitors, and law students, as well as of clerks and government civil servants,[12] and the largest population of surgeons, apothecaries, and stock and insurance brokers of all kinds. Although there were small businessmen and merchants — butchers, brush and broom makers, cutlers, grocers and tea dealers, polishers, and cabinet makers — there were only small numbers of messengers, porters, and errand boys. Equally, there were fewer laborers than in any other district after the City, with relatively few examples of the traditionally female occupations of dressmakers, milliners, or domestic servants.[13]

At the same time, public transport was limited to omnibus routes, which, with one exception, skirted the area. There was one route that went from the Post Office to Sadler's Wells, Islington, and Paddington every fifteen minutes at a cost of 6d, while others went from Bank to Paddington via the Angel and King's Cross or from the Elephant and Castle to Islington via Oxford and Baker Streets.[14] This implies that Phelps had entered an area in which large numbers of people traveled to the City to work or were involved in pursuing established local trades and professions, as well as in the burgeoning building trade. Moreover, the existence of many under the age of twenty in the Finsbury Division attests to the significant numbers of families in the area.[15]

Such evidence seems to throw doubt at least on one element of the myth of Sadler's Wells: that the area in the early 1840s was a degraded one, characterized by blackguards and dominated by a culturally unappreciative working class. The managements of Honner, Greenwood, and Marston before 1844 had already demonstrated the existence of an appreciative and "respectable" body of spectators who were able to differentiate between the responses appropriate to a summer holiday occasion and to the more serious fare offered on an annual basis at a neighborhood theatre. When Phelps, therefore, undertook the management of Sadler's Wells in 1844, it may well have been the case that a respected Drury Lane actor in concert with a respected member of the Islington community were faced not with a theatre looking for an audience, but rather with an audience looking for a theatre whose repertoire would affirm its own self-conscious respectability.

Sadler's Wells prided itself on being the oldest theatre in the metropolis, and its repertoire and those associated with the theatre as performers or staff identified themselves with the local community.[16] The 1839 adaptation of *Oliver Twist* emphasized the connection between Clerkenwell, Pentonville, and the novel; and the period to 1843 saw revivals of *The Ruby Ring*, as well as new plays like *The Fair Maid of Tottenham Court*, *The Clerk of Islington*, and *Claude du Val*, *The*

Highwayman of Holloway, the last on 26 April 1843.[17] Phelps and Mrs. Warner took over a theatre in which most of the patrons sat either in the pit or the gallery. It seated approximately twenty-four hundred and had an extraordinarily deep pit. The number capable of being seated in the fashionable boxes formed little more than 10 percent of the total capacity.[18] To a great extent this configuration would determine Phelps's artistic policy. If he could not persuade people drawn from local inhabitants to occupy the boxes, he would need to rely on volume sales in the pit and gallery. He chose to open with *Macbeth*, which had been presented at Sadler's Wells on a number of occasions: 1840, 1842, and in April 1844, a month before his production. If there was a disturbance at the opening, it may well have been the kind reported at the opening of the earlier 1840 production, when the interference by "two drunken miscreants" was described as an "uproar," which neither the manager Honner nor the police in attendance bothered to quell: they "merely glanced towards the place of disturbance" and took no further action though it did affront "several respectable women" in the gallery.[19] The same report condemns the performance on the grounds of the inadequate company despite the presence of good actors like Cathcart and Marston. This was one aspect Phelps was determined to address.

Phelps and Mrs. Warner assembled a company they could trust and whose abilities would complement each other. For the next eighteen years he pursued a policy calculated, as the Phelps/Warner manifesto of 1844 declared, to make "Sadler's Wells the resort of the respectable inhabitants of the neighborhood."[20] By 19 April 1845, when the winter season closed, it had been "a prosperous season of the legitimate drama."[21] Significance lay in the term "legitimate," as the theatre had certainly been successful under the Honner and Greenwood regimes, especially during the summer.[22] Even before the end of the first year Phelps could afford to perform Massinger's *The City Madam* on 30 October 1844, suitably bowdlerized for his audience who were "superior and intelligent" and included "the presence of a large school . . . a pleasing proof that the exertions of the management are approved of, not merely by playgoers, but by those intrusted [*sic*] with the education and moral culture of youth."[23] By the commencement of the 1845 season, a local newspaper could take considerable pride in the identification of Phelps's policy and the sensibilities of the local population:

The revivals of the olden drama at this theatre . . . continue un-abatedly attractive. We are not altogether surprised at this success; for, if called upon to write the intellectual topography of the me-tropolis and its environs, we should point to the district in which lies Sadler's Wells, as containing a larger proportion of intelligent popu-lation. . . . Islington has been the favoured "biding place of men of genius, especially of artists, for many centuries past, and it maintains this literary and artistical reputation to the present day."[24]

By April 1847, when *Macbeth* was revived, "there was as usual, an attentive, although crowded Monday night audience, who were both liberal and judicious in their applause,"[25] and when it reappeared in September 1847 Jonas Levy could state that "the curtain descended amid a volley of cheers . . . the audience . . . was an indiscriminate one, drawn from all classes of society, and representing the experience of every condition of life."[26] By this time critics were visiting regularly. John Forster had started to go in 1846, Talfourd in 1847; and Dickens certainly saw Phelps's *Cymbeline* in the same year although there is no concrete evidence to suggest that he had been earlier, much less that he had been present at the May opening of *Macbeth* in 1844.[27] From now on critical responses become remarkably similar as critics ex-pressed their surprise and gratification that shop girls, tradesmen, and clerks appreciated Shakespeare better than wealthy and fashionable West End audiences did.[28] Audiences, however, were not necessarily staid or undemonstrative, as descriptions of the pantomime audiences attest.[29] There may also have been a considerable number of younger people who attended Phelps's seasons. On one occasion, for example, for a performance of *The Winter's Tale*, at the benefit of Greenwood, there were numbers of medical students present:

A singular circumstance has attended this theatre latterly. The plays of Shakespeare have been revived here during the two last seasons, thousands of playgoers from all parts of the metropolis, have fre-quented it: and, young gentlemen, who are studying how they can preserve the lives of their fellow creatures at Bartholomew's Hos-pital, have latterly patronised this house, they say because Shake-speare's plays are performed. On the evening of the manager's bene-fit, some sixty or eighty of these students, so called, attended the theatre.[30]

In fact, looking back from the vantage point of 1887, P. P. Hanley felt that Phelps had been responsible for introducing young people to Shakespeare:

> The young people of that time (myself among the number) owe him a debt of gratitude for giving us an opportunity of seeing Shakespeare's plays represented as they should be.[31]

Another factor which may have been of considerable importance is the presence of women in the audience at Sadler's Wells. As early as June 1844, the *Literary Gazette* had commented on their presence:

> A succession of novelty nightly is now to be found in the new management. On Monday *The Stranger* was performed to a full and respectable audience, which consisted chiefly of females. It is astonishing the anxiety of the softer sex to witness this play.[32]

When Greenwood took his benefit in September, the same journal described him as a "great favourite among the ladies, for two-thirds of the audience were of that class."[33] Women, therefore, formed a significant element of the audience. When more working women moved into the neighborhood, especially after 1851, and the numbers of women who were able to stay home declined due to pressures of work, this would have serious implications for the patronage at Sadler's Wells.

Phelps continued the practice already established under Honner of making the theatre available to local charitable bodies.[34] Not only did these occasions cement local relations, but sometimes they attracted fashionable audiences. The *Illustrated London News* (2 December 1848) noticed the benefit for the Italian school in Greville Street, Hatton Garden and mentions that the boxes had "those whose names the public are familiar with as moving in the West End circles." Indeed, the same article found that "the greater portion of the audience . . . were far more accustomed to the light vaudevilles of the St. James's Theatre, and the music of the two opera houses, than the higher class of legitimate drama."[35] Generally Phelps's audiences were drawn from the neighborhood. He did try to raise the quality of theatregoing: he remodeled the theatre in 1846, enlarged the area for box seats, created a dress circle, and insisted that children under three would not be admitted and that children in the pit would pay the full price of 1s. In the summer of 1848 he enlarged the entrance to the boxes and created a separate stairway to the dress circle, together with a new carriage drive and a covered lobby. Clearly there were some in the neighborhood (as well as beyond) who drove to the theatre in carriages. A notice in 1849 of Greenwood's benefit stated that:

> The house presented its usual appearance, every seat being occupied by persons of respectability, indeed, the dress circle was most fashionably attended by ladies elegantly attired, while the private boxes contained many of the most wealthy families in the neighborhood.[36]

A notice of 1853 commented on the fact that a summer visit by Buckstone had been affected by a cab strike, which diminished the numbers in the boxes.[37]

Thus Sadler's Wells became identified as a venue whose patrons, if not from a narrowly-defined middle class, nevertheless exhibited middle-class behavior.[38] They were, in F. M. L. Thompson's description, the "small shopkeepers, traders and dealers"[39] who lived in Clerkenwell and Islington; they were men of lower professional standing than the lawyers and bankers who controlled most middle-class political and reform activity. When Henry Morley, who had remarked in the *Examiner* (15 October) on the solemnity with which audiences had appreciated *A Midsummer Night's Dream* in 1853, reviewed *Twelfth Night* in 1857, he identified the Sadler's Wells audience as one "mainly composed of hard-working men, who crowd a sixpenny gallery and shilling pit. . . . There sit our working classes in a happy crowd, as orderly and reverent as if they were at church."[40] Given the nature of the neighborhood and the presence of numerous churches, the connection between theatre and churchgoers is an important one. Shirley Allen, however, points to a certain confusion in Phelps's mind about the origins of his audiences, which is also mirrored in W. May Phelps's assertion that it was "very erroneous to talk of the audiences being for the most part local."[41] Allen quotes a draft of a letter to the Queen's Master of Revels in which Phelps maintains that Sadler's Wells is situated within "a non-theatrical population — the majority of my audience coming from a distance as a necessity," yet on another occasion he told Richard Horne that his audience were "only local audiences for the most part."[42] Members of the audience, especially those whom Phelps would have designated as "fashionable," did travel from a distance. At an 1849 revival of *King John*, for example, a newspaper account recorded that "the house was filled on Monday with an audience composed of those well-known and honoured in the theatrical and literary circles of London."[43] Yet Phelps's comment to Horne was an admission of the reality that he could not rely on visitors to the area who, if they were unable to obtain transport, found it virtually impossible to reach the theatre, particularly in bad weather:

> Trudging from central London to the precincts of the New River Head (even in the cause of the legitimate drama) during the present uncomfortable weather, with the state of the streets, defying all description, is no joke.[44]

In the final analysis he had to rely on "the more respectable portion of the immediate neighborhood."[45]

The tenure of the theatre by Phelps reached its apogee in the mid-1850s by which time the Sadler's Wells audiences appeared to demonstrate particular characteristics. Richard Lee, writing a biographical sketch of Phelps for the *Theatre* in 1886 described them:

> More than any other they were an audience of students, who came to see presented upon the stage what they had seen and reflected on at home. In the boxes, the pit and even in the gallery, numbers . . . were nightly to be seen checking the text as it fell from the actor's lips by reference to their open Shakespeare.

He goes on to suggest that their allegiance to Phelps could partly be explained by a sense of familiarity: his policy of reviving successful productions for example, was regarded as a demonstration of stability rather than a manifestation of managerial impecuniousness or lack of imagination:

> The charm which drew them to the theatre was not their unfamiliarity, but on the contrary, their perfect intimacy with the play which they went to see; novelty in their sense meaning new readings, not new plots.[46]

Phelps had already established for himself a work pattern whereby his season ended at Easter and he could sublease the theatre during the summer and into September. He was also quite prepared to terminate his winter season early. The *Theatrical Journal* noted in 1855:

Three weeks before Easter, and the season at Sadler's Wells has terminated; as each successive one arrives so does it fall shorter of its allotted time. Originally, the setting in of the hot weather was the only cause of an impoverished audience, . . . and now the doors are closed a fortnight prior to Passion Week. . . . The termination of the run of the pantomime seems to bring in its rear small receipts, cold audiences, and premature closing, and we cannot help thinking some exertion should be made by Messrs. Greenwood and Phelps to meet and overthrow this difficulty.[47]

Phelps's success at Sadler's Wells partly obscures the fact that he was able to offset his production costs by opening the theatre to visits by other companies, including opera, and for the use of public meetings and concerts during the summer, at complete variance with the literary drama that dominated the theatre during the season from September onward. Indeed, it may well have been in his interest to ensure that the two seasons were distinctly different. This raises the question whether the summer repertoire attracted a different audience to the theatre. The 1854 summer season had featured an African opera company, musical burlettas, farces, opera seasons with Sims Reeves and the Pyne-Harrison Opera Company, Pell's Ethiopian Serenaders, and visits by Mrs. Keeley as Jack Shepherd. Such entertainments were intended no doubt to attract summer audiences, who had not succumbed to the increasingly affordable holiday excursions to the seaside at Margate or Brighton.[48] That such excursions might indeed influence audience attendance is implicit in references to excursion trains and the opportunity to spend eight hours at the seaside which figure prominently in the 1861 pantomime.[49] Indeed the pantomimes from 1855 onward draw attention to significant neighborhood problems that would seem to be substantiated by the findings of the 1861 census: the ongoing presence of watchmakers and the printing and publishing trade; anxieties about the increases in population, which find expression in references to suburban villas and the need to discover "refined retreats"; the importance placed on schooling in an area that featured numbers of schools, churches, and a house of correction; the spread of warehouses, especially those related to the furnishing, hardware, and cutlery trades; telegraph and government offices as a source of employment, particularly for the numerous clerks in the area; and milliners' shops as outlets for the large increases in women working as hat and dressmakers.

Phelps's last original role at Sadler's Wells opened the 1859 season – Bertuccio in Tom Taylor's verse drama *The Fool's Revenge* capitalized on Verdi's well-known *Rigoletto* (his operas *La Traviata* and *Il Trovatore* had featured in the 1858 summer opera season at Sadler's Wells) and offered Phelps a role combining Renaissance revenge with Victorian paternalism. The bills for the play announce that the sale of wine, beer, and spirits was not permitted within the walls of the theatre:

> Two matters affecting the regulation of the audience part of the theatre deserve notice at our hands. The fees to the bonnet attendants in the boxes have been abolished; this is a very great relief, as many a paterfamilias will thankfully discover. The other matter is that of all the theatres of London only Sadler's Wells and the Princess's have declined the license for the sale of wine, beer and spirits. . . . We heartily congratulate Messrs. Phelps and Greenwood on having preferred the respectability of their theatre to the gain which they might have made by sacrificing it.[50]

The pantomime that year, *Harlequin Hans and the Golden Goose*, was to be Greenwood's last production as well. References in the pantomime to boarding houses reflected the spread of lodging houses and the provision of board for the large numbers of workmen and clerks in the area; while references to the police station obliquely reflect the presence of police and prison warders who serviced the Clerkenwell House of Correction immediately to the south of Sadler's Wells.

Greenwood, announcing his decision to retire early in 1860, prompted an advertisement by the management in the *London Gazette* that the theatre would be available to let. Phelps was quick to justify this action at his benefit on 17 March 1860, on the grounds of his partner's imminent retirement. Nevertheless he vowed to carry on. Although Phelps admitted that various offers had been made to him to take a theatre "in what some people called . . . the 'fashionable' part of town . . . he could not bring himself to leave the pleasant old boards of Sadler's Wells. (Great cheering)."[51] He would indeed continue, but would appear less frequently. On 28 January 1862 the lease of the theatre was put up for auction. It was described thus:

> The first-class long leasehold property . . . covers a large area of ground, in a very populous and respectable neighborhood, and has excellent access from St. John's street-road and Arlington-street,

with a large area or court yard, affording unusual facilities for carriage visitors. The Theatre is brick-built, slated and tiled, admirably
arranged, tastefully embellished, and approached by a portico; the
auditory is planned so as to secure a good view of the stage, as well
as acoustic facilities, and comprises the dress circle, with seats for
one hundred and two persons; the boxes, to accommodate one hundred and fifty persons; six private boxes; roomy pit, to accommodate one thousand persons; the gallery to hold eight hundred to one
thousand persons. There are two refreshment saloons, and a good
box office.[52]

The notice also itemizes the income and disbursements: £1,000 per
year payable as rent which, after ground rent and taxes had been paid,
left a surplus of £510.15.5. On the face of it, the owner of the lease, if
not the manager, stood to make a reasonable profit after the rent of
£1,000 per year was received from the theatre's tenant. Phelps had paid
this in ten monthly payments, so that the subleasing of the theatre during the summer months would have helped to offset the costs of his
winter season. On the basis of the figures, a full house at Sadler's Wells
would return £120 per performance.[53] In fact, the theatre's lease was
not taken up and Phelps would need to wait until the end of the summer before he could sell his tenancy to Catherine Lucette.

Why then did Phelps give up? He was fifty-eight years old and his
noticeable absences since 1860 suggest that his wife's illness, as well as
the retirement of his partner, had precipitated the decision to change.
Just as influential must have been the opening of Deacon's Music Hall
at the Hugh Myddelton Tavern immediately opposite the front doors of
the theatre in 1861 and of Collins's Music Hall in Islington Green just
north of the Angel in 1862. In order to contextualize the possible importance of these music halls, it is necessary to consider some of the
demographic changes that had occurred in the 1840s and 1850s.

Between 1841 and 1851 there had been little change in the growth
of population in those streets whose inhabitants might have regarded
Sadler's Wells as their local theatre. Thus for example an arterial road
like St. John's Road had increased merely from 1,000 to 1,240 (24%); a
major cross street like Spencer Street, which linked St. John's Road
with Goswell Street, from 378 to 434 (12.9%); Gloucester Road, which
ran north from St. John's Road to the New River Head, from 325 to 365
(10.9%) and Arlington Street, which passed the rear entrance of the

theatre, from 301 to 338 (10.9%). These modest increases complemented a process of gradual change in the diversity of the occupations and professions in the streets themselves. Thus St. John's Road,
a natural magnet for coachmakers, conductors, cab proprietors, and
small shop owners, had by 1851 increased its services for travelers by
adding coffee shops and lodging houses, while additional shops had
created a demand for errand boys and shop assistants. Many of those
who had lived on an independent income (eighty-four in 1841) had
gone together with their servants. The street also attracted clerks working for ship brokers and banks in the City as well as for local merchants. The proliferation of clerks also spread to Spencer Street to join
the solicitors, schoolmistresses, and watchmakers who had lived there
since 1841. By 1851, Gloucester Road housed craft-based artisans, together with their domestic servants and young families, a police sergeant, a nonconformist minister, and carpet warehousemen, along with
their shopmen and servants. Closer to Pentonville Road and the Angel,
Arlington Street maintained its numbers of livery stable keepers, os-
tlers, and cab drivers, while increasing the numbers of shops. Northampton Square, south of the theatre, in 1841 had a population of 238
made up of established clerks working in the City, merchants, a solicitor, a barometer maker, a jeweler with eight apprentices, various small
shop owners, and eight people living off independent incomes and employing servants. In 1851 it had in fact marginally decreased in population: only one independent income holder remained and some of the
clerks had left. On the other hand it had gained a Wesleyan minister, a
general practitioner, and a surgeon, as well as six watchmakers.[54] In
other words, the profile of the neighborhood remained a stable one,
based on its watchmakers, jewelers, printers, and workers in the book
trade (compositors, book folders, etc.), as well as those who served the
needs of travelers and local residents: shops, doctors, lawyers, licensed
victualers, tailors, bootmakers, dressmakers, and milliners.

Nonetheless, dramatic change had occurred in the 1850s. The population of Islington had risen from 95,329 in 1851 to 155,341 in 1861 (a
rise of 62.9%), of which 85,274 (54%) were female and 70,067 (45%)
were male.[55] Increasing numbers congregated around the major north-
south roads including numbers of unskilled workers and transients, especially commercial travelers. Large houses were subdivided to accommodate lodgers who worked in the City or in local industries or who
were unemployed. In St. John's Road the numbers increased to 2,763

(122%), made up of young families whose adults worked in trades not hitherto represented: painting-brush makers, meat salesman, packers, wharf officer, wire workers, warehousemen, barmen. Clerks, shop assistants, commercial travelers, and servants now far outnumbered those who had supported the carriage trade. Nevertheless, although numbers quickly increased in almost all streets, the evidence does not necessarily suggest a completely new profile. Arlington Street, for example, rose to 591 (74%), yet its composition reflected the earlier period of cab proprietors and stable keepers, with additional clerks, dressmakers, tailors, and those in the book and printing trades. Claremont Mews, close to Pentonville Road, had been an enclave entirely given over to cabmen and coachmakers in 1841. It remained so in 1861, although again the presence of boarders attests perhaps the need to supplement incomes by this time. Northampton Square had doubled in the period to five hundred (110%). The Wesleyan minister, the watchmakers, the teachers, the jewelers, and the goldsmiths had remained, but there were now cooks, fur merchants, milliners, warehousemen, shoe manufacturers, gas fitters, a lodging house keeper, laborers, and outfitter's assistants as well. This suggests that the potential audience base of 1851 in Clerkenwell and Islington, the "steady traders"[56] in jewelry, watches, gold and silver, shoes and clothing, continued to exert a considerable presence in 1861 – indeed many retired skilled artisans still continued to live in the area – but they were being swamped by young families, lodgers, and people with uncertain work habits, like commercial travelers. Already there were speculators who were buying houses and providing inadequate lodging for families: a William Vaughan, for example, who owned eight houses in Adelaide Square, let out rooms at 2s 6d per week. He was fined 20s for allowing families of more than four to inhabit one room.[57]

The increases in population certainly suggested changes in work habits that might impinge on leisure as well. Skilled artisans, teachers, doctors, and lawyers may well have maintained regular work patterns. Similarly shops closed regularly at 8:30 P.M. during the week, with a closing time of 10:30 P.M. on Fridays, and some stayed open until midnight on Saturdays. Shopkeepers and their assistants, if they attended Sadler's Wells at all, would have patronized it at half-price in the early part of the week. Phelps, however, made few concessions to half-price entrants: his program began at 7 P.M. with the major revival of the evening, followed by the afterpiece. Thus shop assistants would only have seen the last part of the opening play at 9 P.M. The only time that the program was adjusted to meet the exigencies of their work schedule occurred during the pantomime season when the pantomime followed an opening piece. Phelps's managerial policy to begin the evening with the main play obviously was aimed at those who would be able to attend at full-price. Nevertheless, Sadler's Wells as we have seen, had a large gallery capable of returning £25 when full and a pit with a capacity to return £55. The increases in the numbers of shops and shop assistants in the area by 1861 would have meant that a larger proportion of local residents were being potentially excluded from arriving at the theatre before half-price. The presence of waiters, laborers, journeymen, and commercial travelers meant that there were considerable numbers of those with irregular work practices affected by seasonal fluctuations and even by weather conditions. This would have again militated against regular playgoing habits, even if we imagine that the inhabitants of crowded lodging houses had a taste for performances of *Hamlet, King Lear*, or Sheridan Knowles's *The Hunchback*.

By 1861 transport facilities appeared to have improved: in 1857 the *Islington Gazette* found the notion of remoteness a difficult one to sustain:

Our distance from the Court end of the town is so greatly exaggerated, that it might be as well to give some real notion of it . . . that Islington-green is *within* an eighteen-penny fare of Her Majesty's Theatre in the Haymarket.[58]

In 1860 the *Sunday Times* was urging people to see Phelps's revival of *The Tempest*:

Sadler's Wells is a far way off to the resident of a central or westend locality, but the cab and omnibus now penetrate every metropolitan artery, and we, therefore, would strongly advise the lovers of the legitimate drama to pay a visit to it, and see *The Tempest* admirably produced.[59]

While in 1861 the *Islington Gazette* was noting that:

Our advertising columns of this day contain the prospectus of a new Omnibus Company, which promises so much that is necessarily interesting to Islingtonians. . . . It has been for a long time somewhat difficult, and at all times a too expensive affair, to travel per omnibus from some parts of the parish. The latter of these disagreeables will be removed by the new company; and, doubtless, if entire success should follow their efforts, the removal of the former will soon follow.[60]

The remarks are cumulatively revealing. The area was still regarded as a remote one, requiring a cab fare from central London that exceeded the cost of a full-price pit seat at Sadler's Wells. Plentiful omnibus routes existed, but they followed the arterial roads like St. John's Road, which still left theatre patrons with a walk of 250 yards from the Angel and remained expensive. Cheap fares were needed, but such fares would tend to facilitate the movement of workers in and out of the area, especially the clerks who worked in the City.[61] It still remained problematic whether they would succeed in attracting visitors to the area at night.

These population and transport factors suggest, therefore, that in 1861 Sadler's Wells was less isolated, but still inaccessible to those outside the area by reason of expense, except for those audience members who could afford the price of a cab. Omnibus transport after setting down, involved a walk along streets whose condition was variable, to a theatre whose situation required directions. The relatively stable audience base of local residents, to which Phelps had largely catered and whose composition was noted by journalistic visitors, was being destabilized by newcomers whose work practices were irregular and who therefore might be attracted to the informality of the new music halls, with their more flexible programs and their tolerance of smoking and drinking. Phelps's decision to ban the sale of liquor at Sadler's Wells was probably a deliberate attempt to exclude such an audience and to retain the sense of respectability in which he took considerable pride. Such factors help to explain some of the contradictions that Phelps felt about the exact composition and provenance of his audiences, to which we have referred earlier. If the theatre was to succeed after Phelps's departure, it would require a managerial policy that took account of the changing local population, and continued to attract its traditional patrons, yet utilized new strategies to combat the attractions of other local competitors. At the same time, the theatre's reputation as a venue for legitimate drama needed to be preserved to attract visitors who mourned the end of the Kean management at the Princess's in 1859 and the departure of Phelps in 1862. It proved to be an impossible task. Yet the failure of managements that succeeded Phelps led to a new mythopoeia. The extraordinary nostalgia with which critics remembered the Phelps management provoked the invention of a golden age that had somehow been lost and that was followed by a new iron age of commodification. Even the managers who followed Phelps subscribed to a belief that they could preserve this golden age merely by replicating Phelps's repertoire and, more significantly, that they had inherited the audiences that he had succeeded in "reforming."

The post-Phelps era started unhappily. Catherine Lucette, who became the sole lessee for the new 1862–3 season, retained members of Phelps's company, invited William Creswick to play Hamlet, and actively tried to woo new audiences.[62] By the beginning of the following season, however, the lease had been bought by Robert Edgar and his wife Alice Marriott, who consciously tried to emulate Phelps's artistic policy. She brought back Henry Marston and his wife together with Edmund Phelps and opened with *The Hunchback*, and *Othello*, played Mrs. Haller in *The Stranger*, and revived *The Corsican Brothers* and Lytton's *Richelieu*, in which Marston played the Phelps roles. Perhaps rather prematurely, she headed her playbills with "the unprecedented success of the legitimate drama to its acknowledged home" [*sic*].[63] Yet when the burlesque of *The Bohemian Girl* appeared in July 1864, the *London Review*, though admitting that the performance was "quite equal to the average extravaganza produced in the West-end theatres," added rather ominously:

Why such a production should have been transported in the dog-days to a dying theatre like Sadler's Wells, which has been beaten in the theatrical race, since the withdrawal of Mr. Phelps, by the superior energy shown by the proprietor of the Grecian and other managers of local theatres, is more than we can tell.[64]

More critical by this stage, however, was the state of the theatre itself. Nothing had been done since Phelps had left. The auditorium was deteriorating and W. H. C. Nation, who subleased the theatre for the summer season in 1866, promised that the theatre would be "thoroughly cleansed and re-decorated. New orchestra stalls, dress circle seats and pit seats to be recovered and new entrance for the stalls. The stalls would have spring-stuffed seats and backs and equal to those of the best West End theatres."[65] Reviewers pointed to the attractiveness of Nation's transformation of Sadler's Wells and piously offered the hope that his repertoire, which included productions of Jerrold's *Time Works Wonders* and Boucicault's *Dot*, would bring back an appreciative audience. For a while, this seemed to bear fruit:

> In Mr. Nation's hands the character of the performances and the "quality" of the audiences have both greatly improved . . . filling the stalls and boxes with a class of persons who were rarely seen under the old *regime*. . . . The 4s stalls at Sadler's Wells are now filled with the fashionables of Islington, whose gloves and opera-cloaks are really unexceptionable.[66]

Robert Edgar renewed his lease of the theatre in 1867 for twenty-one years and the 1867–8 season began with a performance of *Azaël*, which had been seen at Drury Lane seventeen years earlier, with Marriott this time playing the title role. Phelps and Creswick were persuaded to return and contribute towards a benefit for those who had suffered in a Fenian bomb explosion at the House of Correction in 1867. Though the performance included *The Man of the World* and *The Jealous Wife*, plays which had not been performed since Phelps's management, the occasion was not a success. No doubt many of those who remembered Phelps's performance were no longer there and the program was an austere and old-fashioned one, hardly calculated to win over a new audience. A new season opened on 13 March 1869 under the management of W. Stanley with a mixture of professional and amateur actors from the Kemble Club, performing *Macbeth*, Lytton's *Lady of Lyons*, Tobin's *The Honeymoon*, and Planché's *Charles XII*. Lacking any sense of direction, the audiences Stanley attracted had little respect for his repertoire or his actors. The *Theatrical Journal* reported:

> The efforts of [the Kemble Club] . . . in the tragedy of Macbeth were not as happy as in other and less difficult pieces that we have seen them in, nor did they have the fair hearing to which all honest and painstaking amateurs are entitled, for a more truly, we may say, blackguardly assemblage of roughs never infested the gallery of a theatre, even in the worst days of transpontine lawlessness. Making every allowance for overflowing animal spirits, and an occasional flash of mythological wit uttered under beery influences on Saturday night, such coarse, dirty remarks fell from the lips of one of the

ringleaders of the noisy gang perched aloft should never be allowed in the walls of a playhouse. . . . We hope Mr. Stanley will station a policeman in the gallery.[67]

Edgar returned from America to open the new 1869–70 season. His company included Edmund Phelps and as a consequence he was able to induce Phelps to return for a series of six performance commencing 27 September. In the event, Phelps could only perform twice, a sore throat preventing him from playing Bertuccio although he did play Othello. It would have struck him as ironic that Sadler's Wells was once again announcing that a bar would be placed on the landing outside the boxes to serve "refreshment of the best quality at public house prices." Alice Marriott returned in early January and "made her reappearance in the house where she has for a long period as manageress and actress . . . [and] . . . maintained worthily the highest position in the favour of the patrons of the theatre."[68] Yet again her season comprised revivals of *The Hunchback*, *The Lady of Lyons*, and Milman's *Fazio*. She also was supported by a second-rate company. Significantly, Edgar sublet the theatre to Edward Weston for the summer season. Weston had a music hall background: he had started Weston's Music Hall in Holborn and was associated with the Bedford in Camden Town. In the five days between the closing of the winter season and his reopening on Easter Monday 1870, Weston needed to refurbish the theatre. As a consequence, it had:

> undergone a transformation as complete as desirable, and from a dirty, dingy little hole had been changed into a light and elegant summer Theatre. The whole place has been thoroughly cleansed – an operation which it much needed. The walls have been redecorated, the chairs and stalls recovered, the boxes hung with new and light curtains and drapery, and the saloons, as well as the flooring of the dress circle and stalls recarpeted.[69]

By July matters had become worse: the *Era* reported tersely that Sadler's Wells "opened for the season last Saturday but since that evening it has been closed. The *ungrateful* public presented under £4 to the treasury."[70]

The 1870–1 season opened under the management of Pennington who had supported Alice Marriott during the previous season. He was determined to present a repertoire that emulated that of Phelps: *Vir-*

ginius, *Lady of Lyons*, *Richard III*, *King Lear*, *Hamlet*, and *Othello*. Initially the response was heartening:

> This old and favourite theatre – still holding a name for the legitimate drama – was opened on Saturday last. . . . The first night of the season under the management of Mr. Pennington, commenced auspiciously, there being a crowded and fashionable audience present such as is seldom seen so early in the season.[71]

Audiences similar to those who had seen Phelps's seasons may well have attended:

> *Virginius*, as produced at Sadler's Wells, is an intellectual treat, and patronised by a numerous and attentive audience betokens a return in the taste of the public to that more healthy class of entertainment which we so fondly believe was the delight of a bygone age.[72]

The *Theatrical Journal*, for example, was delighted to record a return of respectability and respect for the text at a performance of *King Lear*.[73]

After Edgar died in 1871,[74] the lease was taken up by Frederick Belton, an experienced actor who had worked at Drury Lane under E. T. Smith's management and had a considerable provincial reputation, but no managerial background. He did away with all fees and gratuities to theatre staff and it seemed possible that he might be able to attract those "residing in the various squares of this locality near to the theatre."[75] Playbills now notified patrons that tickets for the theatre could be bought in advance at all the railway stations in London and the suburbs, which suggested that Belton wanted to attract an audience from further afield than the local squares. In fact even local benefits, so much part of Phelps's "local" policy, were failing to stimulate much interest.[76] By September 1872 the theatre had a new manager, Delatorre, who was operating the Victoria as well. He dropped prices: the gallery, 4d; pit, 6d; pit stalls, 1s; boxes, 1s 6d; and reserved circle 2s 6d. A private entrance, open on Saturdays and Mondays at 5:30 P.M., allowed patrons to enter for a gallery price of 7d with an extra 6d to all other parts of the house.[77] There was little that he could do to compete with the success of Deacon's Music Hall where: "The excellent management evinced in the retention of a good company and in superior arrangements for the comfort of visitors, brings the desired effect, large and well-satisfied audiences bearing ample testimony to the fact."[78] By

1874 the theatre was to be wound up as a business and converted into public baths. The condition of the theatre had now badly deteriorated:

> Both within and without it certainly has a most dejected aspect. The New River, once overhung with trees and grassy banks, has been vaulted in. Bricks and mortar have all around taken the place of "flowery meads," and the stained walls and broken windows of the building itself gives a ruinous and dilapidated appearance to it. The ruin, however, is only "skin deep"; in the main the building is still sound, and whether as baths and washhouses or as theatre, will stand yet for many a long day.[79]

On 31 August 1875 the unexpired lease was sold at public auction for £1,020, although the theatre would remain effectively dark until Mrs. S. F. Bateman bought it in August 1878 and opened it as the New Sadler's Wells on 9 October 1879. She had just left the Lyceum, which Henry Irving took over, so this was a venture intended to provide a new venue for her two daughters, Kate and Isabel, who had previously achieved some success at the West End theatres. In a letter that she wrote to Irving shortly after acquiring the lease, Mrs. Bateman stated that she intended to run Sadler's Wells "as a country theatre – low prices, pantomime stars or star companies and perhaps a drama production every year." She anticipated that "no special gifts are required for the conduct of such a place" and described the Sadler's Wells neighborhood as "much improved – [and] is without a place of amusement and the facilities for getting to Sadler's Wells by trams and omnibuses have greatly increased."[80] The refurbishment was an expensive one. She completely rebuilt the theatre, installed a covered carriage-way facing St. John's Terrace and a colonnade in Arlington Street, both of which were to enable patrons easy access to stalls, family circle, and private boxes; two separate entrances to the gallery to allow access to both front and back rows independently. C. J. Phipps's architectural improvements including a raked pit were also much praised. Patrons of the stalls and boxes would enter a vestibule with a flooring of Morris-inspired pomegranate patterns, with wall hangings, pictures and statuary. Although prices to the gallery returned to their earlier 6d, Mrs. Bateman was now charging 7s 6d for orchestra stalls. Her programs, for which she charged 1d, carefully identified the various transport options and provided a map which showed the train stations and the distance

from the Angel. Although there were by now plentiful numbers of omnibuses, as well as trains, which could take people to London Bridge,
Paddington, Oxford Street, and Brompton until midnight, the notice
points out the distance to King's Cross Station was half a mile and the
Angel, 250 yards. The only public transport that would drop patrons at
the door of the theatre were carriages and cabs — her playbills indicate
that carriages could be ordered for 11 P.M.

Mrs. Bateman began her season with a revival of *Rob Roy*, presumably to show off the stage's new machinery and to create a sense of
celebratory occasion.[81] Notices pointed to the scenery, to the fact that
two hundred supernumeraries had been employed as highlanders, pi-
pers, dancers, drovers, and soldiers, while the music would be sung by
accomplished vocalists, assisted by a chorus of thirty trained singers
and a large orchestra.[82] *The Entr'acte* praised the new theatre:

> For many years Sadler's Wells was in a disreputable condition . . .
> and had been an arena for the occasional rendez-vous of prize fight-
> ers; but now it is a handsome, roomy, tastily-decorated [sic], and
> altogether well-appointed theatre.

But it wondered whether the expenditure of money should perhaps
have gone on a theatre in "a more favourable situation." More point-
edly, it found the play old-fashioned and certainly insufficient to take
up a whole evening, especially if there was no starring male actor to
play the lead:

> persons who ordinarily sit in stalls and dress-circle will not go a
> couple of miles out of the ordinary theatre-market to see "Rob
> Roy," unless there are a star actor or two in the cast.[83]

Equally, when she revived *Macbeth* and the plays of Tom Taylor —
Lady Clancarty with Isabel Bateman and *Mary Warner* with Kate Bateman — there would have been little to attract playgoers from outside
the area, particularly those who might see Sadler's Wells as offering an
alternative to West End theatregoing. Kate Bateman, after all, had been
seen as Lady Macbeth opposite Irving at the Lyceum and as Mary Warner at the Haymarket and Olympic theatres. Those performances had
been received respectfully rather than enthusiastically. Moreover, her
performances at Sadler's Wells were supported by an inadequate company which evoked unfortunate comparisons with that under Phelps.[84]

More pertinently, Shakespeare was not drawing in those patrons whose presence would justify the refurbishment. *The Entr'acte* remarked:

> we are disposed to believe that this kind of performance is not the one calculated to make a commercial success of Sadler's Wells. What this *locale* demands are stirring dramas and cheap prices. The *raison d'être* of seven-and-sixpenny stalls at Clerkenwell is not clearly defined. And when stalls are empty night after night, they do not favourably advertise the theatre.[85]

It was an astute observation, which drew attention to the inadequacies of the Bateman management. Mrs. Bateman had little idea about the neighborhood, either the composition of its inhabitants or the fact that Sadler's Wells had a number of competitors in easy traveling distance from each other. She had sought to establish a theatre that would draw patrons from outside the area, patrons willing to pay the prices she was asking. She had reduced the gallery capacity to eight hundred and had abandoned half-price, while commencing the performances at 7:30 P.M. Yet the plays she was producing had all been seen within the previous ten years at West End establishments in which Kate Bateman had performed. Moreover, the improvements in transport now enabled local residents easy access to the West End:

> Theatre lovers who follow the fortunes of the current management of Sadler's Wells Theatre will be agreed that Mrs. Bateman is worthily proceeding in the footsteps of the late Mr. Phelps, and is thoroughly deserving of public recognition and support. Since the theatre has been under her care she has produced the sort of pieces well suited to the taste of such an active and intelligent audience as the skilled handicraftsmen of Clerkenwell and the genuine middle class of Islington compose. These good folk go to the play partly for amusement, and also, as they modestly put it, to improve their minds. Unlike some West End audiences, they have not taken pleasure to satiety. They do not run after sensations and stars, nor are they clamorous of too much and too fine elaboration of detail in the works presented to them. Mrs. Bateman conducts Sadler's Wells on the principle of a first-class provincial theatre.[86]

Apart from its patronizing tone, the newspaper evaluation contributes to the creation of a new kind of mythology, that which posited an audience frozen in a moment of history. The very fact that two contemporary observers could suggest, as seen above, completely conflicting assessments of potential Sadler's Wells audiences implies a considerable degree of uncertainty about the nature of the local population. It is quite likely that neither writer was resident in the area. Had they been resident they would have been aware that the Clerkenwell/Islington area was in a state of transition.

By the end of the period the districts of Clerkenwell and Islington showed the conflicts and contradictions that had been present in an inchoate form in 1861. Charles Booth described the area between Goswell Street and St. John's Road, for example, as housing a range of people "from the comfortable artisan class to the lowest grades of labor";[87] the block between St. John's Road and Amwell Street which included Sadler's Wells contained "many decent shopkeepers and artisans and some well-to-do people. Houses are bad in one spot, very crowded with casual laborers and mechanics in a state of wretched poverty."[88] To the west of Amwell Street, which still formed part of the theatre's catchment area, the classification describes it as an area where the "great majority . . . vary from the well-to-do class employing servants to a comfortable and respectable class of skilled mechanics, clerks and professional men. There are some cases of poverty, but no extreme want is felt."[89] The closer to the City and Clerkenwell Green, the greater the proportion of lower-income earners. Thus the area to the west of St. John's Road including Northampton Square and Myddelton Street had "some decent streets filled with comfortable tradesmen, artisans, warehousemen, etc.," but there was also a "good deal of struggling poverty and migratory habits, partly caused by drink."[90] Similarly, the district immediately north of the theatre near the Angel contained "generally a respectable and comfortable working class of ordinary character, with a mixture of laborers, porters, costers, and others in poorly paid work."[91] The area surrounding Goswell Street, which stretched from Clerkenwell Road to the south and Pentonville Road to the north, had one of the highest percentages of poverty in London.[92] Moreover, in terms of the Clerkenwell area as a whole, Booth's analysis quantifies its continued association with the watch and metal industries among men and with women working from home in areas like dressmaking, and matchbox, envelope, and tie making. He also points out that there were many women who also came into the area daily to work in shops and factories.[93]

{ *Nineteenth-Century Audiences* }

Perhaps just as revealing is the article that appeared in the *Daily Telegraph* (17 October 1881), entitled "The 'Roughs' of Islington." It gives an account of a Sunday evening in Upper Street, Islington, the main shopping street that started at the Angel, and identifies the presence of numbers of what it calls "roughs" who harass people coming out of church services by deliberate obstruction. Their activities, the article states, have been a constant source of disturbance for at least twelve years, assisted by the "peculiarly dim" gas street lighting which impeded intervention by police. The roughs are joined by:

> scores of girls of tender age, ranging, seemingly, from twelve to sixteen years.... Judging from their attire, they appear to be the daughters of industrious people of the mechanic class, whose position in life enables them to dress their children in a respectable manner. From the circumstances of these young girls banding together in parties of three or four, or perhaps as many as half a dozen, it may be presumed that the companionship is not promiscuous, and that however distant the localities where they severally live, these Sunday evening excursions are prearranged, and with an understood purpose.

What this reinforces is a collision between generations and between the claims of respectability and sobriety identified with Sunday church-going and youthful rebelliousness. Perhaps these were the "degraded sports" to whom Towse referred in his description of the population surrounding Sadler's Wells. It is hard to imagine that a theatre presenting *Othello* or *Mary Warner* would have had much to offer such inhabitants.

Mrs. Bateman died in January 1881, in the middle of a severe winter in which snow blocked access to theatres and forced many to close.[94] She had been, as the *Daily Telegraph* sympathetically commented, a "prophet crying aloud in the wilderness"[95] but a misguided one who had made little or no attempt to evaluate her audience. Not only had she miscalculated the composition of the local neighborhood, but she had tried to turn back the tide:

> since the days of Greenwood and Phelps a complete revolution has taken place in things theatrical; the generation of play-goers that had hung delightedly on the lips of *their* oracle had passed away, tastes had changed, audiences had persistently turned their faces westwards — and failure was the result.[96]

The fluctuations in the fortunes of Sadler's Wells implies the ongoing connection between the changing role of a specific theatre and the changing nature of a specific locality. The theatre had started as a place of entertainment for summer visitors coming from outside the area, expecting informality as well as novelty and a tolerance of "uncivilized" behavior in a rural retreat. The realization that businessmen and their families were moving into the area of Islington from the beginning of the nineteenth century to complement a population that largely depended upon the movement of livestock and the servicing of a transport industry, changed the role of the theatre, so that a year-long season could respond to the entertainment requirements of a resident community. By the early 1840s, this resident community was a mixed one, including professional men and women, who practiced as doctors, teachers, clergymen, and lawyers; annuitants of independent means; shopkeepers; skilled artisans in gold and silver; a growing body of clerks who worked in the City; medical students; and families. Phelps intervened at a time when this community was seeking the means to express and see expressed its own identity and cultural values. It would have accepted J. L. Towse's belief that the theatre was indeed "an agent of the higher civilization . . . the one human institution . . . whose peculiar privilege it is to illustrate and enforce the soundest principles of art, morality, and social law, under the seductive guise of entertainment."[97] The community's satisfaction with Phelps's stable policy was compounded with a self-satisfaction, particularly as visitors expressed their surprise and delight at the resurgence of a taste for literary drama and were to be found "in the first row of boxes:"

> faces and dresses that do not hail from Islington . . . who have spread the theatre's reputation throughout England or who, attracted by that reputation, have not allowed questionable company to discourage them from seeking the unquestionable pleasure the place affords.[98]

The period after Phelps, however, saw a succession of managers who all too readily subscribed to the belief that once the audience's taste had been reclaimed, it would not change. They saw little reason to question the veracity of this belief or to evaluate the significance, for repertoire or managerial policies, of the changing work practices and living habits of an increasingly destabilized population.

5. The Queen's/Prince of Wales's Theatre

he Queen's Theatre was the only neighborhood theatre within the borough of St. Pancras, which stretched from Hampstead to Camden and Regent's Park and into the vicinity of Tottenham Court Road and areas north of Oxford Street. To the west was the Marylebone Theatre and to the east was Sadler's Wells, both too far away to be within easy walking distance. Originally built in 1785 as a concert room, it was subsequently known as the New, the Regency, the Theatre of Variety, and the West London, finally becoming the Queen's in 1831. That it was attracting a local audience in the early 1820s is implicit in a clipping, which states:

> All the minor theatres are brushing up for the holidays. The East London Theatre astonished the Minories and Wapping. The Regency Theatre . . . turns itself into the West London Theatre to delight the inhabitants of Clipstone and Howland Streets.[1]

Under Thomas Dibdin in 1829 the theatre sought a more fashionable audience,[2] while throughout the 1830s its fortunes varied. In 1830 the *Theatrical Observer* (19 April 1830) commented:

> This pleasing little place of amusement is proving a favourite speculation as its crowded audiences nightly testify; indeed, the present company has imparted a respectability to the concern it has not possessed for years (of course excepting the French seasons).

However, the lessees, Thomas Melrose, John Kemble Chapman, and Alexander Lee, became the victims of their own success, when Charles Kemble, manager of Covent Garden Theatre, attempted to have the theatre closed on the legal grounds that it was in breach of its license as a minor theatre. According to one account, the theatre had been in a deplorable state when the three took it over, but, although they had improved on the standard of entertainment there, a legal loophole prevented them renewing their contract. The landlord, a Mr. Perry of Charlotte Street, had forced their resignation and let the theatre "to a junta determined on behalf of the major theatres to restrain the minors to dancing and singing." [3] In fact the patent theatres had lost their case and in late December the theatre, now under George Macfarren, who had aspirations to turn it into an English Opera house, announced its reopening in January 1831 in terms that implied its intended clientele should be both a respectable and a local one. The announcement was addressed to "the NOBILITY and GENTRY, the HEADS of FAMILIES, and the PUBLIC generally" and claimed for the theatre "a degree of respectability and good taste, unsurpassed by any rival establishment." The interior was to be remodeled, but "with a view to increased comfort and convenience rather than enlarged accommodation." As further reassurance to the more respectable members of the community it was announced that "a new gallery door will be opened in Pitt Street [the road at the back of the theatre] by which means the hitherto unavoidable inconvenience and mixture of company will be prevented." The construction of twelve new family boxes was emphasized as was the theatre's desire to appeal to "the inhabitants of the vicinity – and families in particular." [4] Prices were 4s for boxes, 2s for pit, and 1s for gallery; the repertoire consisted of operas, concerts, and melodramas. Macfarren's management lasted for seventeen months; he was followed by a succession of managements, including that of Louisa Nisbett. Yet whatever its aspirations and despite visits by such celebrated performers as Madame Vestris and William Dowton, an announcement on 29 July 1833 implied that the Queen's was attracting a minor theatre type of audience. Prices were reduced to boxes, 1s 6d; pit 1s; and gallery 6d; the playbill affirmed that, "in consequence of the general depression of the times, and in order to afford the inhabitants of the West End of the town an opportunity of witnessing Theatrical Representations, upon the same scale of *economy* as other Minor Theatres," it would adopt the same sort of reductions as those of the Surrey, Pavilion, Garrick, and Sadler's Wells. [5] The repertoire also implies a local interest in titles such as *The Tobacconist of Tottenham Court Road* (September 1833).

In 1838 the sale of the Queen's Theatre was advertised: described as "a theatrical property of considerable importance to any speculator as it is free from any charge, incumbrance or ground rent," it offered the opportunity of "considerable profit." The full description of the lot announced that:

> This elegant and pleasing little Theatre under judicious and skilful management might unquestionably be rendered exceedingly attractive and profitable. A talented manager, with an efficient Corps Dramatique, would invariably meet with liberal encouragement, a fact which elsewhere has been abundantly proved. The Theatre has long been known to the Public and the situation is decidedly superior to many that could be named. It comprises a considerable plot of ground – and although its space for some departments of the drama is somewhat confined, yet for all the purposes connected with the Representation of Vaudevilles and performances of that character, for which this theatre is eminently calculated, ample accommodation has been found. The Building is substantial with considerable frontage to Tottenham Street, Portico and Entrance saloon, leading to the 2 Circles of Boxes containing about 1000 persons, Eleven commodious Private Boxes, a capacious and comfortable Pit containing sitting-room for nearly 500 Persons.

The announcement also praised the arrangement of the stage and its accommodation for an orchestra, its suitability for minor pieces, and the theatre's snugness. Moreover, other advantages included:

> Its skilful internal arrangement, which commands a perfect view of the stage from every part [and] its convenient size, ensuring those two desiderata "HEARING and SEEING."

Two small houses in Pitt Street were connected to the theatre, furnishing extra dressing-rooms and a greenroom.[6]

Even after the sale, the fortunes of the theatre still varied. In February 1839 the Olympic Theatre Company appeared briefly. Prices were boxes, 4s; pit, 2s; and gallery, 1s, which implies that a relatively fashionable audience was expected. By April 1839 George Wild had become manager, reduced the pit and gallery prices to 1s and 6d respectively and instituted a repertoire largely of melodrama and burlesque. Then in September 1839, Charles James James, a theatrical scene painter, became manager and was to remain as lessee and later joint-lessee for thirty-six years. He had, says, E. L. Blanchard, already "established in England and America a reputation not only for artistic ability, but also for strict probity."[7] The commencement of James's management was hailed by the *Theatrical Journal* (4 January 1840):

> If Mr James does not make a fortune, we shall be surprised, every novelty offered by this theatre, appears to be highly approved of by its numerous patronising frequenters. Surely, Mr James has hit the taste of this neighborhood to a nicety. The success of this little theatre is only another proof of what we have always asserted, let the management be good, and success is certain.

Its only subsequent concern was that the quality of acting did not match that of the scenic department. At the commencement of James's second season, the *Theatrical Journal* (3 October 1840) commended it as "the neatest and one of the most respectable of the minor establishments in London." James appears to have been scrupulous in regard to his audience, even informing those buying tickets for a crowded house that the standing room in the pit was poor, before taking their money.[8] As a scenic artist James was able to oversee a high quality of visual presentation in his theatre: "the scenery alone is worth a visit," wrote the *Theatrical Journal* (20 November 1841), and his diorama for that year's pantomime was compared with the work of Clarkson Stanfield.[9] As a manager he also replaced any piece that was unsuccessful almost immediately. On April 13, 1844, the *Theatrical Journal* noted:

> Mr James, the proprietor of the Queen's stage, is one of the safest whips on the road, and a journey down Tottenham Court Road, will repay the seeker after amusement. The Queen's stage has never yet been upset under this gentleman's guidance. He is civil, obliging, and very enterprising, offering to the visitors who may occupy the box seats, comfort and respectability, and to those on the roof, a ceaseless variety of amusement during the journey, which generally begins about seven, and ends towards midnight. The fares are exceedingly low, there being so much competition of late with other stages of heavier weight, and rail-roads who wait for no one.

Melodrama followed melodrama, perhaps because the local audience was relatively small.[10] Although there were occasional long runs (such as *Old London Bridge* for eight weeks in 1849), the majority of plays lasted only for a week or a fortnight. James's "style of management cannot be said to have been of a very ambitious character, but want of variety could never have been a complaint with his patrons, and each piece was represented with as much completeness as his resources would allow," wrote the *Era* (16 April 1848). Nautical, domestic and gothic melodramas predominated, among which were *Susan Hopley*, *Jack Sheppard*, and *Oliver Twist*, although Shakespeare and the legitimate drama were occasionally performed.[11]

The Queen's seemed generally to be aiming at a clientele similar to that of the Britannia, City of London, and the Victoria, if its repertoire was anything to go by. A police report of 1843 describes its audiences as "persons in the neighborhood, of an inferior class to the persons in the City of London."[12] Its longest running production was the annual pantomime, usually with scenery by James. Some of the melodramas and pantomimes included scenes set in familiar locations, presumably predicated on arousing the interest of a local audience. Thus, in the 1850s, *The London Mechanic* included scenes set in a mansion in Fitzroy Square and in a pawnbroker's shop in Tottenham Court Road, while *Cinderella* included a cab stand and Tottenham Court Road as settings. The 1841 pantomime had one scene in a shop in Tottenham Street[13] and *Polly Put the Kettle On* (1843) included scenes located at the Chinese Pagoda in Hyde Park, at the Emporium in Regent's Street, and in Ould's Oil Establishment, Tottenham Court Road. *Seven Dials or The Beggars of London*, based in an area only ten to fifteen minutes walk south of the theatre, was advertised as "introducing the various localities connected with it and its immediate vicinity, spots so familiar that cannot fail to be recognized by any at all acquainted with its neighborhood."[14] *The Lawless of London*, *The Great Metropolis*, and *Daughters of Midnight or The Mysteries of London* were among other plays that exploited the London setting.

In the 1860s fewer original melodramas were presented at the Queen's Theatre. Plays by Hazlewood that had originated at the Victoria or Britannia (*The Detective*, *Waiting for the Verdict*, *Aurora Floyd*, *Lady Audley's Secret*, *The Workgirls of London*) were performed, and sometimes the playbill stated that permission had been granted by the Britannia to stage certain dramas such as *Jessie Vere* and *The Dark House*. The plays of other dramatists associated with the Britannia such as Frederick Marchant and William Travers were also performed. Such a policy implies either a declining or changing audience or a reluctance, on James's part, to commission original plays. John Hollingshead, writing in the *Sketch* (29 June 1898), suggests that the small size of the theatre made it impossible to compete with the Whitechapel Pavilion and Victoria Theatres in the staging of melodrama and that "it welcomed a new management and a new policy." Although it is unlikely that the three theatres were in competition for the same audiences, the uncompetitive size of the theatre, as melodrama became more and more sensational, may well have been a factor in determining James's acceptance of an approach by Marie Wilton, when she was looking for a theatre of her own. On 18 February 1865 playbills announced the last four weeks of the present season and the present scale of prices. A month later, on 18 March, the season closed with *The Corsican Brothers* (with limelight effect) and *The Detective*.

The Queen's policy of presenting popular melodrama did not altogether satisfy W. B. Donne, the Examiner of Plays at the Lord Chamberlain's Office, to whom new plays were submitted for licensing. He objected to licensing *The Blood Spot or The Maiden, The Miser and The Murderer* in 1858 on the grounds that it belonged to "a class of Drama now nearly extinct on the stage . . . in which highway robbery, burglary and larceny form the staple interest." In Donne's view these sorts of dramas, which had been almost eradicated from the stage, were "extremely prejudicial to the younger portions of the pit and gallery." [15] A few months later the Queen's again aroused Donne's ire during his annual inspection of the London theatres, because it "was scandalously dirty and very defectively ventilated. I find that it goes in the immediate neighborhood by the name of the dust-hole," wrote Donne and made it clear that the manager should be informed of the problem when he received his license. [16] By 1860, C. J. James had certainly taken to heart Donne's concerns, for Donne's annual report states:

> In 1858 a very unfavourable report was made of the condition of this theatre as regards security, accommodation and cleanliness — In 1859 very considerable improvements in all these respects were recorded. In 1860 — not a single note is required, and the Queen's Theatre is only remarkable for its good ventilation, general commodiousness and proper cleanliness. The manager has found the benefits of improvement and intends to continue to improve his theatre — He has nothing to complain of as to business. [17]

Moreover, the business is just what Donne would have hoped for (although James may have been spinning him a bit of a yarn):

Mr James [writes Donne] is now desirous of bettering the kind and character of his Dramas — He finds now that his Theatre is clean, well ventilated and well appointed, that a better class of person begins to frequent his pit and boxes.[18]

In 1861 the only remarks Donne felt necessary on the Queen's was that the improvements and the present condition of the theatre reflect the greatest credit on the lessee."[19] This is substantiated by the *Era* (17 November 1861), which commented:

This very compact and remarkably well-ordered little Theatre is pursuing "the even tenor of its way" in its quiet and unostentatious manner — just the sort of manner which, if we mistake not, denotes it being what is understood in commercial phraseology as "well-to-do in the world." Mr C. J. James . . . is a man as shrewd as he is enterprising, and knows exactly how to manage to keep up the celebrity of his establishment, to earn credit for his Management, and to increase the exchequer. Although voluminous Tragedies and five-act Comedies are not within the scope of the Theatre before us, yet Dramas and Melodramas, Farces, Operettas, Comediettas, and the like, flow in constant profusion, and well succeed in drawing very respectable houses.[20]

Nevertheless, in 1863 and 1864 the Queen's was praised again for its "excellent condition,"[21] which means that, when Marie Wilton became manager and renamed it the Prince of Wales's Theatre in 1865, the theatre already had achieved over several years some of the reforms for which Wilton claims full credit in her various memoirs. Interestingly, James, who was the longest surviving manager in London by this time, remained joint lessee for a further ten years and was regularly present front of house as the theatre's acting manager after Wilton took over, although he seems to have supported her fight to have her name included on the playbill as manager.[22] In fact, it was probably James's business knowledge rather than that of the increasingly absent H. J. Byron which kept the theatre going. James's son, Charles Stanfield James, was employed as the Prince of Wales's scene painter until his death, when he was replaced by Hawes Craven, who painted the scenery for *Play* in 1868.

The repertoire of the Prince of Wales's Theatre, which initially both exploited and attempted to liberate Marie Wilton from her reputation in burlesque, became quickly associated with the plays of Tom Robertson. *Society, Ours, Caste, Play, School,* and *The M.P.* were immaculately presented between 1865 and 1870 by the Bancrofts in settings as familiar as those in which their audiences lived, and with a surface veneer of everyday realism, which was then quite original. Even the dialogue seemed more colloquial than that of other plays, although plotting and characterization were really quite conventional. Robertson's plays were so popular that their runs could be continued from one season into the next and several of them were effectively revived for further long runs. Between 1865 and 1885 (including the Bancrofts' tenancy of the Haymarket) *School* was acted 800 times; *Ours,* 700 times; and *Caste,* 650. The weekly and fortnightly changes of repertoire at the Queen's were replaced by the long run, which in itself allowed the Bancrofts the opportunity for the meticulous staging that attracted audiences to their theatre. Maynard Savin suggests that one of the reasons for the success of Robertson's comedies at the Prince of Wales's Theatre was what today we might describe as "commodity fetishism":

> Capitalising on bourgeois value judgements and the bourgeois predilection for material objects, he was in a fair way to set a new style. With an array of domestic properties, he would provide audiences the thrill of recognition, thus satisfying the acquisitive, possessive instincts of the middle classes, which was finding expression elsewhere in cluttered interior decoration, what-nots, and ginger-bread friezes. The themes of his plays, meanwhile, would flatter the class-consciousness of the bourgeoisie by suggesting that individual worth might leap caste lines.[23]

The Bancrofts claimed that their appeal was to "the refined and educated classes," who were "as ready as ever to crowd the playhouses, provided that the entertainment given there was suited to their sympathies and tastes."[24] That these classes might, however, be undiscriminating is implicit in the *London Entracte*'s (16 July 1870) comment that Robertson's *M.P.* "continues to draw full houses, but why?"

Although the Bancrofts' success was predicated on their performances of Robertson, they also achieved it with a number of other plays, including Byron's *War to the Knife,* W. S. Gilbert's *Sweethearts,* and Bulwer Lytton's *Money.* All bore the Prince of Wales's hallmark, "realism," which Martin Meisel defines as "realism understood as truth

{ *Nineteenth-Century Audiences* }

to the everyday textures and tones of middle class life."[25] Yet this formula was less than effective when applied to the classics. According to the *London Entr'acte* (24 April 1875):

> In "The School for Scandal" — which, as a whole, was indifferently played here — Mrs Bancroft created some little interest by the wealth of accessories used. The usual properties were replaced by costly realities, and would-be aristocrats went to see so much valuable lace, to be taught how to raise a tea-cup, and to dance a minuet. Now Shakespeare is attempted to be embellished on the same principle; but, if we mistake not, the bard will have his revenge. "The Merchant of Venice" was never intended as a decorative drama, but the management of the Prince of Wales's would make it one.

In other words the detail which gave credibility to Robertson's dramas seemed superfluous when applied to Sheridan and Shakespeare. The material trappings may have appealed to the bourgeoisie, but in other ways revealed the artistic hollowness of the Bancrofts' achievement. Ellen Terry, who played Portia, recalled how some of the costumes worn in the production actually provoked laughter from some members of the audience.[26] Indeed, a decline and lack of direction, at least as far as repertoire was concerned, dates from Squire Bancroft's sole assumption of management in 1875 (although the theatre also suffered a profound loss from Robertson's premature death in 1871). Although a production of Tom Taylor's and Charles Reade's *Masks and Faces* was being prepared during the autumn of 1875, it was noted that the number of empty stalls at the theatre "show that for a time at least (it is) deserted by its old clients."[27]

Lynton Hudson, who describes how Marie Wilton acquired "the lease of a bankrupt and almost derelict theatre in the noisy and squalid district of Tottenham Court Road, then beginning to collect a shabby and shady foreign population,"[28] claims that the comedies of Robertson:

> drew into the theatre a new *clientele* from the drawing-rooms of Society, a fashionable and more fastidious public, whose cultivation was of great importance to the future of the theatre. Not least important was the readiness and ability of this new public to pay higher prices for their seats.[29]

Hudson's "foreign population" may be derived from Filon, who also wrote of the "ill-fed and ill-famed Frenchmen" who were congregating in the area at the time.[30] Although the 1871 census reveals a relatively high number of continental Europeans in St. Pancras, with 1,111 French and 1,317 German/Prussians, census returns for individual streets do not suggest that any ghettoes had formed in the neighborhood of the Queen's Theatre. Although some local streets, such as Percy Street, show 29 inhabitants of French origin in 1861 and 33 in 1871, the majority of inhabitants were still London-born.[31] On another level George Rowell considers that the Bancrofts' "feat in coaxing back polite society into an unfashionable playhouse was substantial" and argues that it was the rise of the music hall, which "began at this time to draw off the violent element in the audience," which made this possible.[32] Yet, according to Russell Jackson, quoting *The Times* (11 April 1867), the theatre may have continued to attract at least the respectable poor:

> Let it be remembered that the Prince of Wales's Theatre, though it has been fashionable for two years, is by no means in a fashionable neighborhood, and that the gallery must be peopled by many of those working men who patronized it when it was the humble Queen's. That such an assembly is pleased with an exhibition of a most undemagogic kind is a fact worth noting by those who take an interest in the real operative of London.[33]

Daniel Barrett also suggests that, although (in the Bancrofts' own words), "the house was thronged with intellectual and cultural adherents, many of whom were by no means theatregoers as a general rule":

> The old Queen's playgoers did not completely forfeit their place in the new theatre . . . with the gallery alone accounting for 240 of the possible 814 seats, almost a third of the audience must have been working class and firmly entrenched.[34]

Interestingly, Jackson expresses surprise that such audiences would have tolerated the portrayal of working-class characters like Sam Gerridge in one of the Prince of Wales's most popular plays, Tom Robertson's *Caste* (1867), whereas Barrett argues that Gerridge is a sop to the working-class members of the audience. Barrett also claims that the Bancrofts "never intended to dispense entirely with the traditional pit and gallery audiences, but considered them an integral part of their public."[35] Whatever the case, neither account offers anything more than surmise as to exactly who it was who attended the gallery at this theatre from 1865 onwards. According to the *Daily Telegraph*, reviewing *Society* on 14 November 1865:

> The lower as well as the upper sections of society will find some familiar features quickly to be recognised; and while the plebeian occupant of the gallery will readily appreciate the very intelligible humour of the comedy, the most aristocratic patrons of the stalls will decidedly approve the moral lesson it enforces.[36]

Marie Wilton asserts that there was a great crowd awaiting on the day the theatre reopened, but it was obviously not the local audience she described in her memoirs, for "The inhabitants of Tottenham Street had, doubtless, never seen such a display of carriages before."[37] The *Era* (17 April 1865) thus described the opening night audience:

> On Saturday evening . . . the theatre was filled with an audience comprising a very significant assemblage of those moving in the best circles of society – it can at once be recorded as an event already recognised by the neighborhood as marking an important period in local history. No one on Saturday night could have traversed any of the thoroughfares leading towards the street in which the Prince of Wales's Theatre is situated without observing signs of popular commotion in the vicinity. Approaching the great centre of attraction, the curious investigator into the cause would have seen a singularly dense crowd, and heard a remarkably loud chorus, in which a popular street tune and the most fervent expressions of loyal enthusiasm on the part of the juvenile inhabitants of the district were curiously allied. This vast concourse, evidently remaining under a general impression that the members of the Royal Family were distributed among the various vehicles arriving at the doors in rapid succession, lined the roadway on each side to see the carriages pass, and exhibited an interest in the unusual sight which of itself indicated how great a change had taken place in the thoroughfare. Even the humblest shopkeeper seemed to have made some little effort to bring his establishment into increased harmony with the increased dignity of a building henceforth likely to be associated with brighter prospects for the dwellers around.[38]

In effect the old audience turned out to watch the arrival of the new! Yet the question remains as to who, exactly, constituted these old and new audiences.

The Queen's/Prince of Wales's Theatre was situated close to Tottenham Court Road, north of Oxford Street and southwest of Euston Station, in an area whose population had expanded in the 1830s. Close by was the Scientific and Literary Institute (used for Chartist meetings in the 1840s, although it later became a venue for illusionists and a dancing academy). The rookeries of St. Giles, partially dispersed when Oxford Street was extended to High Holborn, were not far away, but hardly characterized the immediate vicinity of the theatre. Their proximity may have added lustre to the Bancroft myth of triumph in adversity, but we should remember that the Princess's Theatre was even closer to their original site. The audiences during James's management were arguably local, drawn in part from the tradesmen, shopkeepers, and workers who lived in the vicinity. Francis Edwards refers to James's tenancy as "the Jacobite period in the history of the house" when it was run "on East-end-cum-Transpontine lines, for the entertainment of Tottenham Court Rd and its vicinity."[39] Even in the 1830s the point was made that the Queen's "afforded the inhabitants of the West End of the town an opportunity of witnessing theatrical representations as cheaply as at the other minor theatres."[40] An examination of actors' addresses provides evidence as to the theatre's accessibility: benefit bills show actors living close to the theatre in Fitzroy Square, Grafton Street, Portland Place, Euston Square, Tottenham Court Rd., Bloomsbury, and Regent Street (all a short walk away); some lived slightly further afield in Somers Town, Camden Town, and Hampstead Rd. to the north; Long Acre to the east; and, to the south, Soho and the Strand. All of these locations were within adequate walking distance of the theatre. Among audience members, P. P. Hanley recalls visiting the Queen's as a boy when he lived in Camden Town.[41] In 1843 a petition for a theatre in the vicinity of Camden Town and Somers Town was opposed by University College, partly on the grounds that the Queen's Theatre already served that vicinity and partly because the building of another theatre nearby "would be injurious to the discipline of the college and morals of the students," since most resided locally and were free from parental controls.[42] Among streets contiguous to the proposed new theatre, Grafton Street East was described as "a respectable street . . . inhabited by respectable tradesmen and lodging house keepers, who let to young men such as clerks, and students of the university," while Tottenham Place was "a poor neighborhood consisting of the working class of persons."[43] In 1859 a police report argued against licensing the Cabinet Theatre on the grounds that "it would no doubt be frequented by the low population of Somerstown, Lower Islington" and further arguing that both the Queen's and Princess's Theatres were already within easy reach of the inhabitants.[44] The previous year another report had implied that a license was not needed as Sadler's Wells Theatre was only three-quarters of a mile to the east and the Queen's a mile to the west.[45] Indeed, J. B. Howe, who lived in Somers Town as a boy in the 1840s, states that he divided his time between Sadler's Wells, the Queen's Theatre, and the Albert Saloon in Shepherdess's Walk, and even recalled following Marian Rogers, a Queen's actress, to her front door in Grafton Street several times after the performance. By day he worked as shop boy to a fishmonger in Jermyn Street in the West End.[46] The local associations of the theatre are further implied in a newspaper report in the late 1830s that after the performances both performers and audience members could be found drinking in the Hope Tavern, also in Tottenham Street.[47] Locations for the sale of tickets for benefits also imply the theatre's catchment area: many addresses in the immediate vicinity are given on playbills, as are addresses in Soho, Bloomsbury, Marylebone, and Covent Garden, although addresses further away are also given occasionally. By and large such evidence corroborates the local appeal of the theatre, while indicating audiences may sometimes have traveled there from further afield for special occasions.[48] Interestingly, the Queen's is one of the few minor theatres that never provides information about local transport on its playbills, presumably because it was small enough to survive without recruiting spectators from outside the immediate neighborhood.

Within the Tottenham Court section of St. Pancras, in the immediate vicinity of the theatre, lived a small population of just under twenty-five thousand men and women in 1841, rising to between 27,000 and 28,000 ten years later. The majority of local male inhabitants were employed as shoemakers, carpenters, tailors, bricklayers, painters, plumbers, glaziers, shopkeepers, cabinet makers, upholsterers, and laborers; of the few women in employment, many worked as domestic servants, cooks, charwomen, milliners, seamstresses, washerwomen, manglers, and laundry keepers. In 1861 the majority of inhabitants in the St. Pancras parish as a whole continued to be employed in industrial and domestic trades; in 1871 a large proportion of the local population were still employed as mechanics or in trades involving fabrics and textiles. Tottenham Court Road was known for its garret-masters and furniture makers, although the Meaux brewery, on the corner of Oxford Street and Tottenham Court Road, also provided employment for local residents.[49] In 1851, St. Pancras provided homes for one of the largest groups of actors and actresses resident in London, more even than the Strand, which was a much more central location for performers to dwell in.[50] In effect the immediate vicinity of the Queen's Theatre appears to have been populated by the Sam Gerridges, Esthers, and Pollies of Robertson's *Caste* rather than by the more genteel Hawtreys or D'Alroys.

Yet the proximity of the University of London and its hospital, the long association of the streets around the Queen's Theatre with notable artists, and the fashionable quarters available just across Tottenham Court Road in Bloomsbury, not to mention the proximity of Regent's Park and the more fashionable streets around Portland Place, provide evidence that, within walking distance of the theatre, two communities existed side by side, even though the nonprofessional community appears larger in census enumerations, as was arguably the case with Sadler's Wells. Thus streets like Percy and Charlotte Streets had housed a number of well-known artists (often Royal Academicians), engravers, surgeons, engineers, and musicians in the 1830s and 1840s. Fitzroy Square could boast M.P.s, clergymen, aristocrats, physicians, architects, theatre managers (including Alfred Bunn and C. J. James), Pre-Raphaelite painters, and army and navy officers among its inhabitants. A few hundred yards away in Gower Street lived artists, surgeons, professors, clergymen, barristers, and writers. C. J. James also lived for a time in Euston Square, whose inhabitants also included William Rossetti and the journalist, Thornton Leigh Hunt.[51] In other words, there was an educated, professional community living close to the theatre throughout 1840 to 1880. Moreover, the audiences who attended the Prince of Wales's Theatre from 1865, and the social circles in which the Bancrofts mixed, came from exactly this professional community, albeit from a wider area than that described above. The point remains, however, that two communities were enfolded together, often separated by only a few hundred yards. If Gerridge or Polly might have lived in the immediate vicinity of the theatre, D'Alroy and Hawtree may well have been only a brisk walk away.

The addresses of those celebrities whom we know visited the theatre help to establish where individual members of the Prince of Wales's audiences came from. Some of them lived relatively nearby in Portland Place or Bloomsbury; for example Wilkie Collins lived nearby in Gloucester Place, Portman Square, William Creswick in Bloomsbury Square, George Vandenhoff in Gower Street, Sir William Fergusson in Hanover Square, and Anne B. Procter (Barry Cornwall's widow) in Weymouth Street, Portland Place. Others lived in Bayswater, Kensington, Knightsbridge, Holland Park, and Pall Mall. John Ruskin traveled from Denmark Hill in south London. Frederick (later Lord) Leighton traveled from Holland Park Road; W. Frith (who had once lived locally), from Bayswater; Walter Lacy, from Knightsbridge; Ellen Kean, from Kensington Gardens; Fanny Kemble, from Connaught Square; and the lawyer, Sergeant William Ballantine (formerly a local resident), from Pall Mall. Ballantine had formerly lived in Gower Street and had actually been born in nearby Howland Street. (Of all of these only Ruskin lived a significant distance away.) The Bancrofts themselves lived just the other side of Regent's Park in fashionable St. John's Wood, moving closer in to Cavendish Square in 1875. From St. John's Wood the Bancrofts were able to drive through Regent's Park to reach the theatre. From their new home they were within walking distance.[52] An eighteen-year-old Pinero, then resident at 69A Great Queen St., visited *School* in October 1873.[53] Thus the inhabitants of southwest and west London, of St. John's Wood and Regent's Park, of the area of London immediately south of the Park and west of Tottenham Court Road, and, of course, of Belgravia, must have been among the theatre's patrons after 1865. Indeed an early playbill for the Prince of Wales's Theatre announces that tickets can be purchased in advance in St. James Street, New Bond Street, and Regent Street.[54]

Undoubtedly some members of the audience would have walked to the theatre; many others would have relied on some form of transportation. Oxford Street, Regent Street, and Tottenham Court Road, as well as the New Road (later Euston Road) to the north, were major arterial routes not only well served by omnibus (the closest route followed Oxford and New Oxford Streets between Paddington and Cheapside),[55] but also well-suited for private carriages and cabs. That carriages could set down and pick up easily must have been important: presumably the one-way system operating when Vestris leased the theatre was again put into practice. In 1839 her advertisements had announced, "Coaches to set down and take up with their horses heads towards Tottenham Court Road."[56] Moreover, the theatre's location meant that it could attract the carriage trade without causing traffic congestion.[57] Geographically, it is surely no accident that the most fashionable theatre of the 1850s, the Princess's, located in Oxford Street itself, was closer to the Queen's than any other theatre. As early as 1843 it had attracted audiences from outside its immediate vicinity. A police report of 1843 describes this audience as "fashionable, better class of Tradespeople – Housekeepers etc. Not confined to the neighborhood."[58] Later the small Court Theatre in Chelsea (close to Brompton, Knightsbridge, and Kensington) was a venue to which the Bancrofts' protege, John Hare, would also attract fashionable audiences. Indeed Squire Bancroft suggests that the competition afforded by the Court was not a particular threat to the Prince of Wales, "both being small outlying theatres." Rather it was the adoption of similar programs, policies, and furnishings by other West End theatres, such as the Holborn, the Queen's, the Gaiety, the Vaudeville, the Globe, the Opera Comique, the Folly (subsequently Toole's), and the Avenue, that really provoked competition and led to the Bancrofts' departure to the Haymarket in 1880.

Despite Marie Wilton's disparaging claims about the state of the theatre and its audiences in 1865, many improvements had taken place previously and may even have influenced her decision to take over this particular theatre. George Grant's 1849 description of the Queen's may be an exaggeration, but it also suggests why its location may have been advantageous, despite the Bancrofts' comments:

> Placed in a most respectable neighborhood, the audience is always genteel, fashionable, and frequently very numerous.[59]

The *Era* (15 April 1865) also felt the neighborhood was propitious:

> Situated in the very center of a thickly-inhabited district, the respectability of which was acknowledged even in the very term which Theodore Hook thought he had contemptuously employed when he called it "the region of Silverforkia" – with no similar establishment in the vicinity, and with a neighborhood strongly influenced by theatrical predilections – the new undertaking will be commenced with the most encouraging prospects and under the most influential patronage.

The same account also implied that, although James had creditably preserved the respectability of the establishment, it "catered rather for the general public than those more refined audiences which it is the evident object of the new management to attract to the building." Equally, the significant part played by the nearby Princess's Theatre, only a few minutes' walk away, in reclaiming fashionable audiences for the theatre during the 1850s, must have suggested to Wilton that this might be an appropriate venue for her new venture. Whatever claims were made about Tottenham Street and its vicinity, the area was less disreputable than some parts of the traditional West End, easier of access, and probably safer. Moreover, the Princess's Theatre had accustomed audiences to visit that particular part of town. The *Era* (26 September 1865) in fact implies that the enterprise had extended the boundaries of the West End:

> Once the least known, and now admitted to be one of the most conveniently situated and tastefully appointed places of amusement in the metropolis, the Prince of Wales's Theatre would hardly be recognised as having more than the site to identify it with the old Queen's; and, filled as it was last night with an audience not less numerous than fashionable, the gay appearance of the interior must have completely re-assured aristocratic visitors, most doubtful of topographical boundaries, that they had strictly observed the rules of stringent etiquette in seeking amusement in what is now somewhat indefinitely called "the West-end."

According to E. L. Blanchard, it was the proximity of the Prince of Wales's (situated as it was in one of the most densely populated areas of London) to the aristocratic quarters of the town, that attracted Marie Wilton to this particular theatre.[60]

In fact, the changes made to the auditorium immediately prior to the 1865 opening, including more stalls replacing seats in the pit, must have enhanced the appeal of the theatre to the visitors described above. The *Era* (16 April 1898) recalls how "those blue stalls with the white antimacassars, those bright pretty curtains and tasteful carpets, were seen for the first time in a theatre." Commenting thirty-three years after the event the journal adds:

> It requires an effort of mind at the present date to realise the full meaning of this statement. We are so accustomed nowadays to have everything done in the most artistic and luxurious way at our theatres that we take all the cleanliness, cushionings and artistic sur-

roundings as a matter of course. But before 1865, and for some time after, the keynote of the English theatre was slovenliness – The seats were often shabby and dusty, and carpets were considered effeminate luxuries. It was impossible when passing from a comfortable well-furnished house to a theatre, not to feel the latter was prepared for the reception of a class of patrons indifferent to comfort, cleanliness and taste.[61]

A more extreme version of the transformation is recorded in the *Sportsman* (13 January 1879), which recalled a time when:

> Its portals were surrounded by the vendors of strong-smelling "eatables" and when its patrons were not content unless they carried with them to their seats a variety of comestibles, portions of which were for consumption, and the remainder for utilisation as missiles to be shied at the players on the stage or at the occupants of the pit. . . . These were the days when the consumption of fried fish between the acts was in perfect accord with the "etiquette" of the boxes – That theatre was lowly enough then, and it is possible that in those days there were people who prognosticated that it could never be reformed. One only has to visit it now to learn how radically all has been changed. We have a bijou little house of the drama, elegantly and ornately fitted, replete with comforts and luxuries, and patronised by as high a class and select a circle as one could wish.

Interestingly, what is "radical" and "reformed" about the theatre is its transformation from a venue for working-class audiences with a propensity for fried fish into a luxurious resort for the upper classes. Similarly *Dramatic Notes* for the same year talks of "its *elevation* [our italics] to the rank of the most fashionable and best frequented theatre in London."

Yet, this transformation did not occur overnight. Standing room was certainly still available at the new theatre, as it had been under James. Clement Scott recalls how he, Tom Hood, and other members of what he calls the "light literary division" could only obtain standing room at the back of the dress circle on the first night of *Society*.[62] A description of the theatre by a member of the audience who had attended *Society* in 1865 and sat in the pit, indicates that the social segregation of audience members was still in its infancy:

I was gravely introduced to a dingy portico, at the dingiest extremity of which is the pit door of the theatre, by a dweller in Euston-rd, who declared with a seemingly offensive vehemence, that "that was the house for acting". In those days, the pit was eighteenpence, and the bill twopence. The occupants of the pit were for the most part native and to the manner born, and a very pleasant manner it appeared after you had recovered your shape and temper after the outrages afflicted on both at the narrowest of narrow doors, a manner that was not altogether unmixed with lemonade, ale, and bottled stout, which potables were dispensed with nightly circumspection and despatched by an Eleanor Gwynne of matronly aspect, who, very properly, also vended oranges. Beyond the barrier which separated — say Euston Road from Tyburnia — I beheld wave upon wave of that useful article of domestic furniture, the British Anti-Macassar — In those days the toe of the eighteenpenny peasant came preciously near the heel of the seven-and-sixpenny courtier; yet his kibe was galled not.[63]

However, by the end of the Bancrofts' tenure fifteen years later, the gulf between playgoers had widened and the pit was no longer resorted to by local inhabitants, according to this writer. Further, the consequences of the Bancrofts' reforms are tellingly illustrated by a reviewer of *Caste*, when it toured to the Standard Theatre, where "the cold though confirmed approval of the Prince of Wales's audience was replaced by storms of impulsive applause."[64] By 1879 evening dress was usual, if not de rigueur, in the stalls, which even in 1872 had been described as sufficiently commodious that "ladies with elegant toilettes . . . will have no fear of crushing or derangement."[65]

Clement Scott alludes to the support the theatre received from the theatre critic of *The Times*, John Oxenford, and from the proprietor of the *Daily Telegraph*, J. M. Levy, through their favorable responses to the Bancroft incentive. Not only did the encouragement of the establishment press help in attracting a new audience to the Prince of Wales's Theatre, but the imprimatur of royal approval, as manifested in the occasional visits to the theatre by the Prince of Wales and other royalty, also attracted fashionable society. Dickens, Gladstone, Disraeli, and Lord Lytton were among celebrities of the day who visited the theatre. Richard Henry Dana recalls an evening at the theatre when not only the Gladstones were present, but also Lord Frederick and Lord Edward Cavendish, Lady Lyttleton, and Earl Spencer. But Daniel Barrett is probably right when he says that, although royalty and aristocracy "lent an air of sophistication and prestige to the Prince of Wales's Theatre that was especially exhilarating to well-bred, middle class spectators . . . they would never make up a large portion of the audience." Indeed, it was the professional middle class (writers, surgeons, lawyers, artists, politicians, and others) who, through the evidence of correspondence and demographics, were probably the theatre's most regular patrons.[66] *The Theatre* (1 July 1885) claimed that "a cheerful knot of intelligent and theatre loving barristers," who had become firm friends on the Northern Circuit, "had not a little to do with the early success of the Prince of Wales's audience." Many of these, as young Templars, had previously flocked to the Strand to see Marie Wilton in burlesque and continued their support when she moved to Tottenham Street. Many artists and writers visited the new theatre, including Wilkie Collins, Comyns Carr, and Val Prinsep. Furthermore, the long runs may also have been due to another factor: the appeal of the performances to "lovers of good acting." "Theatregoers regard the representations at the Tottenham-street theatre in much the same light as dabblers and amateurs in classical music look upon the program of the Monday popular concerts," commented the *London Entr'acte* (5 October 1872), "and would account it a dereliction of duty on their part if they did not grace the entertainment with their presence pretty often." Indeed, it was reported within two months of the opening of *Caste* in 1867 that some spectators had already witnessed it five or six times.[67] A description of a first night at the theatre in 1877 implies its broad appeal to playgoers:

> Crowds at the doors of Pit and Gallery, bringing back associations of Boxing Night, and carriages rolling successively up to the Box entrance, suggestive of the approaches to the Italian Opera at the height of the London season, would have assured anyone within sight of the Prince of Wales's Theatre on Saturday that among every class of playgoers deep interest had been taken in the new managerial program put forward on that occasion.[68]

Yet, according to the *Daily Telegraph* (18 September 1871), "many who would hesitate to acknowledge themselves members of the regular playgoing community have a mental reservation in favour of this establishment."[69]

In 1863 the Queen's most expensive seats had been 1s 6d in the front circle (which seated 80). The stalls seated 120 at 1s, while there were 220 seats in the boxes and upper boxes at the same price. The pit contained 700 seats at 6d each and the gallery 90 at 4d. Its nightly takings if full were £50.[70] Initially, under Marie Wilton, the theatre reduced its seating by one-third – largely in the pit. The management had obviously been cautious, perhaps because they were initially unsure of exactly the sort of audience they would attract: of a total capacity of 840 places, 500 were still devoted to the pit and gallery (the latter now holding 200), while the stalls seated only 90; the amphitheatre, 40; the dress circle, 120; and the private boxes, 64.[71] Prices were now 6s for the stalls, 3s for the dress circle, 1s 6d for the pit, and 6d for the gallery, the front rows of which became amphitheatre seats at 1s, while private boxes ranged from one to two guineas. By December 1868 stalls were 7s; the dress circle, 5s; the pit, 2s; and the amphitheatre, 1s 6d. By 1875 stalls were 10s; the dress circle, 6s; and the pit, 2s 6d. (Thus within ten years the sale of several rows of stall seats provided an income equivalent to what had formerly been the theatre's entire takings.) In 1865 the doors opened at 7 P.M. and the performance commenced at 7:30 P.M. In time performances commenced at 8 P.M. Children in arms were not admitted and all other children were charged for. A clipping for January 1872 states that bonnets could not be worn in the private boxes, stalls, or dress circle, and audiences were requested to remain seated until the curtain had actually fallen at the end of the play.[72] Despite the increased prices (and the consequent social reengineering of the audience), the demographics of the immediate neighborhood changed little after Marie Wilton took over the theatre. Tottenham Street provided much the same retail outlets in 1880 as it had in 1850.[73] Shopkeepers, tradesmen, dressmakers, and laborers continued to reside in the district as before,[74] but there was no longer a minor theatre specifically catering for them or for their fellow-workers in central London.

Marie Wilton's transformation of the Queen's into the Prince of Wales's Theatre was an astute move, for it soon became one of the most fashionable and frequented theatres in town, although we should be wary of assuming that its typical audience was as glittering as the first night audiences, including the "representatives of arts and arms, and a considerable sprinkling of the half-world which at the present time delights to flaunt it on first nights,"[75] reported in the press. However, the theatre's success must have left some members of the local audience bereft of immediately accessible (and varied) theatrical entertainment. Where did they go? To the Music Hall? To other neighborhood theatres, such as the Marylebone? The only other places of entertainment in the immediate vicinity were the Princess's, which, after the Keans, provided a mixture of fashionable melodrama and Shakespearian revivals, and the Oxford Music Hall, which, despite its relatively cheap admission charges, was hardly courting a local working-class audience.[76] Just across Oxford Street in Soho was the tiny Royalty, which was now gaining a reputation for burlesque and, under Richard D'Oyly Carte's management, was to be the venue for Gilbert and Sullivan's first successful collaboration, *Trial by Jury*. This also catered to fashionable audiences and was unlikely to provide alternative venues for the dispossessed audiences of the Queen's. To the northeast was the somewhat disreputable King's Cross Theatre. One of the most likely explanations is that the old Queen's audience was dispersed across the West End: instead of attending a new performance once a fortnight in the immediate neighborhood, it visited the galleries of a range of theatres, seeking novelty despite the abundance of long runs.[77] On the other hand the local audience may already have declined and this may have been behind James's decision to lease the theatre to Marie Wilton, although the evidence of the census suggests otherwise.

DEFLATING THE MYTH

As the Prince of Wales's, the theatre received superlative reports from W. B. Donne, the Examiner of Plays: in his view it was an example of how his annual inspections had contributed not only to the comfort and security of the audience, but raised the character of the performance as well:

> Some years ago the Queen's now the Prince of Wales, was of a low order both as to the character of the performances there and as to the provisions for public accommodation. The manager, however, Mr C. J. James, has for the last eight or nine years made from time to time such improvements in his house as to render it now one of the most handsome and commodious of the small theatres in Lon-

don. The character of the performances has risen with the improvement of the house, and under the management of Miss Wilton the Prince of Wales theatre has become a place of resort for the upper classes as well as for regular playgoers.[78]

From 1867 to 1869 the Prince of Wales's was praised fulsomely by Donne – "perfect order," "perfect state," "deserving the highest commendation" – and in 1870 he wrote – "superlatively good – nec (ultra) – until next year!! – when doubtless there will be something better than best."[79] In one report he referred to a parallel improvement in the neighboring Royalty Theatre, which in the 1850s, as the Soho Theatre, had probably been in competition for the Queen's audiences. Theodor Fontane's description of the audience (clearly from "the lower strata of society") in the 1850s must also be relevant to the Queen's Theatre, since the two theatres were relatively close.

> Dean Street [where the theatre was situated] is a cross-street of Oxford Street and a part of the former Latin quarter, the students' and artists' district of London. I doubt whether all these streets that converge on Soho Square still have a claim to be distinguished by this title. At least I saw no faces in the audience that could lay claim to being the property of a painter. There was no shortage of models, though. But the fact that this was a lower-class – even "doubtful" audience – gave this performance (*Richard III*) a special charm.[80]

Yet, just as Marie Wilton had taken over the old Queen's Theatre, so another popular burlesque performer, Patti Oliver, took over the Royalty. In 1868 Donne wrote:

> it should also be noted that two Theatres within the last two years – the Prince of Wales and the new Royalty in Dean St, Soho – have risen considerably in the class of Theatres as regards the Performances given in both of them.

He went on to attribute the long runs at these and other theatres to "a general improvement in the character of the more popular plays," adding:

> The long runs are not the effect of mere whim on the part of the audiences neither of mere luck on the part of the authors and managers. The public is not only a judge of what it likes, but in the main a good judge also of what is good. And in two instances – those

of the "New Royalty" and the "Prince of Wales's" Theatres – the improvement morally no less than dramatically in the plays has been the cause of raising these Houses in the scale of public entertainment.[81]

Donne's dreams of reforming the drama seemed to be bearing fruit.

Yet the consequences of the "reforms" instigated by the Bancrofts and approved of by Donne are thrown into perspective by the comments of veteran playgoer, P. P. Hanley:

It would seem that anything is good enough for the pit and gallery folk, who are obliged to arrive early, for since stalls were introduced, a poor place at the best can only be obtained in the pit; in many theatres it consists almost entirely of seats under the boxes, in a most oppressive atmosphere. One theatre has done away with the pit entirely, and in the galleries of most houses several seats are fenced off and converted into amphitheatre stalls; so that the gallery visitor, who pays one shilling for his admission, is relegated to a position, where, if it is a large theatre, the actors look like pigmies. Going to the play is now a very expensive luxury and, unless you book seats beforehand, there is really no comfort, and it is not everyone who can afford to do so. For myself, I must say, if the present system had been adopted in my young days, fond as I was (and am) of the theatre, my visits would have been very few and far between.[82]

Hanley's complaint concerning the abolition of the pit is a direct consequence of the Bancrofts' actions. In 1880 the Bancrofts, at Squire Bancroft's instigation, took over the management of the Haymarket Theatre. The decision to do so was partially motivated by financial reasons – the Haymarket had a much greater audience capacity – and partly traditional – the Haymarket was still regarded as the premiere venue for English comedy. However, the reforms that they undertook at the Haymarket, especially the abolition of the pit, provoked a first-night outcry. Bancroft justified the changes on the grounds of practical business sense. A number of letters of support appeared in the *Era* (8 February 1880). "A Dramatic Lounger" recalled the days when a visitor to the Haymarket pit "did not trouble himself much about the aspect of the Theatre so long as there was a good play and good acting. Hard benches, smoky lights, keen draughts, dingy scenery, a shrieking orchestra, rough companions, and other disagreeables did not hinder the playgoer from sitting out a good play well acted."[83] However, given the additional expenses now incurred in mounting plays and the generally higher quality of comfort and accommodation expected in theatres, galleries, and concert halls, it was perhaps inevitable that, if an audience could fill the pit at stalls prices, then the pit would have to go. Indeed, "A Pittite" wondered if other managements should not follow suit, especially as Bancroft had provided the second circle at the prices previously paid for admission to the pit. After all, in the pit, "The visitors are packed away under the first circle, the flooring of which is barely a yard above their heads. And what is the result? With a full attendance the atmosphere soon becomes simply awful, and comparable only to the famed Black Hole of Calcutta. The occupants are packed like the oft-quoted sardines in a box. Their legs have no stretching room: egress and ingress are matters which are absolutely impossible without the risk of torn garments, and general discomfort; and there is, as a rule, for a seat a hard, bare board without a back."[84] Yet, unlike the pit audience, the stalls audience seemed dull, passive, incapable of demonstrative emotional response or enthusiasm. As correspondence in such journals as the *Era* and *The Theatre* indicates, some playgoers felt this was an advantage. Further marking the separation of audience from actor at the Haymarket was the new proscenium, which reminded observers of the frame for a figure-painting.

In analyzing the audiences who attended the nineteenth-century London theatres it is important that we consider the subtexts running through our source materials and the attendant myths created by them. Just as we must question and even treat with mistrust such sources as Dickens, not to mention national and local newspapers, reminiscences and memoirs, and playbills, yet also draw on them for evidence; so we must remember that, despite their value as a source, the Lord Chamberlain's Papers reflect very strongly Donne's mission to improve the drama by attracting "a better class of person" to the theatres. Although they provide a splendid primary source for historical reconstruction, they do this within the unfolding narrative of Donne's social, moral, and literary objectives. Thus the story of the Prince of Wales's Theatre is not only about the successful attraction of a better class of audience to what was formerly a minor theatre — it is also a story about another audience that went missing.

There are several myths that have to be exploded. One is the notion that the Queen's was a "Dust-hole," a disreputable flea-pit, worthy of notice only when transformed into a mecca for high society by the Bancrofts. It had in fact been a successful "minor" theatre, catering to the artisan and working population of central London for a quarter of a century prior to the Bancrofts' arrival. The second myth is that the Prince of Wales's Theatre effected an overnight change in audience composition. In fact the reputation of the Prince of Wales's Theatre after 1865 owed something to the work of Charles Kean at the Princess's Theatre in the 1850s, certainly socially and quite probably through its geographical proximity. Michael Booth suggests that Kean's management "marked the beginning of the end of a drama based upon the support of popular audiences, without significant participation from the fashionable, the socially respectable and the intellectually cultured segments of the population," and is surely correct in viewing the social success of the Bancroft management as only "a confirmation and an extension of an earlier trend."[85] The third myth is that the Bancroft management set out to be socially exclusive. This is unlikely: the number of gallery and pit seats retained at reasonably low prices suggests that they were expecting a mixed and partially local audience initially. Lastly, the notion that the replacement of popular melodramatic fare by the mildly snobbish plays of Robertson was an evolutionary moment in British theatre is only acceptable if all kinds of prior assumptions are already in place.

The myth of the Prince of Wales's Theatre is a myth of reclamation involving a theatre, the drama, an actress, and an audience. In reclaiming the Prince of Wales's Theatre, Marie Wilton also reclaimed herself. Her autobiography refers to the social ostracism and ignominy endured by her actor-father, who came from a respectable middle-class family, and by herself and her siblings. Her distress and humiliation at appearing in "travestie" (or cross-dressed) roles is also well-documented: one motive behind her entry into management was to escape the obligation otherwise imposed upon her to play such roles. Through her successful management of the Prince of Wales's Theatre and her marriage to the affluent and respectable Squire Bancroft, an actor in her company, she redeemed her past and that of her family. The prodigal daughter and her starving family were forgiven their transgressions and allowed back into polite society. By the mid-1880s, according to T. H. Escott, the actress "who ten or fifteen years ago was dancing a breakdown on the burlesque stage, finds herself seated today between the Premier and a prelate at the dinner-table of a peer . . . the incarnation of everything which is orthodox in British matronhood."[86]

Mythic configurations dominate our received view of nineteenth-century British theatre. This can be seen in popular genres, such as melodrama and pantomime, which move towards the possibility of the reclamation of a golden age or the achievement of a utopian future, founded upon a naive oversimplification of the social, economic, and moral realities of the age. The desire for a restoration or re-creation of a more literary or "legitimate" drama fulfils similar objectives, as "illegitimacy" is confounded and displaced by the redemptive power of "legitimized" high art. Similarly, the function of the theatre in relation to its audience is also mythically encapsulated, whether in Dickens's desire for social improvement or Donne's to reclaim the social and literary status of the theatre. What we learn from their accounts is strongly influenced by their personal agendas, yet their work provides a context in which concepts, such as "social control," now largely discredited, or Foucault's notion of the disciplinary nature of nineteenth-century institutions are seemingly validated. However, if we reclaim Bentham from Foucault for a moment and clamber out of the panopticon, it may be worth remembering that Bentham's own view, embodied in the greatest good for the greatest number, allowed those seeking recreation much greater autonomy amid much less restraint, even if the moral efficacy of such recreations, as substitutions for more dissolute pastimes, is also prefigured in his work. The post-Benthamite urge to impose greater control on and channeling of the spectator's pleasures inevitably influences the way in which theatre audiences were subsequently depicted, but should make us all the more inclined to question rather than endorse the accuracy of these later accounts.

The myth of the audience in need of reclamation or enlightenment, to be achieved through the redemptive power of theatre, implies a social, moral, and aesthetic problem that needs solving and a consequent need for discipline and control to achieve its resolution. It is essentially reductive, establishing passivity and obedience as desirable qualities to be facilitated through cultural and aesthetic means. Within the nexus of social relationships, which inexorably underpin the mythic tendencies explored here and which impinge on all forms of communal recreation, Gareth Stedman-Jones warns us against mistaking archival silence for historical passivity.[87] It might be worth rethinking the nineteenth-century spectator as a sort of theatrical tourist or even, within the context of Shakespearian bardolatry and Sadler's Wells, as a sort of pilgrim. In such a reconstituting, there is always a danger of inventing new traditions and establishing new myths. Nevertheless, the assumption that audiences are agencies that are acted upon rather than acting for themselves informs the ideological imperatives underlying many of the most familiar descriptions of nineteenth-century audiences, a factor often ignored by subsequent commentators, who have elevated such descriptions to documentary status. Yet the cases of both Sadler's Wells and of the Prince of Wales's Theatre suggest that not only should we be wary of such evidence, but that we should also seek to unravel the mythic patterns through which such questionable views are mediated.

Part Four

"THEATRIC TOURISTS" AND
THE WEST END

6. The West End

he West End, an area demarcated less by its geography and demography than by its cultural and commercial status, emerged in the period 1840 to 1880. Strictly speaking, at the turn of the nineteenth century, the west end of London denoted all the areas of London immediately to the west of Temple Bar and the City bounded by the Thames to the south and Oxford Street to the north. The positioning however in the eighteenth century of the two large patent theatres, Drury Lane and Covent Garden, immediately north of the Strand, and the King's Opera House and Haymarket theatre adjacent to the fashionable and aristocratic neighborhood of St. James's, initiated a process of centralization which would progressively define the West End as London's entertainment district. The monopoly granted by the letters patent insured that occasional or regular playgoers or aficionados of music theatre were compelled to travel to this entertainment district. Protected by a monopoly and geographical centrality these theatres felt themselves invulnerable. The period to 1843 however saw neighborhood theatres erected in the rapidly expanding suburbs whose geographic distance from the patent theatres allowed them to mount legitimate drama with legal impunity. It also saw entrepreneurs, responding to the huge increase in London's population, challenge the authority of the patent theatres by erecting theatres like the Lyceum and Olympic in their immediate vicinity. The passing of the 1843 Theatre Regulation Act not only abolished this monopoly, which gave Drury Lane and Covent Garden the privilege of performing legitimate drama, but also recognized the significance of the population growth that the old dispensation could no longer satisfy and the role of neighborhood theatres in responding to demands for theatrical entertainment. It set in train a series of events that radically changed the relationship between theatres and their patrons in the West End. The diaspora to the suburbs particularly by those who might have patronized the centrally located theatres, the increased distances that militated against regular theatre-going, the challenge of other forms of private entertainment all con-tributed to a destabilization whose effects were particularly felt by the former patent theatres. Their cultural position as repositories of a "na-tional drama" became no longer tenable; nor could they be assured of an undisputed call upon the allegiance of a known and quantifiable audience. Thus the period after 1843 saw deliberate attempts to attract new audiences to the West End using strategies based not upon cul-tural but rather upon commercial imperatives. It is this process that we investigate.

We have accepted as axiomatic Michael Booth's insistence upon the need to investigate the changing relationship between theatres and their patrons and the influence of the connection between neighbor-hood, work practices, and cultural habits upon that relationship. As well, we have recognized that many "unwarranted conclusions about the drama and public taste" have derived from the imposition of the-atrical values appropriate to the West End upon London theatregoing generally.[1] Yet as we approach the evidence for the West End that might demonstrate the veracity of the view held by Booth, Rowell, and others that the progress of the West End theatre particularly after 1850, is marked by its embrace on the part of a middle class and a return by 1880 of a self-consciously fashionable society, wishing to see its val-ues reflected on stage, the evidence becomes elusive and to an extent problematic. What makes it problematic is that these views, in fact, reflect the results of a concerted effort on the part of both journalists and theatre managers in the period to paint a picture of theatre's even-tual triumph over adversity — religious opposition, urban degradation, "mob rule and working class domination" — and of the acceptance by a general public of its right to respectability and cultural leadership. The evidence is elusive because, unlike much of the material that in-forms our accounts of other theatres, accounts of West End theatre-going are provided not by quasi-social investigators or by those looking for manifestations of the redemptive power of the theatre in reclaiming a literary taste, but rather by those whose cultural habits were deter-mined by fashion or by the need to earn a journalist's income. More-over, the absence of material in the Lord Chamberlain's papers points to the fact that the office had little interest in West End audiences un-like its preoccupation with those in the East End or in Lambeth.

Thus the reviews by Henry Morley, Sala, Blanchard, Clement Scott and even Dickens in his early years do not represent the views of the occasional playgoer, but those of a working journalist, and, as we have seen elsewhere in the case of Dickens, often a journalist with a social or cultural agenda. Unlike their reviews or comments about theatres outside the West End, which reflected their reactions as cultural explorers confronted by denizens with whom they were unfamiliar, their general lack of interest in West End audiences mirrors their familiarity with them. Only rare occasions like disturbances prompted comment that stood outside their reporting of the quality of the performances or that of the play. The fact that such disturbances were rare, of course, reflects the pall of respectability and fashionable impassivity, which took shape in the early nineteenth century and thickened after 1850. Harold Perkin points to what he calls the Moral Revolution, which changed all aspects of the English "national character":

> Between 1780 and 1850 the English ceased to be one of the most aggressive, brutal, rowdy, outspoken, riotous, cruel and bloodthirsty nations in the world and became one of the most inhibited, polite, orderly, tender-minded, prudish and hypocritical.[2]

Thus, reports about theatregoing tend to focus on the performances, the costuming both on and off the stage, the comfort or discomfort of the theatrical ambience, and the presence of notable patrons and the general aura of respectability. While it may be true that at the end of our period "the working class [had] by no means disappeared from the theatre, even from the West End,"[3] their presence is rarely noticed by theatrical observers. Perhaps the West End as a whole participated in the sort of erasure that we have noticed in the case of the Prince of Wales's theatre under the Bancrofts. This is not to say that such reports should be ignored or regarded suspiciously, but we should position them within a broader investigation of the changing identity of the West End itself, or rather the ways in which this identity was fashioned and manipulated.

Some of the most significant evidence is provided by the responses contained within the Parliamentary Select Committee minutes in 1832 and subsequently in 1866. From these we become aware of the problems that confronted the large patent theatres in the period before the passing of the Theatre Regulation Act in 1843 and the fears held by theatre managers in the 1860s concerning the proliferation of music halls and their effect upon audience attendance. The evidence also points to the significant contribution made by visitors to London to the composition of West End audiences. Theatres which were successful tended to be those with a well-defined repertoire or those whose managers were able to match their repertorial choices and their policies about admission prices and performance times to the needs of their particular neighborhoods. As we have seen in the cases of the Sadler's Wells and Prince of Wales's theatres, commentators viewed with approbation the existence of a respectable and even fashionable audience, who supported well-run theatres offering productions that flattered their discernment and dramatic taste. The managements of these theatres, together with the success of Charles Kean's tenure at the Princess's in the 1850s, appeared indeed to indicate a reclamation of theatrical taste, on the part of a class of theatregoers, which might justify a belief in the theatre's economic viability. That such a belief became prevalent can be seen from the boom in building that took place from 1866 and continued until the end of the century. At the same time such evidence also points to a radical change in perceptions about the theatre of particular relevance to the West End: the shift from a theatre that prided itself on its national relevance to one whose concerns and policies were primarily commercial.

Part of this self-confident commercial speculation can be attributed to the huge increase in the population of London in our period. The growth in population had been centrifugal and the census returns from 1851 to 1871, for example, suggest that the population of the West End declined, at least in the narrowly defined area bounded by Drury Lane to the east, Regent Street and Piccadilly to the west, Oxford Street to the north, and the Thames to the south, as people moved either further west or to the northern and southern suburbs. The explosion in West End theatre building after 1866 suggests that a centripetal force was being exerted, which increasingly attracted audiences drawn largely from those who lived in the provinces and new suburbs of London, who saw themselves as "theatric tourists" (to borrow James Winston's description) and who regarded the West End primarily as a tourist attraction. If this is the case, then reference to the motivations that underpin tourism, an emerging industry in the period after 1840, may well be useful in determining the kinds of audiences that frequented the West End. Equally, the success or failure of theatres like Drury Lane may well have to do with factors of particular relevance to the habits and expectations of tourists: accessibility, security, respectability, and glamor. In modern terms the study of tourism has been defined as the analysis of "the geography of consumption outside the home area; it is about why people travel to consume . . . it is concerned with what makes tourists travel, what determines how far and in what direction they move."[4] Such practices may offer some insight into why people traveled to the West End to indulge in the consumption of a product that became increasingly conspicuous in our period.

Nevertheless, the absence of any new theatre building in the period between 1843 and 1866, despite the huge increases in the population of London, implies a period marked by uncertainty, exacerbated by the financial depression that stretched from the 1830s to the end of the following decade. Fashionable people had indeed progressively moved further away from what had been traditionally regarded as the cultural center of London to the suburbs of north and west London. The theatres most affected by this centrifugal movement to the periphery were the large patent theatres, Drury Lane and Covent Garden, which had enjoyed a privileged position. Part of the sense of uncertainty can be attributed to the fact that, unlike the neighborhood theatres, which relied upon regular playgoers drawn from their immediate communities, the West End began to lose this audience base. This certainly underpins the legal wrangling which marks the period prior to 1843 between "major" and "minor" theatres in London, and the absence of a body of regular playgoers was to have an enduring effect upon managerial strategies in the West End.

The single event which accelerated the process of reevaluation was the unprecedented success of the Great Exhibition of the Works of Industry of All Nations, which attracted 6,063,986 visitors to London in the five months from May to October 1851. Like a magnet it had drawn all classes to Hyde Park at the western end of London from the suburbs, the English provinces, and overseas. John Cole, the biographer of Charles Kean, commented that "London for several months was occupied by the French."[5] Such visitors were prepared to pay the minimum admission price of 1s (from Monday to Thursday), 2s 6d on Fridays, and 5s on Saturdays, and to view the Crystal Palace where a hundred thousand objects were displayed, including machinery, tapestries, gold watches, fine porcelain, pianos, and the largest sheet of plate glass ever made – a combination of applied arts, technology, and markers of middle-class taste.[6] In effect, the Exhibition was a huge theme park and its patrons were tourists, all of whom had traveled from their homes by walking, or by bus, train, cab and boat. In order to reach the Exhibition visitors passed "men with trays of bright silvery looking medals of the Crystal Palace, and filling the air with the cheepness [*sic*] and attractiveness of their wares" and "girls and women with round wicker sieves piled up in pyramids with oranges as well as brown-looking trotters, spread on white cloths."[7] These could be supplemented by the food and drink offered discreetly inside by Messrs. Schweppe, who succeeded in making a profit of £45,000 by October 1851. Despite the huge numbers of visitors, the behavior of the crowds appeared to be exemplary: there were in all twenty-five arrests for pickpocketing and petty larceny.[8] The exhibition itself was divided into courts reflecting the prowess of the individual national contributors. Cole was amazed that:

> By crossing from one department to another, you were as completely in the country designated, as if the carpet of Prince Houssein had actually annihilated time and space and carried you there in a minute. . . . The whole formed a scene of realized enchantment, an animated cosmorama, to lose yourself in for a month . . . and to think of it for ever after.[9]

Among these stood Pugin's Medieval Court, in which "authentic" medieval artifacts were reproduced; where sculptured groupings of a nubile Greek slave being sold "to some wealthy eastern barbarian before whom she is supposed to stand, with an expression of scornful rejection mingled with shame and disgust,"[10] and an Amazon attacked by a tigress were "staged." As we will see when considering Kean's productions at the Princess's, Dean MacCannell's notion of "staged authenticity," which in modern terms denotes one of the major strategies used to construct and define tourist spaces, will offer provocative parallels.

The significance of the Great Exhibition was not lost on West End theatre managers: what had been particularly impressive was the sense of occasion that drew people to London, the respectability of its patrons, a pervasive sense of wonder that encompassed both the Crystal Palace itself and variety of its inclusions – both competitive and yet complementary – and the opportunities for making money by juxtaposing rational amusement with visceral satisfaction. In these terms, the success of the West End might depend upon the recognition that perhaps the decrease in regular playgoers could be offset by turning the West End itself into an elaborate theme park, whose uniqueness might attract a body of visitors from other places, whether those places were the suburbs of London, the provinces, or other countries. To achieve this the places of entertainment needed to identify themselves precisely (like the Exhibition's German, English, or American exhibits); they needed to be supported by a network of food outlets (restaurants and bars inside or outside the theatres); and safe and convenient access needed to be guaranteed, whether by public transport or for those who might wish to walk in the area. Above all, the West End needed to establish itself as extraordinary, offering entertainment that could not be offered elsewhere.

From this perspective, the history of the West End in our period becomes not a teleological one of middle-class and fashionable reclamation. Rather, it shows a deliberate attempt on the part of managements and journalists, many of whom were to an extent beholden to managers for their income, to construct a "Crystal Palace," which would lure an increasingly assertive middle class to a theatrical theme park to flatter its sensitivity and cultural perspicacity or to satisfy its craving for luxurious spectacle. Thus the protests against the incursions of the music hall at the 1866 Select Committee hearings and the evident fear that audiences might be drained away can be seen in the light of theatre managers anxious that the legitimate entertainments of the newly-emerging "theme park" were being threatened by fresh entrepreneurs, less than scrupulous about its emerging image. At the same time, the burst in theatre building after 1866 demonstrates a confidence that the strategies of higher prices, long runs, and glamorous casts in often trivial plays held the keys to ongoing success. In this they were generally proved right, and by 1880 the respectability of the West End theatres was unimpeachable. Theatres like Drury Lane and the Lyceum were even seeking to legitimize their positions by aspiring to become manifestations of a "national theatre," purveying expressions of populist aspiration or "art," positions which found their apogee during the managements of Augustus Harris and Henry Irving respectively.

The case of the West End may be a unique one in our examination of London theatre audiences. It may perhaps be viewed not as a neighborhood seeking a theatrical expression of its values, but rather of a theme park constructed in order to promulgate values which would attract audiences from elsewhere. If "orientalism" is a metaphor that may help us to understand the fascination with the Other of the East End, then "occidentalism" might serve as a term for the West End. Visitors to the West End could marvel at the quasi-historical past as in the antiquarian revivals of Charles Kean's Shakespeare; the elaborate Scottish settings that dressed versions of Walter Scott at Drury Lane; the Irishness of Boucicault's *The Shaughraun* or *The Colleen Bawn*; and the introduction of familiar objects on stage at the Prince of Wales's or Haymarket theatres and the hansom cabs on the stage of Drury Lane. All of these could be seen in theatrical surroundings that catered to a sense of occasion, while at the same time either affirming the accessibility of a different world — the Other made familiar — or celebrating the materiality of the familiar world. Much of the informality of early Victorian theatregoing had disappeared by 1880 in the West End. Theatre managers were unanimously determined to create an environment appropriate to the new and mobile leisure society, which was then emerging. Though the Society of West End Theatre Managers was not officially formed until the Edwardian period, the statement of its role merely enshrined practices which had been evident by 1880: "to enable proprietors of West End London theatres . . . to be in touch with one another, and to facilitate concerted action in any matters generally connected with the welfare or the carrying on of those theatres." [11]

LOCATION, DEMOGRAPHY, AND TRANSPORT

Investigations of London theatres outside the West End have drawn evidence, for example, from police reports, the Lord Chamberlain's papers, the comments of social and theatrical observers, and the demographic and statistical information supplied by census returns. Much of this sort of information is missing when we turn to the West End, in particular the evidence for a locally based audience as distinct from one made up of visitors to the area. Nevertheless, an examination of the "geography" of the West End may allow us at least to surmise about a local audience and to suggest how the emphasis on creating facilities and opportunities to attract visitors may have effectively displaced it.

In formal terms, the boundaries of the West End could be defined as those parts of London immediately west of Temple Bar, bounded by the river to the south, by Holborn and Oxford Street to the north, but extending as far as Kensington to the west. It thus included the notorious rookeries of St. Giles's, Holborn; the area south of the Strand to the river; parts of St. James's, Westminster, especially the area round the Abbey; the Hungerford and Covent Garden markets; the various attractions of Leicester Square and the Haymarket; the aristocratic gaming houses of Almack's and Crockford's in the Pall Mall and Piccadilly areas; as well as the town residences of wealthy aristocrats, which dotted not only the areas immediately adjacent to Piccadilly, but also the areas from Hyde Park to Kensington. Thus the area to the west of Temple Bar exhibited a sprawling demographic composition that reflected the extremes of wealth and poverty. Transport and accommodation details, however, suggest a much more circumscribed area, accessible from the east via Fleet Street and the Strand, which followed the natural boundary provided by the river; from the west via Piccadilly or Regent's Street; and from the south via Westminster and Waterloo Bridges. Access from the north was impeded by the maze of narrow streets which flowed from Oxford Street through Seven Dials to Leicester Square and from Broad Street, Holborn, to Drury Lane. It is this more circumscribed area that would house the West End "theme park" that developed in the period after 1840.

Certainly the marketplace component had been in existence since the eighteenth century. Even as early as 1782 the Strand appeared to be an endless succession of shops, each advertising its wares with large, gaudily painted signs.[12] Some years later the *Penny Magazine* described Oxford Street:

> Shops of every character are to be found in it; the baker and the confectioner, with their open windows, and smoking buns, . . . the fishmonger drenching his shop with water . . . the public house, at the doors of which stable-boys, footmen, and working men may be seen entering or emerging; the coffee-shop; the trunk maker; the hosier, . . . the saloon-like place where the mercer unrolls his silk; the little stalls at the edge of the pavement, loaded with cabbage and cauliflower, green peas and new potatoes.[13]

Geographically then the West End was bounded by long-established shopping streets: Oxford Street to the north, which in the earlier part of the century comprised small shops and businesses, servicing the poorer areas of the St. Giles's parish at its eastern end, as well as the more wealthy hinterland of Portland Square and Regent's Park at its western end; the fashionable shops of Regent Street, which linked with those of Piccadilly; the Strand, which in the late eighteenth century reflected a similar composition to that of Oxford Street. The history of these streets from the 1830s onward is, of course, a history of shopping gentrification and concentration, particularly as large department stores and specialized shops targeted visitors from outside London, the Continent, or the United States, as well as the fashionable shoppers from the wealthy suburbs of Belgravia, Kensington, Chelsea, or Regent's Park, who came to an area where they could combine business with pleasure.

The southern boundary to the West End created by the river, was crossed from 1833 by three bridges. Westminster Bridge led to the western perimeter, but until the construction in the last quarter of the century of Northumberland Avenue, which facilitated access to the Strand, its value was more as a toll-free bridge to the popular theatres of Astley's or the Surrey for those living immediately in the St. James's Square area or from further afield. As we have seen, Lambeth developed into a densely populated working-class area and the Waterloo Bridge's toll, lasting until 1878, inhibited all but those who needed to cross it in order to work in the West End area. The last bridge was the Hungerford, built in 1833, to enable direct access to the Hungerford Market from Lambeth. Its lifespan was relatively short and its purpose defeated by its failure to attract housewives for whom it was intended, to cross the river.[14] Thus the failure of these bridges to open up the West End area together with the fact that the West End was further confined by some of the most desperate slums, (which stretched east from Wardour Street to the north of Leicester Square, through the Seven Dials and Long Acre, to the St. Giles's rookery at Drury Lane), served to emphasize the West End as an island. Indeed, the entire area could be seen as an area of ostentatious opulence, surrounded to the north, east, and south by areas that had been abandoned by the wealthy. Even in Westminster as late as 1850, Westminster Abbey and the Houses of Parliament were immediately adjacent to the slum areas around Dean Yard, Pye, and Orchard Streets.[15]

Inevitably, people who visited the West End were struck by the evident wealth of those who frequented its shops and entertainment emporiums and their contrast with those who lived in the areas located immediately adjacent. Writing in 1835, Charles Dickens described the area of Seven Dials, immediately to the east of Soho, which a visitor to Leicester Square and Saint Martin's would have traveled through or deliberately skirted, as one of squalid people living in squalid conditions in houses that once had been handsome and lofty.[16] By 1852 matters had not improved. Thomas Beames pointed out the contrast between the area just north of Drury Lane, the center of the St. Giles rookery (with its lodging houses, street dealers, crossing sweepers, mendicants, and country tramps), and the luxury displayed in the shops of the Strand.[17] Foreign visitors were also quick to identify the great contrasts between the facade of the emerging West End "theme park" and its hinterland.[18] In 1853 the German visitor Max Schlesinger corroborated the impressions of Dickens and Beames.[19] Similarly, Hippolyte Taine, who visited England in 1858 and subsequently in 1871, found himself astonished at the sheer scale of London, the monumental buildings and the palatial houses on the edges of Hyde Park,[20] but was appalled at the adjacent poverty, which he compared unfavorably to the bad quarters of Marseilles, Antwerp, and Paris. He was equally affronted at the numbers of prostitutes who frequented the Haymarket and the Strand.[21]

Nor were the places of entertainment themselves exempt from the presence of gin and prostitution. Flora Tristan had responded to this as early as the 1830s, when she saw prostitutes crossing Waterloo Bridge, and making their way to the West End to carry on their trade, particularly at the approaches to the theatres.[22] At half-price "throngs of prostitutes and men of every station crowd into the theatre – the women go wherever they please, will even sit next to you with the smell of gin they exhale with every breath." Despite efforts to make the theatre lobbies more elegant, the presence of prostitutes militated against "many decent men and women . . . frequenting the place."[23] Even in the 1860s, after restaurateurs and theatre managers had spent large sums on glamorizing their establishments, West End theatres could still be seen as islands in a dark sea of badly illuminated and treacherous surroundings.[24] One theatregoer remembered, that Wych, Newcastle, and Holywell Streets, close to the Olympic and Drury Lane theatres, were not visited unaccompanied after dark and that it was quite possible to be assaulted by "footpads" in the dimly-lit Drury Lane.[25] Yet this element of danger might also be seen as part of its attractiveness, especially to those groups of men who frequented the clubs and were essentially looking for a good time:

The West end of London was at the time infested by dens of iniquity, known as "night houses," where the young members of the aristocracy might be seen night after night paying 15 shillings a bottle for gooseberry or rhubarb champagne. Several of the most notorious of these houses were in Panton Street, off the Haymarket. . . . The locality was a historical one in the annals of London dissipation . . . the modern Panton Street, since the suppression of the night houses, and the building of the Comedy Theatre, has been the most decorous and reputable of thoroughfares. But its morals were scarcely unimpeachable in the year 1859, and for a few years afterwards.[26]

Despite the fact that these eyewitness accounts obscure their social agendas, as we have seen in our discussions of theatres in other parts of London, they do identify components of the West End audience. Moreover, the high contrasts that were accentuated between wealth and poverty in the West End areas mask the fact that, for example, lodging houses need not necessarily be identified with squalor or shiftlessness. The area immediately to the south of the Strand, for instance, housed many professional people: Craven Street, to the west of the Hungerford Market housed solicitors, doctors, the office of the Commissioners of Metropolitan Roads, and the coroner of the Queen's Household, while lodging houses intended for reasonably affluent tourists in the period to the 1860s were also to be found.[27] Villiers Street, had physicians, railway and civil engineers, journalists, artists (including Clarkson Stanfield and William Etty), and architects. Wellington Street to the north had the offices of journals like *Household Words*, while the Adelphi Terrace, and Robert and John Streets housed the offices of organizations like the Royal Literary Fund, the Royal Society of Arts, the Colonisation Commissioners for South Australia and the New Zealand Colonisation Company, as well as a mix of journalists, architects, and engravers.[28] Indeed, the census abstracts for 1861 list approximately the same percentage of professional as commercial classes in the Strand area. Thus the class that included local government officials, civil servants, and persons involved with the arts and sciences (including actors for the first time) were as prominent as those involved in the buying and selling of goods.[29.] In the St. Martin's area, the professional percentage living there was even greater.[30]

Throughout the period, evidence like the census returns points to the coexistence in the West End of tradesmen, laborers, booksellers, washerwomen, apprentices, skilled artisans like gold- and silversmiths as well as a foreign population of French and German migrants working as confectioners, restauranteurs, teachers, domestic servants, and merchants.[31] Such evidence should alert us to a slightly different form of essentializing that we have been resisting in our discussions elsewhere. The West End, particularly in the period 1851 to 1880, saw the rapid development of an entertainment district geared towards visitors with money in their pocket to spend either on shopping or the enjoyment derived from visiting theatres, exhibitions of technical achievement, and art galleries. The rhetoric of social commentators tends to identify a binary whereby an economically driven entertainment area is contrasted with the squalid poverty surrounding it. However, the census returns and ownership records of houses suggest the parallel existence of a resident community of hard-working men and women, pursuing a craft-based living in various small businesses, and a middle-class professional group attached to government bodies and commercial institutions together with artists, musicians, and actors. This settled, resident community can be contrasted with the high proportion of unmarried lodgers residing in St. Giles's and the evident value of properties around the Strand with the statistic that St. Giles's had a lower property value than even that of Whitechapel.[32] While considerable attention is paid to the return of fashionable audiences to the theatres, the interest by the commentators in those who might have sat in the pit or galleries is very slight. The demographic composition of those who lived locally however may well suggest that it formed a more considerable proportion of those audiences than previously estimated. At the same time, the relentless drive towards West End exclusivity eventually made the attendance of local residents of little interest to theatre managers and their publicists.

Even at the beginning of our period there were strong indications that this local population might be destabilized or displaced. This process can be directly attributed to the changes in modes of transportation, which facilitated access to the area. We have seen how important walking to theatres and places of amusement remained in the period: the evidence of John Coleman, for example, who recalled visiting the Queen's, the Olympic, and the Yorkshire Stingo in Paddington when he lived at Westbourne Green, near Paddington, and worked at Devonshire Place, just south of the Thames:

We dined at six, and as soon as I could leave I was off to the play. There was not a theatre in London I did not visit. There were no penny omnibuses in those days so in most instances each visit to the play was attended by a walk of six or eight miles.[33]

The Victorian habit of walking persisted throughout the nineteenth century, outliving the improvements in transport, and provided the passing trade upon which West End shopping relied. In *Cruchley's Picture of London*, an 1841 guide for the occasional visitor to London, we find an outline for a "plan for viewing the principal objects in the metropolis in the most advantageous manner and shortest time," intended for visitors who were prepared to walk considerable distances.[34] Thus, for example, the fourth day's route starting from Charing Cross, encompassed Covent Garden markets, Drury Lane Theatre, and the British Museum in Great Russell Street, skirting St. Giles's, visiting the Inns of Court in Holborn, traveling to King's Cross, thence through Gower Street past London University College to Tottenham Court Road, crossing Oxford Street to Wardour Street and Leicester Square, and finally down Coventry Street to the Haymarket and back to Charing Cross. At no point is any transport suggested. In fact the only reference to transport occurs in the seventh day's route, which suggests an omnibus to Whitechapel Church and a steam boat to Greenwich.[35]

Though omnibus routes at this time were plentiful for those who had business either in the City or Whitehall, the West End was less well served. In 1841, for example, numerous omnibus routes passed from the Bank through Cheapside, Fleet Street to Charing Cross and thence to the Haymarket and Regent Street. On the other hand, omnibus routes from the west started at Paddington but skirted the West End, traveling via Islington and thence down Goswell Street or City Road to the City and, via London or Southwark Bridges to the Elephant and Castle in Newington. Some did return using Westminster Bridge to reach Charing Cross. There was no north-south access except by hackney coach through narrow streets or by walking from Oxford Street south. This contributed to making the West End an island requiring a degree of effort to approach.[36] In the same period, hackney coach fares were expensive: fare from the Gloucester Coffee House in Oxford Street to Covent Garden or Drury Lane was 1s 6d; from the Paddington terminus of the Great Western Railway, 3s; from Russell Square or Westminster Bridge, 2s; from Clerkenwell Green, 2s. This was appreciably more than the omnibus fare of 6d.[37] By 1837 omnibuses were already an established mode of transport to convey professional and commercial classes to work in the City. By 1851, however, the Waterloo omnibus line was making the point that it could convey passengers into the heartland of the West End, hackney cabs had become cheaper and passengers were being encouraged from western suburbs like Chelsea and Knightsbridge, Islington to the north, Brixton to the south, and Whitechapel to the east.[38] By 1885 there were more than 100 omnibus lines serving the center of London, although the absence of direct north-south access to the West End remained the obvious inconvenience to visitors.

Equally significant perhaps in the period was the influence of railway expansion. In 1841, *Cruchley's Picture of London* could only point to the absence of convenient railway connections. W. P. Frith remembered that while in 1889 a journey from Leeds to London took four hours, "fifty years ago the quickest Royal Mail passage occupied never less than twenty-four hours, and sometimes, in snowy weather especially, much longer."[39] Moreover, the sense of the West End as an island inaccessible by train would not be resolved until after 1860 when the recommendations of the 1846 Select Committee on Railway Termini to exclude the building of terminuses within the metropolis would be overturned.[40] Between 1855 and 1875, however, the spread of train lines allowed visitors to the West End or commuters to the City, particularly from suburbs to the south and west of London, to reach Charing Cross station (built in 1864 on the site of the Hungerford Market), as well as Westminster (through the newly built Victoria station opened in 1860). By 1885, *Baedeker* could direct visitors to the newly completed "inner circle" underground run by the Metropolitan Railway Company (completed in 1884) and the fact that travelers from Kent, Greenwich, and the southern suburbs of Lewisham, Beckenham, and Bromley could use the Charing Cross station to bring them directly into the West End, while the underground brought people from Brompton and Kensington to the west and from the Tower of London, Whitechapel, and London Bridge to the east every 5 to 10 minutes during the day and every 15 minutes after 8 P.M. until nearly midnight in both directions.[41] Thus by 1867 the omnibus was being replaced as the major means of passenger transport. By the mid-1870s railways had overtaken it by three times the volume of traffic. In many cases the omnibus's accessibility in terms of depositing people outside their destinations offset the train's greater speed. Yet although first class on the railway was more expensive than the omnibus fare, third class was often cheaper. A third-class fare, for example, between Cannon Street and Charing Cross was 2d in 1866. John Fowler giving evidence to the Select Committee on Railway Schemes (Metropolis) 1864 suggested that:

> the character of the omnibus traffic is lower than it was and on the railway we have a higher and lower class than originally travelled by omnibus. We carry many who would not ordinarily travel by omnibus, and we carry, in the third class, many persons who are rarely seen on omnibuses.[42]

In fact by 1874 of the 28,000,000 journeys on the Metropolitan underground line, 64 percent of passengers traveled third class at a cost of 1d between adjoining stations.

Thus part of the process of destabilization of the resident West End community can be attributed to the huge increase in a traveling public using the new modes of transportation. While the centrifugal movement to the suburbs was met by new railway and omnibus links, which allowed regular commuters easier access to their workplaces especially in the City, a new and irregular group of visitors who did not form part of a working community were also encouraged into central London. In 1841, prior to these developments, it was possible to suggest certain recurring patterns of habit and behavior: shops opened at 8 A.M.; City cashiers and clerks began work at 10 A.M.; their dinner hour took place between 2 and 3 P.M.; Regent Street shops did most of their business between 4 and 5 P.M.; and by 6 P.M. business had finished, which in turn enabled eating houses in the West End to plan their opening hours to cope with the influx of people from the City. Shops closed by 9 P.M., which signaled the opening of shellfish shops and supper rooms.[43] Such a pattern, of course, enabled a degree of planning with implications for the places of entertainment, which could predict that, for example, a significant proportion of theatre audiences would be made up of those who shopped in Regent Street in the late afternoon, clerks and others from the City who finished work at 6 P.M., and shopkeepers and their assistants who were able to attend at half-price. Henry Solly, the future Unitarian minister, for instance, worked as a clerk in a broker's office in Leadenhall Street. He finished work at 5 or 6 P.M. and regularly went to Covent Garden to see Fanny Kemble or Macready.[44]

As yet the suburban audience may not have been a sizeable one, given the cost and uncertainties of public transport.[45] This, however, was going to change rapidly, and can be measured by changes in the facilities offered to the new visiting population. Though the large hotels attached to railway terminuses did not emerge until the boom of the 1860s, even by 1841 visitors could be pointed towards fashionable hotels like the Clarendon in New Bond Street, Warren's in Regent Street, and Wright's in Piccadilly, as well as comfortable, if not elegant, hostelries associated with the mail coach runs, like the Golden Cross at Charing Cross. Visitors could also go to taverns like the Crown and Anchor in the Strand, the British Coffee House and Tavern in Cockspur Street, and the Cocoa Tree in St. James's Street. Inevitably, however, at this period the concentration of taverns and hotels was to be found on the perimeter of the West End especially in the City. Board and lodging houses were particularly designed for bank and commercial clerks in the City while those in the West End were intended to service "the accommodation of gentlemen visiting London for pleasure, members of Parliament, public functionaries, etc" and were available in a range of prices from £1 11s 6d to £4 per week.[46] Ten years later, it was estimated that the lowest scale of expenses for a trip to London lasting eight days was £3 13s 4d per person, made up of a return railway fare of £1, eight breakfasts at 9d, eight dinners at 1s, eight suppers at 9d, a bedroom with boot cleaning at 1s 2d per night, beverages at 8d per day, and amusements including trips on the Thames at £1 for the period. Obviously such an expenditure was not seen as a regular occurrence, since it represented a week's income even for an established member of the middle class earning a minimum of £150 per year.[47]

In 1862, *Cruchley's New Guide to London* lists the usual tariff for first-class West End Hotels as 2s 6d for a bed (5s with a private sitting room), 1s 6d for "attendance" by chambermaids, 2s 6d for breakfast, 5s for dinner, and 2s for tea (i.e., high tea in the evening). By 1885 the numbers of hotels serving the West End were legion, but the first-class ones, which excluded the station hotels – "more suitable for passing travellers, who wish to catch an early train, than for those making a prolonged stay" – were now only accepting prior bookings, and were regarded as expensive, with bedrooms from 3s to 10s, breakfast 3 to 4s, dinner 5 to 10s, with service charges 1s 6d to 3s per night, clustered round Regent Street, Piccadilly, and the western extremity of Oxford Street near Hyde Park. Boarding houses by this time had been supplemented by private apartments. They were regarded as a more economical alternative to hotels for those making a prolonged stay in London, given that for a sum between 30s and 40s per week upward, they offered all food and accommodation. *Baedeker*, however, suggested that private apartments of furnished rooms with families would be more appropriate for short-term visitors. The most expensive apartments in the West End charged between £2 and £15 per week and were located in the streets leading from Piccadilly, though less expensive ones could be found in the streets off the Strand. *Baedeker* also quotes charges for visitors who were prepared to travel from districts further afield – Bloomsbury for instance had lodging houses charging 15 to 21s per week while suburban bedrooms and board could be obtained for 10s per week. The guide recommended that such visitors would be likely to require only breakfast and tea in their rooms and to patronize the pastrycook's shops, oyster rooms, and restaurants elsewhere.[48] Restaurants in the West End responded as well to this change in clientele and their new habits. The dinner hour by 1885 now took place between 4 and 8 P.M., after which many of them closed, though some of the "less pretentious establishments" retained the older habits by having opening hours between noon and 5 or 6 P.M. Many of the restaurants were now also significantly placed adjacent to theatres: the Gaiety Restaurant on the Strand offered dinner from 5:30 to 8 P.M. at a fixed price of 3s 6d; the Criterion at Piccadilly Circus operated by Spiers and Pond offered the same with a French dinner at 5s. Similar restaurants were to be found near the Adelphi and Vaudeville theatres while the Albion and Old Drury tavern were in the immediate proximity of Drury Lane Theatre.

WEST END AMUSEMENTS

Accommodation, food outlets, and transport facilities provided the infrastructure that enabled visitors to indulge themselves in those amusements offered in the West End.[49] The West End at the beginning of our period resembled a rather haphazard fairground, with each booth displaying its wares for a passing trade. In 1841 visitors were pointed towards the Gallery of Practical Science off the Strand, the Museum of the Zoological Society in Leicester square, the displays at the Egyptian Hall, Piccadilly, the Polytechnic Institution in Regent's Street, the National Gallery in Trafalgar Square, the Cosmorama, Regent's Street, the permanent Fancy Glass Exhibition, the Strand, and the Panorama in Leicester Square. Most of these charged 1s per person as an entry fee and some, like the Cosmorama, and the Leicester Square panorama, closed either at dusk or at 6 P.M. Others continued into the evening – the Polytechnic was open until 10:30 P.M., the Adelaide Gallery in the Lowther Arcade until 10 P.M., the Egyptian Hall in Piccadilly from 7 to 9 P.M.[50] After dark, visitors were free to enjoy the most significant amusement which the area offered, the theatre.

Prior to 1866 fifteen theatres located in the West End represented 41.7 percent of the capacity of all metropolitan theatres. After 1866 the boom in theatre building that resulted in the construction of the Holborn on the northern periphery of the West End; the Globe and Opera Comique in Wellington Street off the Strand; the Gaiety, Vaudeville in the Strand itself; and the Criterion in Piccadilly Circus, increased those numbers by over 25 percent to 52.2 percent of the overall 1866 figures. In 1866 it was calculated that London music halls and entertainment galleries could accommodate 79,300 people per day (excluding the Crystal Palace, which could accommodate 100,000 per day). At the same time, metropolitan theatres could offer a total of approximately 53,518 places. The fifteen located in the West End could accommodate 22,345: by 1866, this had risen by 5,643 to 27,988 at any one time.[51]

Cruchley's Guide in 1841, at the start of our period, identified those theatres that it regarded as preeminent: the patent theatres, Drury Lane and Covent Garden, and the King's Theatre, or Italian Opera. The last was described as "the most fashionable evening resort of our nobility and gentry" where "persons attending the pit are expected to appear full dressed; that is, frock coats, coloured trowsers [*sic*], boots, etc., are not admissible." The theatre's prices reflected this appeal to exclusiveness: the performances commenced at 8 P.M. and admission prices were half a guinea to the pit (although prior booking at a bookseller dropped the price to 8s 6d), and 14s 6d to orchestra stalls. Drury Lane and Covent Garden are recommended more for their impressive architecture and interior fittings than for the excellence of their dramatic offerings. Drury Lane's saloon, which communicated with the box lobbies, is described as forming "a promenade, rather celebrated among the bachelor community for its frail attractions." At this stage, admission to Covent Garden was more expensive than to Drury Lane.[52] Both commenced at 7 P.M., as did the Haymarket whose price mirrored those of Drury Lane. The Haymarket was singled out for its comedy and the fact that "every line is distinctly heard." Its comic reputation was shared by the Adelphi in the Strand, which under the Yates management, had identified it as "a favourite resort of the laughter-loving gentry . . . [and] one of the most fashionably attended of the minor theatres."[53] The Lyceum, rebuilt after a disastrous fire in 1829, was not operating as a theatre but as a site for promenade concerts, charging 1s to all areas except the balcony circle at 2s. Like the opera, the concerts began at 8 P.M. On the other hand, some of the other so-called minor theatres appeared to be flourishing: the Strand theatre located at the eastern perimeter of the West End, opposite Newcastle Street, whose entertainments included "operas, burlettas and ballets," and the Olympic theatre, where elegant entertainments finished earlier than those at other theatres, had much to commend them. Indeed the Olympic is described as the "most elegant and most flourishing establishment of its class in London."[54] The only other theatres selected in 1841 were the two theatres to the north of the West End: the Princess's, which had just been built on the site of the Queen's Bazaar and which was only open for promenade concerts although it was intended to have dramatic entertainments during the summer, and the Queen's Theatre in Tottenham Street. Somewhat presciently, though the latter was described as having experienced considerable vicissitudes, "the excellent situation in which it stands ought to ensure it a genteel and fashionable audience, under the influence of good management."[55]

Although the prices of the boxes, and even admission to the pit at full price, suggest their appeal to a more affluent audience, half-price admission to the galleries was no more expensive than theatres in neighborhoods like Lambeth or Whitechapel. Lower prices over the Christmas holidays also suggest a desire to attract larger numbers including families. In 1841 therefore, it would be incorrect to assume that the West End theatres were in a position to exclude less affluent patrons such as the local working community. Yet the process of commercialization and exclusiveness that would isolate the West End was becoming evident. An indication of this can be measured by the erosion of the pit and the substitution in theatres of stalls placed in what was, after all, the best position to view what was happening on stage. In 1849, Drury Lane introduced three rows of orchestra stalls in front of its pit. This was a relative novelty outside the opera. The pit, moreover, had always been the most egalitarian section of the theatre. Yet by 1866 all the West End theatres had introduced stalls, and by 1874, they had discontinued the practice of half-price.[56] An article in *House-hold Words* on the opening of the New Adelphi under Benjamin Webster in 1859 had earlier identified the significant improvements that Webster had introduced at his theatre: the stalls in the pit as well as in the galleries now made it suitable for families, as did the discontinuation of half-price and the introduction of women as ushers.[57] The issue of half-price, a relic of popular theatregoing, is a significant one, and one to which we will return in the context of the commercialization of the West End. Half-price had always catered to those whose work practices prevented them from attending the theatre before 8:30 or 9 P.M., or to those who simply could not afford either the time or money to pay full price. It also appealed to patrons for whom the theatre was merely part of their nightly entertainment. Montagu Williams, a distinguished barrister, who had been an avid theatregoer from his youth, found the abolition of half-price regrettable: "how pleasant it used to be, after dining at one's club, to saunter round to the theatre at nine o'clock, and, for instance, see Robson [at the Olympic] in "Retained for the Defence", "The Thumping Legacy", or one or other of the little pieces in which he was so entertaining!"[58] The abolition of half-price and the consequent demand that all playgoers pay the full price of admission was an obvious act of discrimination intended both to exclude those like local shopkeepers and their assistants who might not have been able to afford full price, and to inhibit casual playgoers to whom theatregoing was merely an after-dinner bon-bon. In order to insure the highest box office return particularly in the case of the stalls and boxes, the attendance of such patrons was irrelevant or at least unreliable.

By the early 1880s the numbers of theatres in the immediate vicinity of each other had risen to twenty-three. The Haymarket area now had four theatres, together with the Alhambra and Empire music halls in Leicester Square and the Royalty in Soho, but the biggest concentration occurred in the Strand. In addition to Covent Garden, Drury Lane, the Lyceum, and the Olympic, lying just off the Strand, the existing Adelphi and Strand theatres had been augmented by seven more. The only theatre remaining to the north was the Princess's, since the Prince of Wales's had closed in 1882, and the Holborn, built in 1866, had burned down in 1880. With the exception of the Adelphi, which commenced at 7:15 P.M., all other theatres commenced between 7:30 and 8 P.M. By this time the price of a stalls seat was uniformly either 10s or 10s 6d, with the gallery at 1s, with the exceptions of the Globe in Newcastle Street, Drury Lane, the small Royalty theatre in Dean Street, and the Alhambra, which all retained a 6d gallery.[59] The uniformity of prices was complemented by one of repertoire. With the exceptions of Drury Lane, the Lyceum, the Princess's, and the Adelphi, and the two opera houses, Covent Garden and Her Majesty's (formally the King's), all the other theatres based their offerings on comedy, opera bouffe, operetta, burlesques, and farce – in effect, manifesting all the characteristics of a themed environment.

Up to the 1830s regular theatregoers – local residents, those who patronized the West End regularly after work, or those who lived in sufficient proximity to gravitate naturally to the area for their leisure – helped to sustain theatres even after fashionable audiences declined. Progressively, however, this support evaporated as well, and the decrease in regular patrons was the cause of much of the theatrical insecurity that prevailed until at least the end of the 1840s as a result of the free enterprise that the Theatre Regulation Act had promoted. Nevertheless, a core of inveterate theatregoers remained throughout the period even if their evidence tends to reflect the practices of journalists or the habits of a wealthier clientele. Dickens's playgoing, for example, spanned the gamut of West End taste. He wrote on one instance to an actor, William Mitchell, whom he met while on his tour of America in 1842, that he had been "a very staunch admirer" and had seen him at the Queen's, Covent Garden, the Strand, and the St. James's in the 1830s, in plays as various as a burletta by Henry Mayhew, a burlesque opera by Gilbert à Beckett, a military spectacle by Planché, and J. T. Haines's farce *A House Divided*.[60] He wrote to Macready in 1848: "I am going to take Drury Lane – the Strand – the Olympic – the Victoria – Sadler's Wells – and the Marylebone. I don't mention the Haymarket, because (though I am going to take that too) it's a mere fleabite."[61] Again when he was staying at the offices of *All the Year Round* by himself in 1860, he wrote to say that he was "taking a stall at a Theatre every night,"[62] including the Christmas pieces at Covent Garden and the Lyceum. On the occasions he didn't accompany his family to see, for example, Hollingshead's farce *The Birthplace of Podgers* and *Tartuffe* at the Adelphi, he went with Clarkson Stanfield, Mark Lemon, Daniel Maclise, Wilkie Collins, or John Leech, all of whom were his artistic or journalistic friends, to see plays which included Tom Taylor's *Still Waters Run Deep* at the Olympic or Webster in *One Touch of Nature*.

Although they did not form part of Dickens's circle of friends, the records of theatregoing by George Eliot and Anthony Trollope within the period are remarkably, but not surprisingly, similar. Both went to see Kate Bateman in *Leah, the Forsaken* at the Adelphi in 1864, although George Eliot sat in a box with G. H. Lewes while Trollope preferred the stalls.[63] At that performance they would probably have met George Augustus Sala, together with Horace and Augustus Mayhew and Charles Kenney: Sala maintained that they went "at least three times a week to the stalls at the Adelphi for the express purpose of weeping bitterly over the woes of the persecuted Hebrew maiden."[64] Eliot also visited the Lyceum from her house in The Priory, Regent's Park to see Charles Dillon as Belphegor in 1856 and also in 1878 when she saw Irving as Louis XI and was accompanied by her niece. She also ventured out to the St. James's to see a French company in 1853, to the Princess's to see Charles Fechter as Hamlet and Stella Colas as Juliet in 1856 and 1862 respectively, and to Drury Lane to see a matinee session of the pantomime — she was surprised to see the theatre full of children on this occasion.[65] Despite the Haymarket company's reputation for comedy, Eliot found her visit in 1853 to be "a dreary amusement," and she had little respect for the "wit" of the performers.[66]

Montagu Williams as a young man was a theatregoer of catholic tastes who saw most plays from the pit. He went to the Adelphi to see Wright and Webster, to the Lyceum when it was managed by the Keeleys and, subsequently, Eliza Vestris and Charles Mathews, to the Olympic for Robson as we have seen, to the Princess's to see Charles Kean's Shakespeare revivals, as well as his production of *The Corsican Brothers*, and finally to the Haymarket, where he saw Taylor's *The Overland Route* and Sothern as Lord Dundreary in *Our American Cousin*. He also devotedly followed Marie Wilton from the Strand to the Prince of Wales's theatre. He made a practice of attending first nights and, in so doing, was aware that the same people seemed to be present in the stalls and boxes at all major openings. Laura Hain Friswell, the daughter of the essayist and critic James Hain Friswell, was just such a person. She mentions that in the 1860s and 1870s, she and her family went to the theatre three or four times a week, habitually sat in the boxes, and usually walked to the theatres from their house in Great Russell Street, Bloomsbury. She was equally at home at the Prince of Wales's (to see Robertson's *Caste*) and the Princess's theatres as in the Surrey (to see Slous's *True to the Core*) or in Sadler's Wells (to see Henry

Marston as Iago opposite Phelps).[67] In her case, she and her family appear to have followed actors who formed part of her circle. William Creswick, who lived close to her in Bloomsbury Square, had invited her to the Surrey. Marston and Irving were also family friends, and it was Irving who invited the Friswell family to the openings of Byron's *Dearer than Life* at the Queen's Theatre in Long Acre in 1868 and *The Bells* at the Lyceum in 1871.

Yet while this evidence implies the continuing presence of professional men and women who were actively involved in earning their livings through journalism or the law, it begs the question whether they could be regarded as typical theatregoers. Outside their circle the evidence of those who personally visited the West End is scant although it offers some tantalizing glimpses of a much more heterogeneous audience. Arthur Munby, for instance, went on occasions to the theatre with his mistress Hannah, a domestic servant, and gives us a rare personal glimpse of the gallery. We find him in the Haymarket in 1860:

> met my Juno at the Haymarket Theatre to see Tom Taylor's ingenious and spirited piece *The Overland Route*. We went to the gallery, of course; Hannah had never been to any other part of a theatre except once, when "William the groom" took her with an order to the boxes — actually the boxes! — at Astley's. Poor child! She did not presume to recognise me in the street, but waited above in the Gods. As for me, to stand in the mob at the gallery door in the Haymarket, to sit in the gallery among the "roughs" by the side of a maid of all work, and drink with her out of the same bottle between the acts — is not this the very nadir of vulgarity and degradation?[68]

His comments reveal a middle-class man out of place in the gallery and very aware of a class distinction. At the same time, Hannah found the gallery totally appropriate. In a letter to Munby, she tells of visiting the gallery at the Princess's together with her friend Ann and meeting a young man and his sweetheart who gave them ale, ginger beer, and oranges.[69]

Frederick Wilton living at 91 Nichol's Square, a short distance from the Britannia theatre in the East End, visited the West End on a number of occasions. It shows that it was perfectly feasible to visit the West End from the East End and that the numbers of such visitors may have been significant. He went together with his daughter Jessie to the Prince of Wales's Theatre in 1865 to see Robertson's *Society*, and after

{ *Theatric Tourists and the West End* }

West End Audience. From Illustrated Sporting and Dramatic News,
10 November 1881.

seeing his friend the actor Frederick Dewar, walked home at midnight.
On another occasion they went to see Dewar as Captain Crosstree in
Burnand's burlesque of Jerrold's *Black Ey'd Susan* at the Royalty Theatre. He mentions in his diaries that the excursion cost them 1s 10d by
bus.[70] In 1868 his wife and daughter went to the Marylebone Theatre
by the new Underground. Given that they made the journey at the request of the Britannia's manager Sarah Lane to see if a performer,
Mary Saunders, would be suitable for the theatre, the journey was
probably paid for, but he mentions that it cost them 4s 7d, a considerable outlay to a man whose income was £2 a week, supplemented to an
extent by his wife's pension of £7 10s per quarter from the Royal General Theatrical Fund.[71] On other occasions, he went to the Queen's
Theatre, Holborn, to the Alhambra, the Haymarket, the Vaudeville,
and the Lyceum to see performers like Irving, Buckstone, Charles Mathews, Jefferson, or Phelps.[72]

Whether any of these accounts reveal the typical West End theatregoers remains unclear. Most reveal that they had an interest in the plays
or players, the result of personal contacts or professional loyalties. In
fact, their evidence suggests that going to the theatre in the company
of one's family or social circle was an important feature. Equally, it
suggests that the West End attracted a socially mixed audience that

may have preserved elements of popular theatregoing. Their habits demonstrate both catholicity and similarity: they support actors whom they know or admire, wherever they happen to be appearing, regardless of the play itself, and, apart from occasional forays to the opera, they tend to patronize the same West End theatres — the Haymarket, the Adelphi, the Olympic, and the Strand, in particular. None of them however could be designated as West End tourists — most worked as journalists in the area or had direct connections with the theatre business or indeed lived close by.

7. A National Drama: A National Theatre and the Case of Drury Lane

he year 1843 was a watershed for the large patent theatres. No longer able to command by right, they also came to realize that the market for "legitimate" drama was shrinking. Or rather that they would need to ask whether there was a viable market for legitimate drama at all, and if there was, who would be attracted to it. The response of the patent theatres proved an unsatisfactory one. In an effort to determine the viable market and to keep their large companies employed and therefore profitable, managers were perpetuating the practice of indiscriminate competition. They had tried to combat the popularity of the "minor" theatres in the period before 1843 by absorbing the popular forms of melodrama and burletta. Now with a level playing field where all challengers were welcome, they faced each other. They were attempting, said one commentator, to "succeed by commixing every species of entertainment – huddling together tragedy, comedy, farce, melodrame, and spectacle – and striving by alternate exhibitions to draw all the dramatic public to their respective houses." This was creating a disastrous competition with unfortunate artistic results:

> tragedy and comedy are simultaneously played at Drury-lane, Covent-garden, and the Haymarket; while opera runs against opera at Covent-garden and Drury-lane; the three refuse to limit themselves to any one species, and perform all pieces indiscriminately, with corresponding imperfection.[1]

In the period of theatrical free trade after 1843, tensions would be exacerbated between the received traditions of theatregoing and the developing self-conscious respectability of the middle class, and between the commercial imperatives of theatrical speculators and the belief that the role of the theatre lay in the propagation of social cohesiveness through its preservation of a national literary drama.

By 1847, however, Covent Garden had become exclusively an opera house and the Haymarket could rest on its laurels as the identifiable home of English comedy and a venue for visiting stars. Drury Lane, however, had little to show after Macready's management ended in 1843. Nevertheless, it continued to be regarded as a cultural icon and the symbol of a "national theatre" despite dwindling audiences and often futile attempts by managers to recall its former glories. Yet just as an examination of the motives behind the 1809 Old Price Riots at Covent Garden reveal the possibility of organized transgressive behavior in the auditorium, so there is much to suggest that Drury Lane played its part in acting as a virtual or symbolic public sphere during the troubled period of the 1840s, reproducing in its auditorium a simulacrum of actions occurring in the public sphere of mass politics. By the 1840s the physical location of Drury Lane was a culturally "eccentric" one in that, with the drift of those who considered themselves members of the fashionable classes increasingly to west London, Drury Lane found itself on the eastern periphery of a cultural district rather than at its center.[2] Yet its symbolic significance could be harnessed to good effect, particularly its size and its proximity to the southern portions of Clerkenwell where mass Chartist protest was taking place. An instance of this occurred in 1848 in what came to be known as the Monte Cristo riot, the last occasion that Drury Lane would act as a site for a political and cultural debate in our period. On 3 June, *The Times* announced that the Parisian Théâtre Historique would perform Alexandre Dumas's own version of his hugely successful novel *The Count of Monte Cristo* over two nights commencing on Monday 12 June, just as the Chartist leaders announced a nationwide demonstration for the same date. Potential theatregoers in 1848 as well as the authorities were well aware of the revolutionary spirit that was sweeping Paris and continental Europe generally.[3]

Prior to this date, there had already been signs that some kind of organized theatrical resistance was being contemplated. The *Spectator* referred to "large placards" being posted everywhere, "which at first look like new manifestations of Chartism, but on closer inspection they turn out to be appeals to the British authors and actors, calling upon them to resist the foreign invasion by petition."[4] On Monday 12 June, an organized disturbance occurred before the curtain rose. Tin whistles had been distributed and shouting, which drowned out the performers, continued for three hours.⁵ Umbrellas were put up in the pit; people in the boxes were singled out and pursued outside the theatre and there was considerable evidence of the involvement by those whom *The Times* called "persons of standing and respectability in the histrionic profession."⁶ Spectators wore placards inserted into their hats saying "No English authors or English actors are allowed to exercise their talents in Paris." George Augustus Sala contributes a revealing account of the disturbances:

> On the first night of Monte Cristo something like an "O.P." riot took place. I was in it, on the anti-Gallican side. I was a pugnacious youth with a great capacity for quarrelling and getting my head punched; and I think that on the evening in question I emerged from the auditorium of Drury Lane with my clothes torn half off my back, my hat crushed into a pulp and my visage decorated with at least one black eye, most assuredly not of a lovely appearance. The turbulent pittites hooted the French actors, threw potatoes and cabbage stumps from the adjacent market onto the stage, and even pelted with analogous missiles Albert Smith and a strong party of Gallicans who were seated in the front row of the dress circle.⁷

On 13 June, two men, Charles George and William Harrison, "respectably dressed young men," as well as Harry Linden and William Attwood, described as actors, were found guilty of riot. On 14 June the disturbances resumed: pit benches were overthrown, decorative box panels were torn off, and banners were waved. There were more arrests, in particular Sam Cowell, whom *The Times* identified as the "leader of the rioters."⁸ He had been at Drury Lane on both nights and indeed had pulled off his coat to make himself conspicuous. Cowell had started off in the boxes and then moved to lead the demonstration from the pit. The following day the House of Commons received a petition from Benjamin Webster, the proprietor of the Haymarket, complaining of the great hardship brought about by the country being overrun by foreign dramatic performers. At the same time, Charles Mathews, joint lessee together with his wife Madame Vestris of the Lyceum theatre, was contemplating taking out an injunction against the Théâtre Historique.

Thus spectators going to the theatre on 12 June were bombarded by placards announcing the nationwide Chartist day of dissent, those proscribing its London manifestations, and those which could be taken for Chartist notices but which were, in fact, condemning the French theatrical invasion of Drury Lane and fighting a rearguard action against free theatrical trade. Certainly the spectators who decided to go to Drury Lane were prepared for an affray. Though the evidence identifies the presence of actors and a few men who may have been clerks in City offices, their numbers may well have consisted of those who had been sworn in as special constables to protect West End property. Sala records that he joined Benjamin Lumley, the manager of her Majesty's Theatre in the Haymarket, who had brought his backstage crew armed with wooden truncheons. They were part of a contingent that included "the assistants of nearly every tradesman in Piccadilly and Regent Street, together with the tradespeople themselves, bankers and solicitors and their clerks, actors, and doctors, and 'men about town.'"[9] That the incidents at the theatre like those described by Sala, were surrounded by expressions of strident nationalism and xenophobia is supported by the evidence of the broadsheets and placards.

There is little evidence, however, to suggest that those arrested were motivated by a fervent concern for things English. More significantly perhaps, there is also little evidence to suggest that they were starving dramatic authors or actors. Sam Cowell was a popular and successful performer and Attwood was a member of the Olympic Theatre company. At the same time, it is equally difficult to imagine Drury Lane filled with French-speaking enthusiasts of Dumas, unlike the much smaller St. James's theatre, located on the western periphery of the West End, which did cater to just such a clientele. Considerable numbers of French supporters entered the lists on behalf of the Théâtre Historique, many of whom were women: the newspapers disparagingly called them well-known French prostitutes. The arrested individuals, however, were not the French supporters. Thus the Monte Cristo riot may imply that the spectators' reception of the Théâtre Historique's performances was influenced by political circumstances and that it was manipulated by sections of the theatre industry for their own ends.[10] Or rather, that the theatre space was being used to dramatize the dilapidation of a national institution whose state could be obliquely attributed to royal neglect. The terms used in the riot remarkably echo those used in the streets and in the press: the fear of invasion, the dereliction of responsibility on the part of the ruling class, the depressed economic circumstances, and the rights of free speech and assembly.

The events of 1848 at Drury Lane reveal another side of the maneuverings that were taking place as a direct result of theatrical deregulation. The inability of Macready to identify Drury Lane as "a national house" for "a national drama" left the field open to a number of theatrical contenders who realized that the strident nationalism in the streets might be harnessed to their own advantage. At the same time Queen Victoria was sufficiently disturbed by the talk of assassination in the streets and the turmoil generally in continental Europe, to intervene in order to hasten the arrests of Chartist leaders. If the theatre, therefore, had the potential to be a site for the crystallizing of republican sentiments, it might equally be utilized as a means for "diverting attention from more dangerous subjects."[11] Perhaps it was timely to act: early in 1848, at the instigation of Prince Albert who sought to develop a Court theatre not unlike those in Germany, the Queen discussed the desirability of inviting an acting company to Windsor. She attended Charles and Ellen Kean's benefit at the Haymarket on 3 July, and, even-handedly, signaled her intention of being at Macready's farewell on 10 July, before he left on a tour of the United States. Sometime round 13 July, Queen Victoria invited Charles Kean to Windsor Castle in December 1848 for the commencement of what would be designated the Windsor Theatricals. Coincidental with the Queen's invitation to Charles Kean to become the "Master of the Revels" at Windsor, was the publication of Effingham Wilson's *A House for Shakespeare: A Proposition for the Nation*[12] in which he proposed that the government should support a specially designated theatre "where the works of Shakespeare, the world's greatest moral teacher, may continually be performed."[13] In addition, such a theatre would serve as a home for the "legitimate drama," a role which Drury Lane had obviously relinquished, and would set a national standard for popular education and literary excellence.[14] Such a theatre in the middle of the West End would confer "on the cultural practices housed there a legitimacy . . . denied to performances of the same text in a peripheral space."[15] Charles Kean felt that his royal appointment gave him an imprimatur to erect just such an edifice. As well, these maneuverings provide an important theatrical perspective to the thinking that informed the construction of the Great Exhibition.

At the same time, the years immediately preceding the opening of the Great Exhibition were not propitious. On 29 March 1849 the Olympic theatre burned down, and Drury Lane closed early on 30 March. All the theatres in the eastern part of the West End were doing badly,[16] and there was generally a sense of desolation. It is little wonder that theatre managers hoped that the promise of the Great Exhibition would herald a new age. There is much to suggest that many, however, were totally unprepared for it. When James Anderson undertook the management of Drury Lane in 1849, he admitted quite frankly:

> there was much excitement respecting the wonderful structure which was being raised in Hyde Park for the Great Exhibition of the following year, and my friends strongly urged me to take advantage of the situation by becoming managers of some London theatre. The opening of the Exhibition would bring thousands of strangers to the Metropolis, who must, I was told, go to the theatres in the evening, if only to rest themselves after standing on their legs all day. Foreigners would rush to see Shakespeare well acted, especially Germans . . . and the Americans, who adore the drama, were expected to come over in crowds.[17]

His artistic policies, however, which merely replicated the repertoire of his mentor Macready — *The Merchant of Venice*, *As You Like It*, Sheridan Knowles's *The Hunchback* and *The Love Chase*, Shakespeare's *Othello*, and Schiller's *Fiesco, or, the Revolt of Genoa* — reveal that Anderson was choosing plays, not with a potentially new audience of Germans and Americans in mind, but rather on the basis of a loosely constructed repertoire of plays that he knew well and in which had played successfully in the provinces. His policies were predicated upon the existence of an English audience unchanged since the eighteenth century, and sharing the same cultural values. As Leigh Hunt noted with some regret in 1850:

> Forty or fifty years ago people of all times of life were much greater playgoers than they are now. They dined earlier, they had not so many newspapers, clubs, and pianofortes; the French revolution . . . had not yet opened a thousand new channels of thought and interest, nor had the railroads conspired to carry people, bodily as well as mentally, into as many analogous directions. Everything was more

concentrated, and the various classes of society felt a greater concern in the same amusements.[18]

Before Drury Lane could hope to resume its position as "a national theatre," managers would need to attract a new audience consisting of disinterested spectators weaned away from the pianofortes of their drawing rooms and bringing with them the inquisitive habits that the railroads had begun to foster.

We have earlier referred to J. W. Cole's account of the "invasion" of London by French tourists during the Great Exhibition. He also remarks on the effect of such visitors upon theatres generally:

> nearly all [places of amusement] reaped an abundant harvest, principally gathered in from the visitors and foreign strangers . . . at least five-sixths of the audiences were composed of foreigners and holiday excursionists from the country.[19]

Kean probably benefited most from the Exhibition, partly because the Princess's theatre was situated on Oxford Street, one of the two main thoroughfares between Hyde Park and the West End, and partly because it was the closest of West End theatres to the Exhibition.[20] Even before his management, however, the theatre had already attracted reasonably affluent and respectable audiences. At the same time what differentiated Kean's management was his concerted attempt to match in the theatre the Exhibition's image as a tourist site and to redefine the role of the theatre as an element in an emerging West End "theme park." Kean's meticulously authentic spectacles replicated theatrically the actual physical evidence that "surrogate tourists" might find in the Courts of Industry and the Medieval Court at the Crystal Palace, or at sites like the British Museum's Nineveh Court, where authentic archaeological artifacts were displayed. Yet at the Princess's, "theatric tourists" could marvel at a different kind of authenticity. Archaeological findings and the Medieval Court could, as it were, come to life: their simulacra gained an immediacy and authenticity by their integration with the fictional lives of the characters on stage. It forms a principle that site managers have recognized ever since in what Daniel Boorstin rather magisterially calls the construction of "pseudo-events."[21] Moreover, the elaborately detailed program material which Kean gave to his spectators provided tourist "markers" to enable the experience to be judged and revived afterwards. Queen Victoria's patronage of both the Exhibition and the Princess's theatre further cemented the points of similarity between the two theme parks.

On the other hand, Charles Kean's management of the Princess's theatre from 1850 to 1859 signaled a radical change to the idea of a "national drama." He was able to take advantage of the collapse of Drury Lane as a venue for legitimate drama and of the relegation of Shakespeare to Sadler's Wells in the suburb of Islington. He provided instead a site where tourists could feel that they were acquiring cultural capital, and which accorded directly with the aspirations of an up-wardly mobile middle class. Kean's antiquarian and spectacular recrea-tions of Shakespeare or Byron made the past immediate and accessible, and the results would affect all future productions of the "national drama" as the equally spectacular presentations by Chatterton at Drury Lane and Irving at the Lyceum corroborate. Indeed, managers like Ir-ving, who followed Kean's lead, would come to recognize that the ac-quisition of status and prestige, a powerful force in tourist motivation, could be harnessed for their own ends. Spectators were now being redefined as informed and educated tourists who were seeking new knowledge or at least its representation. This recognition by socially conscious managers began the process of site sacralization that would define the West End as London's preeminent theatre district, and contribute significantly to the commodification of nineteenth-century theatre.

W. E. Gladstone, an inveterate theatregoer, went to see most of Kean's productions of Shakespeare as well as *The Corsican Brothers*. On the other hand, the Queen's taste was rather for Boucicault's adap-tation of the Dumas novel – she saw it four times – than for Shake-speare.[22] Interestingly, Gladstone's theatrical habits complement prac-tices that we have noted in the case of Montagu Williams. As a busy parliamentarian, Gladstone was not always able or inclined to eat early in order to view the entire performance. He appears to have seen the entire programs at the Princess's on only six of the nine occasions on which he visited. He saw what must only have been portions of *The Winter's Tale* (3 July 1856), *The Tempest* (8 August 1857), and *King Lear*, on the second occasion that he saw Kean's performance (10 June 1858): his diaries note that he saw the first two between 9 and 11 P.M. Fashion-conscious audiences undoubtedly responded to the example of royal patronage and were also in a position to view the performances critically, although not from the perspective that Kean would have intended. Lady Charlotte Schreiber noted that after an early dinner on 27 November 1857, she "went up to London" to see *The Tempest*. She admitted that her party had good stalls, but she found them too close to the action: "the dresses were so dirty that it was quite disgusting to look at them. When they were fresh the stage may have looked pretty. . . . The acting throughout was infamous."[23] Cole refers to numbers of clergymen who came to Kean's productions of Shakespeare: on one occasion (3 May 1859) half-a-dozen clergymen attended his *Henry V* and in a letter to Kean, one of them commented that he had provided them with a memorable lesson in elocution.[24] The evidence for gallery audiences, however, at the Princess's is scant. Richard Schoch refers to a letter from George Bartley to Kean in 1857 in which he refers to his housekeeper Eliza and her sister being there.[25] There is, however, little in the evidence of both fashionable and other visitors to the Princess's theatre to support Richard Schoch's argument that in Kean's displays "the historically conscious nineteenth-century theatre found its audience an aggregate of strangers and tried to transform them into a collectively constituted national subject."[26]

In the meantime, the question of what was to happen to Drury Lane, in the light of diminishing audiences, was becoming an urgent one. When E. T. Smith became the theatre's manager in 1852, there was talk that the Duke of Bedford's interests might be better served if the theatre were demolished and the land sold for redevelopment. Unlike all the other West End theatres that were each striving to define their niche in the new marketplace, Drury Lane was a large theatre that preserved the conditions of popular theatregoing. In 1854 Dickens wrote to his friend Miss Burdett Coutts once again requesting the use of her box at Drury Lane, saying that he had "a morbid curiosity to see a new phase that is to be presented there, in the decline of a place that I once had a great interest in."[27] In 1860, announcing the forthcoming season under E. T. Smith's management, the *London Review*, under a heading "Old Drury" wrote:

If we wanted a forcible illustration of the fallen condition to which the stage has been reduced by the inevitable operation of an open trade in plays and play-houses, we should point to the spectacle presented by this house at the present moment. It has everything in its favour that prestige, ample means and resources, and a clear stage can bestow. It can command whatever talent is to be had in town or country; and it has a complete sweep of the unoccupied domain of legitimacy. But out of all these advantages, the utmost that can be accomplished is the presentation of . . . pieces . . . which are calculated to flourish, not in this vast area, but in such snug domestic houses as the Strand or the Olympic.[28]

These observations reflect the perception that the Drury Lane Theatre had failed to live up to certain expectations. Dickens's disappointment of course stems from the fact that he had been an assiduous supporter of the theatre during the management of Macready and had seen Macready give his final performance there in 1851. The resonances, however, of the sequence of failed managements as well as the nostalgic comments by writers suggest a more complex problem. Obviously there were factors that militated against Drury Lane forming part of the West End success story in our period. Mismanagement may form part of the story but location, a failure to establish its repertoire as distinct and unique in a climate of increasing tourist discrimination and selectivity, and changing audience taste may well contribute the rest. The terms "Old Drury" and "the National Theatre" are used indiscriminately in the period, the one measuring present achievements by evoking past and often illusory triumphs, the other measuring present deficiencies by allusion to the perceived absence of a theatre whose very fabric might embody national aspirations.

Smith was faced with the unenviable task, as all commentators noted, of winning back an audience that had moved elsewhere. He realized that the cause of legitimacy at Drury Lane was lost and this would color his decisions for the next ten years. These were much resented by observers like Dickens who were looking for someone to assume Macready's mantle, and to whom Charles Kean's Shakespearian revivals appeared as mere manifestations of vulgar cultural self-aggrandizement. Rather than try to cultivate the ambience of a private space, Smith determined to capitalize upon the theatre's potential as a popular venue available to all. He indicated that he would reduce prices, abolish boxkeepers' fees, dress the boxkeepers in scarlet livery so that they could easily be identified, and that he would offer refreshments in the saloons at prices calculated to persuade audiences to buy them at the theatre rather than at competing public houses outside.[29] He opened on 27 December 1852 with a version of *Uncle Tom's*

Cabin by Fitzball and a pantomime by E. L. Blanchard, *Harlequin Hu-*
dibras; or, Dame Durden and the Droll Days of the Merry Monarch
with reduced prices: stalls, 4s; dress boxes, 3s; other boxes, 2s 6d; pit,
2s; lower gallery, 1s; upper gallery, 6d; with no half-price to pit or
galleries.[30]

Smith also seems to have initiated the practice of regular matinee
performances of the Christmas pantomime and these attracted and
would continue to attract large numbers of children, as George Eliot
noted some years later.[31] During his second season, he developed his
matinee practice so that there were regular Wednesday performances
of his evening programs. Thus on 30 September 1853, the *Theatrical*
Journal noted that in addition to children from the Duke of York's
school, there was a general audience made up of "families resident in
the neighborhood of the metropolis, who could not conveniently remain in town to the late hour at which the evening performance terminated." The extension of the practice of matinee performances also
proved attractive to the more affluent:

> The Wednesday morning performances, being highly patronised, will
> be repeated. The house has been well attended and a great number
> of the nobility have witnessed the performances this week.[32]

He invited the children of the St. Martin's and Holborn Public Schools
and those of the Children of the Jews Orphan School in Whitechapel
to a matinee on 23 November. It was an astute strategy intended to
reach parents and school superintendents whose patronage might be
attracted through their children. By 1859 the matinee performances
had established themselves as a regular feature. We find for example, a
matinee performance of the pantomime being given to the Licensed
Victuallers School and to soldiers who had been awarded medals for
the Crimean War:

> The children were accompanied by Mr. Smyth, Governor of the In-
> corporated Society of Licensed Victuallers; Mr. Rowntree, past gov-
> ernor of the same, and a considerable number of the trustees and
> committee . . . who with the school-master and school-mistress sat
> with the 150 scholars in the first rows of the pit. The Crimean men
> of seven or eight hundred, occupied the upper boxes, while the dress
> circle was filled with family parties and supporters of the licensed
> victuallers' excellent charities.[33]

On 11 March 1859, two hundred Greenwich pensioners saw a revised version of Jerrold's *Black Ey'd Susan*, retitled *William and Susan*. They had been admitted free, and "Mr. Wheatley, the Greenwich omnibus proprietor, very liberally gave his omnibus free of charge."[34]

Obviously Smith had realized early that there was little point in trying to emulate theatres like the Lyceum or Strand, but rather that Drury Lane's position had to be reestablished using other means. For example, he used Mark Lemon's adaptation of *Fanny the Little Milliner*, called *The Begging Letter*, as a curtain-raiser for his 1853 pantomime. Critics noted with surprise that this play, a transpontine drama of horror, was enthusiastically received by the audience. Smith's determination to win new patrons as well as the hearts and minds of those who lived in the immediate area, was further expressed by his distribution of soup to two hundred poor people every Tuesday and Friday at the theatre after Christmas.[35] It was an unusually severe winter, and although Douglas Jerrold may well have been right to disparage Smith's gesture as a publicity stunt, it was an extremely effective one, which drew people to the doors of Drury Lane.[36] In 1854, Smith achieved another publicity coup. He announced a charity matinee on 8 March under royal patronage intended to help the wives and children of soldiers who had gone to the Crimean War. Again astutely, given the proximity of Drury Lane to the City, Smith solicited the support of the Lord Mayor and Sheriffs of London, who arrived in state at the theatre on the day to join the aristocratic patrons – the Duchesses of Inverness and Montrose, the Marchioness of Aylesbury, and Lady Palmerston amongst others – and the Duchess of Cambridge and the Princess Mary. The performance opened with an elaborate tableau for the national anthem sung by soloists and chorus and accompanied by the band of the Royal Household Cavalry. Smith's achievement was a considerable one especially in the light of its evident symbolism. He had placed Drury Lane, at least for the moment, once more at the center by drawing together the aristocracy from the West End and the traditionally democratic representatives from the City, which now also included the most influential businessmen in the country. Moreover, the scale of performance on a patriotic occasion, which included a state procession in the streets, particularly suited the dimensions of Drury Lane.

Smith's own background as a man of business and a property speculator brought him much closer to the magnates of the City than to the aristocrats of Kensington, and Belgravia, and this would color many aspects of his populist policies at Drury Lane.[37] In this context, his introduction of opera at cheap prices was a significant West End innovation: it was certainly not intended for the traditional opera audiences. His aggressive entrepreneurial policies enabled him to produce Meyerbeer's latest opera *L'Étoile du Nord* on 26 February 1855, thereby beating Covent Garden by four months, and *La Sonnambula* on 16 April, performed by an Italian company in Italian. "We do not see any reason why a cheap opera should not obtain a footing in this country," wrote the *Era*.[38] In May he reduced his prices of opera even further: he lowered gallery prices to 6d, dress circle to 2s 6d, the second circle boxes and pit to 1s, and stalls to 4s, with private boxes seating two people to 10s 6d, and with those seating four to £1 1s. Surprise was registered by the newspapers, which felt he was taking cheapness too far, although they agreed that a new audience was being attracted to an entertainment traditionally appropriated by the wealthy.[39] In fact by 10 June:

> The houses have been good, particularly in the economical quarters, and it is surprising and gratifying to see with what attention the sixpenny spectators listen to these long musical performances, which, unrelieved and unexplained by intelligible dialogue, can be enjoyed on the strength of the music only. . . . The lessee would do well to print a small handbill elucidatory of the plot, for the use of the pit and gallery visitors.[40]

Smith's profitable season demonstrated the efficacy of his policy, although at a dinner in his honor, Smith made no secret of the fact that should operatic taste flag, he would reinstate horsemanship at a moment's notice.[41] Smith realized that a completely new audience now could be offered the kind of treatment hitherto reserved for an affluent aristocracy. Indeed, the whole necessity of tailoring theatrical openings to the practices of a fashionable "season" was itself being called into question:

> A certain number of rich and influential families . . . leave London for the country or the Continent at the end of July or the beginning of August, and of these the majority do not arrive in London until the middle of May. The period known as "the season" becomes shorter and shorter every year and already, to many persons, lasts only two months. . . . Some families dread the expense of London life, which is constantly increasing. . . . Then the railways enable

persons who have estates in the country to come to London much oftener than they would have found convenient many years since, and there are not the reasons which formerly existed for staying in the metropolis when once there. . . . [T]he fact is that the present fashionable season lasts scarcely longer than from the middle of May to the middle of July. . . . The fact is that we have a large and rich public . . . ready at any time to support any entertainment that is really good, and this quite independently of the fashionable few who only remain in the metropolis during the two or three hottest months of the year.[42]

Smith had realized that the key to Drury Lane's success lay in a policy of commercial populism. Yet the pressure to establish a "national theatre" continued. After Samuel Phelps retired from Sadler's Wells in 1862, he was invited by F. B. Chatterton to perform Byron's *Manfred* on 10 October. Moreover, Chatterton was able to persuade him to remain as the theatre's resident star in Shakespeare from 1864 until 1869. As Daniel Barrett has suggested, Chatterton's determination to have Shakespeare figure prominently under the new management was prompted by his desire to have the theatre as the London home of Shakespeare during the 1864 Tercentenary year and for it to become, in fact, a National Theatre.[43] Phelps's supporters did indeed follow their favorite actor to Drury Lane, enabling *The Times* to assert that: "Drury Lane is now indisputably the house of the poetic drama. . . . The revival of a tragedy at Drury-lane is now anticipated as an important event by hundreds of persons who not long since would have regarded it with utter indifference. A *prestige* is restored that has much of the practical virtue of a patent."[44] Yet Chatterton's policy proved commercially unviable.

Chatterton's decision to put on Andrew Halliday's *The Great City* as the Easter attraction in 1867 would prove to be much more influential, signaling the position that Drury Lane would come to occupy in the West End, while initiating a tradition that would identify the theatre once more as a quasi-national venue. The play's popularity was enormous and stemmed from its celebration of contemporary London, and also "the fact that a real hansom cab, a real horse, and an absolutely convincing driver appeared on the stage . . . [which] caused first a thrill of excitement and then a complete sensation."[45] It thus complemented

the celebration of the mundane, which we have noted in the con-
temporaneous policies of the Bancrofts at the Prince of Wales's. The
Drury Lane playbill for 1 June 1867 stated "THE GREAT CITY has
been witnessed and pronounced by ONE HUNDRED AND FORTY
THOUSAND persons to be the most interesting, exciting, truthful and
successful Drama of modern times."[46] When its season ended on 16
August it had drawn crowds reputedly totaling 386,000 people, the
same drawing power as the Crystal Palace. The following season began with Halliday's adaptation of Walter Scott's *The Fortunes of Nigel*,
set in Jacobean London. The play was a calculated "hybrid between
pure legitimacy and thoroughbred sensationalism . . . and showed that
the policy of tacking by steering a popular course, yet sailing with the
wind of classicalism, was, at any rate, a prudent one in its results on
the treasury."[47] Depictions of London, the *Spectator* suggested, were
more than a "coarse morbid liking to see in the theatre some familiar
street":

> The passion . . . is the sign of a new-born desire to idealize the
> unique metropolis in which we live and work. . . . The impossibility
> of living in more than a part of London, – the majority of its in-
> habitants hardly going beyond certain restricted areas in their or-
> dinary life, and making an excursion into remoter regions as they
> would into a distant country, – tends to increase the desire for the
> stage representation of what people live amidst, but do not really
> see as the people of a compact little city may see and know almost
> every feature in the aspect of their residence.

The play depicted on stage a Fleet Street and a Strand existing at a
time when "the English nation . . . [had been] awakened to the consciousness of national strength and life."[48] By realizing a Jacobean
world on stage Chatterton was accomplishing a trajectory between two
periods of "national consciousness," an aim which, in aesthetic terms,
the advocates of a literary national drama had failed to achieve.

This commenced a pattern whereby Chatterton would begin each of
his seasons with an autumn melodrama, and, until 1874, these would
be provided by Halliday's adaptations of Scott, all of which proved profitable.[49] By now the prices of the more expensive seats at Drury Lane
had risen: private boxes ranged from 1 guinea to 4 guineas; stalls, 7s;
dress circle, 5s; first circle, 4s; balcony, 3s; pit, 2s; though the lower

gallery remained at 1s and upper gallery 6d. These prices prompted Boucicault to write to the *Era* and complain generally about the high cost of admission to West End theatres. The letter prompted a flurry of responses from the various managers, who argued that cheaper prices were now impossible, and that in any case the market would ultimately determine prices. In particular, Andrew Halliday, probably representing Chatterton's interests, argued that:

> to reduce the price of the stalls to 2s 6d. or 3s. would be to drive away the class of persons who now occupy those seats. It is well known to managers that the regular patrons of the stalls cannot be induced to occupy the dress circle, though the seats are quite as comfortable as the stalls, and the price is less. The dress circle again, is occupied by a distinct class of playgoers, who are genteel and select in their way – well-to-do middle class folks, who consider themselves a cut above 2s. company.[50]

Drury Lane was responding to the West End lure of commercialization, and when the 1873 to 1874 season commenced with Halliday's version of *Antony and Cleopatra*, the surrender was complete. It marked the end of a "literary" Shakespeare, and the confirmation that the identity of Drury Lane was that of a theatre of spectacle and perhaps, given the paucity of actors whose talents could not transcend "the furious noise of preparation for 'heavy sets' behind the scenes," that "Shakspeare [*sic*] can only be presented as it is now – in the form of a pageant."[51] It was the logical outcome to the commodification of "the national drama" that Charles Kean had initiated. The practice, on the other hand, of a spectacular autumn melodrama, followed by an equally spectacular pantomime, would be continued by Augustus Harris after 1880.

Yet even though Chatterton and Harris could make fortunes out of Drury Lane, the conditions which surrounded this revitalized icon had changed little. "A Rambler" in the district immediately surrounding Drury Lane noted the appalling living conditions of a porter at the theatre who earned 17s a week and lived together with his wife and four children in a room twelve feet square for which they paid 3s 6d per week. He described their living conditions and those of the others living on wages of less than 15s a week and who could not afford to pay 2d to travel to work let alone the 6d gallery at Drury Lane itself, as characterized by a "poverty which abounds in this unfortunate locality, . . . deeper, and more grinding than almost any I have witnessed."[52] He may as well have been describing the rookeries of the 1830s. Drury Lane had indeed succeeded in reestablishing itself, but its audiences were drawn from among tourists, who responded to it as a nationalist rather than as a "national theatre."

THE COMMERCIALIZATION OF THE WEST END

In his book about Charles Kean, J. W. Cole remarked that the huge numbers of London visitors to the Great Exhibition prompted theatre managers to extend the runs of their productions, and that this had disadvantaged regular playgoers: "that the same pieces were repeated night after night with little thought of variety, was a tolerable proof of continued attraction, and also that the attraction rested with the strangers."[53] Though local residents in the West End may still have continued to attend the theatres on an occasional basis, the emergence of a tourist industry progressively inhibited and ultimately excluded them. Regular playgoers (by definition not tourists), who in the period before 1850 responded to frequent program changes in a variety of theatres, found themselves from the 1860s faced by more theatres performing a much narrower repertoire for longer runs.[54] Just as their choices were being eroded, so regular playgoers found themselves constrained by practices such as the abolition of half-price, the subdivision of the auditoriums into exclusive economic zones defined by orchestra and dress circle stalls, and later starting times, all of which effectively marked the demise of informal theatregoing. These theatrical practices, moreover, were geared to maintaining a steady flow of constantly new audiences, animated by the same sense of predictable occasion and demanding comfort and reassurance – the new tourists. By this stage, managers needed to take little note of regular patrons since "the enormous increase in the size of London, and the existing facilities for reaching it from all country parts, have had the effect of multiplying the number of playgoers."[55]

At the end of 1851 the Crystal Palace was dismantled and moved to Sydenham in south London, where it would remain as a constant reminder to theatre managers of the theme park's continuing attractiveness. In the same year Macready retired from the stage, leaving the "national drama" in the hands of Charles Kean. As well, Charles Morton opened the Canterbury Music Hall in Lambeth, thereby entering the lists as another threatening competitor to the primacy of theatregoing. To some theatre managers, however, the music hall might have appeared as a godsend, just at the time when West End theatres were trying to eradicate the practices of popular theatregoing. If working classes could be siphoned off by the music halls, the way might be left clear for theatres to define themselves as respectable and middle class, unencumbered by contact with those whose knowledge of social observances and manners might be suspect. However, as the evidence presented to the Select Committee in 1866 would show, such a result was far from certain.

The evidence submitted to the Select Committee on Theatrical Licences and Regulations revealed the extent to which theatre managers generally, and West End managers in particular, felt that they were being challenged by the competition of the music halls.[56] The stridency of their protests implies that they felt the music halls had depleted their theatres of a significant section of their audiences. In the leadup to the Select Committee's deliberations, theatre managers had memorialized the Lord Chamberlain. They argued from a position that would appear merely protectionist[57] and increasingly specious: that the ability to smoke and drink while watching a performance in a theatre would be "degrading to the Drama, foreign to its character and purpose, and will tend to lower the social and artistic status of its professors," and, whereas the music halls "are notoriously the resort of women of bad character, many of whom are admitted gratis, and there ply for hire . . . this class of visitors has for many years been carefully excluded from theatres."[58] Such a position whereby theatres took a moral and cultural high ground was difficult to sustain, particularly when a large hall like the St. James, capable of accommodating five thousand patrons daily, was able to attract a "superior class" comprising "ladies and children" during the day, and the "aristocracy and nobility" in the evening, to performances by the Christy Minstrels.[59] Perhaps significantly, the Committee's evidence does not include an input from Chatterton who was managing Drury Lane at the time. He may have been distancing himself from the position of West End managers, which appeared to be a new manifestation of protectionism, and was particularly awkward for him as the manager of one of the former patent theatres. The evidence does, however, show the importance managers were placing upon respectability, and the fact that tourists now included not only overseas visitors, but large contingents of provincial as well as suburban patrons, whose tastes and habits were attuned to regarding the West End as part of cultural sightseeing.

There was, however, something disingenuous about Webster's and Buckstone's protestations that the music halls had drawn off sufficient half-price patrons to the galleries or pit to warrant the discontinuation of half-price. After all, at Webster's Adelphi, the gallery audience only represented a fifth of his theatre's capacity. Much more likely was the determination on the part of significant audience numbers to go to the theatre late, so that the main attraction now needed to start later, preceded by a curtain raiser.[60] It was more cost-effective to adapt the program to meet the habits of those who would be likely to take a box or stalls seat, than to take a gallery audience into consideration. Yet Dion Boucicault felt that "the large sums of money which have been made by managers in pits and galleries of theatres lately, has been principally due to the pits and galleries of the theatres being recruited from the music halls."[61] On the other hand, Astley's theatre, which had always relied on a substantial proportion of its audiences arriving from elsewhere, had abandoned half-price, even though E. T. Smith, who was now managing the theatre, was failing miserably. In fact, the evidence suggested that there was little distinction between music hall and theatre audiences at least among those who might patronize the pit and stalls. The West End music halls attracted artisans with their wives and daughters, shopkeepers, and young "idle" men, many of whom especially on a Saturday night could be found either at the Alhambra or in the galleries of Drury Lane. Even Webster was forced to admit that "many people of the same class go to music halls as well as theatres."[62] This overlap of audiences was noted by Frederick Stanley who was representing London music hall proprietors: he thought that portions of the same audiences might go to either the music hall or the theatre on different occasions but that it was unlikely that either audience would go two nights in succession.[63] The absence of regular or closely repeated attendance at either the music hall or the theatre reinforces one of the repeated assertions before the Committee, that theatres could no longer rely on a supply of regular theatregoers.[64] E. T. Smith agreed that the numbers of "people who go to the theatre every night" was finite.[65] Buckstone protested that at the Haymarket:

I can only keep on the Haymarket as a legitimate comedy theatre; and that class of entertainment is not suited to the galleries; our pit is full, and our boxes are full, but the galleries and the slips are not so full when we have a high-class comedy.[66]

The protestation reveals not only a strong desire to maintain a class difference between the theatres and music halls, which the evidence for a cross-fertilization seemed to be thwarting, but also to identify gallery audiences as essentially lacking in literary taste. Yet as we have seen the Haymarket's audience comprised both classes: Frederick Wilton, Arthur Munby and his mistress Hannah, as well as Montagu Williams, had seen Tom Taylor's *The Overland Route* and Gladstone refers to visits he made with his family on a number of occasions, which more often occurred at 9 P.M. Indeed, he also saw *The Overland Route* on 18 April 1860.[67]

We have seen that a feature of popular theatregoing at all London theatres had been the absence of prebooking for both the pit and the gallery. From a managerial perspective, the failure to implement an effective system of prebooking prevented managers either from planning ahead, or putting in place strategies to encourage regular playgoers. Some efforts, however, were being made: John Hollingshead pointed out to the Committee that the Haymarket was currently advertising that seats could be booked a month in advance and that in the case of a popular piece, a fortnight in advance was obligatory.[68] Of course, it had always been possible to reserve box seats in advance of the performance — at the opera this had been obligatory — and tickets could be purchased either at the theatre's box office or at designated booksellers and libraries between 10 A.M. and 4 P.M. The pit and the gallery, however, traditionally depended on regular theatregoers who were prepared to endure the discomfort of a rush at the opening of the doors, or who responded to impulse buying on the night, and the very absence of booking enabled those whose work practices prevented them from reaching the box office, to just turn up for the performance. Pit patrons in the West End continued to be as resistant to the French notion of a queue as the gallery audiences at other theatres:

Even though it might be difficult to make English people submit habitually to the system of the *queue*, there would, we think, be no objection on the part of the most independent pleasure-seekers for a little guidance in order to prevent their crushing each other to death. . . . A visit to the pit of a London theatre is a pleasure in which no man with a heart complaint, or a woman in an interesting situation, can safely undergo.[69]

Yet pit and gallery audiences continued to enjoy the melee of the last minute, or to rush the doors with little apparent regard for life and limb, making financial control of the box office a difficult one. It was this lack of financial control that undoubtedly explains, in part, the incursion of orchestra stalls, and the lack of attention paid to the galleries. As John Pick has pointed out, when prebooking became the norm for West End theatres in the period after 1880, this effectively contributed to the further marginalization of the working class, whether that class resided in the immediate neighborhood of the West End or traveled from elsewhere.[70]

The minutes of evidence also point to two crucial elements that had their impact upon theatregoing. Patrons were seeking to identify particular theatres with their particular kinds of entertainment, in order to allow them to make decisions about "where to find the particular class of performance that they wish to see."[71] This factor had been identified as early as 1850, and certainly formed part of tourist preplanning. The other element was the undeniable presence of the large traveling population. John Hollingshead declared:

> I believe that most of the London theatrical audiences are likely composed of country people; the old Metropolitan playgoer lives out-of-town, and does not go so much to the theatre as he used to; the provincial people come up to the town, and fresh audiences are created every night.[72]

Horace Wigan, the manager of the Olympic, after stating that playgoers generally had increased in number, agreed:

> I think it has increased in London, very much so, and it is constituted of an entirely different class; that is to say, I do not believe that Londoners support London theatres; they are in very great proportion supported by the population *viagère*.[73]

The comforts and expectations of these "travellers" needed to be taken into account. They were certainly prepared to take theatres to task if their comforts were not seen to. This can be attested from letters which were written to the Lord Chamberlain from dissatisfied patrons, who had visited the West End from suburbs reasonably close to the West End, like Sloane Square, Streatham, and Barnes.[74] In these particular cases, patrons wrote to complain that access to the stalls and dress circle at the Lyceum and Drury Lane had been blocked by chairs in the passageways. Other discomforts that managers needed to address or control included the venality of box-keepers, poor ventilation, and the weather conditions. Dickens had been outraged, when he arrived late at Her Majesty's Theatre to hear Jenny Lind in Donizetti's *The Daughter of the Regiment*, at the failure of the box keeper in the 1840s to recognize his name, and the temerity of the assistant in demanding a fee to ascertain whether Dickens's wife and sister had in fact arrived at their box.[75] He was equally taken aback when he discovered that the numbered stalls at the Olympic did not reserve him a particular stall, but merely referred to the numbers present. He left when he discovered that he had sat in a seat previously occupied and subsequently reclaimed by a person who had obviously gone for refreshments during a break in the action.[76] George Eliot preferred going to the opera largely because "the house is airy and the stalls are comfortable."[77] Flora Tristan, who had noted the presence of prostitutes at theatres in the 1830s, found the theatres, lit by gas, to be excessively hot in summer and cold in winter. She also found that the gas caused giddiness, particularly the lights in the candelabras fixed to the three tiers of boxes.[78] Things were no better at some theatres thirty years later:

> Bad ventilation and villainous draughts [*sic*] are perhaps two of the major annoyances and inconveniences to be met with at a playhouse . . . either it is too hot from the concentrated heat arising from the respiration of the accumulated audience, or it is too cold from an excessive draught admitted through the doors from the staircase or passage.

The writer in the *Theatrical Journal*, singles out the lower gallery at Drury Lane as particularly cold, and the gallery of the Princess's as suffocatingly hot.[79] On another occasion, the Olympic was targeted in 1866 by a patron who had come from Kensington, and complained about the "heat and foulness of the atmosphere," going on to say:

> I am myself a man in the vigour of manhood, and was accompanied by a gentleman of the same age, and although we desired to witness a particular incident in the play, we were unable to remain

in the Theatre more than a quarter of an hour in consequence of the heat and the unwholesomeness of the atmosphere: if there are means of ventilation which I could not discover, they are certainly insufficient.[80]

He wrote this in November, no doubt coming late to a crowded performance in early winter.

In fact, weather was a factor that would affect attendance not only of a George Eliot. We find, for instance, in the Lord Chamberlain's papers, reference to the difficulties facing residents of Camberwell, Dulwich, Brixton, Norwood, Clapham, Kennington, and Balham, who not only find the West End expensive, but impracticable in winter.[81] Notoriously, cabmen would charge exorbitant fees to exploit the hazardous conditions.[82] A fine night in summer could also inhibit theatregoing:

A fine night is a *bête noir* to theatre managers. . . . The stalls and balcony are not so much affected as the cheaper parts of the house, for the people who come from the country to do the London season . . . can afford to occupy seven shilling seats.[83]

At theatres that habitually finished late, like the Haymarket, audiences started to leave before the performance had ended. Smith at Astley's tried to ensure that his performances were over before 11 P.M. so that patrons who "come up to town on purpose" could catch the 11 P.M. train.[84] Those who worked in the City needed to be up early and most suburban business men were in bed by 11 P.M. during the week. Those who missed the last train from London required a stay at a lodging house or the hire of a carriage, which prohibitively cost between 25s and 30s.[85]

Yet the full effect of the influence of tourists on West End theatres had hardly been estimated. Many managers were still indulging in practices which were demonstrably out-of-date. For example, the sense of a theatrical "season," which had been geared to terminate when fashionable Londoners left the city, was now irrelevant:

Although London managers have long ceased to provide for purely London audiences, and the old resident playgoer . . . is pushed by the spread of building into distant suburbs . . . many theatrical directors still act as if they were supported by their former patrons, who used to dine early, believe in the theatre as an institution, and did not live at Richmond, Finchley, Tottenham, or Reigate. The hay-making season and harvest time are looked forward to with some misgiving, an admission that country visitors are now large supporters of London playhouses, but more restlessness is shown when the railways appeal to the public by publishing their arrangements for summer pleasure traffic. Though those whose business it is to watch theatrical audiences can see no reason why Londoners going out of town should affect the welfare of entertainments largely fed by countrymen pouring into town, many managers think otherwise, and about the middle of June we hear of "last nights" and unusual "benefits."[86]

This pattern of West End attendance would remain the norm from now on. By 1871 Thomas Purnell could point not only to the fact that "the requirements of the present age" made serious drama unsuitable but also:

> The chief supporters of our theatres are country people, incited by the advertisements and criticisms they have seen in the London papers; those of the nobility afflicted with 'ennui' who have no engagement for the night; busy professional men who come at fixed intervals with their families; by men who go to the theatre from habit . . . and a large number of greengrocers and other shopkeepers, who have received orders for displaying playbills in their windows. These are the ordinary patrons of the drama, and it is their taste which has to be considered.[87]

Purnell's comments corroborate the evidence of the Select Committee: there were now few regular theatregoers and tourists were increasingly motivated by the West End's advertising strategies. These strategies, moreover, spread into the suburbs as well as the provinces. Transurban omnibuses carried billboards announcing West End openings, hoardings at building sites across London were plastered with details about West End productions, and advertisements appeared in national papers, trade magazines like the *Era*, as well as local papers like the *Manchester Guardian*, informing readers about companies being sent out with versions of West End successes. Those who could not afford to become West End tourists found that they could see approved touring versions of successful plays by a Robertson or Boucicault at local theatres. Like armchair travelers, suburban or provincial "surrogate tourists" could share in the experience of those who had actually been to the West End. There was little room for high art in a climate where theatre was attended on an occasional basis as a reward for services (like Purnell's shopkeepers), where the theatre provided a temporary antidote for boredom (Purnell's ennui), or where businessmen indulged their families at ritualized occasions like the annual pantomime.

Finally, to return to the 1866 Committee, which noted the growing significance of the matinee audiences. The experiment that E. T. Smith had started successfully at Drury Lane would have repercussions on patterns of playgoing, as well as suggesting the existence of differing and potentially lucrative markets drawn from fashion-conscious as well as suburban audiences.[88] Indeed, Frederick Strange felt that matinee playgoers formed a different class of audience, one that was prepared to pay 4s for a stall seat. Until the 1870s, however, the matinee program would merely be a daytime version of the evening performance. John Hollingshead claimed that he had been the first to offer a totally different program when he managed the Gaiety theatre after 1868. The costs of mounting a different program still made it unusual enough in the late 1870s to deserve comment. Yet the benefits and advantages of such an arrangement were obvious. By the end of our period, matinees were offered by most West End managers and typical audiences could be identified:

> The audience which patronises the theatrical matinée presents various features, which are distinctively and peculiarly its own. . . . It is conspicuous for the blending of the professional and theatrical element with the decorous suburban. . . . There are, too, the invalids of both sexes, who love the stage, but to whom the night air is the deadliest of foes . . . [and] those, lastly, who inform you that they never go to theatres on principle, but they occasionally make an exception in favour of afternoon performances. . . . Thus it is that the theatrical audience which affects the matinee is a motley composition of parsons and players, severely devout spinsters, superior men, and strong-minded women . . . the London lounger and the country cousin.[89]

Such comments again offer evidence of how middle-class habits might impact upon theatregoing. It was therefore necessary to take these into account:

It is easy to see what a boon these *matinees* are, especially to suburban playgoers. They can go quietly after lunch at home, or in town if they live too far off, and get back comfortably in time for dinner. There is no fear about catching the last train, or getting a cab or omnibus. . . . Then again a morning performance gives children a chance of being taken to the theatre. . . . It may be added also that, in the present foggy and unpleasant weather for example, there are worse places in which to spend a November afternoon than a comfortable and well-lighted theatre. It is not pleasant to go into a playhouse in the middle of a bright summer day, where the glare of the footlights contrasts unpleasantly with the sunshine without; but it is a very different thing in winter, when home may be dull, when the streets are uninviting, and when the theatre affords a welcome means of distraction.[90]

Thus the evidence before the Select Committee, while it tended to undermine some of the comfortable assumptions held by managers, at least in the West End, about the working-class basis of music halls, simultaneously reinforced the fact that the future of the West End lay in manipulating seat pricing, or half-price admission, so as to emphasize the exclusivity of theatres. Moreover, the conditions of theatregoing needed to reflect the sense of comfort and well-being that visitors associated with their own private spheres of activity, who were participating, in Nelson Graburn's phrase, in "the tourism of the timid."[91]

Yet such a ritualized occasion as the pantomime did preserve some of the older practices of popular theatregoing – the raucous interchanges between gallery, pit, and boxes; the tossing of orange peel and nuts by gallery members at those in the pit, about which Pückler-Muskau had complained in 1826; the sense of social occasion for all – though it remains unclear whether the descriptions of pantomime audiences in the 1860s or 1870s genuinely reflect their actual composition or whether reporters were creating an imaginary *theatrum mundi* comprising the "ordinary patrons of the drama." Thus, for example, in a picture of the Drury Lane pantomime of 1866 we find, in addition to the "famous general and his family," the author and his literary friends, the drama critic, and the "swell";[92] reference to a fictitiously named "Mr. Sittyman," whose name betrays his origins in trade or commerce:

a hard-working merchant . . . a dull, steady plodding man . . . a man who's home by the six o'clock omnibus to Peckham with the regu-

Drury Lane, first night of pantomime. "Boxing Night—A Picture in the National Gallery," by George Cruikshank, from 400 Humorous Illustrations, London, originally published in 1836.

larity of clockwork and whose only dissipation in the year is this one visit to the theatre with his children on boxing night.[93]

His wife and family are imagined as having caught a cab from home to the theatre in order to meet him after work. They sit in a box, and the writer indicates that other boxes have been taken by a "Mr. Louis Nemo," who "made a fortune supplying hot-water bottles to the army during the Crimean War," and who now wishes to enter Parliament, as well as a "Joseph Nemo," who is the local greengrocer. The names signal the author's attitude that they are both "nobodies" in a world of fashion. The presence of a junior clerk who is accompanied by country relatives and by whom he is intensely embarrassed in his quest for fashionable status, is also noted.[94] A less socially loaded description of a similar occasion at Drury Lane is to be found in the *Licensed Victualler's Gazette*:

> crammed from floor to ceiling . . . an epitome of London life. The little Arabs in the sixpenny gallery clinging to the rails for dear life . . . the young clerks and "young ladies" from the telegraph offices in the upper boxes, the substantial tradesmen's wives in the pit, the exquisitely dressed children in the dress circle, the cosy family parties in the private boxes including a grandfather and a three

year old darling, and the languid swells and haughty beauties in the stalls.⁹⁵

Such material, though seductive, in that it purports to reflect the reality of Victorian theatregoing on a particular and very traditional occasion, contributes to the elusiveness and lack of specificity of the actual evidence. Nonetheless, we do know that popular theatregoing died hard: the costs of West End theatregoing, the erosion of the sense of communal festivity and interaction between actors and spectators, the substitution of a private social ritual for a public one, all troubled theatrical observers.

A series of discussions took place in 1878 in the journal *The Theatre*, an organ that very much represented West End theatregoing values, which illustrated this uneasiness.⁹⁶ An article in the September issue on "the cost of playgoing," took managers to task for their failure to take into consideration the class of theatregoer who potentially would form the backbone of the theatregoing public.⁹⁷ Though the managers are not named, the focus is undoubtedly the practices of the West End and the economic obstacles that precluded a middle-class audience from frequent attendance. As a point of departure, the article refers to a typical family, in which the husband earned in the vicinity of £400 per year, and who intended to take his wife from his home in the suburbs, "in which most of his class live," to the theatre "with the comfort which is a lady's right." The writer imagines that the playgoer would buy two tickets to the dress circle, at a cost of between 5s and 6s a seat, and a program for a further 6d, and pay 6d each for the obligatory cloakroom facilities. The article concluded that, with the addition of refreshments and the cost of the journey itself, "the night's amusement leaves very little change out of a sovereign." Within this income bracket the article places all the "educated middle classes of small means and refined habits" including "professional men, and artists, and authors, and students of every kind except the small minority which has made out of art, or science, or study, an income equal to that of the uncultured tradesman."⁹⁸ Clearly the writer was implying that even the reasonably affluent occasional visitor, who formed a sizeable element of the new tourist class, might have to think twice before visiting the West End. The same financial constraints affected any serious, and by inference, regular theatregoer. The sentiments expressed are echoed in Frederick Wedmore's comments in the *Academy* in 1880. He regarded the "pronounced growth of luxurious expenditure" as the principal reason for the exclusion of regular playgoers from West End theatres. Instead of the theatre being "a general amusement and a method of cultivation," it had become "a costly indulgence for those who have richly dined,"[99] a view generally supported by Walter Besant, writing a few years later:

> The people of London have in great measure lost their taste for the theatres, because they have gone to live in the suburbs. Who, for instance, that lives in Hampstead and wishes to get up in good time in the morning can take his wife often to the theatre? It takes an hour to drive into town, the hour after dinner. The play is over a little after eleven; if he takes a cab, the driver is sulky at the thought of going up the hill and getting back again without another fare; if he goes and returns in a brougham, it doubles the expense. Formerly, when everybody lived in town, they could walk. Again, the price of seats has enormously gone up. Where there were two rows of stalls at the same price as the dress circle — namely, four shillings — there are now a dozen at the price of half a guinea. And it is very much more the fashion to take the best places, so that the dress circle is no longer the same highly respectable part of the house, while the upper boxes are now 'out of it' altogether, and, as for the pit, no man knoweth whether there be any pit still.[100]

Indeed, an urbane discussion about the necessity of the pit at West End theatres took place in the pages of *The Theatre* during 1880,[101] arising out of two occasions on which those who were accustomed to sitting in the pit created a disturbance. The first took place on 31 January, when the Bancrofts did away with the pit at the Haymarket (to which we have referred earlier), and relegated its habitues to a euphemistic "second circle." The second was the ejection of a group of young men who had occupied the first row of the pit at the Vaudeville on 29 May to see Albery's *Jacks and Jills*. They had found little to please them either in the play or the performances, and had tried to stop the play. The management with the assistance of the police ejected them. On the surface, the disturbances might appear to be little more than expressions of dissatisfaction with theatrical conditions and accepted conventions. Moreover, the urbanity of the discussions in the pages of *The Theatre* sprang from the fact that the journal tried hard to maintain a balanced argument: after all an organ of West End theatre governance was taking issue with managerial decisions made by its own members. The contributors to the first "symposium" were all named representatives of West End theatre: the author, Frank Marshall, the manager, John Hollingshead, the author/manager/actor H. J. Byron, as well as the editor and critic Clement Scott, who included a reprint of his article written for the *Era Almanack* in 1875, in which he had argued for the significance of the pit.[102] The contributors found themselves in a dilemma. On one hand, the abolition of the pit at one of the oldest theatres in London, known for its retention of conservative values, signaled the unmistakable end of a tradition of popular theatre, and was therefore to be deplored. On the other, the huge rentals of West End properties demanded a quick financial return for managers, especially in smaller theatres like the Haymarket. It was perhaps a little too accurate and too revealing, however, for Marshall to have Bancroft declare:

> The public for which I cater consists almost entirely of persons willing to pay more than five shillings for their seats, and they would not like to come into contact with the vulgar herd who pay less; therefore, following the example of those East-End theatres which cater for a public the majority of whom will not pay more than a shilling for their seat, I devote the greater part of my house to the majority of my patrons.

Contributors to the second "symposium" included David James and Thomas Thorne, the managers of the Vaudeville, who had assisted in the expulsion of the pit troublemakers, and had justified their actions in terms of their concern for the holders of stall seats, and Joseph Knight, the critic for the *Athenaeum*, who used the occasion to urge understanding for the financial burden shouldered by managers faced with a hostile reception. This discussion was a less comfortable one, because it involved both the inalienable right of audiences to reject shoddy, boring, or inadequate productions, and the intervention of police at the request of the managers to eject "a mischievous body of young men" who had forgotten "that a theatre means a serious undertaking and expensive responsibility to its management,"[103] and had taken exception to what James and Thorne called "superficial errors and inevitable 'slips' on the play's first night."

In both cases the behavior can be attributed to a resistance on the part of those who had traditionally occupied the best position in the theatre, to being marginalized either to a gallery, euphemistically labeled an "upper circle," or to an area behind those who could flaunt their economic superiority in the stalls. As all the contributors to *The Theatre* recognized, many of the fashionable stall occupants remained totally uninterested in the action on stage. The pit was traditionally egalitarian and some of the protest was undoubtedly class-based, just as the reaction on the part of the management was driven by financial concerns. After all, West End managers were habituated to noisy, male latecomers in the stalls who interrupted the action, made up of "scions of hereditary legislators, . . . baronets, guardsmen, and their hangers on," as well as "gentlemen whose days are given to commercial pursuits in the City, and whose evenings are devoted to enjoyment at the West End." Moreover, they did contribute economically far more than those who sat in the pit: "whatever their demerits . . . without their support the assistance of society alone would be insufficient for the material prosperity of the stage."[104] The discussion in *The Theatre* took little interest in the gallery audiences: by now, the financial return to managers in the West End of a full gallery was negligible by comparison with that of a full stalls or dress circle.

St. John Adcock's description of a West End audience, leaving the theatres of the Haymarket and Strand in 1901, reads curiously like that of an enthusiastic "pittite" who had been present for a performance of *Macbeth* at Covent Garden in 1837. At the end of the performance in anticipation of a supper of "oysters and porter" the "pittite" describes the audience preparing to leave:

> A modified wish to be gone is evinced by the audience at large, during the progress of the last scene; while many are on their legs, employed in shawling, cloaking, buttoning up their greatcoats. . . . Then follows the bustle of departure. . . . Loveliness remains impatiently shivering on the threshold [of the box portico], while gallantry runs to and fro in search of her ladyship's carriage. Then we have the call for hackney-coaches . . . the hoarse responses of the coachmen; the vociferations of footmen; the fiery zeal of link-boys.[105]

In Adcock's description immaculately groomed and bejeweled men and women are picked up by private carriages, which have been waiting in the side streets; others leave by cab or omnibus, including ladies in opera cloaks. Most leave for home, but many oyster bars and confectioner's shops are patronized by those "who have flocked in from pits

*"Leaving His Majesty's Theatre," St. John Adcock, "Leaving the London
Theatres" in George R. Sims, ed.,* Living London *(1901).*

and galleries, with a sprinkling from the dress-circles." The unfashionable elements are to be found in the "humbler public-houses" — men
with their wives or "sweathearts [*sic*]" consuming alcohol and a sand-
wich or pie in the company of young City clerks and shop assistants.[106]
By this stage, however, such a description, like those of the Drury Lane

pantomime audiences, may well be the product of nostalgia and wishful thinking.

We have been investigating what happened to West End theatregoing after the dissolution of the patent monopoly, and have suggested that there were two fundamental changes that need to be addressed. The first is a shift from popular theatregoing to theatregoing as a middle-class and fashion-conscious leisure activity, propelled by some of the same concerns that motivate a tourist industry. The second is from a perception of the theatre as animated by cultural expectations, to one of the theatre motivated by commercial imperatives. At the same time, we have noted that the West End possessed little of the strong community or neighborhood basis that underpins our discussions of all the other theatres. Yet, at the end of our period, the West End, in the upholstered ceremonial occasions at Irving's Lyceum or in the jingoistic autumn melodramas and Christmas pantomimes at Drury Lane, did succeed in creating a surrogate or symbolic community, comprised of people with few geographic or spatial ties, but linked by a sense of belonging and common values. In this respect the West End and the values that it promulgated helped to create "an imagined community." It became the locus for the dissemination of nationalism and embodied the imperial values of the British nation-state.[107] It is therefore hardly surprising that the issue of a "national theatre" should be revisited at the end of our period. After all, 1878 saw Henry Irving deliver a paper at the Social Science Congress advocating the establishment of a theatre in which ideal standards would be substituted for commercial imperatives,[108] and 1879 saw the publication of Matthew Arnold's influential *Nineteenth Century* article, which drew attention to the comparative advantages the Comédie Française enjoyed as a state subsidized theatre. It was perhaps ironic that he should have drawn his inspiration from a French company, which had in fact been invited by John Hollingshead to perform at the Gaiety, a theatre usually identified with burlesque.[109]

CONCLUSION

London theatre audiences in the mid-nineteenth century were so diverse that generic definitions are clearly inappropriate. This diversity existed not only across London but also within specific theatres and neighborhoods. Indeed, London theatre audiences were far more mobile socially and physically than previous accounts have implied. Yet in the past such audiences have usually been defined in terms of binaries based on the notions of "center" (the West End) as opposed to the "periphery" (south London or the East End, for example). Such oppositions, which rely on the conflation of class and topography, preserve rigid stratifications, the inadequacies of which are demonstrated in this study. We have suggested that it is perhaps time to reinvent Victorian audiences and the language by which we describe and conceptualize them. In particular it is time to break away from the notion that the word "audience" can be used in a generalized or generic way in any discussion of the Victorian theatre. Our examination of specific neighborhoods and individual theatres demonstrates the difficulty of making broad assumptions of any kind, of even the notion that an audience for a specific theatre is representative of a specific community. Indeed, at a time when the very concept of community is being contested in scholarly discourse, it is significant that we have found it less difficult to discuss a theatre's relationship with its neighborhood than to identify a specific community for which it catered.

Our investigation of London theatre audiences in the mid-nineteenth century is particularly indebted to the work of Michael Booth, who has clearly outlined some of the issues with which a study of this nature should engage:

> Generalising about nineteenth-century audiences is, in the absence of a great deal more evidence than is presently available, a risky business, especially when it also leads to possibly unwarranted conclusions about the drama and public taste. It is also difficult to generalise about the conventional divisions between the audience in box, pit and gallery, because at different prices and in different lo-

cations the social composition of the audience could differ widely. Nevertheless, the social and cultural implications of a play performed at a Victorian theatre, and therefore the play itself, cannot be completely comprehended unless one is aware of the audience for which it was performed, and that audience will change, theatre by theatre, district by district, decade by decade. This is so in the West End as in the East, or in any theatre district. The Victorian audience lived its own culture and its own network of economic and social relationships; it did not exist only in auditoriums for the benefit of the scholar. It lived in a wider society of which the theatre was a small part; fully to understand it means knowing something of its social and cultural habits, jobs, wages, cost of living, places of residence, class status, means of transportation, patterns of migration and settlement, moral and political outlook – anything that goes to make up complete human beings living at a chosen moment in history who came together for the collective but usually incidental purpose of seeing a play.[1]

We have tried to identify aspects of "the wider society" to which Booth refers and to give them the weighting which he feels they deserve. We have also gained much from Clive Barker's pioneering study of the audiences at the Britannia Theatre: in many ways it provides an admirable model for the sort of quantitative investigation we have undertaken.[2]

We believe that only by assembling the sort of quantitative data for which Booth calls can we effectively ask challenging questions about the mid-Victorian audience and dislodge some of the prior qualitative judgments that have all too easily been accepted as primary evidence without reference either to context or ideology. In so doing we are advocating neither a vapid empiricism nor a return to the essentialism that has dogged earlier accounts of Victorian audiences. Rather we believe that all evidence has its value, and that we must engage with the fullest range of quantitative data available before moving on to more qualitative analysis. The more we know about nineteenth-century audiences (or the more we are aware of the inadequacies of previous sources), the more we are likely to avoid the ahistorical assumptions made by those who eschew the thorough investigation of documentary sources. Yet, even after such investigation, we remain aware that what we offer is informed speculation.

{ *Conclusion* }

This study has entailed the thorough examination of public records, police reports, census returns, newspaper accounts, playbills, transport timetables, communications networks, biographies, autobiographies, diaries, indeed any source that might broaden our understanding of mid-Victorian theatre audiences. We have assumed that actors' addresses on benefit bills may tell us something about a theatre's accessibility in general or that the existence of a toll on a bridge crossing the Thames may have some bearing on theatre attendances in a specific neighborhood. We have found that careful analysis of communications networks or of census returns may often destabilize categorizations of audiences based on prejudicial social assumptions. In effect we have followed Lawrence Stone's argument that quantitative data "uses as ammunition apparently precise, testable data, which have to be either confirmed or rejected on logical and scientific grounds, instead of strings of selective quotations from favourable sources."[3] In so doing we have discovered that many of the press and police reports, not to mention the familiar accounts by Charles Dickens, G. A. Sala, Henry Mayhew, and others, have created a mythopoeic impression of the nineteenth-century audience. Whether or not such accounts were well intentioned, they reveal contemporary agendas and prejudices that actually obscure the possibility of reconstructing such audiences. (We should however make it clear that our own concerns are interpretative and historiographical; we are not advocating reconstruction per se, which we deem to be impossible.)

In investigating the audience through systematic analysis of quantitative data, we have tried to remain open to the discursive approaches provided by recent theoretical models.[4] Nevertheless, we have chosen to avoid some of the more obvious models available to us, insofar as we have qualms about the sustainability of their application across our field. Foucauldian discourse, for instance, not only sits uneasily in any discussion of nineteenth-century English theatre,[5] but has also been turned into far too closed a system for our particular needs. The same applies to the "carnivalesque": Bakhtin's concept may have a lot to offer, superficially, to a study of this nature, but it is also in thralldom to its own specificity. We do not deny that issues of order, disorder, discipline, power, coercion, subversion are relevant to any investigation of nineteenth-century audiences, but we have preferred not to let these concepts overdetermine the scope of this particular study. Nevertheless, we would hope that this study might well contribute to future discussions of audiences in which such concepts are debated. If we were to take this study further theoretically, it would be more along the lines made possible by Bakhtinian dialogics and around the models provided by Michel de Certeau, both of which allow for a more open and contested discussion of spectatorship. As Angela C. Pao suggests, de Certeau's shift of emphasis to the manipulation of a representation "by users who are not its makers . . . and the secondary production hidden in the process of its utilization" (*L'Invention du Quotidien*) provides a useful antidote to Foucault's privileging of "*les appareils producteurs.*"[6] J. S. Bratton has also provided a useful discussion of the "negotiations" that occur in popular nineteenth-century theatre, again encouraging a less restrictive interpretation of the power relationship between performance and spectators.[7]

The guiding principle behind this study has been to dismantle the myths and ideologically driven constructions through which the composition and behavior of nineteenth-century audiences have been conveyed to us. We hope that we have forever exploded the simplistic assumptions that have previously informed the categorization of West End, East End, and Surrey-side audiences in the nineteenth century. In this respect popular journalism has a lot to answer for and Dickens is the chief culprit. Just as Dickens invented the Victorian tradition of Christmas, so he invented an image of the Victorian theatre, which lived on in popular memory and tradition, but which is not always substantiated by other available evidence. Nevertheless, he created the formulas by which popular audiences were to be described throughout the Victorian period. Even the reliability of public records needs to be scrutinized, particularly during W. B. Donne's period as Examiner of Plays. Donne had such a specific agenda for the theatre and for the audiences he wished it to attract that we must view all documents skeptically, not as primary evidence, but as potentially tainted by the ideological agendas embodied in the theatrical functions of the Lord Chamberlain's Office.

In sum, there was no such thing as a Victorian audience, but rather a variety of audiences, embodying a wide range of perspectives. We can never be sure who exactly constituted these audiences, because even social demography can only suggest possibilities; it cannot provide definitive answers. Yet, even if social demography cannot tell us exactly who attended London theatres in the nineteenth century, it can at least broaden or even redefine prior perspectives. Thus there is little evi-

dence to support the rigid class segregation of theatres by neighborhood, a notion to which some earlier commentators have subscribed.
We have established that, for example, East End theatres like the Pavilion Theatre in Whitechapel, especially, and even the Britannia Theatre in Hoxton attracted audiences from different social backgrounds,
while the socially diverse audiences at the Surrey Theatre and Astley's
Amphitheatre, south of the Thames, make it impossible to define them
simplistically as working-class theatres. Similarly, by reference to social
demography we have revealed that the overnight transformations of
Sadler's Wells and the Prince of Wales's Theatres and their audiences
by Samuel Phelps and Marie Wilton respectively, so long a part of the
folklore of nineteenth-century English theatre, are at the very least
highly questionable. Evidence such as census returns has enabled us
to demonstrate that assumptions like the correlation between a repertoire of nautical melodramas at the Surrey Theatre and a neighborhood filled with sailors living in its vicinity is flawed as is the notion of
a typical West End theatregoer. In fact all the theatres to which we have
referred illustrate that local audiences, as well as those who visited from
outside any given area, contributed to a diversity that represented an
extremely broad social and economic spectrum.

Our investigations have revealed a complexity of cultural phenomena interacting with the theatres we have selected for study. These
findgings challenge the mythologies (along with their ideological implications) through which the histories of these theatres have been
told. In particular, the goal of social amelioration through the evolutionary progress of such phenomena as the drama, a peculiarly Victorian ideal, has somehow been transmuted into an orthodoxy in most
subsequent critical accounts of the Victorian theatre. This has affected
the way in which audiences have been discussed and has created the
sorts of mythic patterns that we have challenged. It has been our intention to break through such barriers and find out a little more about the
people who attended the London theatres in our period. As Dickens
said, "the people . . . *will be* amused somewhere." To discover who
these people may have been, and their relationship to the amusements
that they craved, has been the basis of this study. Indeed, it is our contention that any studies of "amusements," theatrical or otherwise, are
only validated by equal engagement with the people, individually and
collectively, for whom they were devised.[8]

NOTES

INTRODUCTION

1. Earlier studies of theatre audiences like those of Allardyce Nicoll and George Rowell have tended to privilege the theatres of the West End and to have identified their values as universal ones and the preserve of a particular class. See A. Nicoll, *A History of English Drama 1660–1900*, Vol. 4, *Early Nineteenth Century Drama 1800–1850*, 2d ed. (Cambridge: Cambridge University Press, 1970) and *A History of Late Nineteenth Century Drama 1850–1900* (Cambridge: Cambridge University Press, 1946); and G. Rowell, *The Victorian Theatre 1790–1914*, 2d ed. (Cambridge: Cambridge University Press, 1978). To be sure, since Nicoll and Rowell first analyzed nineteenth-century audiences, a number of critics have questioned the orthodoxies that they had established or have opened up alternative modes of exploration. Of particular relevance are Joseph Donohue, *Theatre in the Age of Kean* (Oxford: Basil Blackwell, 1975), and the three studies by Michael Booth, in Michael R. Booth, Richard Southern, Frederick and Lise-Lone Marker, and Robertson Davies, *The Revels History of Drama in English, Vol. 6, 1750–1880* (London: Methuen & Co Ltd., 1975); in "East End and West End: Class and Audience in Victorian London," *Theatre Research International* 2, 2 (February 1977), 98–103; and in *Theatre in the Victorian Age* (Cambridge: Cambridge University Press, 1991), which have usefully mapped out some of the additional territory that any investigation of nineteenth-century audiences must necessarily explore.

2. In many ways the patent theatres were national theatres; they brought to one place a cross section of the community and provided one of the few public forums, as Marc Baer has shown, in which dissent could be expressed, M. Baer, *Theatre and Disorder in Late Georgian London* (Oxford: Clarendon Press, 1992).

3. See the Select Committee on Public Houses, 1852–3 in *British Sessional Papers: House of Commons* (London, 1853), xxxvii, Minutes of Evidence, 445, which suggests that these strategies were less than successful in a climate of free trade.

4. 22 November 1865, LC1/153, Lord Chamberlain's Papers (LCP), Public Records Office (PRO).

5. A Journeyman Engineer [T. Wright], *Some Habits and Customs of the Working Classes. By a Journeyman Engineer* (London 1867; repr. New York 1967), 198–9.

6. *The Victorian Music Hall* (Cambridge: Cambridge University Press, 1996), 62–3.

7. Patterns of leisure are discussed by J. Mekeel, "Social Influences on Changing Audience Behavior in the London Theatre, 1830–1880," Ph.D. thesis (Boston University, 1983); concepts of middle-class respectability by G. Best, *Mid-Victorian Britain* (London: Fontana, 1979); the changing definition of the middle-class in J. Rule, *Albion's People: English Society 1714–1815* (London: Longman, 1992),

F. M. L. Thompson, *The Rise of Respectable Society: A Social History of Victorian Britain 1830–1900* (Cambridge, MA: Harvard University Press, 1988), E. P. Thompson, *The Making of the English Working Class*, rev. ed. (London: Penguin Books, 1991); the emergence of the lower middle class in G. Crossick ed., *The Lower Middle Class in Britain 1870–1914* (London: Croom Helm, 1977). Changes in the structure of theatre buildings to accommodate the increasing sense of class division can most clearly be seen in Richard Leacroft, *The Development of the English Playhouse* (London: Methuen, 1973) with his references to the contemporary nineteenth-century concerns that appeared in *The Builder*.

8. In preparing this book we have consulted a number of studies of other historical periods, in particular, Andrew Gurr's *Playgoing in Shakespeare's London*, 2d ed. (Cambridge: Cambridge University Press, 1996), J. J. Lynch, *Box, Pit and Gallery: Stage and Society in Johnson's London* (Berkeley: University of California Press, 1953), H. W. Pedicord, *The Theatrical Public in the Time of Garrick* (Carbondale: Southern Illinois University Press, 1954), and Leo Hughes's *The Drama's Patrons* (Austin, University of Texas, 1971). As well, we have consulted recent theoretical models relating to audience behavior and composition as proposed in Susan Bennett, *Theatre Audiences: A Theory of Production and Reception*, 2d ed. (London: Routledge, 1997); Marvin Carlson, "Theatre Audiences and the Reading of Performance," in Thomas Postlewait and Bruce McConachie, eds., *Interpreting the Theatrical Past* (Iowa City: University of Iowa, 1989); Susan R. Suleiman and I. Crosman, eds., *The Reader in the Text: Essays on Audience and Interpretation* (Princeton: Princeton University Press, 1980). Interesting material that allows a useful comparison to be made between nineteenth-century audience reception and that of contemporary television is to be found in John Fiske, "Moments of Television: Neither the Text nor the Audience," in E. Seiter et al., eds., *Remote Control* (London: Routledge, 1989) and Nicholas Abercrombie and Brian Longhurst, *Audiences* (London: Sage, 1998).

1. THE SURREY AND THE VICTORIA THEATRES

1. "The Passing of the Surrey Theatre," *Southwark Recorder*, 30 July 1904.

2. *The Times*, 29 August 1823, quoted in Frances Fleetwood, *Conquest: the Story of a Theatre Family* (London: W. H. Allen, 1953), 141.

3. Royal Surrey Theatre Playbills, Theatre Museum.

4. Quoted in William G. Knight, *A Major London "Minor": the Surrey Theatre 1805–1865* (London: Society for Theatre Research, 1997), 149 (no source given).

5. Letter, dated August 10th, 1827, quoted in George Raymond, *Memoirs of Robert William Elliston, Comedian* (London: 1846), 2, 496–7.

6. Royal Surrey Theatre Playbills, Theatre Museum.

7. *Report from the Select Committee on Dramatic Literature: With Minutes of Evidence* in *British Sessional Papers* (1831–32), VII, 95.

8. Ibid., VII, 146.

9. "The older settlements south of the river, Lambeth, Kennington and Southwark had been developed far beyond the capabilities of the Parish Vestries to provide clean water and sewage facilities and suffered heavily. Those people who could

afford it — perhaps the same people who could afford the full price of a box at the theatres — moved out to the developing suburbs of Battersea, Wandsworth, Tulse Hill and Norwood." Knight, *A Major London "Minor,"* 101.

10. George Speaight, ed., *Professional and Literary Memoirs of Charles Dibdin the Younger Dramatist and Upwards of Thirty Years Manager of Minor Theatres* (London: Society for Theatre Research, 1956), 156.

11. *Thirty-Five Years of a Dramatic Author's Life* (London, 1859), 1, 256. The *Times* 8 July 1835 refers to the private boxes at the theatre remaining empty, further complaining on 28 December 1835 that, in consequence of the admission of "gallery people" to the private boxes, "respectable parties will not be in a hurry to take seats in them."

12. A. C. Sprague and Bertram Shuttleworth, eds., *The London Theatres in the Eighteen-Thirties* (London: Society for Theatre Research, 1950), 58–60.

13. *English Melodrama* (London: Herbert Jenkins, 1965), 102–3.

14. "British Heroism and the Structure of Melodrama," in J. S. Bratton et al., *Acts of Supremacy: The British Empire and the Stage, 1790–1930* (Manchester: Manchester University Press, 1991), 47.

15. "He Never Shall Bow Down to a Domineering Frown: Class Tensions and Nautical Melodrama," in Michael Hays & Anastasia Nikolopoulou, eds., *Melodrama: The Cultural Emergence of a Genre* (New York: St. Martin's Press, 1996), 153.

16. "The Factory Lad: Melodrama as Propaganda," *Theatre Quarterly* 1, 4 (October-December 1977), 22–26. It was subsequently revived under a different title not at the Surrey but at the Victoria in 1846 as *The Factory Lads.* In 1840 the Surrey presented *The Factory Boy* by J. T. Haines.

17. "Radicalism in the Melodrama of the Early Nineteenth Century," in *Melodrama: The Cultural Emergence of a Genre,* 192. Other untested assumptions about the Surrey include Richard Cave's assertion that circa 1870 a strong Irish presence cannot be assumed in the Surrey audience in "Staging the Irishman," Bratton et al., *Acts of Supremacy: The British Empire and the Stage, 1790–1930,* 99 and Alan Downer's, apropos Macready's engagement in 1846 at the Surrey, that its audiences were "the roughest in London," *The Eminent Tragedian: William Charles Macready* (Cambridge, Mass: Harvard University Press, 1966), 281.

18. James Jones and James Dunn, lessees of the Surrey, had rejected Temple West's demands for an increase in ground rental and determined to raise money for the building of a new theatre by public subscription, in addition to their own contributions. Together with Joseph Glossop who had an interest in the East London Theatre and the Waterloo Bridge Company, and with costumes and sets appropriated from the Surrey, they were able to persuade Rudolph Cabanel to design the new theatre; John Booth, *A Century of Theatrical History 1816–1916: The "Old Vic"* (London: Stead, 1917), 4–5.

19. Carlson, *Theatre Semiotics: Signs of Life,* 64–6.

20. Fitzball, 1, 96–7.

21. Eluned Brown, ed., *The London Theatre 1811–1866: Selections from the Diary of Henry Crabb Robinson* (London: Society for Theatre Research, 1966), 89 and Macready's diary entry for 15 August 1833 quoted in John Booth, 41.

22. See London County Council, *Survey of London*, vol. 23, "South Bank and Vauxhall" (London: LCC, 1951), 15–16.

23. Quoted in John Booth, 3.

24. The imposing Church of St. John in Waterloo Road was built in 1824. Thomas Lett, a timber merchant, built a set of fine terraces in Upper Stamford Street after 1815 but they remained untenanted until the 1820s. The Royal Universal Infirmary for Children was built in 1823 and a writer on the substantial houses being built in Belvedere Road commented favourably in 1821 on the way in which old buildings were being demolished and being replaced by "new and elegant houses in their stead," *Survey of London*, 23, 50.

25. *Report from the Select Committee on Dramatic Literature* (1831–1832), VII, 1350.

26. William Hazlitt, "The Minor Theatres," *London Magazine*, III, March 1820.

27. F. G. Tomlins, *A Brief View of the English Drama* (London: Murray, 1840), quoted in Marvin Carlson, "The Old Vic: A Semiotic Analysis," in *Theatre Semiotics: Signs of Life* (Bloomington: Indiana University Press, 1990), 59.

28. H. Barton Baker, *The London Stage: Its History and Traditions from 1576 to 1888* (London: Allen, 1889), 2, 239 and also note Charles Kingsley, *Alton Locke* (1850, repr. London: Cassell, 1967).

29. Charles Dickens, *Sketches By Boz*, Ch. 2, "The Streets-Night" (London: Murdoch, 1838), 40–44.

30. Charles Dickens, "The Amusements of the People," *Household Words*, 30 March 1850.

31. George Augustus Sala, "Nine o'Clock P.M. – Half-Price in the New Cut," *Twice Round the Clock* (London, 1859), 271.

32. "Up in the Gallery," *All the Year Round*, N.S. July 1882.

33. John Hollingshead, *My Lifetime* (London: Sampson Low, 1895), I, 188–9.

34. George Rowell, *The Old Vic Theatre: A History* (Cambridge: Cambridge University Press, 1993), 39.

35. Richard Findlater, *Lilian Baylis: The Lady of the Old Vic* (London: Allen Lane, 1975), 43.

36. E. Walford, *Old and New London* (London: Cassell, 1881–93), 3, 203.

37. The toll remained until 1878 when the bridge was bought by the Metropolitan Board of Works. Although 1s 2d each way might not appear to have been a great sum, according to Mayhew, in the early 1850s a pint of plums, a pair of soles, a quart of mussels or 2 oranges could be obtained from a street vendor for 1d, *London Labor and the London Poor* (London: Griffin, 1864 ed.), I, 11.

38. Charles Knight, *London*, vol. 3, LXI, "Chelsea, Waterloo and Other Bridges" (London: Knight, 1841–4), 168.

39. Report from the Select Committee on Metropolitan Bridges, 1854, 32–33, *British Parliamentary Papers*.

40. Ibid., Appendix, 157.

41. Victoria Playbill, 26 September 1833, Theatre Museum. To an extent the theatre was further disadvantaged by toll gates at Lower Marsh which provided the

quickest access from Westminster Bridge Road to Waterloo Road. A toll remained in force here until the mid-1840s.

42. John Coleman, *Fifty Years of an Actor's Life* (London: Hutchinson, 1904), I, 96. He also remembered a specific instance in which he walked from Westbourne Grove to the Victoria to see Phelps play there.

43. Coburg Playbill, 14 October 1819, Theatre Museum.

44. *Theatrical Journal*, 1 August 1840.

45. Victoria Playbill, 13 March 1843, Theatre Museum.

46. *Sketches By Boz*, 56.

47. Victoria Playbill, 17 June 1848, Theatre Museum.

48. Victoria Playbill, 25 October 1847, Theatre Museum.

49. *South London Press*, 26 May 1866. By 1873 it could report the use of cheap return tickets by the railway companies to lure people away for the Easter holidays (12 April 1873), a prospect made more attractive the following year by "gaily coloured posters" (4 April 1874).

50. Unidentified Clipping, dated 1869, Theatre Museum.

51. Victoria Playbill, 24 December 1878, Theatre Museum.

52. *Select Committee on Dramatic Literature* (1831–2); LC7/5, LCP, PRO; *Era*, 16 June 1861.

53. We have already established that it was located on major thoroughfares, easily accessible via Waterloo, Westminster, and Blackfriars Bridge. We should also take into account Hungerford Suspension Bridge, running from Hungerford Market to Belvedere Rd., Lambeth, which opened in 1845 and was taken down in 1863, when it was replaced by the Charing Cross Railway Bridge. Hungerford was also a major focus of steam navigation on the Thames, the embarkations and landings exceeding two million per year.

54. Between 1829 and 1846, fourteen steamboat companies had crafts in commission on the Thames. The Halfpenny Fare Steamers, which were greatly patronized by the poorer working classes of the metropolis, ran from Dyer's Hall Wharf near London Bridge to the Adelphi, until they were ousted by the suburban railroads later in the century. In 1866 the fare from Lambeth Bridge to London Bridge by steamer was 1d. The steam navigation of the Thames exceeded that of any other river in the world. In 1861, the number of passengers landed and embarked at Old Shades-pier on board the penny boats of the London and Westminster Steamboat Company was 3,207,558. See Frank Burtt, *Steamers of the Thames and Midway* (London: Richard Tilling, 1949), 29, 55–56; J. Timbs, *Curiosities of London* (London, nd), 777; and Donald J. Olsen, *The Growth of Victorian London* (London: Batsford, 1976), 321.

55. Olsen, 319.

56. Playbills, John Howard Library, Southwark.

57. Playbill, 27 January 1872, John Howard Library, Southwark.

58. Unidentified Clipping, dated 25 August 1879, Theatre Museum.

59. *Dramatic Notes*, December 1880. The *South London Times*, 26 December 1867, refers to "both town and country visitors" seeking admission to the pantomime, suggesting another dimension to consider.

60. In 1836, Cornelius Webbe wrote: "In no city in the world will you find a greater population on foot than in the good city of London. . . . The English – cabs, omnibuses and hackney coaches notwithstanding – are a walking people." "Glances at Life in City and Suburbs," in *Four Views of London* (London: Smith, Elder & Co., 1836), 181.

61. *Some Recollections of the Stage by an Old Playgoer* (London: privately printed, 1883), 6.

62. This was not the only visit Hanley recalls: he mentions that he saw Dowton as Cantwell, Vestris and Mathews, and T. Cooke at the Surrey; that under Davidge the Surrey company was "a strong one for melodrama"; and that he subsequently derived great pleasure from Creswick's fine performances at the theatre (Ibid., 6–8).

63. *Lambeth Observer and South London Times*, 9 October 1858; *South London Press*, 8 June 1867.

64. Census of 1841, HO107/1060–1062, 1064–1065, 1083–1086; Census of 1851, HO107/1563–1566, 1569–1571; Census of 1861, RG9/330–332, 334–337, 346, 348–351, 366–367. PRO.

65. *British Parliamentary Papers 1841 Census Abstracts: Enumeration*, vol. 3 (Shannon: Irish University Press, 1971).

66. Interestingly, the provision of juvenile nights during the Surrey pantomime season (when the pantomime was played first) throughout the period under discussion would seem to reflect the large presence of children in the neighborhood. The published census return in Southwark for 1841 records 31,283 (31.8%) children out of a total population of 98,098, *British Parliamentary Papers 1841 Census Abstracts: Occupations*, vol. 5 (Shannon: Irish University Press, 1970).

67. Ibid.

68. A far larger proportion of single people, particularly women, lived in Lambeth.

69. *British Parliamentary Papers 1851 Census Abstracts: Ages, Occupations and Birth*, vol. 8 (Shannon: Irish University Press, 1970).

70. Ibid.

71. Thus in King Edward Street we find two barrister's clerks, a cashier in a solicitor's office, an engineer, a law stationer, a stone mason, a solicitor's clerk, an excise manager, a messenger in the House of Commons, a Parliamentary agent's general clerk, a sculptor, a terra cotta manufacturer, and a vocalist. In Gladstone Street the inhabitants include an accountant, an attorney solicitor, a bookbinder, a GPO letter sorter, a railway clerk, a parliamentary reporter, a schoolmaster, and a silver smith. On the other hand nearby London Street contains bookbinders, chair makers, laborers, plasterers, shoemakers, plate workers, laundresses, and charwomen.

72. In 1841, for instance, 3,390 seamen and 639 watermen lived in east London as opposed to 386 seamen and 272 watermen in Southwark and Lambeth. In 1851, 6,286 seamen were resident in east London as opposed to 713 in Southwark and Lambeth.

73. LC7/5, LCP, PRO.

74. Ibid.

75. In 1851 the distribution of sailors across south and east London (out of a total of 10,111 throughout the metropolitan area over the age of twenty) certainly suggests that a greater proportion was domiciled in east London: 200 (1.9%) in London City; 78 (0.7%) in Shoreditch; 100 (1.1%) in Bethnal Green; 1,025 (10.1%) in Whitechapel; 1,521 (15.04%) in Saint George in the East; 2,083 (20.6%) in Stepney; 1,579 (15.5%) in Poplar; 59 (0.5%) in Saint Saviour, Southwark; 451 (4.4%) in Saint Olave, Southwark; 443 (4.3% in Bermondsey; 74 (0.7%) in Saint George, Southwark; 43 (0.04%) in Newington; 129 (1.2%) in Lambeth; 33 (0.3%) in Wandsworth; 791 (7.8%) in Rotherhithe; 634 (6.2%) in Greenwich, *British Parliamentary Papers: 1851 Census Abstracts: Ages, Occupations and Birth*, vol. 8.

76. *Lambeth Observer and South London Times*, 9 October 1858; *South London Press*, 8 June 1867.

77. Miss Martin, engaged in 1841, lived at 11 Agnes Place, Waterloo Rd.; in 1845 both N. T. Hicks and a Mrs. J. Furzman, who had a benefit at the theatre, were resident at number 5. J. Webster, engaged in 1842, lived at 3 Great Union Street, Newington Causeway; N. T. Hicks in 1843 lived opposite the Circus Gate at 3 Blackfriars Rd.; E. F. Saville, engaged at the theatre in 1844, lived at 41 Doddington Grove, Kennington. Stansbury, the musical director in the 1840s, lived at 5 Melina Place, Westminster Rd. Mr. Neville (1847) lived at 39 Francis Street, Newington; Georgina Pauncefort, who had a benefit at the theatre in 1866, lived at 15 St. George's Rd. Southwark. William Creswick and Richard Shepherd (managers of the theatre in the 1850s and 60s) lived comparatively locally, in Kennington and Clapham Road respectively; the former had moved across the river from Bloomsbury Square, the latter from Brandon Lodge, Brixton. When Davidge was manager of the Surrey he had lived in Charlotte Terrace, near the New Cut, and then in Davidge Terrace, Kennington Rd. Royal Surrey Theatre Playbills, Theatre Museum London and British Library.

78. *Sunday Times* 4 December 1842. Far more actors lived in Lambeth than in Southwark. The 1841 Census records 32 actors in Southwark of the 181 living in Surrey (17.67%); in 1851 the numbers engaged in theatrical and related professions were 56 in Southwark of the 229 living in the county of Surrey (24%).

79. *British Parliamentary Papers 1841 Census Abstracts: Enumeration*, vol. 3. The abstract of census returns for the Brixton Hundreds, which does not differentiate Lambeth, shows 73,777 men and 82,794 born in Surrey; 60,917 men and 79,139 women outside the county, 3,580 men and 3,674 women born in Ireland; 1,647 men and 1,164 women from Scotland. The total population of 115,888 comprises a large proportion of males and females under the age of 15 (32.81%), 14,734 of those are under five years of age (12.71%); 12,321 are between five and ten (10.6%); and 11,076 (9.5%) between ten and fifteen. There are 12,233 (10%) between twenty and twenty-five with a much larger proportion of females to males (7,338 to 4,895 or 59.9% and 40.1%).

80. The increase can further be measured by the fact that in 1831 the total population in Lambeth of 87,856 had numbered 39,545 males (45.1%) and 48,311 females (54.9%), *British Parliamentary Papers: 1851 Census Abstracts: Ages, Occupations and Birth*, vol. 8.

81. Ibid. In 1851, for instance, of the 35,047 males over twenty in Lambeth, 590 worked as domestic servants, 1,218 as shoemakers, 2,362 as laborers (a total of 4,170 or 11.89%); of the 45,275 females over the age of twenty, 6,161 worked as domestic servants, and 2,973 as milliners and seamstresses (a total of 9,134 or 20.17%).

82. In London as a whole in 1851, of a total population of 474,013 males and 493,260 females under the age of twenty and 632,545 males and 762,418 females over the age of twenty, there were 266,311 (34.9%) women older than twenty and 66,840 (13.5%) younger than twenty engaged in the clothing or "personal offices" business (as servants) and 114,476 (24.15%) men over twenty employed as mechanics. Of the women 138,262 were domestic servants and 124,165 were employed directly in the clothing industry. Of the female domestic employees 32,994 (23.8%) were less than fifteen years of age and 32,432 (23.4%) less than twenty years of age, *British Parliamentary Papers Population: Inhabitants: 1851 Census Abstracts*, vol. 8.

83. *British Parliamentary Papers: Population 1861 and 1871 Census Returns: General Reports*, vol. 15.

84. Ibid.

85. Lower Marsh for example had twenty-five butchers with their assistants and five fishmongers in 1861.

86. Certainly the numbers of those who listed no trade or occupation was a high one in the district. James Street, for example, in 1851, had 350 out of 883 and in 1861, 275 out of 590.

87. *The Survey of London*, vol. 23, 41, mentions that Nos. 3–13 Stamford Street (later York Road), which were erected in 1829, housed dramatic agents and, because they were used "as lodging houses for members of the theatrical profession who were in low water; they earned the sobriquet of Poverty Corner."

88. There were, of course, discrepancies between the published and manuscript census returns. According to Tracy C. Davis, the published census for 1861 lists 45 female performers and 69 male performers as resident in Lambeth, while the manuscript census lists 87 female performers and 52 male performers in the same district, "The Theatrical Employees of Victorian Britain: Demography of an Industry," *Nineteenth Century Theatre* 18, 1–2 (Summer and Winter 1990), 16.

89. Davidge lived near the New Cut and died in Walcot Place; Eliza Vincent and Osbaldiston lived in Balham and later West Brixton; J. T. Johnson in 1848 lived at Great Charlotte Street, Blackfriars Road; Eliza Terrey in Upper Stamford Street in 1850; Cony and Blanchard at Chester Place, Kennington Cross in 1841, although Hooper, the acting manager in 1838, chose to live in Cecil Street, Strand. Many visiting artists lived elsewhere: T. Cooke lived in Brompton; Mr. and Mrs. F. Mathews played at the Victoria from Bedford Square.

90. *Sunday Times*, 31 December 1848.

91. *Weekly Theatrical Reporter and Music Hall Review*, 25 January 1868.

92. *Sunday Times*, 13 March 1842.

93. *Sunday Times*, 1 January 1843. This mobility between Lambeth and the East

End can further be seen in reports of disturbances at the Pavilion. In 1869 young men living near Blackfriars Bridge were part of a drunk and disorderly group arrested by the police, *Theatrical Journal*, 20 January 1869.

94. *Weekly Theatrical Reporter and Music Hall Review*, 22 February 1868.

95. The census returns for 1851 show a surgeon living in Waterloo Road and a number in Upper Stamford Street; for 1861 in Waterloo Road and Gibson Street.

96. "Mr. Whelks over the water," *All the Year Round*, 30 June 1866, 589.

97. Playbill, 15 March 1841, John Howard Library, Southwark.

98. Memorandum, LC7/5, LCP, PRO.

99. Prices remained stable and competitive throughout the 1840s and 1850s (boxes 2s; pit 1s; gallery, 6d), but half-price was limited to the boxes only at 8:30, children in arms were not admitted and pass out checks were not transferable. Private boxes were £2.2.0; £1.11.6; and £1.1.0.

100. *The London Theatre in the Eighteen-Thirties*, 72–3.

101. Unidentified Clipping, John Howard Library, Southwark.

102. Letter, dated 20 April 1869, LC1/220, LCP, PRO.

103. LC1/70, 27 November 1859, LCP, PRO.

104. Ibid.

105. By the mid-1860s, however, the opera seasons seemed less successful. W. B. Donne refers to the Operatic Company at the Surrey Theatre being a "misadventure" in a letter dated 14 June 1866, LC1/167, LCP, PRO.

106. Unidentified clipping, dated 21 August 1841, Lambeth Archives, Minet Library.

107. The *Weekly Dispatch*, 17 August 1846 claims Vestris and Mathews are drawing "crowded houses and must make a profit for the theatre despite the high salaries they attract." However, the *Critic*, 4 July 1846 had stated that English audiences of the class prevalent at the Surrey couldn't appreciate good acting, as Vestris and Mathews were playing "always to bad, sometimes to empty houses," yet when *Cinderella* was brought out, the pit was full and there was a good sprinkling in the boxes.

108. W. Knight, p. 250.

109. Unidentified clipping, dated 8 April 1845, Lambeth archives, Minet Library.

110. *An Autobiography* (1885), 72.

111. Ibid., 80.

112. Audiences at Sadler's Wells under Phelps are discussed in Chapter 5.

113. W. Knight, 264. Knight makes it quite clear that the opera seasons were a significant part of the Surrey's repertoire from the early 1840s to the mid-1850s.

114. *South London Press*, 5 October 1867.

115. *Examiner*, 7 October 1871.

116. *Building News*, 10 May 1872.

117. Unidentified clippings, John Howard Library, Southwark.

118. Unidentified clipping, 25 May 1878, Theatre Museum.

119. John Booth, 15.

120. Ibid., 12–14.

121. Quoted in Ibid., 28.

122. Blanchard makes this claim in his account of the theatre which appeared in the *Era Almanack*, 1873, 7–12. He had access to account books and documents that in the four weeks of May 1821, the following were received:

Week ending May 5	£312.19.0
Week ending May 12	£404. 3.0
Week ending May 19	£354. 8.6
Week ending May 26	£402. 4.0

He also mentions that on the evening of Monday 11 June 1821 receipts were £152.2.6 with a weekly total of £523.4.6. However, if the capacity of the house was £325 per night as Thomas Allen claims in his 1829 *History of Surrey*, then Blanchard's figures indicate poor houses. Even the Monday performance represents no more than a half house. Perhaps there is some truth to Glossop's claim made to his rival manager Dibdin that he had lost £2,700 at the Coburg.

123. According to "The Victoria's Last Night," *Illustrated Sporting and Dramatic News*, 19 June 1880.

124. In a letter to the Lord Chamberlain, he suggests that his theatre may have to reduce its prices to compete with the beer shops where costs are between 1d and 3d, LC7/6, LCP, PRO.

125. Victoria Playbill, Theatre Museum.

126. This was attacked in the *Theatrical Journal*, November 1846. "The management of this theatre have reduced their admission to the gallery to threepence, and if the desideratum by so doing was to collect the regiment of "Lambeth blackguards" together, they have certainly gained their object beyond their utmost wishes; such conduct is disreputable and unworthy of the management, the company and the theatre."

127. Victoria Playbill, 15 May 1846, Theatre Museum.

128. On December 21 1866, the playbill for *The Three Musketeers* announced "a lapse of 10 minutes for refreshments which can be had at the Bars at the same price as outside the theatre."

129. Victoria Playbill, 8 February 1868, Theatre Museum.

130. From the early 1880s the Britannia, for instance, started to stage West End successes.

INTRODUCTION TO PART II:

ORIENTALISM AND SOCIAL CONDESCENSION

1. By 1871, 90% of households along Hoxton High St had changed, the larger manufacturers retaining their shops, but living elsewhere. Multiple occupation households also became increasingly common, J. Davis and T. Davis, "The People of the 'People's Theatre': The Social Demography of the Britannia Theatre (Hoxton)," *Theatre Survey* 32, 2 (November 1991), 158–9. Clive Barker's hypothesis that the neighborhood declined (along with the social range represented at the theatre), as the prosperous moved out of the area in the 1870s, is probably correct, although

in 1871 Hoxton's immediate population remained relatively stable in size, while that to the south of the theatre had decreased, "The Audience of the Britannia Theatre, Hoxton," *Theatre Quarterly* 9, 34 (1979), 39.

2. A year earlier the *Saturday Program* 29 April 1876 had referred to "these sturdy sons of toil – men who like on Saturday nights to take their wives and families to the play," quoted in Barker, "The Audiences of the Britannia Theatre, Hoxton," 31.

3. On 7 November 1843 a report from London's K Division of Police described Bethnal Green as "inhabited principally by laboring persons and weavers, who are generally very peaceably disposed," LC7/5, LCP, PRO. In 1824, fifty thousand weavers lived in east London, although the free trading policy of 1866 decimated them and by 1888 their number had shrunk to thirty-three hundred.

4. Andrew Davies, *The East End Nobody Knows* (London: Macmillan, 1990), 31–32.

5. Gartner, *The Jewish Immigrant in England 1870–1914* (London: Allen & Unwin, 1960), 88.

6. Davies, *The East End Nobody Knows*, 47.

7. E. Said, *Orientalism* (Harmondsworth: Penguin, 1978; reprinted 1995), 54.

8. Ibid., 60.

9. Charles Booth, *Life and Labor of the People in London*, vol. 1, *East London* (London: Macmillan & Co., 1889); Walter Besant, *East London* (London: Chatto and Windus, 1901).

10. In the eighteenth century, Garrick had performed at Goodman's Fields and the Royalty Theatre had come into existence; the early-nineteenth century saw the building and catastrophic collapse of the New Brunswick Theatre.

11. *Report from the Select Committee on Theatrical Licenses and Regulations*, 1866, Q1124, 1125, 46. Benjamin Webster praised audiences at the Standard, the City, and the Surrey where he found them "rather better and more attentive than at the West End; they do not converse during the performance." He also found them just as appreciative of high-class or high-quality acting. Q3228, 3229, 181.

12. Unlike their South London counterparts they are not included in Bradshaw's *Guide through London and Its Environs*, 1857, for instance.

13. Memorandum, LC7/5, LCP, PRO. That some of the gallery frequenters of the City of London Theatre lived in the neighborhood twenty years later is confirmed in the case of John Wilkinson, aged sixteen, of 73 Long Alley, Worship Street, a shoe-black who was crushed to death as he ran onto the crowded gallery staircase in November 1863 and a witness, Thomas Samuel Stainbridge, also of Long Alley, LC1/127, LCP, PRO.

14. Petition, 4 October 1843, LC7/5, LCP, PRO.

15. Ibid. Note attached to petition.

16. Memorandum, 23 September 1843, LC7/5, LCP, PRO.

17. *Hackney and Kingsland Gazette and Shoreditch Telegraph*, 31 May 1871 provides a sense of the variety within the East End by the 1870s when it refers to

"classic" Hackney, plebeian Whitechapel, and the "horny-handed masses of Shore-ditch and the East-end generally."

18. Quoted in A. E. Wilson, *East End Entertainment* (London: Arthur Barker Ltd., 1954), 74.

19. Ibid., 146.

20. Henry Mayhew, *London Labor and the London Poor* (London, 1861–62, repr. New York: Dover, 1967), II, 127. J. Balfour, giving evidence to the Select Committee on Public Houses 30 May 1854, refers to the Jews in the vicinity of Petticoat-lane. "I found the Jews on our Saturday night, after the Sabbath, were great frequenters of theatres; the theatres in their quarter are crammed. If you were to go to the theatres near the Jews' quarter, you would find the gallery and pit filled with Jews and Jewesses," *Report from the Select Committee on Public Houses 1854* in *British Parliamentary Papers*, 54. In 1866, Nelson Lee, the City of London manager, gave evidence to the Select Committee, claiming that galleries did not fill up so much on Fridays and Saturdays, because he had lost a large portion of the Jewish audiences to the music halls, *Report from the Select Committee on Theatrical Licenses and Regulations 1866*, Q.5024, 181.

21. Police Report, 22 July 1845, LC7/6, LCP, PRO.

22. Police Report, 22 July 1844, LC7/6, LCP, PRO.

23. Police Report, 20 September 1844, LC7/6, LCP, PRO.

24. Ibid.

25. Police Report, 24 April 1868, LC1/200, LCP, PRO.

26. Letter, 15 October 1872, LC1/263, LCP, PRO.

27. "The Low Theatres of London," quoted from the *Morning Post*, 7 February 1851, LC1/232, LCP, PRO.

28. Letter, 14 April 1870, LC1/232, LCP, PRO.

29. *Hackney and Kingsland Gazette*, 15 January 1870.

30. Police Report, 23 July 1845, LC7/6, LCP, PRO.

31. See John Russell Stephens, *The Censorship of English Drama 1824–1901* (Cambridge: Cambridge University Press, 1980), 62–67.

32. Police Report, 23 July 1845, LC7/6, LCP, PRO.

33. Memorandum, 10 October 1844, LC7/6, LCP, PRO.

34. LC7/6, LCP, PRO.

35. Police Report, 12 July 1847, LC7/7, LCP, PRO.

36. *Memoirs of Mummers and the Old Standard Theatre* (London: *Era*, 1924), 45.

37. Quoted in Allan Stuart Jackson, *The Standard Theatre of Victorian England* (London: Associated University Presses, 1993), 90.

38. Clipping, London Theatres, S. Arnold Collection, Harvard Theatre Collection.

39. Even Theodor Fontane, who is rather more dismissive, was convinced of the popularity of Shakespeare among the lower strata of society, when he sat between a worker from the docks and a grenadier from the Scottish Fusiliers on a visit to the Standard in 1856 to see *Anthony and Cleopatra*, Russell Jackson, ed. and trans., *Shakespeare in the London Theatre 1855–58* (London: Society for Theatre Research, 1999), 17. Over ten years later the *Theatrical Journal*, 3 March 1869, com-

mented that the boxes at the Standard were occupied by "an audience whose evident respectability would do credit to any theatre in the metropolis."

2. THE PAVILION THEATRE, WHITECHAPEL

1. Frances Edwards says the theatre was built at no. 85, on a site intended for a cloth factory, *Playbills: A Collection and Some Comments* (London: privately published, 1893), Pamphlet in Heal Collection.

2. Edwards identifies him as Hyatt.

3. Quoted in Wilson, *East End Entertainment*, 68. According to Wilson, the theatre was soon reported to the authorities, who asked the proprietors "to show cause for keeping a disorderly house." That it was disorderly seemed based on the accusation that the house, which was described by one witness as "fitted up like a theatre such as Drury Lane and Covent Garden," had contravened the statute of George II by the presentation of music and a one-man show. In fact the theatre did have a music license and the case against the managers was dismissed.

4. Ibid., 71.

5. This contrasts with the Surrey, which, as demonstrated previously, shows far less correlation between nautical melodrama and related neighborhood occupations. Nautical melodrama was a popular form of entertainment at a wide range of theatres during this period. See also *Report from the Select Committee into the Laws Affecting Dramatic Literature*, Q2133, 122.

6. Anita Cowan, "The Relationship Between Theatre Repertoire and Theatre Location: A Study of the Pavilion Theatre," in K. V. Hartigan, ed., *All the World: Drama Past and Present*, vol. 2 (University Press of America, 1982), 10.

7. Ibid.

8. *An East-end Chronicle: St. George's-in-the-East Parish Church* (London, 1880), 52.

9. Millicent Rose, *The East End of London* (London: Cresset Press, 1951), 159.

10. *East End Entertainment*, 74.

11. Ibid., 78–9.

12. In 1845, for instance, H. Betty as Hamlet drew so crowded a house that not everyone in the pit and the gallery could actually see the stage, *Theatrical Journal*, 13 September 1845.

13. *London Labor and the London Poor*, IV, 227.

14. Ibid.

15. *East London Observer*, 4 September 1858. The *Builder*, 16 October 1858, gives the pit's seating capacity as 1,750.

16. Inspecting the new theatre in October 1858, W. B. Donne noted the existence of separate entrances to the boxes and pit and to the gallery; the provision of six urinals for the pit and the boxes and three for the gallery; and of four water closets, three for the house, and one for the performers. Report, 20 October 1858, LC1/58, LCP, PRO. The upkeep of the gallery urinal appears to have left something to be desired, judging from Donne's 1860 report on the theatre: "*Gallery* Urinal very offensive and out of repair. Dust bin foul: The latter should be moved from its present place to a corner of the urinal yard." In 1863 the theatre was noted as being

"very dirty," Report, 6 September 1860, LC1/83, LCP, PRO. Indeed, throughout the 1860s the Pavilion was regularly mentioned in the Inspection reports for its dirty condition.

17. Wilson, *East End Entertainment*, 80.

18. Ibid. See also Pavilion Playbill, 30 October 1858, Theatre Museum.

19. The *Observer* elaborated its concerns thus:

Regarded in this light the drama produced at the Pavilion on the opening night would be a standing libel on our intelligence; and we beg therefore to enter our solemn protest at it being so regarded; to inform the dramatic Aristophanes of *Lloyd's Weekly Newspaper*, and all whom it may concern, that we yield "The Sailor's Home" to them as fair game, but that we shall not tamely submit to East London being held responsible for its superlative bathos!

20. *East London Observer*, 22 October 1859.

21. Ibid.

22. Ibid.

23. Cowan, *All the World: Drama Past and Present*, 5–6, quoting John Hollingshead, *Today: Essays and Miscellanies* (London, 1865), II, 306.

24. "Report to the Council . . . Into the State of the Poorer classes in St. George's-in-the-East," *Journal of the Statistical Society of London*, J.S.S.L, II (1848), 200–207, quoted in Cowan, 11. Cowan also draws attention to L. D. Schwarz, who shows (through parish registers and street directories) that in the late eighteenth and nineteenth centuries the people living, for example, in St. George's in the East, Wapping, Limehouse, Shadwell, Ratcliffe, and Poplar, were more likely to be associated with river trade than with any of the major business outlets for the East End (silk weavers, sugar bakers, agriculture, etc.), "Occupations and Incomes in Late Eighteenth Century East London," *East London Papers*, 14 December 1972, 23.

25. There is also evidence that spectators traveled from beyond Whitechapel and its vicinity. A benefit bill for 1848 advertises tickets as available from venues in Tooley Street, Blackfriars Road, The Strand, Covent Garden, and Borough, which suggests that audiences might occasionally travel from the other side of the city and from south of the river to visit the Pavilion, Playbill, 30 November 1848, British Library. An 1862 benefit bill for Robert Ealem, who had been waterman to the Lord Mayor of London, states tickets could be obtained from Bankside, Wapping, Bermondsey, Horsleydown, Greenwich, and Legal Quay, Playbill, 2 April 1862, Bancroft Library.

26. Census returns for streets in the vicinity of the Pavilion Theatre, 1841 & 1851 (HO107/712, 715–717; 1543–1547, PRO).

27. However, Whitechapel and St. George's-in-the-East were home overall to about 14,500 Irish, while Stepney and Poplar housed a further 9,600. About 25% of London's Irish lived in the East End, while about one-third of migrants from the rest of Europe and elsewhere were situated there. Yet over 80% of Whitechapel's population in 1851 originated in London or other parts of England. *British Parliamentary Papers, 1851 Census: Ages Civil Condition Occupations and Birthplaces I*, vol. 8, 34.

28. *East London Observer*, 7 September 1861.

29. Ibid.

30. Ten years later the 1871 census reveals 2,000 occupants of German origin, 2,700 of Dutch origin, and 2,600 of Polish origin – all noted origins for Jewish migration – living in Whitechapel, as opposed to a total of 3,200 migrants from abroad living there in 1851. *British Parliamentary Papers, 1871 Census: Ages Civil Conditions Occupation and Birthplaces*, vol. 18, 26.

31. Census returns for streets in the vicinity of the Pavilion Theatre (RG9/269–271, 274–277).

32. "Report to the Council . . . into the State of the Poorer Classes in St. George's-in-the-East," 200, quoted in Anita Cowan, "Popular Entertainment in London 1800–1840: The Relationship between Theatre Repertoire and Theatre Location." (Ph.D. thesis, University of Washington, 1978), 31.

33. The theatre managers themselves lived in varying locations. In the 1840s Johnson lived in Victoria Place, while Nelson Lee resided in Horsemonger Lane, Borough. Ten years later James Elphinstone lived at 48 Bishopsgate Street and at Redman's Row, Mile End, while his business partner, Frederick Neale, resided in Green St., Whitechapel. When Henry Powell became manager in 1864, he resided in Victoria Park. Morris Abrahams, on the other hand, lived in Whitechapel Road in the 1870s (as he had previously, when he had managed the East London Theatre). As for performers, Mrs. W. West traveled from Southampton Street in Covent Garden in 1848 and Percy Roselle from Woburn Place in Hackney, in 1867, to appear at the Pavilion.

34. Rose, *The East End of London*, 150.

35. Census returns for streets in the vicinity of the Pavilion Theatre (RG10/503–527).

36. Census returns (RG10/503–527, PRO). In reviewing the Pavilion's likely audience, other factors should also be taken into account, such as the late opening of shops and the presence of stalls and hawkers in the Whitechapel Road. Although this may have benefited places of entertainment and vice versa, it also meant that street traders and shopkeepers, plus their assistants, may not have been among those who attended the Pavilion Theatre.

37. "Crossing from Bishopsgate Street to Whitechapel, through a neat and noble road called Commercial Street, we come upon the London Hospital for sick and wounded seamen opposite to which is the Pavilion Theatre, "Unidentified clipping, c.1851, Bancroft Library.

38. Yet when the Oriental Music Hall in Poplar applied for a theatrical license in 1866, a police report stated that "There does not appear to be any objection to the establishment of a Theatre in the proposed situation. The nearest Theatre is the Pavilion, Whitechapel Rd, at a distance of about three miles," Report dated 1 December 1866, LC1/167, LCP, PRO. This suggests that the expanding population to the east of Whitechapel would have preferred their own theatre as opposed to a three-mile journey to the Pavilion.

39. Pavilion Playbill, 9–10 March 1829, Guildhall Library.

40. Pavilion Playbills, 30 January 1860, Guildhall; 30 October 1858, Theatre

Museum; 25 & 26 June 1853, British Library. In 1858 they are advertised as every ten minutes rather than five.

41. *Daily Telegraph*, 28 December 1860.

42. *East London Observer*. The cost of an Easter excursion ticket from Bishopsgate or Mile End to Epping Forest in 1861 was 2s, first class; 1s 6d, second class; and 1s, third class.

43. Ibid., 14 May 1870.

44. 2 January 1867, LC1/185, LCP, PRO.

45. *The Dumb Sailor Boy, Black-Ey'd Susan, The Pilot, The Shipwrecked Sailor and his Dog, Jeffrey the Seaman, Fifteen Years of a British Seaman's Life, Homeward Bound or The Sailor and his Wife, The Union Jack*, and *Ben the Boatswain* are just a small number of examples.

46. 21 March 1835 quoted in Cowan, *Popular Entertainment in London 1800–1840*, 86.

47. Pavilion Playbill, 3 October 1832, British Library.

48. *Wapping Old Stairs or The Child of a Tar* (1830), *Wilkins the Weaver or Bethnal Green in the Olden Times* (1834), *The Man of Mile End or The Assassin of Steben (now called Stepney) Heath* (1834), *Jack Lively: the bold fisherman of Barking* (1835), which included a view of the river at Barking, *Murder of the Mount or Whitechapel 1740* (1836), *Minnie Grey* (1853) with scenes in Epping Forest and Wapping, and *Rail, River and Road* (1871), which included scenes set in a parlor in Mile End Road and at Blackwall Pier, are just some of the plays that may have traded on a local interest amongst spectators.

49. In 1845 the Pavilion, Standard, and Sadler's Wells Theatres were all charging prices ranging from 4s for a private box to 6d in the gallery, whereas the Garrick and City of London Theatres' prices were usually half the amount.

50. Pavilion Playbill, 10 July 1853, British Library.

51. Pavilion Playbill, 14 May 1859, Theatre Museum.

52. In 1863 Sadler's Wells charged 2s and 3s for seats in the dress circle; 1s for the pit; and 6d for the gallery. The Queen's charged 1s for the stalls, boxes, and upper boxes; 6d for the pit; and 4d for the gallery.

53. Pavilion Playbill, London Theatres, S. Arnold Collection, Harvard Theatre Collection.

54. Manuscript Lists, Pavilion Files, Theatre Museum.

55. *East London Observer* (17 May 1862) claimed the lessees:
Have given another proof of their determination to elevate the character of the house, and provide a kind of entertainment worthy of the patronage of the upper class of residents at this end of London, by the engagement of Mr Benjamin Webster, Mr Paul Bedford and other members of the Adelphi company; by the production of the great Adelphi drama of *The Dead Heart* on a scale of liberality, as regards scenery, costume and stage effects, such as seldom has been witnessed at any of our local theatres. The result of this engagement has been an amount of patronage, which shows that such efforts to raise the dramatic taste of the neighborhood are appreciated as they deserve.

56. However, the *East London Observer* (31 December 1870) indicated that all

was not lost, at least at those theatres with competent management, like the Standard and East London:

> If the East-enders are not, as a class, familiar with the glories of Covent Garden and Drury Lane, the ignorance of the West-enders respecting the splendid manner in which the pantomimes at the Standard, East London and other oriental theatres, are produced, is no less characteristic. There is scarcely an East London pantomime which cannot compare with the best efforts of the West; nay in some respects they are superior. If any "swell" doubts this, let him take a cab and drive to the East London Theatre. He will find here an audience — perhaps not quite so select as that of the Gaiety or St. James's, but infinitely more enthusiastic — mustering some two or three thousand strong to behold a pantomime, which would have made a Covent Garden manager of the old school envious.

57. George R. Sims, ed. *Living London*, 3 vols. (London: Knight, 1901), reprinted in Russell Jackson, *Victorian Theatre* (London: Macmillan, 1989), 75–6.

58. Ibid., 76.

3. THE BRITANNIA THEATRE

1. Petition, LC7/5, LCP, PRO. The City of London Theatre was about a mile away.

2. Ibid.

3. *Sam and Sallie* (London: Cranley and Day, 1933), 259.

4. Census returns for Shoreditch 1841 (HO107/704–709); 1851 (HO107/1533–1538); 1861 (RG9/230–249); 1871 (RG10/437–473, PRO).

5. He also allegedly reduced competition by taking over the Albert Saloon in Shepherdess walk, running it down and then closing it. Crauford, *Sam and Sallie*, 267.

6. Britannia Playbill, 27 October 1856, British Library.

7. The adult population of Hoxton Old and New Towns had increased by 33% as opposed to a 25% increase in the rest of Shoreditch since 1841. The majority were locally born, with Kent, Essex, and Ireland providing the largest influx of residents from elsewhere. However, the Irish accounted for only 3% of the adult population in Shoreditch as a whole, as opposed to 16% in Whitechapel, 12.5% in St. George's-in-the-East, 8% in Stepney, and 9% in Poplar, *British Parliamentary Papers, 1851 Census: Ages Civil Condition Occupations and Birthplaces* in vol. 8, 33–4.

8. "The Amusements of the People," *Household Words*, 13 April 1860.

9. It is exactly this sort of thinking that lay behind Sir Richard Mayne's tacit policy of allowing (or at least not actively countering) prostitution in public places.

10. Barker, "The Audiences of the Britannia Theatre, Hoxton," 27. Crauford, 74, claims there was room for 3,200 seated — 4,790 standing. The 1892 *Report from the Select Committee on Theatres and Places of Entertainment* in *British Parliamentary Papers*, Q3074–3075, 208 (George Conquest's evidence on the Surrey Theatre) refers to one-third of the pit's and gallery's capacity in some theatres being standing room. *The Britannia Diaries 1863–75: Selections from the Diaries of Frederick C. Wilton*, ed. Jim Davis (London: Society for Theatre Research, 1992), 189,

refers to hundreds of strangers being on the stage (presumably after the performance was over) when the Two-Headed Nightingale was engaged in 1871 and, in the same year, states the theatre was not only full in the audience part of the house, but in passages as well, for Marie Henderson's benefit (188).

11. In a 1924 letter to the *New York Sun* (14 August 1924) the Rev. W. H. Collinson of the Bronx recalls how, for someone from a poor background like himself, the Britannia was his "graduation school." In the mid-nineteenth century he worked as a potato peeler for 4s per week in a cook shop next to the theatre and visited the gallery whenever he could.

12. "Two Views of a Cheap Theatre," *All the Year Round*, 25 February 1860.

13. "Dickens and the Working class Audience" in Sue-Ellen Case and Janelle Reinelt, eds., *The Performance of Power: Theatre Discourse and Politics* (Iowa City: University of Iowa Press, 1991), 167.

14. Davis and Davis, "The People of the 'People's Theatre': The Social Demography of the Britannia Theatre (Hoxton)," 164–5.

15. "Dickens and the Working class Audience," 169.

16. Ibid., 168.

17. It is very questionable, for instance, as to whether *Lady Audley's Secret* (1863) or *The Work Girls of London* (1864), two of the most frequently performed Britannia melodramas subsequent to Dickens's visit and during a relatively prosperous period in the neighborhood, function in quite this way.

18. A clipping for 1861 refers to the theatre's "hard-working audience, still working hard even in their relaxation," Barker, "The Audiences of the Britannia Theatre, Hoxton," 31. H. Chance Newton also refers to the theatre's "huge working class audience," *Referee*, 27 January 1924.

19. *Letters from a Theatrical Scene-Painter* (London: privately printed, 1880), 81.

20. Ibid., 39. That refreshments were important at the Britannia is clear from its earliest days. See Letters dated 31 July and 5 August 1844, LC7/5; LC1/141; H. Chance Newton, *Referee* 27 January 1924; *Illustrated Times* (11 December 1858); *New York Sun* (14 August 1924); and H. G. Hibbert, *Fifty Years of a Londoner's Life* (London: Grant Richards, 1916), 65.

21. Letter, 29 April 1864, LC1/141, LCP, PRO.

22. *Report from the Select Committee on Theatrical Licenses and Regulations 1866*, Q4422, 156.

23. Wilton's diaries provide a very full account of the working life of the Britannia from 1863 to 1875 and one that has no agenda beyond recording each day's events. As a local resident Wilton again gives the lie to middle-class prejudices about the East End. He read widely (even holding a pass to the British Museum Reading Room), took *The Times* daily, was an enthusiastic chess player, fisherman, and gardener, and was extremely well informed about current affairs. See *The Britannia Diaries*, passim.

24. *The Britannia Diaries*, passim. Other visitors, not mentioned by Wilton, include H. Chance Newton who recounts how terrified he was, when he saw *The Murder of the Italian Boy* at the Britannia at about the age of nine. He was taken to the theatre from his home in Birdcage Walk, off the Hackney Road (*Referee*

20 January 1924). Clement Scott (later the *Daily Telegraph*'s theatre critic) also lived locally as a boy and visited the Britannia. T. Bell, who wrote to the Lord Chamberlain in 1864, complaining about refreshments at the theatre, lived at 5 Bow Square, Bloomfield Street, Finsbury Circus, EC (LC1/141, LCP, PRO).

25. *The Britannia Diaries*, 94.

26. Ibid., 161. "Boy hero" plays were very popular in the 1860s according to the playwright Arthur Shirley, letter to the *Referee*, 27 January 1924.

27. Ibid., 175.

28. Letter, 8 September 1878, LC1/342, LCP, PRO.

29. Ibid.

30. Letter, 19 December 1878, LC1/342, LCP, PRO.

31. LC1/342, LCP, PRO.

32. Letter, 1 January 1879, LC1/343, LCP, PRO.

33. "Rule Britannia," *Entr'acte Annual*, 1885, 4.

34. *The Children of Gibeon* (London: Chatto and Windus, 1887), 99–101, quoted Barker, "The Audience of the Britannia Theatre, Hoxton," 37.

35. Ibid.

36. *The Britannia Diaries*, 73.

37. Ibid., 74.

38. Britannia Playbill, 5 July 1847, S. Arnold Collection, Harvard Theatre Collection.

39. Britannia Playbill, 21 November 1853, British Library.

40. Ibid., 11 August 1856.

41. James Anderson, *An Actor's Life* (London: Walter Scott Publishing Co., 1902), 300, recalls how he did the rounds of the London pantomimes when he was out of an engagement in 1870. The Britannia and Standard pantomimes were both better, in his view, than those at Drury Lane and Covent Garden.

42. *The Britannia Diaries*, 211.

43. Ibid., 162.

44. The *Hackney and Kingsland Gazette*, 4 July 1874 indicates the social differentials when it comments that 64 residents in a thousand were servants in Hackney as opposed to 22 in Shoreditch and 19 in Bethnal Green. Industrialized Hackney Wick, however, was very densely populated. In 1880 (*Hackney and Kingsland Gazette*, 14 May 1880) it was calculated that there had been an increase of population in Hackney and Stoke Newington of almost fifty-five thousand:

It is probably true that a larger proportion of married persons now inhabit the newly built smaller houses than obtained in 1869, owing to the exodus of working people from other parts of London to the comparatively cheaper residences in this district.

45. Clipping from the *Era*, 30 March 1856, London Theatres, S. Arnold Collection, Harvard Theatre Collection.

46. Clipping, Harvard Theatre Collection.

47. *Referee*, 3 February, 1924.

48. *Hackney and Kingsland Gazette*, 31 December 1880.

49. Playbills, 21 November 1853, and 1867, British Library.

50. Jackson, *The Standard Theatre of Victorian London*, 104.

51. Barker, "The Audience of the Britannia Theatre, Hoxton," 30, 36.

52. Barker, 36, suggests that this and the cessation of advertising in *The Times* in 1870 may indicate that the Britannia no longer felt it worthwhile to look further afield for its audiences.

53. Wilton, *The Britannia Diaries*, 143, records the cost of a visit by his wife and daughter to the Marylebone Theatre via this line as 4s 7d.

54. Yet, in the late 1860s, Anderson the Magician appeared at a succession of theatres including the Standard, the Surrey, and the Pavilion, which suggests that there was a sufficiently large audience in East and South London to make these multiple engagements possible. Playbill, undated, New York Public Library. In 1871, F. C. Wilton (*The Britannia Diaries*, 188) reveals that the Two-headed Nightingale drew large audiences to the Britannia, even though they (it) had only just completed an engagement at the Standard. However, when the Britannia Theatre closed for the night in late December 1871 because of Samuel Lane's death, Wilton and his daughter visited both the Pavilion and East London Theatres on the same evening (199).

55. *Hackney and Kingsland Gazette*, 22 April 1878.

56. Davis and Davis, 160.

57. Jim Davis, "Reminiscences in Retirement: Theatrical References in the Post-Britannia Diaries of F. C. Wilton," *Theatre Notebook* 47, 2 (1993), 109. The circumstances are ambiguous here, since the fracas allegedly commenced after one of the party remonstrated over the force used to evict a troublemaker from the theatre.

58. Petition, LC1/32, LCP, PRO.

59. Police Report, 10 November 1853, LC1/32, LCP, PRO.

60. Inspection Report on Stoke Newington Assembly Rooms, 2 February 1869, LC1/220, LCP, PRO.

61. Sometimes several theatres would compete with very similar plays. Thus early in 1866 the Pavilion, East London, and Britannia theatres were all inspired by James Greenwood's *A Night in the Workhouse* to run workhouse plays simultaneously.

62. *Life and Labor of the People in London*, I, quoted in Jackson, *Victorian Theatre*, 67–8.

63. Said, *Orientalism*, 328.

INTRODUCTION TO PART III.

MYTH AND NINETEENTH-CENTURY THEATRE AUDIENCES

1. *A History of English Drama 1660–1900*, vol. 4, *Early Nineteenth Century Drama 1800–1850*, 2d ed. (Cambridge: Cambridge University Press, 1970), 8.

2. Ibid., 11.

3. *A History of Late Nineteenth Century Drama 1850–1900* (Cambridge: Cambridge University Press, 1946), I, 9.

4. See George Rowell, *Queen Victoria Goes to the Theatre* (London: Elek Books Ltd., 1978) for a full account of Queen Victoria's theatrical interests.

5. *The Victorian Theatre 1790–1914*, 2d ed. (Cambridge: Cambridge University Press, 1978), 3.

6. *Tropics of Discourse: Essays in Cultural Criticism* (Baltimore: The Johns Hopkins University Press, 1978), 127.

7. Ibid., 68–69.

8. *Ideology: An Introduction* (London: Verso, 1991), 188.

9. Richard Foulkes, *The Shakespeare Tercentenary of 1864* (London: Society for Theatre Research, 1984), 3.

10. *Household Words*, 4 October 1851, 25–7.

11. J. R. Towse, *Sixty Years of Theater* (New York: Funk and Wagnall, 1916).

12. Towse, 33–4. Towse, however, is collapsing two perspectives of the Clerkenwell/Islington neighborhood so that observations about the area after 1862 become verities that were equally applicable prior to 1844.

13. Towse, 35–6.

14. Michael Williams, *Some London Theatres Past and Present* (London: Sampson Low, 1883), 18.

15. Shirley Allen, *Samuel Phelps and Sadler's Wells Theatre* (Middletown: Wesleyan, 1971), 80. Stephen Remington continues the mythmaking in 1982: he states that an uproar on Phelps's opening night was caused by "various showmen and proprietors of shooting galleries" who had been ordered off the premises by Phelps and that Phelps "eventually succeeded in training the Sadler's Wells audience. . . . His audience, from all walks of life, eventually became thoroughly discriminating and appreciative." "Three Centuries of Sadler's Wells," *Journal of the Royal Society of Arts* 130 (July 1982), 47. There is no evidence to support the presence of shooting gallery owners.

16. W. May Phelps and J. Forbes-Robertson, *Life and Works of Samuel Phelps* (London: Sampson Low, 1886),17.

17. Ibid., 251.

18. *Theatrical Journal*, December 1841; and Cook quoted by S. Allen, 79.

19. LC1/83, Report dated 7 September 1860, LCP, PRO.

20. *Essays on the Drama* (London: John W. Parker & Son, 1858), 87–8.

21. Ibid., 153–4.

22. LC1/58. LCP, PRO.

23. H. Barton Baker, *A History of the London Stage* (London: Allen & Co., 1889), II, 113. E. B. Watson, *Sheridan to Robertson* (Cambridge, MA, 1926), 77; and the Markers in Michael R. Booth et al., *The Revels History of Drama in English*, vol. 6, *1750–1880* (London: Methuen, 1975), lviii, also subscribe to this view of history.

24. Ibid.

25. *Mr and Mrs Bancroft On and Off the Stage By Themselves* (London: Richard Bentley & Son, 1889), 85.

26. Ibid., 86. However, if an entry in *Notes and Queries*, 9th Series, 64, 176, which states she played a sailor boy at the theatre in 1855 is correct, she cannot have been entirely unacquainted with the type of audience to be expected.

4. SADLER'S WELLS THEATRE

1. W. Wroth refers to the significant nearby spas like the Islington Spa, which lasted until 1826; the Pantheon until 1779; Bagnigge Wells, which mounted con-

certs until 1841; St. Chad's Well until at least 1840; White Conduit House, which, rebuilt in 1829, continued to have concerts, farces, juggling, and ballets until 1849; the Belvedere Tea Gardens until the 1850s. *London Pleasure Gardens of the Eighteenth Century* (London: Macmillan, 1896, repr. Shoe String Press, Connecticut, 1979). Also W. Wroth, *Cremorne and the later London Gardens* (London: Elliott Stock, 1907); and E. Beresford Chancellor, *The Pleasure Haunts of London* (London, 1925; repr. Blom, 1971), 385ff.

2. See *New Monthly Magazine*, 1823, quoted by W. J. Pinks and C. J. Wood, *History of Clerkenwell* (London: Herbert, 1881), 539.

3. Wesley had established his chapel in the City Road in 1777; there was a Methodist chapel in Spa Fields dating from 1779; St. Mary's Church in Canonbury had been a center for Church of England evangelism since 1754; Claremont Chapel on Pentonville Road was a Congregationalist chapel from 1819; the Zion Baptist Chapel was built in Chadwell Street in 1823; Upper Rosoman Street had the Catholic church of St. Peter and St. Paul on the site of an earlier High Church building from 1835 together with the Vestry Hall of Clerkenwell from 1814. St. Luke's Hospital for the Insane was established in Old Street in 1787 in the south of the area, the Royal Caledonian Asylum, an orphanage for the children of soldiers and sailors in 1828, and the London Fever Hospital on the Liverpool Road in the north in 1849. The Clerkenwell Parochial Charity School was established in 1828 and stood close to the Lady Alice Owen's school and alms houses, which had existed on St. John's Road since 1613. For further details see Pinks and Wood, *History of Clerkenwell*; and Peter Zwart, *Islington: A History and Guide* (London: Sidgwick and Jackson, 1973).

4. Pinks and Wood, 13.

5. Ibid., 14.

6. The need for change had already been suggested by Thomas Dibdin. In a letter to Lloyd Baker, the ground landlord on 22 December 1817, he tried to negotiate for a decrease in rental: "Sadler's Wells is not nor ever will be what it was; we are considered by the Public as out of Town, and the very great notice the Circus and Astley's have risen into (tho' formally nothing in comparison with the Wells) has decreased the value of our concern considerably." Quoted by Denis Arundell, *The Story of Sadler's Wells*, 2d ed. (Newton Abbot: David and Charles, 1978), 92–3.

7. Unidentified notices and clippings, Sadler's Well's Collection, Finsbury.

8. *The Times*, 16 October 1807 and *Gentleman's Magazine*, vol. 77, 1807, pt. 2, 971; and the *Public Ledger*, 17 October 1807.

9. Unidentified clipping, 20 November 1825, Sadler's Wells Collection, Finsbury. The reference to Mecklenburgh and Russell Squares indicates that the area of Bloomsbury formed part of the theatre's catchment.

10. Unidentified clipping, undated, Sadler's Wells Collection, Finsbury.

11. According to the abstract of the 1841 census returns there were 25,228 inhabited houses; 886 uninhabited and 438 in the process of being built. Nearly 49,000 of the population were under fifteen years of age. *British Parliamentary Papers, 1841 Census Abstracts: Occupations*, vol. 5 (Shannon: Irish University Press, 1970).

12. Ibid. The area also had the largest number of keepers or heads of public institutions.

13. Ibid. There were 346 solicitors and attorneys listed in 1841; 900 in the publishing business; 1,984 watch and clock makers. The relative proportion of domestic servants can be seen by comparing the 8,347 females over the age of twenty so employed and living in the district with the 19,390 living in Westminster and the 29,941 in Holborn immediately south of Clerkenwell. There were also few lodging-house keepers, suggesting at this period perhaps the absence of a transient population.

14. "The Stranger's Guide," *Theatrical Journal*, 1 August 1840, 275. The transport situation hadn't improved by the middle of Phelps's term. An unidentified clipping in the Sadler's Wells Collection refers to the difficulty of reaching the theatre: "It is not in anybody's way. No omnibus, wherever you may be, can take you up, and put you down at the door. . . . The best way for strangers is to put all their faith in the Angel at Islington; and, when there, to trust to the nearest policeman or baker's shop for further particulars."

15. *1841 Census Abstracts: Occupations*, vol. 5. The census statistics list 37,436 males under twenty and 39,455 females under twenty among the 185,174 living in Finsbury, i.e. 40% of the total population.

16. Benefit bills list actors as living in the salubrious area immediately north of the Pentonville Road: Mrs. Barnett, Dorset St., Liverpool Road; Cathcart in Lower Street and moving to Providence Place, Islington. Many lived in Clerkenwell and adjacent to the theatre: Cawdrey, the principal machinist under Honner and Phelps, in Sidney Street, City Road; Marston who had lived in Camden Town but moved in 1846 to Lloyd Square; the dancer Miss Marshall in Lower Rosoman Street; Greenwood who had lived in White Hart Lane Tottenham but moved in 1845 to Vineyard Gardens, Clerkenwell; others like Mr. and Mrs. Collier and Mrs. Watts, as well as Simpson, the box and gallery check taker under Honner lived in Arlington Street.

17. When the theatre was remodeled in May 1841, the playbills draw attention not only to the improvements like the raking of the pit, and the provision of a new stairway to the gallery but also make much of the involvement of named local craftsmen who had premises in St. John's Road and King's Cross and provided upholstery and gilding.

18. In a letter to Spencer Ponsonby, the acting manager Charles Dudley (28 February 1863) described Sadler's Wells as possessing a dress circle seating 80, boxes seating 150, 10 private boxes seating probably another 40, a pit seating 1,100, and a gallery holding 1,000 (LC1/128). He calculated that a capacity audience would return £120.13s. W. May Phelps and J. Forbes-Robertson appear to be wrong in suggesting that the boxes seated between 500 and 600, *Life and Life Works*, 12.

19. Unidentified clipping, Week of 7 December 1840, Sadler's Wells Collection, Finsbury.

20. The playbills quote the manifesto. See also Shirley Allen, 83.

21. *Literary Gazette*, 19 April 1845.

22. *Sunday Times*, 6 and 20 June 1841.

23. Unidentified clipping, Sadler's Wells Collection, Finsbury. This kind of

textual pruning would characterize even his productions of Shakespeare. When Phelps produced *Pericles* (14 October 1854), *Lloyd's Weekly* could report that "the greatest theatrical purists need not be afraid to visit the foul room at Mytilene, since it has been whitewashed and purified by the pen of Mr. Phelps."

24. Unidentified clipping, 10 October 1845, Theatre Museum, London.

25. Unidentified clipping, 7 April 1847, Sadler's Wells Collection, Finsbury.

26. *Lloyd's Weekly London News*, 27 September 1847, quoted in May Phelps, 102.

27. See the letters from Forster, Dickens, and Talfourd in May Phelps, 371, 372, 389. As the letters from Dickens to Phelps show, the literati tried to persuade him to assume the mantle of Macready as an actor-manager who could be attracted inside their circle and be supportive of their literary agenda. Phelps however was a private person who actively discouraged such social recognition despite the fact that professionally he wanted their support and that his bid for the vacant Drury Lane in 1851 signaled an intention to leave Sadler's Wells for more remunerative pastures.

28. F. G. Tomlins in *Douglas Jerrold's Weekly Newspaper*, 1 August 1847; and Allen, 96.

29. For example, the report of the 1844 pantomime in the *Weekly Dispatch*, 29 December 1844, includes a description of the traditional and noisy rivalry between the patrons of the pit and the gallery.

30. *Theatrical Journal*, 29 November 1845.

31. P. P. Hanley, *A Jubilee of Playgoing* (London: Privately printed, 1887), 10. The actor J. B. Howe who lived in Somers Town not far from King's Cross, worked as a fishmonger's shop boy in Jermyn Street in the West End. He mentions that he and his sister had saved up to see Phelps as Hamlet. He claims that as a result of this experience he determined to become an actor. J. B. Howe, *A Cosmopolitan Actor* (London: Bedford Publishing, [1888]), 22.

32. *Literary Gazette*, 15 June 1844.

33. Ibid., 21 September 1844. George R. Sims in his autobiography *My Life*, tells that his father had taken a house in Islington from where he rode to London House in Aldgate Street to work. He also mentions that his mother was a keen theatregoer, – presumably she may have been a frequent Sadler's Wells patron. Clipping, Sadler's Wells Collection, Finsbury.

34. These included such organizations as the Islington Philanthropic Association, the Britannia Friendly Society, the Goldsmiths' and Jewellers Annuity Association, and the Hope Benevolent Institution, as well as occasions like the benefit for the masons employed in the construction of the Houses of Parliament and Nelson' Column in the period before Phelps. Phelps had benefits for the Goldbeaters Philanthropic Society, the Lithographic Printers, the Brassformers, Braziers and Coppersmiths Pension Institution, and the Bishopsgate Benevolent Institution in the period to 1849.

35. The attendance of those who were attracted from their habitual West End theatregoing was recognized as early as 1846. The *Weekly Dispatch*, 19 April 1846, noted: "Some few years gone by, people would have laughed at the idea of this little theatre boasting of the presence of an aristocratic audience – real westenders –

but such it was the fate of the house to witness on Wednesday evening Mr Spicer's play Judge Jeffreys attracted one of the most numerous audiences we ever witnessed with its walls, and well did the visit repay the labor attendant upon the journey from St. James's to Clerkenwell." Henry Spicer's play *Judge Jeffreys* had opened on 16 April.

36. *Theatrical Journal*, 24 May 1849.

37. Ibid., 3 August 1853.

38. *Theatrical Journal*, 31 December 1851.

39. Quoting F. M. L. Thompson, *The Rise of Respectable Society* (Cambridge, MA: Harvard University Press, 1988), 19.

40. Henry Morley, *Journal of a London Playgoer* (London: Routledge, 1891), 138.

41. Allen, 248; and W. May Phelps and J. Forbes Robertson, 13.

42. Allen, 248 quoting *The Theatre*, 1 January 1879.

43. Unidentified clipping, 3 February 1849, Theatre Museum, London. Later commentators attributed Phelps's success to the fact that: "in three months Belgravia, Tyburnia and, indeed, every suburb of fashionable London was at his feet. All the more distinguished in artistic and literary circles felt that not to be present at a first night at the Wells was to be accounted a nobody. Lord Chief Justice Pollock said in 1856 – 'I believe we must look for the drama, if we really wish to find it, in that remote suburb of Islington,'" *Islington Daily Gazette and North London Tribune*, 21 November, 1902. At the same time of course many of these distinguished visitors were on the free list and contributed little to the box office takings. "Reminiscences of Sadlers's Wells," *Islington Gazette*, 11 July 1887.

44. Unidentified clipping, 24 March 1845, Theatre Museum, London.

45. *Literary Gazette*, 23 August 1845.

46. Richard Lee, "Samuel Phelps: a biographical sketch," *Theatre* NS VIII, 1 September 1886.

47. *Theatrical Journal*, 28 March 1855.

48. The *Theatrical Journal*, 3 August 1853, explicitly stated that audiences were the same. When Buckstone visited Sadler's Wells in 1853, it stated that "Such pieces as *Good for Nothing* and the *Rough Diamond* are a treat here where tragedy is so constant before the same audience."

49. E. L. Blanchard's *Cherry and Fairstar, or Harlequin and the Singing Apple*.

50. *Islington Gazette*, 22 October 1859.

51. Ibid., 31 March 1860.

52. Pinks and Wood, 435–6.

53. The auction notice accords with the letter from Charles Dudley in 1863 (see footnote 18).

54. Census returns for selected streets in Clerkenwell and Islington, 1851–61, HO17/1495–1519; RG9/125–199. PRO.

55. *Islington Gazette*, 1 November 1862.

56. *London Review*, 1 February 1862. It described Pentonville as a "sober neighborhood."

57. *Islington Gazette*, 19 March 1859.

58. Ibid., 25 April 1857.

59. *Sunday Times*, 28 October 1860.

60. *Islington Gazette*, 18 May 1861.

61. The first volume of the 1861 census returns published in mid-1862 had noted that "The great increase of houses and population in Islington is attributed to the facility of communication afforded between the northern suburb and the City and West end. In the middle of the day it loses a large portion of its inhabitants who are engaged in the City and elsewhere, as clerks." Quoted in the *Islington Gazette*, 1 November 1862.

62. A playbill for example points to the fact that country visitors to the Cattle Show at the Agricultural Hall were only a five-minutes walk from the theatre, 6 December 1862, Sadler's Wells Collection, Finsbury.

63. Playbill, 1 October 1863, Theatre Museum, London.

64. 30 July 1864, Theatre Museum, London.

65. Notice, 2 April 1864, Theatre Museum, London.

66. Unidentified clipping, 21 July 1866, Sadler's Wells Collection, Finsbury. By 23 July however, J. A. Cave, the manager of the Marylebone theatre, had agreed to bring his entire company in for a six-week season. Prices were lowered to boxes and stalls, 2s; upper boxes, 1s 6d; pit, 1s; and gallery, 6d from Marriott's 2s 6d stalls. He also brought his repertoire of Travers's *Kathleen Mavourneen*, Marchant's *The Blue Dwarf*, Suter's *Dick Turpin*, Hazelwood's *The Casual Ward* and with the help of Nelson Lee attempted to re-create Grimaldi's great 1810 success at Sadler's Wells, the pantomime *Mother Goose*.

67. *Theatrical Journal*, 17 March 1869.

68. *Sunday Times*, 16 January 1870.

69. *Era*, 24 April 1870.

70. Ibid., 31 July 1870.

71. *Theatrical Journal*, 21 September 1870.

72. *Era*, 27 November 1870.

73. *Theatrical Journal*, 14 December 1870.

74. H. Barton Baker, *The London Stage*, II, 218.

75. *Theatrical Journal*, 22 November 1871.

76. On 10 November 1871 the Clerkenwell Volunteer Fire Brigade had taken the theatre to provide funds for a fireman, Joseph Ford, killed at a fire in Gray's Inn Lane: "The procession to the theatre was to consist of a portion of the Clerkenwell Volunteers, the firemen with their engines, and a band of music. At the appointed time (six o'clock) a goodly number of anxious spectators assembled around the theatre, awaiting the coming of the procession. Up to seven o'clock there was no glimpse of this taking place, to the great disappointment of the public, as also to the proprietor of the theatre. The time had now arrived when the performance commenced with a slender but respectable audience," *Theatrical Journal*, 15 November 1871.

77. Playbill for Buckstone's drama *The Green Bushes* (originally performed at the Adelphi in 1845), 30 September 1872, Sadler's Wells Collection, Finsbury.

78. *London Entr'acte*, 1 February 1873.

79. Unidentified clipping, 20 January 1875, Sadler's Wells Collection, Finsbury.

80. Letter to Henry Irving, 21 September 1878. In the same letter, she states her address as 7 Albany Courtyard, Piccadilly, but intimates that she is proposing to take a house "near the Foundling Hospital" and thus closer to the theatre. Quoted in L. Irving, *Henry Irving: the Actor and his World* (London: Faber and Faber, 1951), 305–6.

81. This was the first revival at Sadler's Wells since Honner's management in the late 1830s.

82. Unidentified clipping, 27 September 1879, Sadler's Wells Collection, Finsbury.

83. *Entr'acte*, 18 October 1879.

84. Ibid., 21 February 1880.

85. Ibid., 6 March 1880.

86. "Shakespeare at Sadler's Wells," unidentified clipping, 1880. Sadler's Wells Collection, Finsbury.

87. Charles Booth, ed., *Life and Labor of the People in London* (London, 1902–4; repr. New York: AMS Press, 1970), 2, First series, Table 1 (Classification by school board blocks and divisions compiled in 1887), 18.

88. Ibid., 20.

89. Ibid., 21.

90. Ibid., 18.

91. Ibid., 21.

92. 61% according to Ibid., 2, Statistics of poverty, 31.

93. Booth, 3rd series, vol. 2, 165.

94. *Era*, 29 January 1881. She caught a chill while waiting for one of the convenient omnibuses to which she had referred.

95. 29 March 1880.

96. Barton Baker, vol. 2, 219.

97. Towse, 6–7.

98. Theodore Fontane, *Shakespeare in the London Theatre 1855–58*, ed. Russell Jackson (London: Society for Theatre Research, 1999), 59.

5. THE QUEEN'S/PRINCE OF WALES'S THEATRE

1. Unidentified clipping, 1831, Heal Collection.

2. Unidentified clipping, 1829, Heal Collection.

3. Unidentified clipping, Heal Collection.

4. Ibid., December 1830.

5. Half-price was also abolished, presumably on the assumption that latecomers would be prepared to pay the new reduced price, whatever time they arrived, Queen's Theatre Playbill, Heal Collection.

6. Sale Bill, 27 February 1838, Heal Collection. The seating capacity is probably exaggerated. James Grant, *The Great Metropolis* (London, 1836), 80–81, gives a total capacity of 600–700.

7. *Era Almanack*, 1874.

8. *Theatrical Journal*, 2 January 1841.

9. Unidentified clipping, Theatre Museum.

10. The *Weekly Dispatch*, 2 November 1845, wrote of *Death Wedding*, a new Queen's melodrama staged in 1845, that "It is a near relative of the class of dramas which have been so long dealt with at this house, under the present management, and is nicely suited to those whose mental powers are of the lowest order." This was to be the pattern for the next twenty years, as melodramas with such titles as *The Outcast of the Heath, or Tottenham Court in 1679*, or familiar melodramas from other theatres were performed.

11. This included Maria Atkins as Romeo, Mr. Holt as Hamlet, Eliza Farrell as Macheath, Henry Betty in Shakespeare, N. T. Hicks as Othello and Pizarro, and Hudson Kirby, as well as short seasons when the theatre was leased by other managers.

12. Memorandum, LC7/5, LCP, PRO.

13. Queen's Playbill, 18 January 1841, New York Public Library.

14. Queen's Playbill, 4 June 1849, Heal Collection.

15. Memorandum, 20 May 1858, LC1/58, LCP, PRO.

16. Memorandum, 20 September 1858, LC1/58, LCP, PRO.

17. Report, 12 September 1860, LC1/83, LCP, PRO.

18. Ibid.

19. Report, September 1861, LC1/98, LCP, PRO.

20. Yet on 29 December 1861, the *Era* revealed a somewhat less orderly picture prior to the Boxing Day performance of the pantomime:

> Long before the time of opening the entrances to this Theatre were besieged by an immense crowd, the principal portion of which seemed to comprise "roughs" of the lowest grade and boys of young age, and the scene of uproar that took place was disgraceful, and at one time assumed a somewhat threatening aspect. All respectable persons who wished to enter the theatre could not for a time get near the doors, and, to add to this, fights were of most frequent occurrence, the whole forming a scene of confusion and uproar seldom equalled.

However, an unidentified clipping, 1842, Theatre Museum, referred to "the quietness, good order, and close-packed cheerfulness of the audience." The *Theatrical Journal*, 3 January 1846, refers to the boisterous and unruly boxing night audience, "principally a juvenile" one.

21. LC1/127 & LC1/141, LCP, PRO.

22. Initially James was paid £20 per week for rent for the theatre and for his services as acting manager. Richard Lorenzen's statement that "James not only failed to make his theatre fashionable and to be recognized throughout the city, but also lost enough money to warrant him giving up the theatre after twenty-six years of spasmodic success and failure as a manager," "The Old Prince of Wales's Theatre: A View of the Physical Structure," *Theatre Notebook* 25 (1971), 135, is questionable. James would appear to have been relatively successful and his policies suggest he was not concerned to draw a fashionable audience to the theatre. He was certainly successful enough to be entrusted as acting manager by Wilton.

23. *Thomas William Robertson: His Plays and Stagecraft*, Brown University Studies, vol. 13 (Providence Rhode Island: Brown University, 1950), 58.

24. Marie and Squire Bancroft, *Recollections of Sixty Years* (London: John Murray, 1909), 83.

25. *Realizations* (Princeton, NJ: Princeton University Press, 1983), 355–6. Meisel also argues that Robertson and the Bancrofts "contributed to the creation of a respectable, class-specialized theatre whose descendants are 'Broadway' and the 'West End.'"

26. Clipping from the *Windsor Magazine*, undated, Heal Collection.

27. Unidentified clipping, 30 October 1875, Theatre Museum.

28. *The English Stage 1850:1950* (London: George G. Harrop & Co., 1951), 41.

29. Ibid., 47.

30. Augustin Filon, *The English Stage*, trans. Frederic Whyte (London: John Milne, 1898), 103.

31. Kensington, Marylebone, St. George's Hanover Square, and Westminster all housed larger European communities, "Tables Relating to Foreigners," Table 15, *British Parliamentary Papers: Population*, vol. 18 (Shannon: Irish University Press, 1970). See also Census returns for Percy Street, 1861 and 1871.

32. *The Victorian Theatre*, 2d ed. (Cambridge: Cambridge University Press, 1978), 83. There is little evidence of a violent element in the previous audience and visits to music halls often engendered more expense than visits to theatre galleries.

33. *Victorian Theatre*, 13.

34. *T. W. Robertson and the Prince of Wales's Theatre* (New York: Peter Lang, 1995), 70.

35. Ibid.

36. In fact the composition of the audience may have been more subject to seasonal variations. The *Era*, 31 December 1871, commented, during a revival of *Caste*, that "Although the stalls were not so well filled as usual, the pit and gallery had scarcely standing room on Boxing Night, and the entertainments provided gave the same delight to the general public that had been so repeatedly afforded to the more fashionable frequenters during the height of the London season." Equally a different audience may have attended at different times of the evening. The *Illustrated Times*, 27 October 1866, comments:

> The PRINCE OF WALES's theatre was visited on Saturday last by the Prince and Princess of Wales, the Queen of Denmark, Princess Thyra, and many other notabilities whose names I do not remember. The Prince wished to see "Ours," so he directed, at the last moment, that the burlesque should be played first, to the intense delight of Jones, who had paid to see "Ours," and had to leave by the ten o'clock train for Norwood, and of Brown, who, having seen "Ours" half a dozen times, came in at ten to see the burlesque.

37. *On and Off the Stage*, 89.

38. The *Illustrated Times*, 22 April 1865, gives a less pompous description of the first night audience: "A number of fashionable people, literary and artistic ce-

lebrities, young swells, and very pretty girls gathered together, and formed an elegant audience."

39. *Playbills A Collection and Some Comments*, 4, pamphlet printed 1893, Heal Collection.

40. Unidentified clipping, 1833, Heal Collection.

41. *A Jubilee of Playgoing*, 49. John Coleman cites the Queen's as one of the theatres he visited when he first lived in London and always walked to the theatres he attended. He was based at Westbourne Green, west of Paddington, a distance of three or four miles from Tottenham street, *Fifty Years of an Actor's Life* (London: Hutchinson & Co., 1904), I, 94–6. Some actors also lived at a distance from the theatre: additional addresses include Waterloo Road, Kingsland and Hoxton, but these are exceptional rather than typical.

42. Letters, dated 14 and 17 October 1845, LC7/5, LCP, PRO.

43. Report, 29 September 1845, LC7/5, LCP, PRO.

44. Report, 17 October 1859, LC1/70, LCP, PRO.

45. Report, 3 December 1858, LC1/70, LCP, PRO.

46. Howe, 22–3.

47. *Licensed Victuallers, Their Manners and Their Parlours: The Hope Tottenham Street*, Unidentified clipping, 1839, Heal Collection.

48. Among local societies and individuals that took benefits at the theatre were the Prince of Wales's Universal Philanthropic Society, which met in a Leicester Square Tavern and one of the sufferers from a fire in nearby Howland Street. The Hand and Heart Philanthropic Society held a benefit in 1843 for which tickets could be purchased largely in the vicinity of the theatre and across Oxford Street in Soho. For the 1842 benefit of masons who had been employed on Nelson's Monument, Woolwich Dockyard, and the new Houses of Parliament, tickets were available at many local venues, but also as far afield as Clerkenwell, Camberwell, the City, Pimlico, and Lambeth. A benefit for a local widow and her family advertised ticket sales in the Strand, Soho, Bloomsbury, Regent's Park, Oxford Street, Tottenham Court Rd., Drury Lane, Covent Garden, and Oxford Street. Among benefits in 1855, that for the theatre's band advertised tickets as available at the Blue Posts Tavern in nearby Charlotte Street (in 1857 these were also available at the Hope Tavern), while a benefit bill for Charles Frazer advertises tickets on sale south of the river at the Equestrian Tavern in Blackfriars Road and the Coburg Arms in Webber Street, close to the Surrey and Victoria Theatres. A benefit for a member of a philanthropic society the same year advertised ticket sales not only locally, but as far east as Shoreditch and south of the river in Newington Butts and Stangate. In 1861–2 benefits took place for philanthropic societies based locally in Foley street and Upper Charlotte Street. A benefit playbill, 28 February 1844, New York Public Library, lists two local taverns, the Hope in Tottenham Street and the Blue Posts in Charlotte Street, as well as venues in Rathbone Place and the corner of Goodge Street, all a couple of minutes away from the theatre, as venues for ticket sales.

49. Joyce Mekeel, "Social Influences on Changing Audience Behavior in the London Theatre, 1830–1880," Ph.D. thesis (Boston University, 1983), 131.

50. *British Parliamentary Papers: Population*, vols. 5, 8, 15, and 18; and Census returns for selected streets in the parish of St. Pancras, 1841–1871.

51. See W. Godfrey and W. Marcham, eds., *Survey of London*, vol. 21 *The Parish of St Pancras Part III* "Tottenham Court Road and Neighborhood" (London: LCC, 1949), passim.

52. *On and Off the Stage*, 140, 211.

53. J. Wearing, ed., *The Collected Letters of Sir Arthur Pinero* (Minneapolis: University of Minnesota Press, 1974), 27–8. Shaw states he saw *Caste* at the Prince of Wales's Theatre (Savin, 82).

54. Playbill, 15 April 1865, Guildhall Library. On the other hand a playbill for 29 July 1841 also announces that places and private boxes can be purchased in advance from sources in the same streets.

55. Bradshaw, 1857.

56. Unidentified clipping, 1839, Heal Collection.

57. This was a perceived problem with the new Holborn Theatre, a short distance away. "I quite anticipate stoppage of the traffic about setting down time, by the increase of carriages going to the Theatre turning – and out of Holborn, which would cause confusion and delay to the oncoming traffic," Police Report, 13 May 1865, LC1/153, LCP, PRO.

58. Memorandum LC7/6, LCP, PRO.

59. George Grant, *A Comprehensive History of London* (Dublin, 1849), 308.

60. *Era Almanack*, 1874.

61. The *Daily Telegraph*, 18 September 1871, likened the auditorium to a comfortable drawing room: "Where the refined elegancies of the drawing-room secure entire piece of mind as well as of body, the most scrupulous need not fear to enter." *The Times*, 25 April 1870, referred to the audience "who sit, as in a drawing-room, to hear drawing-room pleasantries, interchanged by drawing-room personages." Quoted in Michael R. Booth, *Theatre in the Victorian Age* (Cambridge: Cambridge University Press, 1991), 53. At the time the *Illustrated Times*, 25 November 1865, satirically described how the "the antimacassars set off coiffures, costumes, and shoulders charmingly."

62. Robertson's son recalls that later the Bohemian members of the Savage Club, to which Robertson belonged, were later given free admission on first nights of Robertson's plays at the Prince of Wales's, where they formed a sort of claque on his behalf, Robertson, 1889, xlvii.

63. *Illustrated Sporting and Dramatic News*, 9 March 1878. Mrs. Bancroft refers to an "Eleanor Gwynne" figure on her first night at the theatre. "When I was leaving . . . to go home, there was a woman with a basket of oranges still standing outside, who, when she saw me, exclaimed, "Well, if this is your haristocrats, give me the roughs, for I've only took fourpence!" *On and Off the Stage*, 90. The gallery too may have attracted some of its old regulars, if the following conversation reported by the critic of the *Illustrated Times*, 22 April 1865, is to be believed:

A lad, evidently a habitue in the gallery of the old Queen's, had descended for refreshments and had met some friends of congenial tastes. "Well, Bill", asked one, "what's the new actors like?" The gallery critic answered, "They're the *cleanest* lot you ever seen". "And the theatre?" "That's clean too". "No!" The inquirers could not believe this last statement; it seemed too impossible. "Is the gallery clean?" "Yes, it's all *beastly* clean!"

64. *On and Off the Stage*, 180.

65. Charles Dickens, *London Dictionary* (London, 1879), 276; *Era*, 29 September 1872.

66. The Bancrofts refer to several doctors and surgeons visiting the theatre, including a Mr. Critchett and Dr. Morell Mackenzie, *On and Off the Stage*, 278. The first night audience of *The Merchant of Venice* included "quite a remarkable number of royal academicians" and among audiences at other times were caricaturists like Linley Sambourne (of *Punch*) and Carlo Pelligrini (Ape of *Vanity Fair*). Lord Russell of Killowen, the Lord Chief Justice, often attended first nights, *The Bancrofts Recollections of Sixty Years*, 101, 103, 206, and 427. Mekeel, 201, suggests members of the demi-monde and of the "military fast crowd," such as Valentine Baker and his friends, were also seen there.

67. *Illustrated Sporting and Dramatic News*, 6 July 1867. Laura Hain Friswell, a journalist's daughter, recalls visiting theatres with her family several times a week, the Prince of Wales's being one of their favourites, Mekeel, 201.

68. *Daily Telegraph*, 2 April 1877. The issue of first nights is a complicated one. It may well be that, at both Sadler's Wells under Phelps and at the Prince of Wales's under the Bancrofts, the celebrities noted in reviews indicated an audience specific to that occasion rather than the regular playgoers.

69. In 1873, when the royal box was required at short notice, messages were sent to the person who had taken the box to ask him to relinquish it. The spectator in question turned out to be a city stockbroker who had booked it, but was away on business. On the evening in question he turned up — not with his wife, who claimed he had gone to Liverpool on business — but with an attractive young lady, *On and Off the Stage*, 175–6.

70. LC1/127, LCP, PRO.

71. LC1/166, LCP, PRO. These figures are contradicted by Diana Howard, *London Theatres and Music Halls 1850–1950* (London: The Library Association, 1970), 216, who states that, after the theatre had been reconditioned in 1865, the capacity was c. 600, the stalls holding 143, the pit 85, the gallery 134, and the boxes 142. This seems far too small to make the theatre financially viable, even with increased prices. Booth, *Theatre in the Victorian Age*, 52, suggests that Marie Wilton deliberately excluded a popular audience from the renovated theatre through her decorations, repertoire, and prices. It seems more likely, however, that the eventual audience was self-selecting and that she kept her options open initially.

72. 24 January 1872, Theatre Museum.

73. Joyce Mekeel, drawing on the London street directory, notes that "one finds on Tottenham Street itself in 1865, five bootmakers, two beer retailers, one pub, . . . three grocers, two timber merchants, a baker, an undertaker, a plumber, and an artist. Fifteen years later in 1880, the pattern remains much the same; there is one more pub, a coffee house, three tobacconists, and a few more grocers" (132).

74. Census Returns for local streets, Parish of St. Pancras.

75. Unidentified clipping, Harvard Theatre Collection, quoted Mekeel, 170–171.

76. The Oxford Music Hall held an audience of two thousand in 1863, LC1/127, LCP, PRO.

77. It seems quite reasonable to suppose that the local audience for the Queen's might well have regularly visited the gallery of the Princess's, for instance. However, that theatre's policy of long runs would not on its own have provided a varied enough repertoire, so spectators would have had to look further afield as well.

78. Report on Inspection of Theatres, LC1/185, LCP, PRO. It is interesting that, in the 1866 report that praised the Prince of Wales's so fulsomely, the Effingham Theatre in the East End was also singled out for praise. Donne praised the Effingham's "thorough cleanliness and order," which meant that all portions of the house were kept fit for an audience. Moreover, comparing it with the Prince of Wales's, he felt that the Effingham "exhibits – if the region in which it stands, Whitechapel – be borne in mind, even more strikingly – the progress of improvement." Donne expressed particular delight that the manager, Morris Abrahams, planned to "provide a handsome Box and Stall entrance, and to separate the better class of the audience from the Pit and Gallery Spectators."

79. LC1/185, LC1/221, LC1/234, LCP, PRO.

80. Fontane, 10.

81. Report on Theatrical Manuscripts, 6 January 1868, LC1/200, LCP, PRO.

82. *A Jubilee of Playgoing*, 113.

83. A correspondent writing to *Notes and Queries* 9th Series XII, 12 December 1903, remembered a time when the few stalls in the Haymarket were protected from the pit by a coarse wooden partition surmounted by a row of iron spikes.

84. In the *Era*, 3 October 1880, a correspondent from Peckham-rye complained that the crush involved in gaining access to the pit of the Lyceum subjected the crowd "to a grinding-down process which can be very little less painful than if the whole mass of people were wedged into a giant coffee-mill and ground down to powder." On finally achieving entrance he felt very much as though he "had been immersed – clothes and all – in a tub of water."

85. *The Revels History of Drama in English*, vol. 6, *1750–1880*, 14.

86. *Society in London* (London, 1885), 299, quoted in Richard Foulkes, *Church and Stage in Victorian England* (Cambridge: Cambridge University Press, 1997), 149.

87. *Languages of Class: Studies in English Working Class History* (Cambridge: Cambridge University Press, 1983), 78.

6. THE WEST END

1. Michael R. Booth, *Theatre in the Victorian Age* (Cambridge: Cambridge University Press, 1991), 10. Moreover, Booth implies that the West End theatregoing is the easiest to define.

2. Harold Perkin, *The Origins of Modern English Society 1780–1880* (London: Routledge, 1969; repr. 1976), 280.

3. Booth, *Theatre in the Victorian Age*, 9.

4. C. Law, *Urban Tourism: Attracting Visitors to Large Cities* (New York: Mansell, 1993), 14.

5. J. W. Cole, *The Life and Theatrical Times of Charles Kean F. S. A.* (London: Bentley, 1859), 2, 5.

6. E. de Maré, *London 1851: The Year of the Great Exhibition* (London: Dent, 1973).

7. Ibid., 37–8, quoting Henry Mayhew, *1851: or the Adventures of Mr. and Mrs. Sandboys . . .* (London: Bogue, 1851).

8. de Maré, 48. On the other hand, there is some evidence to suggest that the apprehensions did not reflect the actual criminality during the Exhibition. A pickpocket interviewed by Mayhew informed him that he had netted £200 during the Exhibition.

9. J. W. Cole, 4.

10. Great Exhibition Catalogue, quoted in de Maré, 71.

11. J. Palmer, ed., *Who's Who in the Theatre* (London: Pitman, 1952), 1849.

12. See *Travels of Carl Philipp Moritz in England in 1782* [1795], repr. London: Milford, 1924, 30.

13. "A Looking Glass for London – No XIV Trade – Regent Street and the shops of the 'West End,'" *Penny Magazine*, 29 July 1837, 282.

14. See G. Gater and W. Godfrey, eds., *The Survey of London*, vol. 23, "The Strand" (London: LCC, 1937), 45.

15. Thomas Beames, *The Rookeries of London* (London: Cass, 1850; repr. 1970), was particularly appalled at the proximity to the wealthiest parts of London of an area populated by ex-sailors, cab men, prostitutes, poor Irish, and counterfeiters, living in squalid lodging houses in which 72 people lived in 6 rooms (127ff).

16. Charles Dickens, "Seven Dials," *Sketches by Boz*, in *Works of Charles Dickens* (New York: Scribner's, 1911), vol. 26, 83–4.

17. Thomas Beames, 29–30.

18. Tracy Davis describes the compact West End as a "semiotic neighborhood" demonstrating a "front" consisting of Mayfair and the various shopping localities provided along Piccadilly, Regent Street, Oxford Street, and Tottenham Court Road, which "provided sites of the formal social performances of the daytime" while its "back," consisting of the Strand, Trafalgar Square, Soho, and Covent Garden, were the sites of the greater informality of evening. This informality deliberately confused the mixture of official and unofficial public spaces and behaviors, *Actresses as Working Women* (London: Routledge, 1991), 140.

19. Max Schlesinger, *Saunterings in and about London*, trans. Otto Wenckstern (London: Cooke 1853), 266–9.

20. "The number of such houses at the West-end is astonishing! The rent is nearly £500; from five to seven servants are kept; the master expends from twelve to twenty-four hundred pounds a year," Hippolyte Taine, *Notes on England*, trans. W. F. Rae (London: Holt and Williams, 1872), 18.

21. Ibid., 36. J. Timbs refers to the numerous lodging houses offering "Lodgings at 3d. a night" in an area described "as if the houses had originally been one block

of stone, eaten by slugs into numberless small chambers and connecting passages," *Curiosities of London*, 1867, 378.

22. Flora Tristan, *Flora Tristan's London Journal: a survey of London life in the 1830s* (London: 1840; trans. Dennis Palmer and Giselle Pinsett, London: 1980), 74-5.

23. Ibid., 179.

24. [Dr. Doran], "In and about Drury Lane," *Temple Bar*, vol. 16, 540-1, describes the contrast between the theatre and its immediate surroundings, and obviously sharpened to make the contrast even greater, the similarity between the attractiveness of the gin shop/theatre and the streets that surround it is clear: "half-drunken" men and women degraded and repulsive, with voices "freighted by blasphemy" fight like animals only to return "into the boozing-kens to find fiery compensation" are contrasted with the "hive of humming industry" that characterizes final rehearsals for a pantomime at Drury Lane: "Outside there was violence, outrage, blasphemy, drunkenness. Inside, boundless activity, order, sobriety, earnestness, hard work, and cheerful hearts."

25. "One of the Old Brigade," *London in the Sixties* (London: Everett, 1908), 73, 76.

26. G. A. Sala, *The Life and Adventures of George Augustus Sala Written by Himself* (London: Cassell, 1896), 331. The contrast between the beacon and its surroundings especially those near Leicester Square is also referred to by John Hollingshead in the second part of the century: "The splendour which distinguished the Alhambra Palace [after 1854], did not extend to the Square, for a more forlorn and disgraceful wilderness could not be found in the lowest parts of London. Dead cats, oyster shells and vegetable refuse encumbered the ground and the Royal Georgian statue in the middle of the great dustbin bore many marks of decay and public disfigurement," John Hollingshead, *My Lifetime* (London: Sampson, Low, 1895), I, 229.

27. G. Gater and W. Godfrey, 36ff. In 1827, Heinrich Heine stayed in a boarding house in Craven Street and bemoaned the fact that his expenditure amounted to a guinea a day.

28. Ibid., 110-113.

29. *British Parliamentary Papers*, Table 83, 1861 Census abstracts estimate that among those twenty years of age and over, a total of 26,137 living in the Strand area, 1,769 (6.8%) were professionals, 1,859 (7.1%) belonged to the commercial class. These figures however need to be set alongside the 11,064 (42.3%) industrial class, which comprises bootmakers, hairdressers, cabinet makers, caterers, butchers, pastrycooks, newspaper agents, and those involved in "mechanical production" and the 10,064 (38.5%) in the domestic class, which included wives, maids, charwomen, and those "entertaining or providing personal services."

30. The same table lists 1,053 professional people or 8.2% of the 14,507 over twenty living in the district.

31. The areas of St. Giles's parish and the Strand both contained substantial numbers of small businesses and manufacturing concerns. Indeed the area round Drury Lane was known for its boot and shoemakers and the area round Long

Acre for carriage builders, *Routledge's Popular Guide to London and its Suburbs* (London: Routledge, Warne, 1862), 27–8. According to the 1851 census abstracts, 248 coach builders lived in the St. Giles's district. The 1851 census abstracts list 772 male shoemakers in the Strand and 748 in the St. Giles parish; 944 and 806 male tailors respectively; roughly the same numbers of printers (452 and 330 respectively); cabinet makers (212 and 277 respectively); goldsmiths and silversmiths (173 and 108 respectively); although the numbers of laborers in the St. Giles's district far outnumbered those in the Strand (1413 as distinct from 410). St. Giles's area also listed 107 law clerks compared to the Strand number of 183. Among the female occupations and trades, both areas contained numbers of washer women (598 in the Strand and 521 in the St. Giles's area) although far fewer than in districts like Kensington, Chelsea, Westminster, or Marylebone. (The abstracts list 2,395 in Kensington, 2,011 in Chelsea, 3,047 in Marylebone.) The Strand and St. Giles's areas were home to 807 and 857 milliners; and 598 and 521 washerwomen respectively. Although there were 2,320 general domestic servants living in St. Giles's and 1,373 in the Strand, these figures are again dwarfed by those in the wealthier residential areas. The 1871 census listed 1,931 persons within the professional classes living in St. Giles's, with 2,443 in the Strand; 13,454 in the domestic classes including wives, with 11,208 in the Strand; 3,618 in the commercial classes with 2,435 in the Strand; 9,462 involved in industrial production in St. Giles's with 8,623 in the Strand. St. Giles's had however 1,497 people living in the area engaged as laborers, apprentices, or shopwomen, which are absent from the Strand returns (1871 census abstracts, vol. 17, table 10). It also lists 1,449 people of foreign birth living in the St. Giles's district (of whom 345 were French and 467 were German) and 1,147 in the Strand (of whom 363 were French and 315 were German), while in the St. Giles's area 136 were American. The German population were principally occupied as confectioners, pastrycooks, cabinet makers, watchmakers, merchants, and tailors and their wives, while the French worked as goldsmiths, musical instrument makers, teachers, domestic servants, and milliners.

32. The 1861 census abstract enumerates a total of 1,321 unmarried lodgers living in the St. Giles's district (vol. 15, table 3) and 1,229 single people living alone (table 33–6). The 1871 census abstract (vol. 17, table 10) values St. Giles's property as £307,237 compared to that in Whitechapel as £315,025.

33. John Coleman, *Fifty Years of an Actor's Life* (London: Hutchinson, 1904) vol. 1, 94–6. He saved 1s a day by not eating lunch and 2s 6d omnibus fares by walking. He also visited Drury Lane and Covent Garden, which were "more dignified," but after a long walk he sometimes found them closed because of a death (e.g., the Duke of Sussex) or financial difficulties (vol. 1, 101). When engaged as an actor at the Standard he regularly walked to Shoreditch from his lodgings in Camden Town (vol. 1, 110).

34. *Cruchley's Picture of London* (London: Cruchley, 1841), 13.

35. Ibid., 264–5, 271–2. The guide offered cautionary advice to strangers to be careful of "sharpers, swindlers, prostitutes, and pickpockets, who are prowling about in all directions to entrap the unwary" especially cigar, tea, and brandy smug-

glers, confidence tricksters offering mock-auctions but above all, to be careful of gambling: "Gaming houses are numerous; some of which hold forth inducements to young men who are resolutely bent on abstaining from play; such as balls, suppers, etc., to which are invited females of prepossessing appearances and doubtful characters." (Ibid., 174).

36. G. A. Sekon suggests that before the late 1870s, through traffic south of Euston Road had been prevented from entering the Bedford estate, which would have made the West End more accessible from Bedford Square and Great Russell Street. This would have prevented the setting up of any public transport lines in the period, *Locomotion in Victorian London*, 49–50 quoted in T. C. Barker and Michael Robbins, *A History of London Transport* (London: Allen & Unwin, 1963), 242.

37. Such costs should be set against the costs of living and incomes in the period. In 1824 it was calculated that a man earning 48s per week with a family of wife and three children would have 4s per week left after all household expenses were deducted; a skilled mechanic earning 33s per week would have 2s 9d left. In 1841, 30s per week enabled a family to live in spartan conditions with 10d left over for all sundries and contingencies. In 1855 a working cutler living in Whitefriars Street kept a wife and four children on £1 16s 9d per week which allowed 1s 2d for all expenses other than basic food, rent, clothing, coal, and light payments, Mrs. C. S Peel, "Homes and Habits," in G. M. Young, ed., *Early Victorian England: 1830–1865* (London: Oxford University Press, 1934), 126–133.

38. E. L. Blanchard, ed., *Bradshaw's Guide through London and its Environs* (London: Adams, 1851), 255–6:

The Waterloo Omnibuses – [start from Camberwell Gate], thence taking Walworth Road (*Amelia Street, Surrey Zoological Gardens*), Elephant and Castle, London Road (*Philanthropic Institution, Blind School*), Waterloo Road (*Royal Victoria Theatre*), Waterloo Bridge (*from this Bridge fine views of London*), Wellington Street, Strand (*Lyceum Theatre, Exeter Hall, Adelphi Theatre*), Charing Cross West (*Lowther Arcade, near Hungerford Market, Suspension Bridge, etc*), Charing Cross (*Northumberland House, National Gallery, Nelson's Monument, Fountains*), Cockspur Street (*Equestrian Statue of George III*), Pall-mall (*Her Majesty's Theatre and Haymarket Theatre*), Waterloo Place (*Duke of York's Column, entrance to St. James's Park*), Regent Street Quadrant, Regent's Street (*209, Cosmorama*), Oxford Street (*Close by the Polytechnic Institution*), John Street, Portland Street, Portland Road, Albany Street (*Colosseum, Diorama*), York and Albany Tavern (*near Regent's Park, Zoological Gardens, and North Western Railway*).

Hackney cabs' journeys from the Great Western railway to Drury lane had dropped to 1s 6d; from Clerkenwell to 1s; and the fares highlight opportunities for travelers from Chelsea, Knightsbridge, and Sloane Square to the west (1s 6d), Islington and St. John's Wood to the north (1s 6d and 2s), Brixton to the south (2s) and Whitechapel to the east (1s 6d).

39. W. Frith, *My Autobiography and Reminiscences* (London: Bentley, 1889), 14.

40. Paddington station on the western perimeter had been built in 1855, King's

Cross to the north in 1852. *Cruchley's Picture of London*, 6th ed. (London: Cruchley, 1841), 236–7, refers to the fact that the London to Manchester railway had begun to operate, but the London and Southampton Railway had only reached Vauxhall, the Great Western railway was only partially open and the portion to Bath had yet to be completed. On the recommendations of the Select Committee see *Report and Minutes of Evidence of Royal Commission on . . . Railway Termini within the Metropolis*, 1846, vol. xvii, 719.

41. *Baedeker*, 30–5.

42. Barker and Robbins, 172.

43. "The World of London," part IV, *Blackwood's Edinburgh Magazine*, August 1841, 204–5.

44. Henry Solly, *These Eighty Years* (London: Simpkin, Marshall, 1893), 220. He saw Macready as Hamlet, Macbeth, Virginius, and Othello in the period 1837 to 1839 and also occasionally went to the opera with his cousins who lived in Great Ormond Street.

45. The composition of a typical lower middle-class suburban household set somewhere in south London at this time is described as comprising the husband, who earned 35s per week and spent 7s per week on rent and who visited the theatre together with his wife once a fortnight. It is unlikely that they would have patronized the West End. The would much more likely have visited the Surrey or Victoria.

46. *Cruchley*, 168–70.

47. *Clark's Guide to the Sights of London* (Chepstow: Clark, 1851). An established clerk, working as a head of department in a bank in the City and who earned £150 per year in 1844, might spend on average £1 19s 4d on excursions and amusements for the whole of the period, Arthur Hayward, *The Days of Dickens* (London: Routledge, 1926, repr. Archon, 1968), 73.

48. *Baedeker*, 6–9.

49. *Cruchley's Picture of London* describes the Strand and Covent Garden "as forming a center to a greater variety of places and objects of curiosity than any other spot in the Metropolis" (12).

50. "Christmas Holidays," *Theatrical Journal*, 28 November 1840, 406.

51. *Select Committee on Theatrical Licences*, 1866, vol. 16, IUP, appendices 1 and 3, 295, 313.

52. *Cruchley*, 85–9. Prices to the dress boxes at Covent Garden were 7s, to the first and second circles, 5s; pit, 3s; and gallery 1s, with half-price at 9 P.M. Drury Lane's prices were 5s to a private box; pit, 3s; lower gallery, 1s 6d; and upper gallery, 1s, also with a half-price at 9 P.M.

53. Ibid., 93. The Adelphi began its performances earlier, at 6:30 P.M. with a half-price at 8:30 P.M. Its price structure of boxes, 4s; pit, 2s; gallery, 1s, slightly less expensive than the Haymarket, might suggest that it was aiming for an audience whose habits were slightly different.

54. Ibid., 96. Prices at the Olympic started at 4s for the boxes; pit, 2s; and gallery, 1s, with half-price at 9 P.M. Prices had evidently been raised since 1840: the *Theatrical Journal* in its guide to Christmas amusements had quoted the Olympic as boxes, 2s 6d; pit, 1s; and gallery, 6d, with half-price to the boxes only, Ibid., 406.

The Strand's prices were 3s, boxes; pit, 2s; and gallery, 1s, with half-price at 8:
30 P.M. Again the Christmas guide listed the pit prices as 1s 6d with half-price at
9 P.M., though these variations may be understandable in the light of the Christmas
audiences all theatres wished to attract.

55. Ibid., 96, 98. Although the promenade concerts at the Princess's were expensive (boxes between 10s and 1 guinea with separate approaches built for them),
the guide signals that the dramatic program would be equivalent to other West End
theatres: boxes, 4s; 3s for boxes in the "second circle"; 2s, pit; and 1s, gallery with
a performance to begin at 7 P.M. The Queen's however was much less expensive:
boxes, 2s; pit, 1s; gallery, 6d with a half-price at 8:30 P.M.

56. *The Box Book Keeper's Guide or London Theatrical and Amusement Directory*, edited by W. Marx (London: Jullien, 1849), is the earliest example of an attempt to provide a box plan for a select number of London theatres. Its plan of
Drury Lane shows seventy-five pit stalls placed in three rows in front of the pit. By
1866, the theatres referred to in the 1841 guide had all introduced this division: the
Adelphi, 394 (which together with the box patrons totaled 61.5% of the house
capacity); Drury Lane, 180 (together with the huge box component of 1,320 making
39.47% of the house capacity); the Haymarket, 60 (which together with its 842 box
seats totaled 49.5% of the house capacity); the Lyceum, 170 (which together with
its 470 boxes total amounted to 42.9% of the house capacity); the Olympic, 100
(together with the box component of 330, equivalent to 37.7% of the house capacity); Princess's, 108 (together with the boxes at 471 making a sum of 36.6% of total
capacity); the Queen's, now renamed the Prince of Wales's, 90 (together with a box
component of 184 making 33.6% of total capacity); and the Strand, 77 (together
with the box capacity of 179 making a total of 23.6%).

57. *Household Words*, 19 March 1859.

58. Montagu Williams, *Round London* (London: Macmillan, 1893), 179.

59. *Baedeker*, 37–40.

60. Letter to William Mitchell, 16 February 1842 in Madeleine House et al., eds.,
The Letters of Charles Dickens (Oxford: Clarendon Press, 1965–98), vol. 3, 64–5.

61. Letter to Macready, 10 June 1848, Ibid., vol. 5, 330.

62. Letter to Mary Boyle, 28 December 1860, Ibid., vol. 8, 354. Dickens was
quite happy on occasions to go by himself to the theatre. He wrote to John Forster
that he had gone to the Princess's to see Boucicault's *Streets of London* and found
it an example "of utterly degraded and debased theatrical taste" though it was
obviously enormously successful. He had also tried to see Menken at Astley's to be
confronted by standing room only, and had seen John Toole at the Adelphi in John
Oxenford's adaptation of Balzac's *Le Père Goriot (Stephen Digges)* among a very
thin audience: "where I couldn't . . . get the house up to Nine Pounds," Letter to
John Forster, 8 October 1864. Ibid., vol. 10, 433–4.

63. George Henry Lewes's journal, 8 February 1864, in G. S. Haight, ed., *The
George Eliot Letters* (New Haven: Yale University Press, 1954–78), vol. 4, 132 and
Anthony Trollope writing to Frederick Chapin, 26 February 1864, in N. John Hall
and Nina Burgis, eds., *The Letters of Anthony Trollope* (Stanford: Stanford University Press, 1983), vol. 2, 1007.

64. [George Augustus Sala], *The Life and Adventures of George Augustus Sala Written by Himself* (London: Cassell, 1896), 411.

65. Eliot, Letter to Sara Hennell, 3 February 1862, Haight, vol. 4, 10.

66. Eliot, Letter to Charles Bray, 9 December 1853, Haight, vol. 2, 17

67. Laura Hain Friswell, *In the Sixties and Seventies* (London: Hutchinson, 1905), 118. She saw *True to the Core* twice, once at the Surrey and then at its transfer to the Princess's. She mentions that the box at the Surrey was so large that it allowed her entire family to dance while the band played quadrilles during the interval.

68. D. Hudson, ed., *Munby, Man of two Worlds: the Life and Diaries of Arthur J. Munby 1828–1910* (London: Murray, 1972), 54.

69. Ibid., 132.

70. J. Davis, ed., *The Britannia Diaries 1863–75: Selections from the Diaries of Frederick C. Wilton* (London: Society for Theatre Research, 1992), 15 December 1865 and 19 December 1867, 100, 136.

71. Ibid., 19 May 1868, 143.

72. Ibid., 18 December 1865, 100; 21 December 1865, 101; 21 and 22 December 1871, 198; 22 December 1869, 167.

7. A NATIONAL DRAMA: A NATIONAL THEATRE AND THE CASE OF DRURY LANE

1. "On the Present state of the Drama," *Cicerone*, 21 October 1843, 42.

2. This had been noticed by 1832. In a letter preserved in the Covent Garden Theatre Letterbook of H. Robertson 1823–49 (BM Add. Mss. 29643), the comment is made that both Covent Garden and Drury Lane are "situated close together, at the farthest possible distance from the circle of respectable suburbs where the most intelligent and best educated portions of society reside, – the Regent's Park and the Clapham Road – Kensington and Stratford – are a tolerable two hours journey from either of these emporiums of the regular Sock and Buskin."

3. Posters were everywhere joined by posted proclamations announcing a veto on the proposed meeting. Forty-five hundred soldiers, 6 field pieces, 3 troops of the Royal Horse Artillery, 400 pensioners, and 4,300 police were mobilized in London.

4. *Spectator*, 27 May 1848, 511.

5. Despite the identification of Dumas with the republican cause in France, the Lord Chamberlain's representative at the 12 June performance, while corroborating the continuous uproar, found nothing objectionable in the play itself, LC7/8, 12 June 1848.

6. *The Times*, 13 June 1848.

7. *George Augustus Sala . . . by himself*, 178. Sala had sided with the theatrical conservatives as early as April. He was sworn in as a special constable to protect West End property in the face of the massive Chartist meeting called at Kennington Common on 10 April.

8. *The Times*, 16 June.

9. G. A. Sala, 181.

10. St. Vincent Troubridge implies that the riot was influenced by the machinations of a theatrical cabal in "Theatre Riots in London," *Studies in English Theatre History* (London: Society for Theatre Research, 1952).

11. *Sunday Times*, 23 April.

12. Effingham Wilson, *A House for Shakespeare: A Proposition for the Nation* (London: Effingham Wilson, 1848).

13. Wilson, 2, quoted in Loren Kruger, *The National Stage* (Chicago: University of Chicago, 1992), 89.

14. Kruger, Ibid.

15. Kruger, 13.

16. A petition to the Lord Chamberlain sought permission to erect a theatre in Drury Lane on the site of the Great Mogul Tavern: "Since the destruction of the Olympic theatre by fire, there is no place of amusement for the vast masses of tradespeople and mechanics residing in the neighborhood" and that with the closure of Drury Lane, there was no "theatrical entertainment for the middling classes except at a great distance," 21 April 1849, LC7/8 PRO.

17. James Anderson, *An Actor's Life* (Newcastle: Scott, 1902), 163.

18. Leigh Hunt, *Autobiography*, ed. R. Ingpen (London: Macmillan, 1903), 1, 152.

19. J. W. Cole, 11.

20. Prior to the exhibition's opening theatres had suffered: "The cold, cheerless state of the weather and the engrossing excitement caused by the approaching inauguration of the Great Exhibition in Hyde Park, have for some weeks past produced an unusual depression in dramatic affairs. . . . The town usually so full of visitors at this time [Easter holidays] has been comparatively empty, as most persons intending to come to London for mere amusement, deferred doing so until close upon the opening of the Great Exhibition, when the theatres were almost forgotten in the immense attraction of the Crystal Palace and its manifold wonders," *Sunday Times*, 4 May 1851. After the opening however the *Theatrical Journal*, 3 September 1851, noted that "although the aristocracy and the court have left the metropolis, the influx of country people who arrive daily to see the sights of London, are so numerous, that they make a balance in favour of the population in London at this period of the year." Almost as soon as Anderson left Drury Lane, the theatre's Committee leased it out to American and French equestrian troupes, managed by Nelson Lee, which, "realized in a few months over seven thousand pounds," J. Anderson, *An Actor's Life*, 199.

21. Daniel Boorstin, *The Image: A Guide to Pseudo-Events in America* (New York: Athenaeum, 1987).

22. Gladstone saw *The Winter's Tale, The Tempest, Richard II* (twice), *King Lear* (twice), *A Midsummer Night's Dream, The Merchant of Venice*, and *Henry V*. Kean used the occasion of his visit to *Richard II* to solicit Gladstone's support for a state subvention, M. R. D. Foot and H. C. Matthews, eds., *The Gladstone Diaries* (Oxford: Clarendon Press, 1974–94), IV and V, passim.

23. Earl of Bessborough, ed., *Lady Charlotte Schreiber* (London: Murray, 1952), sv. 27 November 1857.

24. J. W. Cole, 351–3.

25. Richard W. Schoch, *Shakespeare's Victorian Stage: Performing History in the Theatre of Charles Kean* (Cambridge: Cambridge University Press, 1998), 132. He also quotes the disparaging comments in the *Theatrical Journal* and *Westminster Review*, which upbraid Victoria for her visits in 1852 and 1853.

26. Schoch, 133. Moreover, both Schoch and Kruger make the mistake of perpetuating a binary between theatres and music halls. Both assume a theatre of the middle class and a music hall of the "great unwashed" (Schoch, 129 and Kruger, 91), which as we shall see finds little substantiation as far as the West End is concerned.

27. Letter to Miss Burdett Coutts, 27 February 1854.

28. "Old Drury," *London Review*, 20 October 1860, 374.

29. *Theatrical Journal*, 15 September 1852.

30. Blanchard had written the pantomimes for the Marylebone and in 1852 also supplied those of Sadler's Wells, and the Surrey, Blanchard, *Reminiscences*, 1, 101.

31. Letter to Sara Hennell, 3 February 1862 (*Letters*, IV, 10). See also *Theatrical Journal*, 9 February 1853, and also Clement Scott, *The Drama of Yesterday and Today* (London: Macmillan, 1899), 1, 432–4.

32. *Theatrical Journal*, 23 November 1853.

33. *Theatrical Journal*, 16 February 1859.

34. *Theatrical Journal*, 16 March 1859.

35. *Weekly Times*, 22 January 1854. The *Theatrical Journal*, 25 January 1854, noted that this was still going on in late January when "the theatre has been surrounded daily by hundreds of poor creatures, who have received a loaf of bread and a quart of excellent soup."

36. Jerrold in *Lloyd's Weekly*, 22 January; a satiric lampoon in *Diogenes*, 30 January 1854; and Smith's retort in the *Weekly Times*, 29 January 1854.

37. Coleman recounts that Smith was less than impressed at the beginning of his management by the Court's refusal to retain a Royal box. When five years into his term, the services of Charles Mathews were requested for the Windsor theatricals, Smith is reputed to have declined, saying "if the Court wanted to see Mathews, they could come to Drury Lane." The result was that neither Victoria nor Albert visited the theatre during his management, John Coleman, *Players and Playwrights I have Known* (London: Chatto and Windus, 1888), 1, 103.

38. 22 April 1855. The fact that operas at cheap prices had been offered at the Surrey and Sadler's Wells (during the summer months) may suggest that Smith was hoping to attract outlying audiences back into the center.

39. *Era*, 20 May 1855.

40. *Era*, 10 June 1855.

41. *Era*, 15 July 1855.

42. Unidentified clipping, October 1859, Drury Lane boxes, Theatre Museum.

43. Daniel Barrett, "Shakespeare spelt Ruin and Byron Bankruptcy: Shakespeare at Chatterton's Drury Lane, 1864–1878," *Theatre Survey* 29, 2 (November 1988), 157.

44. *The Times*, 7 November 1864.

45. T. E. Pemberton, *The Kendals* (London: Pearson, 1900), 46.

46. Drury Lane boxes, Theatre Museum.

47. C. L. Kenney, *Poets and Profits at Drury Lane Theatre: a theatrical narrative. Suggested by F. B. Chatterton*. (London: Aubert, 1875), 21, quoted in Barrett, 161–2.

48. "The Fortunes of Nigel at Drury Lane," *Spectator*, 3 October 1868, 1153.

49. Chatterton estimated that he had cleared about £6000 on *Amy Robsart* (1870) and *Rebecca* (the 1871 adaptation of *Ivanhoe*) and £4000 on *The Lady of the Lake* (1872), Coleman, 2, 357.

50. *Era*, "English and American theatres," 30 October 1870.

51. *Sunday Times*, 28 September 1873. See also the *Entr'acte*, 4 October 1873.

52. A Rambler, "Homes of the Poor: Drury Lane Dwellings," *Daily Telegraph*, 6 May 1880.

53. J. W. Cole, 11.

54. It is worth noting that in the period before 1850, only eight plays had achieved a run of 100 consecutive performances. From 1851 to 1860, though this number had only increased to fourteen, one play had performed more than 150 times consecutively. In the following decade these numbers increased dramatically: 25 with a run of 100 performances, 16 with runs to 200, 4 with runs up to 250 performances, and 6 over 300 (effectively an entire theatrical year). Between 1871 and 1881, thirteen West End theatres had plays running for over 300 performances, 4 between 250 and 300, 13 between 200 and 250, 35 between 150 and 200, and 65 between 100 and 150 performances (John Palmer, ed., *Who's Who in the Theatre*, 1805–36. This should be set against the figures for total West End capacity. In 1866, prior to the entertainment building boom, it was calculated that London music halls and entertainment galleries as a whole could accommodate 79,300 people per day (excluding the Crystal Palace which could accommodate 100,000 per day). At the same time, metropolitan theatres could offer a total of approximately 53,518 places. Of the theatres fifteen were located in the West End accommodating 22,345 per performance or 41.7% of all metropolitan theatres. After 1866 with the building of the Holborn on the northern periphery of the West End, the Globe and Opera Comique off the Strand, the Gaiety, Vaudeville on the Strand, and the Criterion on Piccadilly Circus, the number had risen by 1874 by 5,643 to 27,988 per performance or 52.2% of the 1866 figures, an increase of over 25%, *Select Committee on theatrical licences, 1866*, vol. 16, appendices 1 and 3, 295, 313.

55. Thomas Purnell, *Dramatists of the Present Day* (London: Chapman and Hall, 1871), 11.

56. The West End theatre managers felt particularly threatened by the Oxford Music Hall, situated on the corner of Oxford Street and Tottenham Court Road, and the London Pavilion on Coventry Street, both of which had opened in 1861 and were each capable of accommodating two thousand patrons daily. Preeminently however, their attack was aimed at the Alhambra situated in Leicester

Square, which had been in existence since 1854 and could hold five thousand daily, *Select Committee on theatrical licences, 1866*, vol. 16, appendix 3, 313.

57. This dispute had been simmering throughout the 1850s and when music halls like the Canterbury in Westminster Road could afford to buy the paintings of Daniel Maclise, Dickens's friend; *All the Year Round*, 23 March 1861, 558, might well rubbish the dispute as raising the specter of discredited patent monopoly on the grounds that the music hall was helping to educate a theatregoing public and was thus an integral part of rational amusement.

58. LC1/154, 6 April 1865.

59. So the report to the Lord Chamberlain's Office in 1867, LC1/185.

60. Benjamin Webster's response to Q3181, *Select Committee on theatrical licences and regulations, 1866*, 373.

61. Dion Boucicault's response to Q4238.

62. Response to Q3276.

63. Response to Q2890.

64. So Frederick Strange, manager of the Alhambra, F. G. Tomlins, John Poole, manager of the Metropolitan, Edgeware Road, E. T. Smith, and John Knowles, proprietor of the Theatre Royal Manchester. The last was commenting on the presence of workers in Manchester theatres and comparing this to their presence in Drury lane. William Bodkin, the assistant judge for Middlesex, suggested that the poorer classes could indeed be seen at West End theatres in considerable numbers (Q2015).

65. Response to Q3681.

66. Response to Q3545.

67. Gladstone went to the Haymarket at 9 P.M. to see Bayle Bernard's *The Evil Genius* with his sons, 31 March 1856, and also *The Critic*, 25 August 1860, when he stayed from 9 to 11:30 P.M. On this occasion he went at 7 P.M. and left at 10:15 P.M., *Gladstone Diaries*, vol. V, sv.

68. Response to Q5252.

69. *The Times*, 5 January 1865.

70. John Pick, *The West End: Mismanagement and Snobbery* (Eastbourne: John Offord, 1983), 81.

71. Sir Thomas Henry, chief magistrate, Bow St. Police Court, response to question 835.

72. Response to question 5315.

73. Response to question 4591.

74. Letters from F. G. Marshall of Lowndes Street SW, 25 November 1876, LC1/312 PRO; Arthur Field of Leighan Court Road, Streatham, 8 January 1877, LC1/325; S. W. Keene, Barnes, 10 January 1878, LC1/341.

75. Letter to Benjamin Lumley, the theatre's manager, 4 June 1847, *Letters*, vol. 5, 78. Russell Jackson quotes indignant reactions to fees charged in the West End theatres: at the Lyceum in the *Theatrical Times*, 1847, the Olympic in *The Times*, 1855, and the *Era*, 1872, as well as to refreshment overpricing in the *Era*, 1877, although the last should be taken in the context that the playgoer had ordered a bottle of Moet champagne, Jackson, 25, 34–5, 60–1.

76. Letter to William Farren, 25 October 1851, *Letters* vol. 6, 528. Dickens had paid 4s for his stall though he did admit that that he had arrived shortly before 10 P.M. to see the burlesque: Fitzball's *Azael; or the Prodigal in London* with Henry Compton.

77. Letter to Sara Hennell, 11 July 1863, *Letters* vol. 4, 92.

78. Flora Tristan, 178.

79. B. W. W., "Theatrical annoyances and inconveniences," *Theatrical Journal*, 26 December 1855, 411.

80. LC1/167, R. Wood of 3 Holland Villas Road, Kensington West writing to the Lord Chamberlain 3 and 13 November 1866.

81. LC1, 9 December 1858.

82. Frederick Wilton (the stage manager of the Britannia theatre, Hoxton) noted that a couple who had been to the Princess's Theatre during a particularly icy January in 1867 were charged £1 10s by a cab to travel a short distance home. They were obliged to comply "the lady being dressed in Opera Cloak," J. Davis, ed., *The Britannia Diaries*, 41–2. In 1879 fog closed Drury Lane, the Olympic, the Vaudeville, and the Imperial (on Westminster Road) for two weeks, *Daily News*, 15 December 1879.

83. *The Entracte*, 13 June 1874, 4.

84. Response to question 3969.

85. So "Our Suburban Residence" in *All the Year Round*, 21 April 1866. This would remain a constant factor throughout the remainder of the period and beyond. When Sarah Bernhardt performed at the Gaiety in 1882, the length of the performance caused patrons to start preparing to leave, making the last scene inaudible. Moreover, gallery audiences insisted on a performance leaving enough time to go to the pub before it shut at midnight. The *Daily News*, which commented on the length of the Bernhardt performance, mentions that audiences will not tolerate anything that finishes later than 11:20 P.M., 5 June 1882. See the *Referee* on gallery tolerance, 4 September 1882.

86. *London Review*, 11 June 1864, 623.

87. Thomas Purnell, 14.

88. When the Court theatre in Sloane Square put on Robertson's *The Ladies' Battle* for a matinee performance, the *Daily Telegraph*, 17 February 1879, commented: "Hitherto these daytime abstractions, so much affected by Society, and so cordially appreciated by suburban residents, have consisted as a rule, of careful repetitions of the evening program or benefit plays."

89. "Some theatrical audiences," *All the Year Round*, 19 May 1877, 275.

90. H. Saville Clark, "Morning Performances," *Examiner*, 20 November 1880, 1310.

91. N. Graburn, "Tourism: The Sacred Journey," in V. Smith, ed., *Hosts and Guests* (University of Pennsylvania, 1989), 35.

92. On the egregious "stall swell" who enters late and gets bored quickly but who is nonetheless "a pretty harmless and liberal patron of the Stage" see the *Era*, 5 August 1877.

93. "Before the footlights or Sketches of Playhouse Society," *London Society*

Magazine, January 1867, 31.

94. The same kind of social snobbery can be found in the *Era* a few years later, when an observer seated in the stalls, comments ironically on dress circle gentility: "They do not get their dresses from Worth's at Paris, nor from White's in Regent Street, and as to those single-button primrose gloves we should hesitate to say how many months they have been acquiring that dingy hue that all the care in the world cannot guard them from," *Era*, 16 September 1877, reproduced in Russell Jackson, *Victorian Theatre*, 57–9.

95. *Licensed Victualler's Gazette*, 1 January 1876, 11.

96. It had started publication in 1877, and indeed from August 1878 until December 1879, its proprietor was Henry Irving and its editor, his friend Clement Scott. Irving had bought the journal for £1000 to disseminate his own conception of the dignity of the actor's profession and of the theatre practices that he valued, Laurence Irving, *Henry Irving: The Actor and His World*, 349–50.

97. "The cost of playgoing," *The Theatre*, September 1878, 99–103.

98. A full-time working journalist like E. B. Blanchard who regularly wrote many of the London pantomimes as well as articles for the *Era*, the *Daily Telegraph*, and *All the Year Round*, earned £590 15s in 1878, Clement Scott and Cecil Howard, eds., *The Life and reminiscences of E. L. Blanchard* (London: Hutchinson, 1891), 2, 482.

99. Frederick Wedmore, *The Academy*, 7 February 1880, quoted in Russell Jackson, 63.

100. Walter Besant, *Fifty Years Ago* (London: Chatto and Windus, 1888), 126.

101. "Is the pit an institution or an excrescence?" on 1 March, 129–142; and "The police in the pit – can such a system be justified?" in August, 63–76.

102. "A Plea for the Pit," *Era Almanack*, 1875, 80–3.

103. *The Theatre*, August, 64.

104. *All the Year Round*, 19 May 1877, 274–5.

105. "Going to the theatre," *Fraser's Magazine*, March 1837, 382.

106. St. John Adcock, "Leaving the London theatres," in G. R. Sims, ed., *Living London* (London: Knight, 1901), 10–12.

107. See B. Anderson, *Imagined Communities: Reflections on the Origins and Spread of Nationalism* (London: Verso, 1991).

108. See Alfred Emmet, "The long prehistory of the National Theatre," *Theatre Quarterly* 6, 21 (Spring, 1976), 55–62.

109. Matthew Arnold, "The French Play in London," *Nineteenth Century*, August 1879, 228–43; and John Hollingshead, *My Lifetime* (London: Sampson, Low, Marston, 1895), vol. 2, 134.

CONCLUSION

1. *Theatre in the Victorian Age*, 10.

2. "The Audiences of the Britannia Theatre, Hoxton," 27–41.

3. *The Past and Present Revisited*, rev. ed. (London and New York: Routledge and Kegan Paul, 1987), 18.

4. See Tracy C. Davis and Bruce McConachie, "Introduction," *Theatre Survey*

39, 2 (November 1998), 1–5, for a useful discussion of the links between method-
ology, quantitative data, and theory in researching the audience.

5. See, for instance, Deborah Vlock's discussion of Foucault in *Dickens, Novel
Reading and the Victorian Popular Theatre* (Cambridge: Cambridge University
Press, 1998), 1–3.

6. *The Orient of the Boulevards: Exoticism, Empire and the Nineteenth-Century
French Theatre* (Philadelphia: University of Pennsylvania, 1998), 7.

7. See, in particular, "Introduction" and "British Heroism and the structure of
melodrama" in J. S. Bratton et al., *Acts of Supremacy: The British Empire and the
Stage, 1790–1930* (Manchester: Manchester University Press, 1991), 1–61; and
"The Contending Discourses of Melodrama" in J. S. Bratton, J. Cook, and
C. Gledhill, eds., *Melodrama, Stage Picture Screen* (London: British Film Institute,
1994), 38–49.

8. Given the extent of documentary evidence available, there is considerable
scope for further studies in this area. These might include qualitative explorations
of the relationship between the repertoires of individual theatres and their potential audiences (including the sort of cutural negotiation taking place during performance); the discourse of power and of spectacle as configured in the nineteenth-
century theatrical event; and the interplay between theatrical and dramatic forms
and audience response (a possible approach to which Peter Brooks has already
pioneered in *The Melodramatic Imagination*). In addition, further case studies
might include comparative investigations of English provincial audiences, for example, or of theatre audiences located in such urban centers as New York and Paris.

BIBLIOGRAPHY

PRIMARY SOURCES

London, Public Record Office
Lord Chamberlain's Papers (Memoranda, Letters, Police Reports)
   LC1/32, 58, 70, 83, 98, 127, 141, 153–154, 166–167, 185, 200, 220–221, 232, 234, 263, 312, 325, 341–342, 343.
   LC7/5, LC7/6, LC7/7, LC7/8.
Census Returns
   1841 HO107/704–709,712, 715–717, 1060–1062, 1064–1065, 1083–1086.
   1851 HO107/1495–1519, 1533–1538, 1543–1547, 1563–1566, 1569–1571.
   1861 RG9/94–124, 125–199, 230–249, 269–271, 274–277, 330–332, 334–337, 346, 348–351, 366–367.
   1871 RG10/437–473, 503–527.

Parliamentary Papers
Reports
   PP 1831–2 VII, *Report from the Select Committee into the Laws affecting Dramatic Literature.*
   PP 1846 XVII, *Report from the Royal Commission on . . . Railway Termini within the Metropolis.*
   PP 1852–3 XXXVII, *Report from the Select Committee on Public Houses, Hotels, Beer Shops, Dancing Saloons, Coffee-Houses, Theatres, Temperance Hotels, and Places of Public Entertainment.*
   PP 1854, *Report from the Select Committee on Metropolitan Bridges.*
   PP 1854 XIV, *Report from the Select Committee on Public Houses.*
   PP 1866 XVI, *Report from the Select Committee on Theatrical Licenses and Regulations.*
   PP 1892 XVIII, *Report from the Select Committee on Theatres and Places of Entertainment.*
Census Materials (All Published By Irish University Press: Shannon, 1970–71)
   PP 1841, Census Abstracts: Enumeration, vol. 3.
   PP 1841, Census Abstracts: Occupations, vol. 5.
   PP 1851, Census Abstracts: Ages, Occupations and Birth, vol. 8.
   PP 1861, 1871, Census Abstracts, Population: General Reports, vol. 15.
   PP 1871, Census Abstracts, Population: Ages, Civil Conditions, Occupations and Birthplaces, vol. 18.

Special and Local Collections
Bancroft Library, Mile End
   Pavilion Theatre: Clippings and Playbills

British Library
  Add. Ms. 29643, Theatre Letterbook of H. Robertson 1823–49
  Percival Collection (Sadler's Wells)
  Playbill Collection
Finsbury Library, London
  Sadler's Wells Archives
Guildhall Library, London
  Playbills, Maps
Harvard Theatre Collection
  S. Arnold Collection
  Drury Lane, Prince of Wales's, Sadler's Wells, Surrey, Victoria Theatres:
  Clippings and Playbills
Holborn Local History Library
  Heal Collection: Queen's and Prince of Wales's Theatres
John Howard Library, Southwark
  Astley's, Surrey, Victoria Theatres: Clippings and Playbills
Minet Library, Lambeth
  Astley's, Bower, Surrey, Victoria Theatres: Clippings and Playbills
Mitchell Library, New South Wales
  Ms. 1181, Diaries of Frederick C. Wilton
New York Public Library
  Pavilion, Prince of Wales's, Surrey, Victoria Theatres: Clippings and Playbills
Rose Lipman Library, Hackney
  Britannia Theatre: Clippings and Playbills
Theatre Museum, London
  Britannia, Drury Lane, Pavilion, Prince of Wales's, Sadler's Wells, Surrey,
  Victoria Theatres: Clippings and Playbills

Newspapers and Periodicals
  Academy
  All the Year Round
  Athenaeum
  Blackwood's Edinburgh Magazine
  Builder
  Building News
  Church Times
  Cicerone
  Critic
  Daily News
  Daily Telegraph
  Diogenes
  Douglas Jerrold's Weekly Newspaper
  Dramatic and Music Hall Review
  Dramatic Notes
  East London Observer

  East London Papers
  Entr'acte Annual
  Era
  Era Almanack
  Examiner
  Fraser's Magazine
  Gentleman's Magazine
  Hackney and Kingsland Gazette and
      Shoreditch Telegraph
  Household Words
  Illustrated London News
  Illustrated Sporting and Dramatic
      News
  Illustrated Times
  Islington Daily Gazette and North
      London Tribune

Islington Gazette
Journal of the Statistical Society of
   London
Lambeth Observer and South
   London Times
Licensed Victualler's Gazette
L'International
Literary Gazette
Lloyd's Weekly London News
London Entr'acte
London Magazine
London Review
London Society Magazine
Morning Post
New Monthly Magazine
New York Sun
Notes and Queries
Penny Magazine
Porcupine
Public Ledger
Referee

Saturday Musical Review
Saturday Program
Sketch
South London Press
South London Times
Southwark Recorder
Spectator
Sportsman
Sunday Times
Temple Bar
The Theatre
Theatrical Journal
Theatrical Observer
Theatrical Times
The Times
Tower Hamlets Independent
Weekly Dispatch
Weekly Theatrical Reporter and
   Music Hall Review
Weekly Times
Windsor Magazine

SECONDARY SOURCES

Abercrombie, Nicholas, and Brian Longhurst. *Audiences*. London: Sage, 1998.

Allen, Shirley. *Samuel Phelps and Sadler's Wells Theatre*. Middletown: Wesleyan, 1971.

Anderson, B. *Imagined Communities: Reflections on the Origins and Spread of Nationalism*. London: Verso, 1991.

Anderson, James. *An Actor's Life*. London: Walter Scott Publishing Co., 1902.

Arnold, Matthew. "The French Play in London," *Nineteenth Century* (August 1879).

Arundell, Denis. *The Story of Sadler's Wells*. Newton Abbot: David and Charles, 1978.

Baer, M. *Theatre and Disorder in Late Georgian London*. Oxford: Clarendon Press, 1992.

Baker, H. Barton. *A History of the London Stage*. London: Allen, 1889.

Bancroft, Marie and Squire. *Recollections of Sixty Years*. London: John Murray, 1909.

[Bancroft, Squire and Marie]. *Mr and Mrs Bancroft On and Off the Stage By Themselves*. London: Richard Bentley & Son, 1889.

Barker, Clive. "The Audiences of the Britannia Theatre, Hoxton." *Theatre Quarterly* 9, 34 (1979).

Barker, T. C., and Michael Robbins. *A History of London Transport*. London: Allen and Unwin, 1963.

Barrett, Daniel. "Shakespeare Spelt Ruin and Byron Bankruptcy: Shakespeare at

Chatterton's Drury Lane, 1864–1878." *Theatre Survey* 29, 2 (November
1988).

Barrett, Daniel. *T. W. Robertson and the Prince of Wales's Theatre.* New York:
Peter Lang, 1995.

Beames, Thomas. *The Rookeries of London.* London: Cass, 1850, repr. 1970.

Bennett, Susan. *Theatre Audiences: A Theory of Production and Reception.*
London: Routledge, 1997.

Besant, Walter. *East London.* London: Chatto and Windus, 1901.

Besant, Walter. *Fifty Years Ago.* London: Chatto and Windus, 1888.

Bessborough, Earl of, ed. *Lady Charlotte Schreiber.* London: Murray, 1952.

Best, G. *Mid-Victorian Britain.* London: Fontana, 1979.

Blanchard, E. L., ed. *Bradshaw's Guide through London and its Environs.* London:
Adams 1851, 1857.

Boorstin, Daniel. *The Image: A Guide to Pseudo-Events in America.* New York:
Athenaeum, 1987.

Booth, Charles, ed. *Life and Labor of the People in London.* London, 1902–4,
repr. New York: AMS Press, 1970.

Booth, J. B. *A Century of Theatrical History 1816–1916: the "Old Vic."* London:
Stead, 1917.

Booth, M. R. "East End and West End: Class and Audience in Victorian London,"
Theatre Research International 2, 2 (February 1977).

Booth, M. R. *English Melodrama.* London: Herbert Jenkins, 1965.

Booth, M. R. *Theatre in the Victorian Age.* Cambridge: Cambridge University
Press, 1991.

Booth, M. R., et al. *The Revels History of Drama in English VI: 1750–1880.*
London: Methuen, 1975.

Bratton, J. S., "The Contending Discourses of Melodrama." In Bratton, J. S.,
J. Cook, and C. Gledhill, eds. *Melodrama, Stage Picture Screen.* London:
British Film Institute, 1994.

Bratton, J. S. "Introduction" and "British Heroism and the Structure of
Melodrama." In Bratton, J. S., et al. *Acts of Supremacy: The British Empire
and the Stage, 1790–1930.* Manchester: Manchester University Press,
1991.

Brown, Eluned, ed. *The London Theatre 1811–1866: Selections from the Diary of
Henry Crabb Robinson.* London: Society for Theatre Research, 1966.

Burtt, Frank. *Steamers of the Thames and Midway.* London: Richard Tilling,
1949.

Carlisle, Janice. "Dickens and the Working-Class Audience." In Case, Sue-Ellen,
and Janelle Reinelt, eds. *The Performance of Power: Theatre Discourse and
Politics.* Iowa City: University of Iowa Press, 1991.

Carlson, Marvin. "He Never Shall Bow Down to a Domineering Frown: Class
Tension and Nautical Melodrama." In Hays, Michael, and Anastasia
Nikolopoulou, eds. *Melodrama: The Cultural Emergence of a Genre.* New York:
St. Martin's Press, 1996.

Carlson, Marvin. "Theatre Audiences and the Reading of Performance." In

Postlewait, Thomas, and Bruce McConachie, eds. *Interpreting the Theatrical Past*. Iowa City: University of Iowa Press, 1989.

Carlson, Marvin. *Theatre Semiotics: Signs of Life*. Bloomington: Indiana University Press, 1990.

Chancellor, E. Beresford. *The Pleasure Haunts of London*. London, 1925, repr. New York: Blom, 1971.

Clark's Guide to the Sights of London. Chepstow: Clark, 1851.

Cole, J. W. *The Life and Theatrical Times of Charles Kean F. S. A.* London: Bentley, 1859.

Coleman, John. *Fifty Years of an Actor's Life*. London: Hutchinson, 1904.

Coleman, John. *Players and Playwrights I Have Known*. London: Chatto and Windus, 1888.

Cowan, Anita. "Popular Entertainment in London 1800–1840: The Relationship between Theatre Repertoire and Theatre Location." Ph.D. thesis, University of Washington, 1978.

Cowan, Anita. "The Relationship Between Theatre Repertoire and Theatre Location: A Study of the Pavilion Theatre." In K. V. Hartigan, ed., *All the World: Drama Past and Present*. Washington: University Press of America, 1982.

Crauford, A. L. *Sam and Sallie*. London: Cranley and Day, 1933.

Creswick, W. *An Autobiography*. London: Henderson, 1885.

Crossick G., ed. *The Lower Middle Class in Britain 1870–1914*. London: Croom Helm, 1977.

Cruchley's Picture of London. London: Cruchley, 1841.

Davies, Andrew. *The East End Nobody Knows*. London: Macmillan, 1990.

Davis, Jim. "Reminiscences in Retirement: Theatrical References in the Post-Britannia Diaries of F. C. Wilton," *Theatre Notebook* 47 (1993).

Davis, Jim, ed. *The Britannia Diaries 1863–75: Selections from the Diaries of Frederick C. Wilton*. London: Society for Theatre Research, 1992.

Davis, Jim, and Tracy C. Davis, "The People of the 'People's Theatre': The Social Demography of the Britannia Theatre (Hoxton)," *Theatre Survey* 32, 2 (November 1991).

Davis, Jim, and Victor Emeljanow. "New Views of Cheap Theatres: Reconstructing the Nineteenth-Century Theatre Audience." *Theatre Survey* 39, 2 (November 1998).

Davis, Tracy C. *Actresses as Working Women*. London: Routledge 1991.

Davis, Tracy C. "The Theatrical Employees of Victorian Britain: Demography of an Industry." *Nineteenth Century Theatre* 18, 1–2 (Summer and Winter 1990).

Davis, Tracy C. and Bruce McConachie. "Introduction." *Theatre Survey* 39, 2 (November 1998).

Dickens, Charles. "The Amusements of the People (1)." *Household Words*, 30 March 1850.

Dickens, Charles. "The Amusements of the People (2)." *Household Words*, 13 April 1850.

Dickens, Charles. *London Dictionary*. London: 1879.

Dickens, Charles. *Sketches By Boz*. London: Murdoch, 1838.

Dickens, Charles. "Two Views of a Cheap Theatre." *All the Year Round*, 25 February 1860.

Dickens, Charles, and R. H. Horne. "Shakespeare and Newgate." *Household Words*, 4 October 1851.

Donne, W. B. *Essays on the Drama*. London: John W. Parker & Son, 1858.

Donohue, Joseph. *Theatre in the Age of Kean*. Oxford: Basil Blackwell, 1975.

Douglass, Albert. *Memoirs of Mummers and the Old Standard Theatre*. London: Era, 1924.

Downer, Alan. *The Eminent Tragedian: William Charles Macready*. Cambridge, Mass: Harvard University Press, 1966.

Eagleton, Terry. *Ideology: An Introduction*. London: Verso, 1991.

Emmet, Alfred. "The Long Prehistory of the National Theatre." *Theatre Quarterly* 6, 21 (Spring 1976).

Erle, T. H. *Letters from a Theatrical Scene-Painter*. London: privately printed, 1880.

Estill, R. "The Factory Lad: Melodrama as Propaganda." *Theatre Quarterly* 1, 4 (October–December 1977).

Filon, Augustin. *The English Stage*, trans. Frederic Whyte. London: John Milne, 1898.

Findlater, Richard. *Lilian Baylis: The Lady of the Old Vic*. London: Allen Lane, 1975.

Fiske, John. "Moments of Television: Neither the Text nor the Audience." In Seiter, E., et al., eds. *Remote Control*. London: Routledge, 1989.

Fitzball, E. *Thirty-Five Years of a Dramatic Author's Life*. London: Newby, 1859.

Fleetwood, Frances. *Conquest: The Story of a Theatre Family*. London: W. H. Allen, 1953.

Fontane, Theodore. *Shakespeare in the London Theatre 1855–58*, ed. and trans. Russell Jackson. London: Society for Theatre Research, 1999.

Foot, M. R. D., and H. C. Matthews, eds. *The Gladstone Diaries*. Oxford: Clarendon Press, 1974–94.

Foulkes, Richard. *Church and Stage in Victorian England*. Cambridge: Cambridge University Press, 1997.

Foulkes, Richard. *The Shakespeare Tercentenary of 1864*. London: Society for Theatre Research, 1984.

Friswell, Laura Hain. *In the Sixties and Seventies*. London: Hutchinson, 1905.

Frith, W. *My Autobiography and Reminiscences*. London: Bentley, 1889.

Gartner, L. P. *The Jewish Immigrant in England 1870–1914*. London: Allen and Unwin, 1960.

Gater, G., and W. Godfrey, eds. *The Survey of London*, 16. London: LCC, 1937.

Godfrey, W., and W. Marcham, eds. *Survey of London*, 21. London: LCC, 1949.

Grant, George. *A Comprehensive History of London*. Dublin, 1849.

Grant, James. *The Great Metropolis*. London: Saunders and Otley, 1836.

Gurr, Andrew. *Playgoing in Shakespeare's London*. Cambridge: Cambridge
University Press, 1996.

Hadden, H. *An East-end Chronicle: St George's-in-the-East Parish Church*.
London, 1880.

Haight, G. S., ed. *The George Eliot Letters*. New Haven: Yale University Press,
1954–78.

Hall, N. John, and Nina Burgis, eds. *The Letters of Anthony Trollope*. Stanford:
Stanford University Press, 1983.

Hanley, P. P. *A Jubilee of Playgoing*. London: Privately printed, 1887.

Hanley, P. P. *Some Recollections of the Stage by an Old Playgoer*. London:
privately printed, 1883.

Hayward, Arthur. *The Days of Dickens*. London: Routledge, 1926 repr. Archon,
1968.

Hibbert, H. G. *Fifty Years of a Londoner's Life*. London: Grant Richards, 1916.

Hollingshead, John. *My Lifetime*. London: Sampson, Low, Marston, 1895.

Hollingshead, John. *Today: Essays and Miscellanies*. London, np, 1865.

House, Madeleine et al., eds. *The Letters of Charles Dickens*. Oxford: Clarendon
Press 1965–98.

Howard, Diana. *London Theatres and Music Halls 1850–1950*. London: The
Library Association, 1970.

Howe, J. B. *A Cosmopolitan Actor*. London: Bedford Publishing, [1888].

Hudson, D., ed. *Munby, Man of two Worlds: the Life and Diaries of Arthur J.
Munby 1828–1910*. London: Murray, 1972.

Hudson, Lynton. *The English Stage 1850:1950*. London: George G. Harrop, 1951.

Hughes, Leo. *The Drama's Patrons*. Austin: University of Texas, 1971.

Hunt, Leigh, J. H. *Autobiography*, ed. R. Ingpen. London: Macmillan, 1903.

Ilseman, Hartmut. "Radicalism in the Melodrama of the Early Nineteenth
Century." In Hays, Michael, and Anastasia Nikolopoulou, eds. *Melodrama:
The Cultural Emergence of a Genre*. New York: St. Martin's Press, 1996.

Irving, L. *Henry Irving: The Actor and his World*. London: Faber and Faber, 1951.

Jackson, Allan Stuart. *The Standard Theatre of Victorian England*. London:
Associated University Presses, 1993.

Jackson, Russell. *Victorian Theatre*. London: Macmillan, 1989.

Kift, Dagmar. *The Victorian Music Hall: Culture, Class and Conflict*. Cambridge:
Cambridge University Press, 1996.

Kingsley, Charles. *Alton Locke*. 1850, repr. London: Cassell, 1967.

Knight, Charles. *London*. London: Knight, 1841–4.

Knight, William G. *A Major London "Minor." The Surrey Theatre 1805–1865*.
London: Society for Theatre Research, 1997.

Kruger, Loren. *The National Stage*. Chicago: University of Chicago, 1992.

Law, C. *Urban Tourism: Attracting Visitors to Large Cities*. New York: Mansell,
1993.

Leacroft, Richard. *The Development of the English Playhouse*. London: Methuen,
1973.

London County Council. *Survey of London*, 23. London: LCC, 1951.

Lorenzen, Richard. "The Old Prince of Wales's Theatre: A View of the Physical Structure." *Theatre Notebook* 25 (1971).

Lynch, J. J. *Box, Pit and Gallery: Stage and Society in Johnson's London*. Berkeley: University of California Press, 1953.

Maré, E. de. *London 1851: The Year of the Great Exhibition*. London: Dent, 1973.

Marx, W., ed. *The Box Book Keeper's Guide or London Theatrical and Amusement Directory*. London: Jullien, 1849.

Mayhew, Henry. *London Labor and the London Poor*. London, 1861–62, reprinted New York: Dover, 1967.

Meisel, Martin. *Realizations*. Princeton, NJ: Princeton University Press, 1983.

Mekeel, Joyce. "Social Influences on Changing Audience Behavior in the London Theatre, 1830–1880." Ph.D. thesis, Boston University, 1983.

Moritz, Carl Philipp. *Travels of Carl Philipp Moritz in England in 1782* [1795]. repr. London: Milford, 1924.

Morley, Henry. *Journal of a London Playgoer*. London: Routledge, 1891.

Nicoll, Allardyce. *A History of English Drama 1660–1900*. Vol. 4, *Early Nineteenth Century Drama 1800–1850*. Cambridge: Cambridge University Press, 1970.

Nicoll, Allardyce. *A History of English Drama 1660–1900*. Vol. 5, *Late Nineteenth Century Drama 1850–1900*. Cambridge: Cambridge University Press, 1946.

Olsen, Donald J. *The Growth of Victorian London*. London: Batsford, 1976.

Pao, Angela C. *The Orient of the Boulevards: Exoticism, Empire and the Nineteenth-Century French Theatre*. Philadelphia: University of Pennsylvania, 1998.

Pedicord, H. W. *The Theatrical Public in the Time of Garrick*. Carbondale: Southern Illinois University Press, 1954.

Pemberton, T. E. *The Kendals*. London: Pearson, 1900.

Perkin, Harold. *The Origins of Modern English Society 1780–1880*. London: Routledge, 1969.

Phelps, W. May, and J. Forbes-Robertson. *Life and Works of Samuel Phelps*. London: Sampson Low, 1886.

Pick, John. *The West End: Mismanagement and Snobbery*. Eastbourne: John Offord, 1983.

Pinks, W. J., and C. J. Wood. *History of Clerkenwell*. London: Herbert, 1881.

Purnell, Thomas. *Dramatists of the Present Day*. London: Chapman and Hall, 1871.

Raymond, George. *Memoirs of Robert William Elliston, Comedian*. London: np, 1846.

Remington, Stephen. "Three Centuries of Sadler's Wells." *Journal of the Royal Society of Arts* 130 (July 1982).

Rose, Millicent. *The East End of London*. London: Cresset Press, 1951.

Routledge's Popular Guide to London and its Suburbs. London: Routledge, Warne, 1862.

Rowell, George. *The Old Vic Theatre: A History*. Cambridge: Cambridge University Press, 1993.

Rowell, George. *Queen Victoria Goes to the Theatre*. London: Elek, 1978.

Rowell, George. *The Victorian Theatre 1790–1914*. Cambridge: Cambridge University Press, 1978.

Rule, J. *Albion's People: English Society 1714–1815*. London: Longman, 1992.

Said, Edward. *Orientalism*. Harmondsworth: Penguin, 1978; repr. 1995.

Sala, George Augustus, *The Life and Adventures of George Augustus Sala Written by Himself*. London: Cassell, 1896.

Sala, George Augustus. *Twice Round the Clock*. London, 1859.

Savin, Maynard. *Thomas William Robertson: His Plays and Stagecraft*. Providence RI: Brown University, 1950.

Schlesinger, Max. *Saunterings In and About London*, trans. Otto Wenckstern. London: Cooke, 1853.

Schoch, Richard W. *Shakespeare's Victorian Stage: Performing History in the Theatre of Charles Kean*. Cambridge: Cambridge University Press, 1998.

Scott, Clement. *The Drama of Yesterday and Today*. London: Macmillan, 1899.

Scott, Clement, and Cecil Howard, eds. *The Life and Reminiscences of E. L. Blanchard*. London: Hutchinson, 1891.

Sims, G. R., ed. *Living London*. London: Knight, 1901.

Smith, V., ed. *Hosts and Guests*. University of Pennsylvania, 1989.

Solly, Henry. *These Eighty Years*. London: Simpkin, Marshall, 1893.

Speaight, George, ed. *Professional and Literary Memoirs of Charles Dibdin the Younger Dramatist and Upwards of Thirty Years Manager of Minor Theatres*. London: Society for Theatre Research, 1956.

Sprague, A. C., and Bertram Shuttleworth, eds. *The London Theatres in the Eighteen-Thirties*. London: Society for Theatre Research, 1950.

Stedman-Jones, Gareth. *Languages of Class: Studies in English Working Class History*. Cambridge: Cambridge University Press, 1983.

Stephens, John Russell. *The Censorship of English Drama 1824–1901*. Cambridge: Cambridge University Press, 1980.

Stone, Lawrence. *The Past and Present Revisited*. London and New York: Routledge and Kegan Paul, 1987.

Suleiman, Susan R., and I. Crosman. eds. *The Reader in the Text: Essays on Audience and Interpretation*. Princeton, NJ: Princeton University Press, 1980.

Taine, Hippolyte. *Notes on England*, trans. W. F. Rae. London: Holt and Williams, 1872.

Thompson, E. P. *The Making of the English Working Class*. London: Penguin Books, 1991.

Thompson, F. M. L. *The Rise of Respectable Society: A Social History of Victorian Britain 1830–1900*. Cambridge, MA: Harvard University Press, 1988.

Timbs, J. *Curiosities of London*. London: Horton, 1871 [1855, 1868].

Tomlins, F. G. *A Brief View of the English Drama*. London: Murray, 1840.

Towse, J. R. *Sixty Years of Theater*. New York: Funk and Wagnall, 1916.

Tristan, Flora. *Flora Tristan's London Journal: A Survey of London Life in the*

1830s, trans. Dennis Palmer and Giselle Pinsett. London: 1840, London: Prior, 1980.

Troubridge, St. Vincent. "Theatre Riots in London." *Studies in English Theatre History*. London: Society for Theatre Research, 1952.

Vlock, Deborah. *Dickens, Novel Reading and the Victorian Popular Theatre*. Cambridge: Cambridge University Press, 1998.

Walford, E. *Old and New London*. London: Cassell, 1881–93.

Watson, E. B. *Sheridan to Robertson*. Cambridge, MA: Harvard University Press, 1926.

Wearing, J., ed. *The Collected Letters of Sir Arthur Pinero*. Minneapolis: University of Minnesota Press, 1974.

Webbe, Cornelius. *Four Views of London*. London: Smith, Elder, 1836.

White, Hayden. *Tropics of Discourse: Essays in Cultural Criticism*. Baltimore: Johns Hopkins University Press, 1978.

Williams, Michael. *Some London Theatres Past and Present*. London: Sampson Low, 1883.

Williams, Montagu. *Round London*. London: Macmillan, 1893.

Wilson, A. E. *East End Entertainment*. London: Arthur Barker, 1954.

Wilson, Effingham. *A House for Shakespeare: A Proposition for the Nation*. London: Effingham Wilson, 1848.

[Wright, T.] *Some Habits and Customs of the Working Classes. By a Journeyman Engineer*. London 1867, repr. New York: Blom, 1967.

Wroth, W. *Cremorne and the Later London Gardens*. London: Elliott Stock, 1907.

Wroth, W. *London Pleasure Gardens of the Eighteenth Century*. London: Macmillan 1896, repr. Connecticut: Shoe String Press, 1979.

Young, G. M., ed. *Early Victorian England: 1830–1865*. London: Oxford University Press, 1934.

Zwart, Peter. *Islington: A History and Guide*. London: Sidgwick and Jackson 1973.

{ *Index* }

Factory Lad, The, 5, 6
Fair Maid of Tottenham Court, The, 113, 114
Fairbrother, B. S., 16
farce, 25, 27, 39, 112, 120, 143, 188, 193
Farrell, 55
Faust, 95
Fazio, 129
Fechter, Charles, 189
Fenchurch Street Station, 67
Fenton, Frederick, 38
Fergusson, Sir William, 151
Fiesco, 198
Fifteen Years in a British Seaman's Life, 69
Fitzball, Edward, 5, 6, 203
Folly Theatre, 152. See also Toole's Theatre
Fontane, Theodor, 159
Fool's Revenge, The, 121
Fortunes of Nigel, The, 207
Foucault, Michel, 79–80, 163, 229
Frampton, Frederick, 38
Friswell, James Hain, 189
Friswell, Laura Hain, 189
Frith, W. P., 151, 181
Frou-Frou, 87
Furzman, Mrs. J., 16

Gaiety Theatre, 152, 184, 185, 217, 225
Garrick Theatre, 47, 48, 50, 67, 70, 74, 94, 97; audience composition at, 47, 48, 50, 67
George, Charles, 195
Gideon, Johnny, 87
Gilbert and Sullivan, 98, 158
Gladstone, W. E., 155, 200, 212
Glossop, William, 11, 12, 33
Glynn, Isabella, 30
Great City, The, 206
Great Exhibition, 171–73, 197–98, 199, 209
Great Metropolis, The, 141
Great Western Railway, 180
Grecian Theatre, 32, 48, 75, 84, 87, 91,

94; audience behavior at, 85; audience composition at, 48, 84–85
Greenwood, James, 99
Greenwood, John, 111
Greenwood, Thomas, 101, 113, 114, 115, 116, 117–18, 121, 135
Grimaldi, Joseph, 112
Guy Mannering, 69

Haines, J. T., 24, 35, 188
Hall, Mary, 19
Halliday, Andrew, 206–8
Hamlet, 37, 113, 125, 130
Hanley, P. P., 15, 117, 148, 160
Hansbury, Thomas, 6
Hare, John, 152
Harlequin Hans and the Golden Goose, 121
Harlequin Hudibras, 203
Harris, Augustus, 33, 173, 208
Harrison, William, 195
Harwood, George, 84
Haymarket Theatre, ix, 101, 125, 132, 144, 152, 160, 167, 174, 185, 188, 189, 190, 191, 192, 193, 194, 195, 197, 211, 212, 215, 221, 222, 223
Hazlewood, Charles, 141
Hazlitt, William, 10, 12
Hemyng, Bracebridge, 57, 70
Henderson, Marie, 83, 87
Henry IV Part 1, 30
Henry V, 201
Her Majesty's Theatre, 29, 125, 174, 188, 196, 214
Hicks, Newton Treen, 35
Hollingshead, John, 10, 85, 142, 188, 212, 213, 217, 222, 225
Homeward Bound, 68
Honeymoon, The, 128
Honner, Mrs. Robert, 15, 16
Honner, Robert, 15, 16, 112, 113, 114, 115, 117
Hood, Tom, 154
Hope, Henry, 75
Horne, Richard, 102, 118–19

transport (*continued*)
126, 206, 215, 219, 221; by coaches
and carriages, 4, 12, 14, 151, 156, 215,
223; by ferries, 14; by omnibuses, 4,
12, 13, 14, 15, 66, 67, 70, 71, 85, 89,
90, 132, 151, 180–81, 204, 216; by
railways, 13, 14, 15, 31, 37, 64, 66, 67,
89, 90, 181–82, 206; by steam boats,
12, 14, 15, 37; and tolls, 11, 12, 39,
176; by trams, 66, 67, 71, 90; by underground railway, 67, 90, 181, 191;
by walking, 12, 15, 40, 66, 75, 89,
119, 148, 151, 179–80, 187
Travers, William, 141
Traviata, La, 121
Trovatore, Il, 69, 121
Trial by Jury, 158
Tristan, Flora, 177, 214
Trollope, Anthony, 189
True to the Core, 26, 31, 189
Tully's English Opera Company, 61
Twelfth Night, 118
Two Locksmiths, The, 24

Uncle Tom's Cabin, 202

Valentine and Orson, 110
Vandenhoff, George, 151
Vaudeville Theatre, 152, 184, 185, 191,
221, 222
Venice Preserv'd,, 25
ventilation, 54, 74, 110, 214, 215
Vestris, Eliza, 28, 151, 189, 195
Victoria station, 181
Victoria Theatre, xiv, 3, 6–14, 20–23,
24, 32, 33–40, 46, 69, 79, 90, 112,
130, 141, 142, 188; admission prices
at, 24, 33, 35, 38; audience behavior
at, 34; audience composition at, 8, 9,
10, 12, 14, 22, 33, 35; communications and transport at, 11–14, 33; and
competition with other theatres, 6,
33; demographics of population
near, 20–23, 33, 37; location of, 6–
8, 9, 10, 12, 39; refreshments at, 10,

38; repertoire and management of,
33–39
Vincent, Eliza, 36, 39
Virginius, 30, 37, 130

Wade, William, 75
Waiting for the Verdict, 141
Wapping Old Stairs, 15
War to the Knife, 144
Warner, Mary, 113, 115
Waterloo Bridge, 3, 4, 6, 8, 10, 11, 39,
176, 177
Waterloo Bridge Company, 11
Waterloo Station, 10, 13, 14
Webster, Benjamin, 187, 188, 189, 195,
211
Wedmore, Frederick, 220
West End, xiv, 31, 32, 33, 41, 48, 69, 85,
88, 93, 116, 117, 131, 132, 133, 148,
149, 152, 153, 158, 167–74, 193–209,
226, 227, 229, 230; amusements in,
184–92; commercialization of, 209–
25; contrasted with East End 43, 46,
47, 52, 53, 70, 71, 94–95, 186; loca-
tion, demography, and transport of,
174–84
West London, 191
Westminster Bridge, 3, 11
Weston, Edward, 129
Weston's Music Hall, 180
Whistler, The, 15
White Hoods, 38
Whitechapel Board of Works, 63
Whitechapel Needle, 68
Wigan, Horace, 213
Wild, George, 139
Wilks, T. E., 113
William and Susan, 204
Williams, John, 92
Williams, Montagu, 187, 189, 200, 212
Wilton, Frederick Charles, 75, 82–83,
86, 92, 190, 212
Wilton, Marie, 106, 142–43, 145, 147,
153, 156–59, 162, 230. *See also* Ban-
croft, Squire and Marie

Studies in Theatre History & Culture